Effective Practice in Youth Justice

Providing a comprehensive and up-to-date review of research and the implications for practice, the second edition of *Effective Practice in Youth Justice* considers core areas of youth justice practice, such as how to engage young people effectively within the context of recent changes to the youth justice system brought about by the introduction of the scaled approach and the Youth Rehabilitation Order. It also provides an overview of the available research in specific areas of practice, including assessment; planning interventions and supervision; mental health; substance misuse; restorative justice; education, training and employment; and custody and resettlement.

The content has been specifically developed to meet the needs of students taking YJB sponsored courses with the Open University and is required reading for many of these. The book is also an essential resource for professionals working within the youth justice system, those training to work in youth justice, and students taking courses in youth justice or related subjects.

Martin Stephenson is an educationalist and criminologist and is currently a Director with ECOTEC Research and Consulting and Executive Director with Unitas, a national charity that helps young people access, participate and progress in education and training. In these roles he leads on a wide range of research and technical assistance projects in the field of youth inclusion and youth justice.

Henri Giller is Managing Director of Social Information Systems Ltd (SIS). SIS is an independent research and consultancy organisation with over 30 years experience of advising, monitoring and evaluating youth justice initiatives. Dr Giller has been an adviser to the Youth Justice Board on performance management issues for over 10 years and has advised numerous Youth Offending Teams on their policy and practice.

Sally Brown is Managing Director of Inclusive Learning Solutions and has considerable experience of working as a consultant, facilitator, writer and researcher in the fields of youth justice and education. Working with the Open University, she has been closely involved in the development of YJB sponsored courses across a wide range of practice areas.

Effective Practice in Youth Justice

Martin Stephenson, Henri Giller and Sally Brown

Second edition

 Routledge
Taylor & Francis Group

LONDON AND NEW YORK

First published 2011 by Routledge
2 Park Square, Milton Park, Abingdon, Oxon OX14 4RN

Simultaneously published in the USA and Canada
by Routledge
270 Madison Avenue, New York, NY 10016

Routledge is an imprint of the Taylor & Francis Group, an informa business

British Library Cataloguing-in-Publication Data
A catalogue record for this book is available from the British Library

Library of Congress Cataloging in Publication Data
A catalog record for this book has been requested

ISBN: 978-0-415-61075-9 (hbk)
ISBN: 978-0-415-61077-3 (pbk)
ISBN: 978-0-203-83194-6 (ebook)

Project management by Deer Park Productions, Tavistock, Devon
Typeset by TW Typesetting, Plymouth, Devon
Printed and bound by TJ International Ltd, Padstow, Cornwall

Contents

List of figures and tables   *ix*
List of abbreviations   *xi*
Acknowledgements   *xiii*
Preface to the second edition   *xv*

1 Evidence-based practice and effective practice   **1**
Introduction   1
The youth justice context   2
Why has evidence-based practice emerged?   3
The risk society   3
Managerialism and the audit society   7
Research and practitioners   8
'What Works' in youth justice   9
Determining effectiveness   10
Evidence   11
Risk and protective factors   12
The limitations of the 'What Works' approach   15
Implementation   22
Guidelines for more effective practice   25
The role of the practitioner   35
Does guidance work?   36
Reflective practice   37
Conclusions   40
Summary   41
Further reading   42

**2 Assessment, planning interventions and supervision
and the scaled approach**   **43**
The evidence base for assessment, planning interventions and
    supervision   43
The scaled approach   56
The principles of effective practice and assessment, planning
    interventions and supervision and the scaled approach   59
The challenges for practice   69
Summary   70

	Note	71
	Further reading	71
3	**Engaging young people**	**72**
	The evidence base for engaging young people	72
	The principles of effective practice and engaging young people	88
	Conclusions	96
	Summary	96
	Further reading	96
4	**Education, training and employment**	**97**
	The evidence base for education, training and employment	97
	The principles of effective practice and education, training and employment	115
	The challenges for practice	122
	Summary	122
	Further reading	123
5	**Mental health**	**124**
	Introduction	124
	The evidence base for mental health	124
	The principles of effective practice and mental health	133
	The challenges for practice	142
	Summary	144
	Further reading	144
6	**Substance misuse**	**145**
	The evidence base for substance misuse	145
	The principles of effective practice and substance misuse	151
	The challenges for practice	159
	Summary	160
	Further reading	161
7	**Parenting**	**162**
	The evidence base for parenting	162
	The principles of effective practice and parenting	172
	The challenges for practice	181
	Summary	182
	Further reading	183
8	**Restorative justice**	**184**
	The evidence base for restorative justice	184
	The principles of effective practice and restorative justice	195
	The challenges for practice	200
	Summary	201

| | Note | 202 |
| | Further reading | 202 |

9	**Offending behaviour interventions**	**203**
	The evidence base for offending behaviour programmes	203
	The principles of effective practice and offending behaviour interventions	207
	The challenges for practice	216
	Summary	219
	Further reading	219

10	**The secure estate and resettlement**	**220**
	The evidence base for the secure estate	220
	The evidence base for resettlement	224
	The principles of effective practice and resettlement	231
	The challenges for practice	239
	Summary	242
	Further reading	242

| References | 243 |
| Index | 267 |

List of figures and tables

Figures

1.1	A systematic approach to reflective practice	38
2.1	Indicators of level matrix	60
2.2	The cycle of change	64
7.1	Core elements of parenting programmes	177
9.1	Discretion versus accountability	218

Tables

1.1	Effective interventions by youth crime risk factor reduced	16
1.2	*Asset* scores and risk of reoffending	26
1.3	Paradigms in learning	38
5.1	Different agency responses to the same presenting problem	127
5.2	The CAMHS four-tier framework	135
6.1	HAS four-tier framework	153
8.1	Types and degrees of restorative justice practice	190
10.1	Summary of the most and least effective types of treatment regarding recidivism rates	232

List of abbreviations

ABC	antecedents, behaviour and consequences
ADHD	Attention Deficit Hyperactivity Disorder
APIR	Assessment, Planning, Implementation and Review
CAF	Common Assessment Framework
CBT	cognitive-behavioural therapy
CAMHS	Child and Adolescent Mental Health Services
CRISS	Crime Reduction Initiative in Secondary Schools
DARE	Drug Abuse Resistance Education
DBT	dialectical behavioural therapy
DCLG	Department for Communities and Local Government
DCSF	Department for Children, Schools and Families
DfEE	Department for Education and Employment
DfES	Department for Education and Skills
DoH	Department of Health
DPAS	Drug Prevention Advisory Service
DSM-IV	*Diagnostic and Statistical Manual of Mental Disorders*
DTO	Detention and Training Order
EBD	emotional and behavioural difficulties
EMA	Education Maintenance Allowance
ETE	education, training and employment
FE	further education
FFT	Functional Family Therapy
FIP	Family Intervention Programme
FIT	Family Integrated Transitions
GCSE	General Certificate of Secondary Education
GLM	Good Lives Model
GNVQ	General National Vocational Qualification
HMIP	HM Inspectorate of Prisons
IAP	Intensive Aftercare Programme
ICD-10	*International Statistical Classification of Disease and Related Health Problems*, 10th Revision
ICPS	Institute for Criminal Policy Research
ISO	Individual Support Order
ISS	Intensive Supervision and Surveillance
ISSP	Intensive Supervision and Surveillance Programme

LEA	local education authority
LSU	Learning Support Unit
MAPPA	Multi-Agency Public Protection Arrangements
MET	Motivational Enhancement Therapy
MI	Motivational Interviewing
MST	Multi-systemic Therapy
Nacro	National Association for the Care and Resettlement of Offenders
NEET	not in education, employment or training
NICE	National Institute for Health and Clinical Excellence
NTA	National Treatment Agency
OCJR	Office for Criminal Justice Reform
Ofsted	Office for Standards in Education
ONS	Office for National Statistics
PEIP	Parenting Early Intervention Pathfinder
PISA	Programme for International Student Assessment
PRU	Pupil Referral Unit
PSHE	personal, social and health education
PTSD	post-traumatic stress disorder
RBI	Reducing Burglary Initiative
RCT	randomised control trial
RFR	risk factor research
ROSH	Risk of Serious Harm
RoTL	Release on Temporary Licence
SCH	Secure Children's Home
SEN	special educational needs
SIfA	Screening Interview for Adolescents
SL	speech and language
SLC	speech, language and communication
SLCN	speech, language and communication needs
SNASA	Salford Needs Assessment Schedule for Adolescents
SQIfA	Screening Questionnaire Interview for Adolescents
SSP	Safer Schools Partnership
STC	Secure Training Centre
TSA	Trust for the Study of Adolescents
UNCRC	United Nations Convention on the Rights of the Child
WHO	World Health Organisation
YIP	Youth Inclusion Programme
YISP	Youth Inclusion and Support Panel
YJB	Youth Justice Board
YJS	youth justice system
YOI	Young Offender Institution
YOP	Youth Offender Panel
YOT	Youth Offending Team
YRO	Youth Rehabilitation Order

Acknowledgements

This publication was originally based on a series of Readers commissioned by the Youth Justice Board. Acknowledgements are also due to the original authors of the Readers, in particular to: Kerry Baker and Sarah Jones (Assessment, Planning Interventions and Supervision); Alison Clare and Janet Maitland (Mental Health); Fiona Hackland and Bob Baker (Substance Misuse); Sarah Lindfield, Anna Elliott, Janice Kusick and Josie Melia (Parenting); Guy Masters, Paul Crosland, Roger Cullen and Liz Nelson (Restorative Justice); and Tim Bateman (Offending Behaviour Programmes).

Most of these chapters have been substantially changed with elements of guidance removed. This content has also been amended to take account of the latest evidence in the areas covered in light of Henri Giller's review of research in 2006, the YJB Source documents published in 2008 and Dr Caroline Hudson's review of relevant research and policy in the key areas of youth justice practice referred to in this book carried out in 2010.

Particular thanks are due to David Monk of the Youth Justice Board for his commitment to making the book possible in the first place and his continued support for ensuring this second edition.

Preface to the second edition

There have been some significant changes to this edition. These have resulted from the feedback gained from the Open University as it is the main textbook for their principal course on youth justice. Additional influences have been points raised in constructive reviews such as those by Stephen Case and Lisa Romano-Dwyer to whom we are grateful. Policy changes such as the introduction of the Youth Rehabilitation Order (YRO) and the Scaled Approach also necessitated some additional material.

The previous chapters on targeted neighbourhood intervention programmes, mentoring and ISSP have been removed and some of this material has been assimilated into other chapters. There is a new chapter on engaging young people in youth justice interventions and the chapter on assessment, planning, intervention and supervision has been augmented to take account of the introduction of the YRO and the Scaled Approach. All the chapters have taken account of the series of reviews commissioned by the Youth Justice Board (YJB) for their source documents which underpin their Key Elements of Effective Practice (KEEPS) and other relevant publications that have come out since the first edition.

In some ways the timing for this new edition could be better given that the new coalition government is only six months old at the time of going to print. However the requirement to revise the OU course has determined the timing. While the policy direction appears clear, little detail has so far emerged and a Green Paper is expected in early 2011. What is certain though is that the centralised New Labour approach is being dismantled with the YJB to be abolished and an emphasis on local accountability and local priorities rather than centrally set targets. The abolition of the YJB appears set to take place over a protracted period and it is unclear how proactive the role of the new unit in the Ministry of Justice will be or indeed the nature of any regulatory system. For example, significant changes are being proposed in the youth justice assessment system (currently known as Asset), which presumably will take account of both operational experience and cogent academic criticism, but it is unclear as to how far YOTs will be required to use such systems in the future.

The reductions in public expenditure at local authority level will probably see the integration of YOT management structures with those of other services such as Connexions and the Youth Service and the diminution of the YOT role in preventative work. The emphasis on commissioning and outsourcing may well see a significant increase in the delivery of youth justice interventions outside of traditional local authority providers with a move to the private and voluntary sectors. Consequently there is likely to be much greater diversity between local authority areas in terms of resourcing, youth justice interventions and outcomes.

A key policy driver may also be the 'rehabilitation revolution' with far more emphasis being placed on community rather than custodial interventions. This will build upon the very significant reductions in the juvenile custodial population that have occurred in 2009 and 2010. It means that community interventions will need to be more robust (or at least will need to be perceived as such) with the negative consequences of custody receiving far more attention than in the recent past. The three key measures: the numbers of first-time entrants; reoffending rates; and the custodial population will probably continue to be used to measure the effectiveness of the youth justice system.

Despite the significance of these changes much will remain the same as YOT structures will probably largely stay in place, managers will continue to juggle scarce resources and practitioners will grapple with engaging young people and matching their needs to these resources. To this extent issues surrounding effectiveness will not go away and issues surrounding evidence-based practice will remain relevant.

Evidence-based practice has been attacked from several directions. Fundamental criticisms include its alleged inapplicability with regard to explaining the complexities of human behaviours; its prescriptive reliance on certain limited and expensive research methodologies; and the simplistic attraction to policymakers. A relatively pragmatic approach is taken here which is explicit about the shortcomings of the 'What Works' approach and open about the lack of hard evidence to underpin many interventions. However there is an attempt to translate the principles underlying evidence-based practice into a practical framework for practitioners to make sense of the research evidence, limited though it sometimes is.

The audiences for this text include students on the OU youth justice courses, particularly the Certificate in Effective Practice (K208), although hopefully it will be useful for a wider range of people. The learning outcomes of this course have influenced the purpose, content and structure of the book such as the relationship between research evidence and practice and key skills such as critical reflection and acquiring and using the information needed for effective practice in youth justice. Accordingly each chapter reviews the evidence base of effectiveness of each topic, places interventions in the context of evidence-based practice principles and highlights some of the challenges to practice. Each chapter should not be interpreted as a DIY guide to a particular intervention, rather as a summary of relevant research evidence to be filtered through the professional judgment of those working in youth justice. It is not intended to be a comprehensive guide to youth justice, rather to be used to complement some of the excellent texts on the subject which are referenced within this volume.

Evidence-based practice and effective practice

Introduction

One of the success stories of the 1990s in the development of healthcare and policy was the emergence of evidence-based practice. This approach rapidly developed into an international movement. Evidence-based practice has spread across most areas of healthcare such as mental health, dentistry, nursing and physiotherapy. This has now become a theme across social policy with education, criminal justice and social care all being encouraged to be evidence-based. These disciplines and professions have adopted this approach but to varying degrees. In criminal justice the new emphasis on evidence-based practice has converged with the 'What Works' movement. But although some of its more enthusiastic adherents see this as bringing a clearer, more consistent and effective way of working it has been criticised heavily by opponents in various disciplines such as education, youth justice and social care.

This chapter examines critically the underlying assumptions about the nature of evidence and the methodology in this model. As well as looking at the shortcomings of a simplistic 'What Works' approach, it also assesses how far the principles underpinning evidence-based practice in youth justice provide a useful framework for designing and applying interventions by practitioners. This sets the scene for the following chapters which place each topic within the framework of these principles. The role of the practitioner is appraised in the 'What Works' context as is the influence of guidance and reflective practice.

The headline message from government has been that 'what matters is what works' and that practice should be derived from the latest and most reliable research findings. This has an instant, rational appeal. While the small print conceals conceptual difficulties and significant challenges for implementation, the evidence-based practice approach has been promoted vigorously across criminal justice.

The youth justice context

Significant though the structural changes have been since 1998, the present youth justice system did not simply fall out of clear skies with the Crime and Disorder Act. Some of the early rhetoric of the Youth Justice Board (YJB) led to complaints of a 'Year Zero' style (Pitts 2001a) and an 'apparent expurgation of all youth justice knowledge and practice prior to 1998' (Jones 2002: 15). The antecedents of the current system go back at least until the early nineteenth century and many current practitioners were working in this field before 1998. Equally its development is perhaps characterised by certain recurrent themes rather than a simple linear, progressive development of increasingly effective solutions to youth crime. Neither are the size and character of youth justice services a simple reflection of the scale and nature of offending by young people. It has been argued that in effect each society gets the youth justice system it deserves, as how a society defines and reacts to the behaviour of young people 'ultimately tells us more about social order, the state and political decision-making than it does about the nature of youth offending and the most effective ways to respond to it' (Muncie 2004: 303).

This wider socio-political context is often considered crucial to understanding youth crime and youth justice (Hendrick 2006) and this also applies to the current emphasis on evidence-based practice.

For much of its history, youth justice has seen lurches between welfare and justice approaches. Welfarism is derived from the notion that a child should be treated differently to an adult where offending is concerned, with an emphasis placed on meeting the child's needs. In contrast to this, the justice approach focuses on matching the levels of formal intervention to the gravity of the offence rather than to putative needs. There has always been a complex and often confused blend of justice and welfare although the balance between the two has shifted considerably at times. Both have had unintended consequences, with welfare tending to increase formal interventions and control unnecessarily, and justice ignoring individual needs and sometimes human rights.

The current preoccupation with the behaviour of young people is nothing new and what is striking is the recurrent discovery of the degeneracy of youth and how much worse their behaviour is than in some golden age in the past (Pearson 1983). What may be new is the rise of what might be termed 'the politics of behaviour' whereby there is a convergence of the New Labour and Conservative positions on law and order (Downes and Morgan 2002) and across other social policy areas such as education. Linked to this has been the rise of managerialism, central to which has been an emphasis on evidence-based practice.

Why has evidence-based practice emerged?

Like all such movements evidence-based practice is a product of its time. It is derived partly from wider social influences, developments in public services, changing notions of professionalism and practitioner concerns with their effectiveness. Much of the attraction of an evidence-based approach to practice lies in the fact that it is an ostensibly neat and coherent approach to the messy and ill-defined complexities of practice. Politically, it is the epitome of managerialism and purports to be value-free as the application of proven methods to treat the particular social ill. After all, who could possibly argue in favour of what does not work? Perhaps, too, the language of 'dosage' and 'treatment' has been borrowed so readily from medicine because it conveniently supports the idea of offending as a symptom of individual pathology. Despite the confidence of government agencies in this approach many academic commentators have contested it.

> A considerable body of research has been identified demonstrating clearly that a firmly evidence-based approach to the prevention of youth crime is both a realistic proposition and a strategy that can be confidently expected to be successful. (Communities that Care 2001: 121)

> The doctrinaire tyranny of the 'what works' movement is wasting the creativity of the youth justice professionals as it places at risk much of the genuinely good practice undertaken by them. (Bateman and Pitts 2005: 258)

Such is the popularity of evidence-based practice that it runs the risk of being perceived as either simply a fashionable accessory to current practice or a panacea. Before engaging with the notion and detailed implementation of effective practice, it is essential to become familiar with the origins of evidence-based practice in order to understand its strengths and limitations.

The risk society

Commentators agree that one of the defining characteristics of twenty-first-century society is accelerating and often dramatic social change. Societies are increasingly moulded by global rather than national or regional influences. Many fixed and locally based traditions are being replaced by rapid endings and transitions in life and social norms, and with these changes comes a heightened concern with risk.

In a much more unsettled social and economic environment, where lifelong careers and traditional family structures are no longer the norm, coping with uncertainty has become much more important. Dealing with this uncertainty is increasingly defined as an individual rather than an organisational or state responsibility. The interpretation and management of risk is an increasingly important feature of our personal and professional lives. Arguably, evidence-based practice has won so many adherents so quickly because it promises a consistent risk management methodology resting on a platform of knowledge. In some ways, it is essentially a cautious and defensive response to the challenges of modern society.

The evolution of youth justice mirrors these wider trends. Social policy increasingly focuses on children who are 'at risk'. Management of risk is starting to permeate nearly every sphere of activity within youth justice. The start of intervention is itself regulated through a detailed assessment of risk through the *Asset* (Youth Justice Board assessment tool) profile. Interventions that focus on the management of this risk represent a significant contrast to previous approaches such as system management and diversion in the late 1980s and early 1990s, or earlier approaches such as intermediate treatment. The emphasis on the swifter administration of justice reflects not only concerns with more effective management of risk in terms of further offences, but also the impact of uncertainty and more challenging transitions in young people's lives.

The Crime and Disorder Act 1998 and subsequent youth justice reforms reflect the emphasis on the individual in terms of people's responsibility for their actions and the ability to modify their behaviour. Offending Behaviour Programmes, for instance, could be seen as being partly about equipping young people with risk-management skills. Coping strategies and decision-making skills, particularly in relation to planning, are prerequisites for participation in modern society.

Arguably, young people who offend are in even greater need of acquiring such skills. Most of the young people in custody or on high-level interventions such as Intensive Supervision and Surveillance (ISS) will face more complex, significant challenges (e.g. limited access to education, substance misuse) in their lives than will their peers, including much earlier transitions (e.g. leaving home, becoming a parent).

More critical interpretations see this as a manifestation of the tendency of current social policy to focus on the deficits of an individual young person and their responsibility while ignoring the social and economic circumstances of the young people (Goldson and Muncie 2006). Similarly, it is argued that the preoccupation with 'risk' has displaced consideration of 'need', and that actuarial justice as exemplified by the use of *Asset* provides a spurious sense of certainty and reliability over something as troubling and uncertain as the delinquent behaviour of young people (Smith 2006).

The emergence of the risk society has also seen a big shift away from the young person and towards the offence – a focus on the 'deeds' rather than the 'needs'. The increasing concern with minimising risk has led to risk assessments displacing needs assessments in youth justice. More widely the 1998 Crime and Disorder Act introduced a definitive split between child and family welfare and youth justice and many commentators have pointed out the implications this has for this group of highly vulnerable young people.

This is particularly relevant as there is increasing empirical evidence on how childhood and adolescence has become significantly more challenging in the UK. For example, a study by the Institute of Psychiatry shows a 100 per cent increase in the prevalence of emotional problems and conduct disorder among young people since the early 1990s, a trend that was not discernible in either the USA or the Netherlands (Nuffield Foundation 2004). Children's well-being across many countries compares unfavourably in the UK (UNICEF 2007). Compared with our European neighbours young people in the UK are more likely to experience early pregnancy, drug and alcohol misuse, educational failure and incarceration, and much of this literature suggests that there are specific socio-economic conditions that are critically affecting the very nature of childhood in the UK (Dixon and Margo 2006).

These conditions seem to be creating serious problems for many children and young people as they attempt to navigate extended and risky pathways to adulthood, particularly in environments plagued by high levels of poverty and income inequality, economic inactivity, educational failure and social isolation. In response the Labour government introduced wide-ranging measures between 1997 and 2010 to tackle child poverty, social exclusion, neighbourhood disadvantage, educational underachievement and health inequalities with children and young people being viewed as 'vulnerable', 'deprived' and 'excluded'.

In youth justice, however, due largely to the dominant risk discourse, where government has been especially if not more active, it has adopted a very different view of children and young people as 'depraved' rather than deprived, 'troublesome' rather than troubled. Arguably protection of the public has eclipsed children's welfare needs due to the emphasis on risk. The evolution of the Respect agenda under the 1997–2010 Labour government on anti-social behaviour stood in stark contrast to its policies on the education and well-being of children as laid out in Every Child Matters.

Risk factor research (RFR) has become even more attractive to policy-makers than 'What Works' research as through espousing a clear scientific method it has identified those aspects of the lives of young people most associated with offending. Its proponents claim considerable predictive power for this approach and that it exposes the causes of delinquency and points the way to cures. It is attractive to a range of key audiences: 'The list of risk factors for future offending produced by RFR provides academics, policy makers and practitioners with a ready set of targets for intervention' (Case and Haines 2009: 1).

However, as with the 'What Works' evidence, practitioners need to appreciate that the findings of RFR have inherent limitations and are not free from political bias. While the approach and the findings appear straightforward and based on common sense, their applicability to working with individual young people is much more contested (Case and Haines 2009).

Risk factors have been criticised on a number of grounds, particularly for reducing young people who offend to little more than a collection of risks. This carries the potential for both labelling and net-widening (Kemshall

2008). Risk factors are not necessarily either constant or universal. Risk factors associated with certain offences may well not apply to other offences. Equally they may not transfer readily across different ethnic and gender groups.

Predicting delinquent pathways is difficult given the complex social processes and interactions that are involved which over time can produce quite different outcomes than initial risk assessment at a young age might have predicted.

Many of the risk factors established by large-scale studies are only correlates and can rarely be seen as 'causes' of offending. Even where it is established what the temporal order of events was and a given risk precedes offending, this does not explain how and why this translates into offending.

Equally importantly broad-brush studies cannot lead to predictive accuracy for individuals where risk has been aggregated across groups. Through the search for clear and practical findings, such oversimplification may have occurred as to render them almost irrelevant to a practitioner working with a young person in a complex and dynamic environment and possibly without all the relevant basic information.

The potential of risk factor research to provide useful findings for policymakers and practitioners is clear but this potential is yet to be fully realised. Doubts about some aspects of the validity of RFR do not of themselves call the 'What Works' approach into question. It is certainly true that many commentators portray the risk-based approach as forming a complete package that includes evidence-based practice. The simplistic model is that RFR identifies the causes of crime which are diagnosed in the individual through actuarial assessment, which is then prescribed a specific treatment which has been carefully tested and validated, resulting in a 'cure'. Of course in reality the evidence does not and probably never will exist to support this chain of reasoning. Even if the first two links in the chain were abandoned and a needs-led social welfare approach was adopted, many studies that have contributed to the evidence base on interventions would still be valuable. For example, it is hard to argue that being able to access and thrive in education is not a social good and a universal entitlement for young people, and studies which help us achieve that for young people remain relevant in both a needs-based and a risk-based model.

The matching process given all the qualifications about the nature of the evidence on both risks and interventions needs therefore to be handled with considerable caution. In any event, many are very general such as 'organisational change in schools' covering a wide range of interventions nearly all of which are beyond the influence of a Youth Offending Team (YOT) or simply provide overlapping lists. The list does, however, illustrate the differences in empirical evidence underpinning some interventions and is a guide as to the range of interventions that arguably all YOTs should be aware of if not actually providing.

Managerialism and the audit society

In parallel to the increased awareness of risk has been the growth of managerialism in public services. Over the past 20 years, issues such as value for money, effectiveness, accountability and transparency have come to dominate public services. As trust in the traditional authority of professionals has diminished, it has been replaced with reliance on audit and inspection systems.

Evidence-based practice draws much of its strength from an audit culture. For instance, both processes share an overwhelming emphasis on effectiveness and the need to demonstrate accountability and transparency. Both approaches are also characterised by an attempt to reduce complexity to manageable proportions through the introduction of batteries of guidelines, checklists and procedures. Within youth justice, both processes are combined in the Youth Justice Board's Effective Practice Quality Assurance Framework, whereby practitioners audit their own performance within a framework of evidence-based practice.

The perceived challenge to professionalism by the new managerialism as it has been dubbed has evoked a fierce response claiming that 'these developments suggest a wholesale dehumanisation of the youth crime issue, such that the sole purpose of youth justice becomes one of simply delivering a cost-effective and economic "product"' (Muncie 2004: 275). Other commentators have claimed the 'zombification of youth justice professionals' (Pitts 2001a), that 'the professional skills of youth justice practitioners were neutered, and the principled "systems management" of the 1980s was replaced by a technocratic managerialism with no principles or independent rationale' (Smith 2003: 3).

An uncritical defence of professional autonomy, however, may ignore vested interests and the negative effects of many welfare interventions. There is no necessary conflict between an approach that focuses on children's rights and a managerialist and audit culture. Arguably, there is a paucity of information about the lives of many young people who become drawn into the youth justice system. Useful management information is signally lacking, for example, on those young people who are detached from mainstream education. Information flowing into and out of custody is a trickle despite the considerable financial and human costs associated with incarceration (ECOTEC 2001a). Neither is bemoaning the lack of resources devoted to remedying the underlying structural factors behind crime always compatible with railing against managerialist approaches that emphasise effectiveness, value for money and the opportunity costs of interventions. It could just as easily be argued that there is not enough of a managerialist or audit culture within youth justice which would more readily expose under-resourcing or poor performance locally and the low priority given to many of these young people by mainstream services (Stephenson 2007).

While the role of managerialism is part of a much wider debate, several points are worth considering in relation to evidence-based practice in youth justice. Critics of managerialism ignore some key issues such as accountability, equity and service users' choices. Managerialism aims to make agencies and professionals subordinate to the needs and informed choices of the public. In achieving this, services must be accountable to the public for their quality of performance. For instance, the use of targets, standards and performance indicators has received much criticism yet there is a considerable amount of evidence that they have a positive effect on outcomes across public services for marginalised and vulnerable groups of people (ESRC 2009, cited in Brindle 2010). With regard to equity, the fact that young people and families in some areas have fewer interventions available is difficult to justify and identifying these shortfalls potentially enables them to be remedied. Differential use of custody despite similar offences and circumstances, for example, raises issues of accountability, equity and value for money as well as social justice, and identifying and dealing with this problem is entirely compatible with a managerial approach.

Research and practitioners

Although members of the public might reasonably assume that the actions of professionals are determined largely by the most up-to-date and reliable research findings, in reality this is often not the case. Studies across most disciplines indicate that for a variety of reasons many professionals only make relatively limited use of research findings in their day-to-day decision-making.

More significant influences on practice are:

- knowledge gained during primary training;
- prejudice and opinion;
- outcomes of previous cases;
- fads and fashions;
- advice of senior and not so senior colleagues.

(Trinder and Reynolds 2000)

One contributing factor to this situation is that much of the research available to practitioners lacks methodologies which are robust enough or appropriately consistent to be applied confidently. In addition, the volume of available research (irrespective of its methodological merits) can often overwhelm busy practitioners. Also, many do not possess the appraisal skills to assess the validity of the research methodologies employed and the overall quality of the research.

In this context evidence-based practice provides a framework which attempts to:

- narrow the research–practice gap;
- enhance the take-up rate of research by practitioners;
- provide a consistent methodology for researchers.

Some studies suggest that in disciplines such as social work the application of theory or research to practice tends to be, at best, ad hoc. Although judgement, values and intuition are always extremely important, it makes it more difficult for practitioners to make decisions regarding choices where there is a lack of empirical evidence as to the effectiveness of the options. Despite this, it has been argued that the ethos within social work and to some extent probation does not always support an empirical approach.

The YJB embarked on its effective practice strategy to influence practice in a constructive and coherent matter in order to improve outcomes both for young people and the public. It is clear that there were wide variations in such important matters as the quality of assessment at this time, and the introduction of *Asset* and other measures was intended to enhance practice and make it more consistent. In terms of managerialism, it is worth noting that the YJB's relationship with YOTs is not that of command and control. The governance arrangements introduced in 1998 established a balance between the centre and local authorities and deliberately did not go down a national service route. Accordingly, the use of much of the material on effective practice is voluntary as is participation in the relevant training. The accredited programmes approach was rejected by the YJB, which arguably gives practitioners more discretion.

'What Works' in youth justice

The expression 'What Works?' provides a further historical dimension to this discussion. It derives from the title of an article by Robert Martinson (1974: 49) which concluded, on the basis of research existing at that time, that there was 'no clear pattern to indicate the efficacy of any particular method of treatment'. This conclusion was not universally accepted at the time, and Martinson himself acknowledged that the poor design quality of many research programmes might preclude the detection of any positive outcome. Nonetheless, it is only in more recent years that a certain consensus has developed among researchers that some approaches to working with young people who offend seem capable of having an impact on reducing their offending.

Meta-analysis (a statistical tool which facilitates the aggregation of results from different studies) has been used since the mid-1980s to review a large number of research studies which, in combination, confirm a positive overall effect. Clear trends have been detected concerning the ingredients of programmes with higher or lower levels of effectiveness in reducing offending. The term 'What Works' is often used to refer to that body of research knowledge and to the principles deriving from it, although it has now become associated with a much narrower definition with a strictly defined methodology, a concentration on programmes and a specific type of guidance.

Determining effectiveness

Practitioners are beset by a confusing array of ill-defined labels to describe particular interventions or programmes. Just how are 'good', 'best', 'innovative' or 'excellent' practices to be differentiated? Without clear criteria to define and thereby judge the impact of particular practices, how can replicable and sustainable programmes be identified, let alone transplanted to different environments?

The definition and application of effective practice are rooted in the wider concept of evidence-based practice. The term 'effective practice' is not used here as a synonym for evidence-based practice. Rather, it refers to those programmes, processes or ways of working which have the highest level of validation from research and evaluation. Evidence-based practice refers to the wider, cross-disciplinary approach to delivering those products and services that has been validated according to the accepted criteria.

Based on a widely used definition of evidence-based medicine (Sackett *et al.* 1997: 71) the equivalent for youth justice could be:

> the conscientious, explicit and judicious use of current best evidence in making decisions regarding the prevention of offending by individual young people based on skills which allow the evaluation of both personal experience and external evidence in a systematic and objective manner.

This has the advantage of not being constrained by too slavish an adherence to purist 'What Works' methodologies and definitions of evidence and places due emphasis on the role of the practitioner.

The criteria for judging the validity of any intervention can be generic, but effectiveness is determined in the context of the required outcome. This varies considerably and can be contradictory even among allied professions. While meeting the needs of the child is of paramount importance in social work, the primary aim of all interventions in youth justice (as laid down in the Crime and Disorder Act 1998) is to prevent offending. Similarly, interventions which have been shown to increase self-esteem, for example, but not to reduce offending may be deemed ineffective in youth justice terms (although some interventions are effective in reducing offending and as a by-product increase self-esteem).

Evidence-based practice represents a new cultural approach for youth justice services to adopt, but strictly speaking most approaches to preventing offending in the UK must be deemed 'promising' or 'unknown' rather than truly effective.

Evidence

The fierceness of the 'What Works' debate is generated by problems over what constitutes sufficient evidence, the extent to which the scientific rigour of the natural sciences can be applied to youth justice policy and practice and assumptions about the relationship with research evidence and practice. The issue is not whether evidence is significant but the kind of evidence and how different kinds of evidence are valued. Practitioners are continually drawing on a wide range of evidence – from listening to others, observing young people, reading reports, reasoning or reflecting, in addition to research evidence in its different forms. The 'What Works' movement is about establishing particular ways of generating or marshalling evidence.

Relatively little account has been taken about how this and other evidence is transmuted into practice. Arguably there needs to be more emphasis on the fact that evidence can only indicate a balance of probabilities and that there is a significant challenge in reconciling research evidence with knowledge acquired from other sources.

The allegedly selective use of evidence by policymakers has led to a gap between research findings and policy formation and practice development (Goldson and Muncie 2006). This can be compounded by a lack of methodological rigour of some evaluations (Bottoms 2005). Accordingly it may also be that many practitioners may resist 'What Works' research evidence if it is perceived as a tool to enforce government policy. The dialogue between practitioners and researchers is important and may be better serviced by a more flexible approach about what should be valued as evidence. This may be enhanced by more concentration on the application of research methods to practice rather than simply research findings.

The hierarchy of evidence

There are several frameworks for classifying crime prevention interventions according to the extent and nature of the supporting research evidence. For example, Utting and Vennard (2000) use the following four categories.

- *What works* – where a programme has been positively evidenced by at least two evaluations which show statistically significantly different outcomes for participants against a comparable group of non-participants.

- *What doesn't work* – where a programme has at least two evaluations (comparing participants against a group of non-participants) which demonstrate ineffectiveness.

- *What's promising* – where a programme has been positively evidenced by at least one evaluation which shows statistically significantly different outcomes for participants against a comparable group of non-participants.

- *What's unknown* – any programme not classified in the three previous categories.

Such a framework can provide a means of assessing the weight of the evidence base in respect of particular interventions. It is worth emphasising that although the framework specifically mentions crime prevention, it is a hierarchy of validation which constitutes a means by which to judge any aspect of the functioning of the youth justice system.

It is also worth remembering that just because a particular intervention or programme lacks a thorough evaluation it does not necessarily mean that it is any the less effective. What is more challenging, however, is when a team or individual continues with an intervention or programme that the research evidence indicates is likely to be ineffective.

The approach of the 1997–2010 government and of the YJB towards research and evaluation has been criticised on several grounds in that although there has been a tenfold increase in research publications by the Home Office and the YJB in the decade 1997–2007, compared to previous decades it has followed a particular research agenda (Phoenix 2009). This agenda, it is claimed, sought only to reinforce policy priorities and was based on a series of unquestioned assumptions about the youth justice system.

The emphasis on programme evaluations in pursuit of 'What Works' evidence potentially ignores other types of research such as qualitative or theoretical studies which could equally assist policymakers and practitioners and it has been argued that a more imaginative research strategy may be required from the youth justice policymakers in the future (YJB 2008a).

According to the evidence compiled on behalf of the Youth Justice Board (Communities that Care 2001: 124) the characteristics of interventions that may be less likely to be effective include those that:

- are given to those at lower risk of offending and reoffending;

- use vague, unstructured counselling;

- are unable to address multiple problems presented by young people whose offending behaviour is persistent and/or serious, including poor mental health and drug and alcohol abuse;

- are too brief or diluted to establish the conditions in which young people can make sustainable changes in their lives;

- focus on restraint without significant effort in the direction of rehabilitation.

Risk and protective factors

Despite the very different theoretical backgrounds, most studies adopt a risk and resiliency approach in trying to disentangle the causes of delinquency. While risk factors are associated with an increasing likelihood of the commencement, frequency and duration of offending, protective factors reduce the probability of such outcomes despite these risks. Not only do risk factors tend to be interrelated and occur at the same time but they may also be symptoms rather than potential causes. For example, failure at school has often been linked with offending and in this context non-attendance may be highly associated with poor academic attainment, and both may be correlated with delinquency. There are several possible directions of influence. Not being in school could equally be either a cause or an effect of low attainment. Similarly, both risk factors could be the cause or effect of delinquency. Alternatively, an independent variable, such as learning difficulties or high impulsivity, may be creating these intervening variables.

Although there are weaknesses in the evidence relating to the causes of youth crime the body of research particularly that derived from longitudinal studies provides significant insight into the risk and protective factors that lead to some young people developing offending behaviour while others do not. While no single factor can be specified as the 'cause' of offending behaviour it is possible to elicit relatively short series of the main risk factors that, particularly when clustered together in the absence of the most important protective factors, are implicated in the onset and continuation of offending behaviour. A significant criticism of this approach is that it may give too great a weight to individual risk factors at the expense of ignoring socio-economic influences (Goldson and Muncie 2006).

Risk and protective factors model

In order both to take account of the research findings and to provide practitioners with a straightforward approach to implementation it may be helpful to adopt a simple risk and protection model. Within this model the twin objectives are to reduce the exposure to risk and to enhance protective factors identified by the research for children and young people.

These risk and protective factors could be grouped in the following way:

Risk factors	Protective factors
Family factors	Social bonding
School factors	Healthy beliefs and clear
Community factors	standards
Personal, individual or peer factors	Opportunities, skills and
	recognition

(Adapted from Communities that Care 2001)

Risk factors

Exposure to the risks listed below appears to increase significantly the chances of young people becoming involved in crime.

Family	School
Deprivation, particularly low income, poor housing and large family size Conflict within the family Ineffective supervision Passive or condoning attitudes in relation to anti-social and criminal behaviour A history of criminal activity from parents or siblings	Organisational weaknesses in the school Low achievement from primary onwards Lack of attachment to formal schooling Aggressive behaviour, particularly bullying
Community	Individual/peer
A disadvantaged and neglected neighbourhood A lack of attachment to the neighbourhood Ready availability of drugs High turnover of local population	Delinquent peer groups Hyperactivity and impulsivity Attitudes sympathetic to offending Substance misuse

Protective factors

The absence of all or any of the risk factors may afford protection against involvement in offending. A range of protective factors that will safeguard against involvement in crime and mitigate the influence of the risk factors listed above has been identified. These protective factors include:

- being female;

- possessing a resilient temperament;

- being attached to community and school;

- opportunities for developing social and reasoning skills;

- recognition and due praise.

(Rutter *et al.* 1998)

Salience, prevalence and modifiability

There are three important dimensions to risk and protective factors. Evidence is accumulating that indicates how widespread is a particular risk factor such as low attainment in school, i.e. the prevalence. In contrast salience measures how influential is a particular risk factor, such as low achievement beginning in primary school, in predicting the likelihood of offending. The degree to which a particular risk factor can be modified is very important from a practitioner's perspective in deciding which to tackle.

Obviously being a male is a widespread and significant risk factor but is not susceptible to change.

Matching programmes/interventions to risk factors

It is possible to map particular interventions and programmes that have been validated to a greater or lesser extent for their effectiveness against those risks which have been identified as being the most widespread or important for youth crime (see Table 1.1).

The limitations of the 'What Works' approach

Despite its rational appeal the 'What Works' approach has attracted significant criticisms. Although purportedly value free, being the objective application of rigorous research findings to interventions to prevent offending or reoffending, it can be seen as being quite the opposite. 'What Works' is the manifestation of the current political emphasis on competence in delivering hard outcomes to key parts of the electorate (Bateman and Pitts 2005). Under the guise of its apparent simplicity and rigour which enables its messages to be neatly packaged to both the public and practitioner, 'What Works' stands accused of distorting research findings, deskilling and wasting the creativity of practitioners and justifying interventions that increase offending. While the condemnation of the Youth Justice Board sometimes veers into polemic rather than objective analysis, these are cogent criticisms that require discussion.

The 1997 New Labour government through the Crime and Disorder Act 1998 attempted to modernise youth justice and to legitimise its changes. In doing so it not only made some decisive breaks with the past but inevitably through the Youth Justice Board emphasised the failures of both past governments and interventions by practitioners. Evidence-based policy is only the servant and not the master of political priorities. Accordingly, where evidence supported the value of diversion, the ineffectiveness of custody and indicated caution over the effectiveness of ISS which were at odds with political imperatives, it tended to be ignored. This was at times perhaps accompanied by an unwarranted degree of confidence in the success of the post-1998 policy initiatives such as the Detention and Training Order (DTO).

Philosophical issues

One fundamental issue is that 'What Works' is predicated upon the assumption that a straightforward natural science approach is achievable. This positivist approach can lead unwary policymakers into a belief that universal truths can be produced for the social sciences, in this case criminal justice, with the same uniformity and reliability as for physics or chemistry. Certainly this approach has fitted readily into certain aspects of medicine

Table 1.1 Effective interventions by youth crime risk factor reduced

Risk factor	Programme strategy*
Poor parental supervision and discipline	**Pre-natal services; family support using home visiting; parenting information and support; pre-school education;** *after-school clubs*
Family conflict	**Family support using home visiting; parenting information and support**
Family history of problem behaviour	**Pre-natal services; parenting information and support; family support using home visiting; family literacy**
Parental involvement in/attitudes condoning problem behaviour	**Pre-natal services; parenting information and support; family support using home visiting; family literacy**
Low family income/poor housing	**Pre-natal services; family support using home visiting;** *after-school clubs*; housing management initiatives
Low achievement beginning in primary school	**Pre-natal services; parenting information and support; pre-school education; family literacy; reading schemes; reasoning and social skills education; organisational change in schools;** *after-school clubs*; *mentoring*; *youth employment with education*; preventing truancy and exclusion; further education for disaffected youth
Aggressive behaviour, including bullying	**Parenting information and support; pre-school education; reasoning and social skills education; organisational change in schools;** *mentoring*; preventing truancy and exclusion; youth work
Lack of commitment, including truancy	**Pre-school education; family literacy; reading schemes; reasoning and social skills education; organisational change in schools;** *mentoring*; **youth employment with education**; preventing truancy and exclusion; further education for disaffected youth; youth work
School disorganisation	**Reading schemes; reasoning and social skills education; organisational change in schools;** preventing truancy and exclusion
Alienation and lack of social commitment	**Parenting information and support; reasoning and social skills education; organisational change in schools;** *after-school clubs*; *mentoring*; *youth employment with education*; preventing truancy and exclusion; further education for disaffected youth; youth work; peer-led community programmes

Individual attitudes that condone problem behaviour	**Parenting information and support; organisational change in schools;** *after-school clubs; mentoring;* preventing truancy and exclusion; youth work; peer-led community programmes
Early involvement in problem behaviour	**Parenting information and support; reasoning and social skills education; organisational change in schools;** *after-school clubs; mentoring;* preventing truancy and exclusion; youth work; peer-led community programmes
Friends involved in problem behaviour	**Parenting information and support; reasoning and social skills education; organisational change in schools;** *after-school clubs; mentoring;* preventing truancy and exclusion; youth work; peer-led community programmes
Disadvantaged neighbourhood	*Community mobilisation; community policing; youth employment with education;* housing management initiatives
Community disorganisation and neglect	*Community mobilisation; community policing; youth employment with education;* youth work; housing management initiatives
Availability of drugs	**Organisational change in schools;** *community policing;* youth work; peer-led community programmes
High turnover and lack of neighbourhood attachment	**Organisational change in schools;** *after-school clubs; mentoring; youth employment with education; community mobilisation; community policing;* further education for disaffected youth; peer-led community programmes; housing management initiatives

*Strategies in bold are those for which programmes have been evaluated in the UK and shown to reduce the relevant risk factors.

Strategies in bold italics are those for which programmes have been evaluated outside the UK and shown to reduce the relevant risk factors.

Strategies in normal type are those which have not undergone either form of evaluation.

Derived from Communities that Care (2001: 64).

and healthcare. Acute medicine and other areas such as primary care and mental health have been relatively enthusiastic supporters. Yet even within health there are concerns about the displacement by randomised controlled trials (RCTs) of qualitative research looking, for example, at patient preferences and values (Reynolds 2000).

But it has been argued that disciplines such as social work and probation are inherently different from medicine. Here the effect of a 'dose' of intervention is not readily predictable from person to person and where a great diversity of external elements can influence the outcome. This complexity and unpredictability does not always sit comfortably within the rigid methodologies of 'What Works'. As Trinder (2000: 149) concluded:

> ... social work encounters are not straightforward or linear relationships, but multiple, multilayered, relational and complex, and located in a social and political context. Within this framework of the inherently messy and complex nature of social work and probation relationships, classic formulations of evidence are impoverished and potentially constraining.

Randomised controlled trials

In evaluating treatment or intervention measures the most widely recognised research methodology in the evidence-based practice movement is that of the randomised controlled trial (RCT). This is often dubbed the 'gold standard' method of assessing the effectiveness of an intervention. The principal characteristic of an RCT is that the participants are randomly allocated to either the group receiving the intervention or the control group. This is designed to limit bias, particularly where neither the participants, the practitioners or those gathering the data know the difference between groups. A comparison of the changes in outcomes or behaviours between the participants of the two groups reveals the existence and size of any effect of the intervention. If several such studies are carried out with similar findings then there can be considerable confidence in replicating the intervention more widely.

In tandem with the use of RCTs has been the application of meta-analysis, a statistical approach whereby results are aggregated from different studies that use experimental and control groups. This enables a large number of evaluations of different interventions to be combined to assess whether there has been any effect (positive or negative) and to gauge the size of this effect. The advantage of this aggregation is that it highlights the overall effects of interventions while minimising or statistically controlling for small differences between studies. Its strength therefore is in identifying broad patterns of findings in an arguably clearer and more consistent way than more traditional reviewing techniques of research.

In a review of the findings of meta-analysis it was claimed 'that the net effect of "treatment" in the many studies surveyed is, on average, a reduction in recidivism rates between 10 per cent and 12 per cent' (McGuire and Priestley 1995: 9). Given the considerable volume of research involved, these results may appear modest but, for example, similar meta-analysis of many medical interventions such as heart bypass surgery or some cancer treatments reveal effects of this scale.

Criticisms of RCTs

There are significant criticisms of the 'What Works' approach being so heavily dependent on RCTs. This may seem a rather esoteric debate, of little relevance to practitioners, but it does pose important questions about the nature of evidence and its translation into effective practice. Taken together the criticisms undermine an oversimplified approach to devising and implementing a 'What Works' approach but also indicate productive ways forward.

It has been argued that the RCT is much more effective where singular treatments are applied to a well-defined set of subjects with specific outcome targets. This could be deemed simplistic when applied to the complexity of many of the circumstances and interactions within youth justice. To take a practical example: the education and training of young people in custody, which is supposed to be the most important intervention (judged by numbers of hours at least). In the context of evaluating the education of prisoners Pawson (2000: 66) emphasised a series of complexities that undermines an RCT approach:

- Education is not a 'treatment' applied in dosages but a multifaceted and prolonged social encounter involving a range of ideas, curricula and personnel.

- The 'subjects', namely inmates, are hardly uniform and while they do not represent an exact cross-section of society, they do present a mighty range of social backgrounds, a positive jumble of prior educational experience and, indeed, an unfortunate array of offences.

- The rehabilitative 'outcome' of prisoner education is rarely perceived in simple, therapeutic terms but is considered to work *indirectly* via building character, raising self-confidence, acquiring competence, gaining credentials, promoting self-reflection, creating moral standards, improving social skills, enlarging cultural aspirations and so on.

While Pawson dismisses such an approach to answering the question 'Does prisoner education work?' as a 'dangerous oversimplification' he does not abandon attempts to answer it. Faced with the multifaceted nature of education acting on individuals in such chaotic circumstances as is often the case in a Young Offender Institution (YOI) it is arguably much more sensible to be asking questions such as 'why' the education of young people who offend might work, and going on to inquire 'for whom' and 'in what circumstances' and 'in what respects' it appears to work (Pawson 2000).

RCTs are often perceived to be weak at establishing causal connections and there is little attention given to the mechanisms by which change in an individual occurs. Similarly the context is often ignored. As Pring has highlighted, 'such large-scale explanations cannot be sensitive to the complexity and variability of social rules and expectations through which decisions and actions are made intelligible' (2004: 207). The social rules and the institutional framework within which young people and practitioners operate can vary enough to mean that an intervention that might be apparently effective in one context might not be in another. For instance, a similar intervention in a custodial environment might have a very different outcome to one in the community.

A related assumption underlying the quasi-experimental method of RCTs is that the administration of the appropriate intervention dosage to the individual will result in the desired cognitive behavioural change with little consideration of the motivation and predisposition of the individual. Rather than programmes simply working on individuals it has been argued that they must work *through* individuals.

> Potential subjects will consider a programme (or not), volunteer for it (or not), become interested (or not), cooperate closely (or not), stay the course (or not), learn lessons (or not), retain the lessons (or not). Programmes are thus learning processes and, as with any learning process, certain groups and individuals are much more likely to have the appropriate characteristics which will allow them to stay the course. (Pawson 1997: 155)

The blunt nature of the quasi-experimental approach that masks the differences in context and the interactions with individuals perhaps explains why the results of RCTs with matched cohorts of young people can be inconsistent.

Clearly, too, when aggregating many studies through meta-analysis only average measures of changes in recidivism are used. Even on the most effective programmes where recidivism has decreased on average by about 40 per cent this disguises a performance range both above and below this central score. The inference that practitioners can therefore draw is that even when they apply interventions which are rated the most 'effective', the outcomes could range from a complete cessation of offending through to a significant increase. Equally, there may well be individuals who participate in interventions that in aggregate appear to be ineffective, such as custody, who nevertheless find it a life-changing experience.

It is important though in recognising the limitations of the quasi-experimental approach that this is not exaggerated to the extent of committing the 'uniqueness fallacy' as Pring has warned (2004: 208). A false dualism can be created whereby the kind of evidence which relates to the explanation of physical events such as the effectiveness or not of medical interventions is portrayed as inapplicable to the uniqueness of the human condition. While these methodologies cannot at present provide universal truths it is undeniable that much of human behaviour is predictable. Certain types of intervention can be identified that, other things being equal, can have particular consequences.

There are other difficulties with quasi-experimental methods. There are ethical problems in denying potentially helpful interventions, no guarantee that random selection will produce the essential comparison groups, imperfect data-gathering and transmissions systems, and perhaps importantly, strong vested interests. Few managers would go to all the extra work involved in such research and risk exposing their existing interventions as ineffective if they were compared with a comparison group.

RCTs tend to produce guidance for practitioners that relates to interventions with individuals rather than for initiatives that focus on neighbourhoods or cities. In practical terms it is obviously much simpler and less expensive to allocate individuals randomly to different intervention groups than to do so with cities or neighbourhoods. In addition it is far harder to conduct large-scale trials without the design being compromised by the treatment group's knowledge of the intervention and this being transmitted to and affecting the control group (Tilley 2006).

The quasi-experimental approach is not necessarily useful in assisting practitioners to decide what does not work, partly due to its inherent methodological limitations. Commenting on the largely consistently negative findings for Scared Straight and similar programmes (where a young person is exposed to confrontational insights into prison life) Tilley (2006) points out that as there is no understanding of why failures occur then the conclusions must be necessarily limited. He goes on to list the possible explanations. Were the young people not scared? Or did they enjoy being scared and so the experience acted as an inducement? There could have been significant variations within the group with certain subsets being deterred while others were encouraged. Then again the dosage may simply have been too low to make an impact. Perhaps for those already committing offences or inclined to do so the visits removed the mystique of custody, rendering it less scary?

In any event public and political opinion is not necessarily amenable to certain research messages that conflict with common sense or more punitive approaches. One well-known American project highlights this problem – Drug Abuse Resistance Education (DARE). Strong empirical evidence including studies using a random assignment design has indicated that DARE is not effective (Howell 2003). Yet it remains a very large programme employing more than 50,000 police officers lecturing in nearly half of America's elementary schools. One explanation for its continuing popularity despite being apparently a failed intervention is because it is founded on a mistaken belief in the effectiveness of deterrence. It appears that fundamental beliefs in the efficacy of repressive deterrence are irresistible, particularly when combined with an apparent common-sense approach. The zero tolerance approach applied to schools has also been found to be ineffective but this has not restricted its popularity in the United States and its potential spread to the UK (Howell 2003; Smith 2005).

More benign motives can lie behind projects where the evidence does not suggest that they are effective. Flexible provision linked to schools, with the ostensible aim of reintegrating young people, can often counter-intuitively lead to a greater detachment. The youth inclusion programme developed by the Youth Justice Board is a structured youth work programme combining elements of education and personal development targeted on the 50 most at risk young people in a neighbourhood. Referral criteria include poor attendance or exclusion from school. Its targets included reducing recorded crime by 30 per cent and reducing non-attendance and school exclusion each by 30 per cent. The outcomes have, however, included a 6 per cent increase in offending and a significant deterioration in attendance. While this approach might have made common sense from a youth justice perspective, from an educational perspective it ran the risk of providing young people with an easy option educationally and enabled schools to divert young people who may have been challenging in school settings towards more 'appropriate' education provision without resort to exclusion (Burrows 2003).

Implementation

From a policymaking perspective, rigorous, consistent evaluation of pilot projects followed by the refinement of the model and then the faithful implementation of this model subsequently maintained by data returns and inspection appears straightforward. From a political standpoint it is axiomatic that communities and young people should have access to the same quantity and quality of public services. Yet significant and perennial problems with implementation consistently undermine this process.

The inconsistent and limited findings of 'What Works' studies have been attributed to the weaknesses of implementation: 'The results reported in this volume say a great deal about implementation, its problems and its effects on outcomes rather than the true effect of interventions' (Chitty 2005: 79). This is disputed on two counts. Given that an intervention can only have effects if it is implemented this appears an artificial distinction (Smith 2006). Others feel that researchers and policymakers have accused practice and thereby practitioners of poor performance. In this line of argument 'the problem appears to have been more fundamental than this, having its origin in the researchers' understanding of the nature of the human sciences and their beliefs about human nature' (Bateman and Pitts 2005: 250).

This may be overstating the case and certainly ignores the effects of, for example, poor recording and weak exchange of key information between professionals but, equally, over-reliance on a methodology that does not explain how particular outcomes are achieved in detail constrains replicability.

The past decade has seen very substantial increases in expenditure on public services and there have been consistent problems in implementation of initiatives to time, cost and volumes of services. This has a significant impact on evaluating, particularly using more sophisticated approaches such as RCTs which require sufficient numbers of young people who have similar characteristics and antecedents. In youth justice projects that have been set up later than planned, data collection has been limited and referrals lower than expected. These problems would have beset any evaluation strategy but can have damaging consequences within a 'What Works' approach. Where the implementation of new initiatives or interventions has drifted and invalidated the research design, potentially erroneous inferences may be drawn by policymakers. The enormous attrition of participants involved in the Basic Skills Pathfinders programme, for example, meant that the original research intention to judge the impact of improvements in basic skills on offending had to be abandoned and this has led some civil servants to query whether there is any effect rather than to challenge the model of implementation used (McMahon *et al.* 2004).

The disparity between the certainty with which research findings can be hailed by policymakers and the cautious, limited and often ambiguous nature of those findings can be considerable. This is underlined by much of the evaluation commissioned by the Youth Justice Board. The first notable attempt to gather evidence systematically was through the evaluation of initiatives supported through its development fund. These initiatives included cognitive behaviour, restorative justice, substance misuse, education, training and employment, parenting, final warning interventions, and generic preventative services. Each had a separate evaluation and all the national evaluators questioned the extent to which there was evidence of effectiveness (Fullwood and Powell 2004). All suffered from poor data collection, late starts and fewer referrals than the Youth Offending Teams (YOTs) had predicted.

So widespread and apparently endemic are the problems with implementation that what is needed according to Smith (2006) is a theory of implementation. This would assist in disentangling the effects of programme and implementation weaknesses. There may be all sorts of constraints inherent in the circumstances that affect, for example, engagement in groupwork programmes or education, training and employment.

It may be that implementation and project management skills in both central and local government are in relatively short supply compared to the demands of the many initiatives that have been launched. There may also be diminishing returns as an initiative moves from its early stages which tend to attract the most motivated managers and practitioners only to find effects diluted later when the less enthusiastic or downright hostile teams become involved.

While it may be unfair to blame practitioners for the shortcomings of researchers' theories and the over-reliance on methodologies that are important but not sufficient, there is abundant evidence that many practitioners do not always put a premium on recording and data collection. This goes beyond a failure to comply with the managerialist demands of a perceived technocratic government and perhaps partly reflects the lack of a practice culture that is routinely evidence-informed.

Many research studies have been stymied by the lack of the most basic information on key aspects of a young person's life. Studies incorporating large samples of *Assets*, for example, can find problems with the quality of its completion, its transfer when necessary and keeping it up to date (for example, ECOTEC 2001a). These problems persist both within the youth justice system, particularly between custody and community, and between youth justice and key agencies such as education and health (Stephenson 2007). The systemic weaknesses over data exchange continue through time as the recording practices and management information systems are unable to keep pace with the often turbulent lives of young people who appear and disappear within the purview of a range of agencies. Very few studies are able to follow large enough groups of young people who have been in the youth justice system over a significant period of time to judge the longer-term impact of an intervention and to gain insight into why it appeared to have had the effect it did. The use of reconviction data has its limitations and longitudinal studies tend to suffer attrition among the group who have detached from mainstream services.

A major concern about placing too much emphasis on RCTs and meta-analysis is that they tend overwhelmingly to be North American in origin whereas the British equivalents are much more limited both in scope and positive findings (Chitty 2005). Not only does there appear to have been a longer-standing evaluation culture with significant resources devoted to the more costly research methods such as longitudinal studies or RCTs but of course the context and mechanisms for change may be radically different from those of the UK. Despite the 1997–2010 government's espousal of evidence-led policymaking (Cabinet Office 1999) evaluation often appears to be relatively ad hoc and small-scale.

The Crime Reduction Initiative in Secondary Schools (CRISS) programme in the UK comprised a series of school-focused development projects from which it was hoped to identify measures to reduce actual and potential offending by young people. There is a marked contrast in the nature of this initiative compared to some of the American examples. The CRISS programme was relatively short-term (two years), contained a very wide range of rather disparate initiatives (38 projects involving over 100 schools with each school implementing between five and ten separate interventions) and there was a much less rigorous evaluation methodology with a considerable emphasis on qualitative research. Not surprisingly, although a central objective of this programme was the collection of robust evidence, the best that could be achieved were recommendations for promising approaches (Home Office 2004). None of these programmes could be validated using the hierarchy of evidence outlined above.

Given all these difficulties it has to be seriously questioned whether the widespread use of RCTs is actually practicable in the youth justice field, at least at present. Paradoxically the Home Office reaction has been to call for greater methodological rigour in its pursuit of policy certainties (Harper and Chitty 2005). Apparently RCTs are robust enough to ensure 'that our knowledge of "What Works" is truly improved and the existing equivocal evidence is replaced with greater certainty' (Chitty 2005: 82). The Youth Justice Board, although rejecting the strict 'What Works' approach adopted by the probation and prison services, has nevertheless been drawn more closely into the Home Office approach to research.

Guidelines for more effective practice

While the use of RCTs and meta-analysis clearly has limitations, it has enabled a series of principles to be identified regarding the design of effective programmes and interventions. These principles do not provide a prescription of what to do, let alone how to do it, in terms of reducing or stopping a young person's offending. What they offer though is a framework within which projects can be developed and evaluated, or guidelines when constructing a package of interventions. The following seven principles are drawn from McGuire and Priestley (1995) supplemented with that of 'dosage' (Lipsey 1995). Each of the following chapters in this book places the topic covered – restorative justice or mental health, for example – within this framework to illustrate their application in practice.

Principles of effective practice

- *Risk classification* – matching the level and intensity of intervention to an assessment of the seriousness of offending and the risk of reoffending.

- *Criminogenic need* – programmes should focus on those factors that directly contribute to offending, as opposed to more distantly related causes.

- *Dosage* – programmes must be of sufficient intensity and duration to achieve their aims.

- *Responsivity* – matching the learning styles and strategies of young people to the staff working with them.

- *Community based* – learning takes place in a context that is meaningful to the young person, i.e. close to the young person's experiences and life contexts.

- *Intervention modality* – programme content and methods are skills-based, focused on problem-solving with a cognitive behavioural approach. Programme interventions mirror the multiple needs (criminogenic) of the young person.

- *Programme integrity* – effective programmes have a clear rationale. They link aims to methods, are adequately resourced, staff are trained and supported, and there is appropriate monitoring and evaluation.

Risk classification

The evidence suggests that levels of intervention should be commensurate with the likelihood of offending. Therefore those young people deemed to be at greater risk of offending should be placed on more intensive programmes. Equally those of lower risk should receive lower or minimal intervention. This is not simply a matter of the efficient allocation of

25

Table 1.2 *Asset* scores and risk of reoffending

Asset score	*Risk of reoffending*
0–4	Low
5–9	Low–medium
10–16	Medium
17–24	Medium–high
25–48	High

Source: Baker *et al.* (2005).

resources but also because intensive interventions with those at low risk can have counterproductive results and be associated with increases in offending (Nacro 2006). The reasons for this are unclear but may lie in similar explanations as to net-widening whereby labelling and the effects of mixing with more delinquent peers tend to draw a young person further into the youth justice system.

Risk is defined here on an actuarial basis whereby *Asset* uses prior history of offending and a range of other dimensions such as education, family and health to predict the likelihood of subsequent offending. The designers of *Asset* advocate that a banding is used to establish risks of reoffending (see Table 1.2).

Asset scores can therefore be helpful in assigning those most at risk of reoffending to more intensive interventions. Of course *Asset* has limitations. Its predictive accuracy, although similar to actuarial systems for adults who offend, is only about two-thirds. There is much less emphasis in *Asset* on the role of protective factors which may ameliorate risk though this reflects a wider lack of knowledge. The negative aspects of young people's lives tend therefore to be overemphasised. There will often tend to be gaps in the evidence needed for scoring. In matching young people to particular intensities of intervention, *Asset* is a helpful tool but should be used in the context of a practitioner's skills and experience (Annison 2005).

There are dangers, particularly for young children, if an actuarial approach does not take account of existing needs and problems rather than focusing simply on some future risk of criminality. Assessment (of which *Asset* is but one component) underpins effective planning by practitioners who have to make judgements often on the basis of unreliable information.

Criminogenic need

Where young people have particularly chaotic lives, which is a characteristic of many of those in the youth justice system, a practitioner is often faced with such a welter of problems, for example homelessness, substance misuse, family discord and detachment from education, that it is often difficult to set priorities for interventions. This principle stresses the need to distinguish between those problems or features that appear to contribute to or underlie offending rather than those that may be only distantly related, if at all. The criminogenic needs will of course in practice often be difficult to distinguish for a particular individual. Practitioners have to become adept at deciding which are the priority issues to focus on in their work with a young person. This would not mean that those factors apparently more distantly related to offending should be ignored but might mean that a caseworker would broker access to other services rather than deal with them directly.

The assessment process is clearly crucial in constructing a plan with interventions that are targeted effectively at those factors considered most likely to be direct contributors to offending behaviour. The *Asset* assessment revolves around 12 dimensions of dynamic risk factors, each of which is scored according to the extent to which it is considered to be linked to the young person's offending. So both the principle and the *Asset* process are designed through the exercise of professional judgement to lead to planned interventions with clear priorities.

Sentencing of young people who offend is, in effect, based on the principle of proportionality: any punishment imposed by the court should be commensurate with the seriousness of the offence (and previous offending, where this is relevant) (Nacro 2000). In addition, as YOTs become more conversant with *Asset* and the requirement to assess 'risk' factors, the possibility of future risk posed to a community by a young person will become a relevant factor. The view taken by the court of the seriousness of the offending determines the type of order available to the court. Thus, in most circumstances, a custodial sentence can only be made where the offending is so serious that only a custodial sentence can be justified. Similarly, a community sentence can only be made where the offending is serious enough to justify a community sentence. In both cases, the restriction of liberty involved in any court order, as determined by the length of the order and the intensity of intervention, must be proportionate to the young person's behaviour.

While the statutory framework technically applies to sentencing, there are good reasons for adopting a similar approach at the pre-court stage in relation to Final Warning interventions, and when determining the content of a youth offender contract. Article 40(4) of the United Nations Convention on the Rights of the Child (UNCRC), to which the UK is a signatory, requires that young people who offend should be dealt with in a manner 'proportionate to their circumstances and the offence'.

The situation is further complicated by what is commonly referred to as 'the welfare principle'. Section 44 of the Children and Young Persons Act 1933 requires that:

> every court in dealing with a child or young person who is brought before it, either as being in need of care and protection or as an offender or otherwise, shall have regard to the welfare of the child or young person.

The welfare principle is reiterated in Article 3(1) of the United Nations Convention on the Rights of the Child:

> In all actions concerning children, whether undertaken by public or private social welfare institutes, courts of law, administration authorities or legislative bodies, the best interests of the child shall be a primary consideration.

The effect of the Human Rights Act 1998 is to make it unlawful for any public authority to act in any way that is incompatible with the European Convention on Human Rights. YOTs and establishments within the juvenile secure estate clearly fall within the definition of a public authority, and in those circumstances at least two articles of the Convention have potential relevance to planning and delivering interventions to young people who offend.

The right to a fair trial (Article 6) has a broad application. It includes all actions taken, from the arrest of an individual through to sentence. The delivery of an offending behaviour programme at any stage should therefore be a 'fair' response to the young person's behaviour. At one level, this is simply to reiterate the earlier point about interventions being proportionate to the level of offending. In addition, however, it might be argued that Article 6 obliges practitioners to ensure that:

- any programme is appropriate to the young person's circumstances;

- any programme is delivered in a way that maximises the chances of compliance;

- in the case of a Final Warning, where participation in the programme is technically voluntary, the young person's consent is sought.
  (*R* v. *Metropolitan Police Commisioner* and *R* v. *Durham Constabulary* (2002))

Article 8, on the other hand, deals with the right to respect for private and public life. To comply with this Article, an intervention which involves disclosure of personal information or intervention with the young person's family must be justifiable on the basis that it is a reasonable response to the offending behaviour intervention.

The human rights framework is broader than that provided for in domestic legislation. The UNCRC and the United Nations Standard Minimum Rules for the Administration of Juvenile Justice (commonly known as the Beijing Rules) provide more detailed guidance for the delivery of programmes to young people who offend. In general, the overall effect is to suggest that any programme designed to address offending behaviour should be tailored to meet the particular circumstances of the young person, and should form part of an integrated approach aimed at promoting healthy development.

Dosage

Despite its medical overtones this is a straightforward principle, i.e. the amount of contact received by a young person in relation to reducing their offending. This comprises both duration and intensity. In Lipsey's (1995) meta-analysis of the effectiveness of interventions he defined low dosage as interventions that were of 26 or fewer weeks, with less than two contacts per week and a total contact time of 100 or fewer hours. High dosage was more than 100 hours' total contact time over more than 26 weeks with two or more contacts per week. Given the entrenched nature of the disadvantages that many young people in the youth justice system have suffered from or their chronic involvement in harmful behaviours such as substance misuse, it is fanciful to suppose that limited sporadic interventions will have much impact on their circumstances or behaviours. Equally, where the risk classification principle is not observed and young people are targeted who have not offended or are at low risk of reoffending, then a high dosage may increase the chances of offending.

It might be supposed that the volume of interventions would be well established given how relatively straightforward it is to measure compared to other aspects of intervention. This is not the case. The great majority of evaluations lack this important evidence and this is mirrored by similar deficiencies in monitoring returns. Consequently, evaluations often focus on completion rates and their association with outcomes such as reductions in offending. Useful though this is it leaves open the question of just how much intervention is necessary and for how long interventions should last for optimum outcomes.

Even in controlled institutional settings very little is known about the levels of participation and consequent outcomes. In custody the most intensive intervention is supposed to be education or training yet this appears to be extremely difficult to ascertain (Stephenson 2007). Apparently, 'it is clearly still the case that in many establishments reporting systems are not sophisticated enough to provide information on the actual take-up of learning and skills as opposed to what is on offer' (Youth Justice Board 2004c). This confusion between what is planned and what is actually delivered extends more widely within the prison service. The Chief Inspector of Prisons' recent report produced a series of examples illustrating how the hours of 'purposeful activity' were greatly exaggerated in half of the local prisons inspected. With Soviet-style creativity, the prison ship *Weare* even had pre-printed forms containing hours out of cell prepared in advance (HM Inspectorate of Prisons 2006).

These problems may also be commonplace in the community. The evaluation of Intensive Supervision and Surveillance Programmes (ISSP) noted that the monitoring software was used for constructing timetables rather than recording actual delivery and recording non-compliance (Moore *et al.* 2004). Government targets can also exert a powerful influence on returns, perhaps leading to an emphasis on what is planned rather than actually achieved for a young person. For example, the Youth Justice Board's target of 90 per cent of YOT supervised young people being in suitable full-time education, training or employment averages about 75 per cent nationally yet a national census revealed a figure of less than 50 per cent (Youth Justice Board 2006). A lack of detailed registration systems, generous interpretation of counting rules, including counting arranged destinations, may have been behind this.

Despite the importance of programmes it is the individual supervision of a young person that is the spine for interventions. Yet the amount of such supervision appears both poorly recorded and relatively limited (Audit Commission 2004). This is an important but under-evaluated area. The inadequacy of available resources or more often the difficulty of accessing, for example, mainstream services such as education also tends to undermine adherence to this principle. Often managers and practitioners may take refuge in the notion that a young person is so 'disaffected' that they are not yet ready for full-time interventions. Ostensibly reasonable though such assumptions are they ignore the impact of the pervasive low expectations of these young people which tend to be self-fulfilling. These rather convenient assumptions which implicitly attribute responsibility to the young people rather than lack of resources, appropriate provision or engagement skills do not take account of studies such as Hurry and Moriarty's (2004) evaluation of education, training and employment (ETE) projects which demonstrated that relatively high levels of engagement were possible. The one project which achieved this also had recording systems that enabled an analysis of dosage in relation to outcomes and shed light on the possible relationship between literacy and numeracy gains and subsequent reductions in offending (Hurry et al. 2006).

Responsivity

Apart from the issue of special educational needs very different learning outcomes can result for individual young people. This is despite the nature of the topic, the knowledge and skills of the learner, their motivation, their previous experience of learning and the knowledge and skills of the person facilitating this learning. The gap between the theoretical understanding of such individual differences and a practical application in particular learning circumstances has been bridged by a wide range of style constructs.

Differential learning outcomes, despite common contexts, have been tackled by several criminologists. Bonta (1996: 31), for instance, asserts 'offenders differ in motivation, personality, and emotional and cognitive abilities, and these characteristics can influence the offenders' responsiveness to various therapists and treatment modalities'.

Out of the extensive literature that has resulted over many years, academics in both education and criminal justice have adopted learning styles as being useful in understanding and supporting learning. Within education the concept of learning styles appears to be widely accepted and various instruments are employed to assign learners to particular categories.

In youth justice, while managers and practitioners may view formal learning as being largely the province of education professionals there is to some extent a recognition that, for example, interventions that aim to change behaviour depend upon learning. Certainly those academics concerned with the identification of the effectiveness of interventions in preventing offending and reoffending have often embraced the validity of learning styles constructs:

> Programmes work best when there is a systematic matching between the styles of workers and the styles of clients. But on balance the learning styles of most offenders require active, participatory methods of working, rather than either a didactic mode on the one hand or a loose, unstructured, 'experiential' mode on the other. (McGuire 1995: 15)

There are three key assumptions that can be questioned within this principle: that learning styles can be clearly defined and measured and are relatively unchanging for individuals; that matching this learning style with the respective teaching/instructional styles makes a significant difference; and that young people who offend tend to have an active and participatory learning style.

Even bolder claims have been made for the negative impact of a lack of responsivity in education. It has been argued, for example (Hodges 1982), that the urban poor (in America) and young people who offend are more likely to possess a right-brain dominance and be spatial/holistic, visual learners. This is contrasted with the assertion that most learners in society possess a left-brain dominance and are verbal/analytic learners. This chain of reasoning has linked disruptive behaviour, detachment from school, low attainment and associated offending by so many of the urban poor to their inability to learn effectively due to the verbally-based instructional methods that allegedly characterise most American schools.

Although learning styles are meant to be stable psychological constructs, they have been remarkably difficult to assess reliably for any learners, let alone young people who offend. A recent comprehensive literature review commented that despite the weight of material this area was 'opaque, contradictory and controversial' with 'very few robust studies which offer ... reliable and valid evidence and clear implications for practice based on empirical findings' (Coffield *et al.* 2004: 21).

This report concluded that not only were most of the psychometric instruments unreliable and lacking in validity but they were unsuitable for learners with relatively low levels of literacy, which is a common characteristic of many young people who offend.

A more fruitful approach probably needs to take account of the relationship between learners' use of effective learning strategies and their academic attainment (Adey *et al.* 1999: 21). It is possible that children and young people with low academic attainment did not absorb some of the basic learning strategies required for school learning during their primary education.

A report into learning styles and young people who offend (Youth Justice Board 2005a) concluded: '. . . the evidence does not have sufficient weight to justify claims of the existence of a discrete, stable learning styles construct. Indeed it could be constrictive and unhelpful to rely heavily on such a simplistic approach.'

Accordingly, each of the chapters interprets the responsivity principle in terms of understanding and responding to a young person's learning strategies and learning skills. One of the key differences is that unlike putative learning styles, strategies and skills are under conscious control and can be learned and improved upon. The challenge for practitioners here then is, firstly, assessment of a young person's repertoire of learning strategies and skills, and then taking account of it in a subsequent intervention and working as far as is possible to enhance it.

One important element in enhancing a young person's repertoire is the process known as meta-cognition – the awareness of one's own thinking and the control of that knowledge as one engages in a cognitive event. While this approach may seem directly relevant to skill acquisition such as literacy and numeracy it is equally applicable to certain interventions that focus on thinking skills.

It is important under this principle that other factors that may be relevant to the relationship between the practitioner and the young person in facilitating learning are taken into account such as maturity, gender and ethnicity. Similarly the young person's readiness to change is a crucial component depending on what stage of change they may be at (see p. 64 below).

Community based

On balance interventions delivered in the community appear to be more effective than those in custodial or institutional settings. This can be developed further in that interventions carried out closer to a young person's home environment may be more likely to achieve transferable learning. It appears very difficult to enable learning that can transfer between very different environments. This may partly explain the ineffectiveness of custody and also of interventions such as Outward Bound programmes, particularly if delivered in isolation.

Within the community this principle could be taken to include enabling young people to gain access to and participate effectively in mainstream provision, particularly education but also health, leisure and cultural activities such as libraries and museums. The majority of young people in the youth justice system who have any education provided experience it through on- or off-site units (Learning Support Units (LSUs) or Pupil Referral Units (PRUs)) or, post-16, through specialist training providers who cater largely for those who offend. Such settings may share fundamental weaknesses such as the formation of negative or delinquent peer groups, trying to change behaviour out of the original context and marginalisation of staff.

Given that young people will ultimately have to return to mainstream environments such as further education colleges or employment then, arguably, segregated education or training could create more problems than it solves. Similarly small group or one-to-one contacts may be more effective in enabling the transfer of learning if conducted in ordinary community settings, libraries, youth clubs, etc.

Intervention modality

There were consistent findings from Lipsey's meta-analysis (1995) regarding the nature of effective interventions. Those programmes that appeared to be more effective tended to recognise the breadth of challenges facing many people who had offended and to devise a range of interventions to match them – multi-modal. These interventions also had a focus on the acquisition of skills intended to enhance problem-solving, social interaction or other kinds of coping skills. The methods were often drawn from the two traditions within psychology of behaviourism and cognitive theory or a synthesis of the two – cognitive-behavioural.

One important potential application of this principle is that interventions that in isolation have not been demonstrated to be effective, can if combined into a broader, structured approach focused on criminogenic needs, have better outcomes. For example, outward bound activities or sports or arts interventions can be integrated into a wider programme (Chapman and Hough 1998).

This principle has often tended to be dominated by cognitive-behavioural approaches, particularly with adults. The prison and probation services have invested heavily in such approaches through formally accrediting programmes. Many commentators see a disproportionate emphasis on such programmes with Rod Morgan, when Chief Inspector of Probation, warning of 'programme fetishism' (HM Inspectorate of Probation 2002). This is partly because the evidence regarding the effectiveness of these programmes can be questioned: 'While the studies indicate that programmes of this kind have an influence on some offenders, for the majority the programmes *by themselves* are unlikely to deliver the outcomes in reducing offending that have been expected of them' (Roberts 2004: 156). Other factors were seen to play an important part in encouraging desistance, some of which – such as access to employment, training and education, and appropriate accommodation – could be influenced by practitioner intervention (Roberts 2004).

The results of evaluations of the effectiveness of YJB-sponsored cognitive-behavioural programmes had similar messages although some methodological weaknesses and low completion rates limited the findings (Feilzer *et al.* 2004). There are other flaws in the accredited cognitive-behavioural programmes that require other interventions such as the fact that the literacy skills of many of the young people in custody are not of a sufficient level to succeed in these programmes (ECOTEC 2001b; Davies *et al.* 2004). In contrast to the prison and probation services the Youth Justice Board has not adopted an accredited programmes approach, thereby giving more scope for a range of intervention modalities.

Programme integrity

This principle espouses the requirement that there should be an explicit theoretical base to an intervention and that it should be faithfully implemented. One of the explanations given for inconsistent findings of effectiveness of particular interventions is implementation failure. This is seen as potentially masking what might otherwise have been effective interventions (Harper and Chitty 2005). Threats to the integrity of an intervention have been identified as due to drift, reversal and non-compliance (Hollin 1995). Drift refers to the gradual slippage of the aims of the intervention whereby perhaps a lack of clarity over initial longer-term objectives means they are eclipsed by more immediate concerns, or simply the inertia of existing ways of working prevents change. Reversal is where some staff actively work to undermine or reverse a new approach, perhaps because they are operating from a different theoretical perspective or value base (Hollin 1995). Non-compliance is where elements of a new initiative are ignored or replaced by staff so that a customised version emerges that has little resemblance to the original intended objectives and methodologies.

These threats to faithful implementation are largely separate from the exercise of creativity to adopt and improve a particular approach or to fit it more closely to the local context but rather, deliberately or unconsciously, prevent a new initiative from being tested for the first time.

The barriers to faithful implementation can be presented by the organisation, the practitioner or the young person. The culture of particular YOTs or custodial establishments may be inimical to change or have elements of disorganisation that prevent a staff group from effectively implementing a new initiative or intervention as originally intended. This can often include a lack of training, although training by itself will not necessarily turn an ineffective organisational culture around.

Practitioner resistance can spring from several sources. It may be that a particular programme appears so prescriptive as to erode professional autonomy or that evaluation is intrusive and time-consuming.

The engagement of young people in evaluation processes could be considered as part of the wider issues concerning participation and completion of interventions. Knowledge of the nature of engagement is increasing, albeit often from a standpoint of education (Fredericks *et al.* 2004). If particular practitioners are half-hearted in their support of evaluation then it might be expected that some young people would mirror this.

It has been suggested that close researcher involvement in the design and implementation of an intervention leads to a higher level of programme integrity. Lipsey (1995) highlighted that researcher involvement was second only to the type of intervention in being associated with positive effects on reducing offending.

The role of the practitioner

The implicit role of the practitioner in some examples of guidance can appear somewhat mechanical with little scope for the exercise of their expert judgement or discretion. While the methodology of meta-analysis appears insensitive to the influence of practitioners the approach to the implementation of accredited programmes or simplistic 'What Works' guidance has also been criticised for neglecting the importance of effective relationships (McNeill and Batchelor 2002; Tilley 2006).

While research has tended to concentrate on the characteristics of effective programmes or interventions, there is no reason why the particular elements of a practitioner's craft cannot be subject to an evidence-based approach. Unfortunately, most of the research has been on adults who have offended and applying these findings to young people has to be done with great care. The effects of maturation and the very different contexts and opportunities such as access to the labour market could alter the effectiveness of particular practitioner styles and approaches.

In contrast the centrality of relationships is often emphasised in discussions regarding the role of parents. If ineffective parenting, characterised by such features as harsh and inconsistent disciplining, weak supervision and monitoring, and limited positive involvement, has been found to be related to the development of anti-social behaviour then it is a reasonable supposition that equivalent practices by practitioners within schools, custody or YOTs could have similar negative outcomes.

Using the findings from studies of desistance and resilience to explore the effectiveness of the relationship between young people and practitioners, Batchelor and McNeill (2005) highlighted the potential of motivational interviewing and pro-social modelling. While motivational interviewing is not yet supported by convincing evidence as to its effectiveness with young people who offend, it has been found to have positive effects with those who have substance misuse problems, albeit they are older than those in the youth justice system (Harper and Hardy 2000). Within this approach key factors in more effective styles of practice have been identified such as the abilities to express empathy, develop discrepancy (between current and desired behaviour), avoid arguments and confrontation, support self-efficacy and deal flexibly with resistance (Batchelor and McNeill 2005).

Certain principles for effective supervision can also be drawn from pro-social modelling. These principles include: role clarification – being clear about the purpose of supervision (or any intervention), mutual expectations, the tension between control and welfare, the constraints on confidentiality and any scope for negotiating.

There is some evidence with those older young people supervised by probation officers who had been trained in and made use of a range of relationship skills that more positive outcomes including lower reoffending rates were achieved compared to a control group (Trotter 1996).

What must always be borne in mind is that the particular context of the opportunities available to a young person can exert powerful negative influences that can overcome the effects of accredited programmes or defy the exercise of considerable skills and energy by practitioners.

See Chapter 3 for more on engagement.

Does guidance work?

Managers and practitioners in youth justice can sometimes feel besieged by guidance from central and local government and there is an abundant supply from various voluntary organisations. But does it work? In medicine it is claimed that there is strong evidence that guidance and guidelines have little effect on changing the behaviour of doctors to become more evidence-based (Peile 2004). The two major weaknesses with regard to guidance in criminal justice are first that it is widely ignored, and second that when it is not ignored it is poorly followed (Tilley 2006).

The reasons for this appear to be a combination of inherent deficiencies in guidance and barriers to its adoption. Most guidance is very limited in describing exactly how a practitioner can encourage desistance and why it will work with some young people in some circumstances but not with others. Where accredited programmes are concerned the level of prescription has been accused of crowding out the exercise of practitioners' discretion and limiting effective case management, which is reflected in high rates of attrition with very few people completing an intervention (Raynor 2004a).

More fundamentally perhaps is that detailed prescriptive guidance does not tend to reflect that much practice knowledge is not necessarily acquired or used consciously. The classic example of learning how to ride a bike emphasises the tacit nature of some knowledge:

> We cannot learn to keep and balance on a bicycle by taking to heart that in order to compensate for a given angle of imbalance (a), we must take a curve on the side of the imbalance, of which the radius (r) should be proportionate to the square of a 5th of the velocity (v) over the imbalance: $r \sim v2/a$. Such knowledge is ineffectual, unless known tacitly. (Polanyi 1969: 144)

Much of the craft of a practitioner in youth justice when interacting with a young person may be known tacitly. Such knowledge is usually acquired through personal contact and some variation of apprenticeship. The professional training of, for example, medics or teachers is not just about acquiring the theoretical knowledge but finding personal understanding through supervised practice training. Written guidance is therefore intrinsically insufficient to transmit this personal understanding.

In addition to these problems a range of other barriers prevents the ready absorption of research evidence disseminated through guidance. Much guidance flounders on inertia as the perpetuation of routine practices can be a formidable obstacle to change. Equally there can be a tendency simply to reframe traditional practice so that it fits with the latest policy guideline (Burnett and Appleton 2004). Similarly it has been argued that professionals such as teachers bring to teaching a set of beliefs and understandings that are resistant to particular kinds of research evidence (Thomas 2004).

Guidance based on research evidence often has to compete with information and advice from familiar local sources which may be more trusted or perceived as more authoritative. Adopting an analytical, reflective approach that takes into account the latest research evidence with its qualified and possibly ambiguous messages becomes very constrained in these circumstances.

While a considerable amount of energy has gone into amassing evidence of what might be effective in criminal justice, there has been very little research into the most effective processes by which this evidence can be transmitted into the knowledge and skills deployed by practitioners.

The stance adopted here is to encourage a more systematic incorporation of social science evidence into the tacit or craft knowledge of practitioners rather than claiming that practice is little more than the application of formulaic guidance or recipes. If a particular kind of evidence is seen to be imposed on practitioners through official guidance as the only means of achieving effectiveness it is unlikely to be accepted. Rather the research evidence set in the framework of the same principles of effectiveness is being made available to add to the evidential storehouse of the youth justice practitioner. Some of the more vitriolic attacks on the perceived approach of the New Labour government's initiatives in youth justice saw an imposition of a crude and ultimately ineffective 'What Works' approach.

Some critics of the 'What Works' movement come dangerously close to indulging in what Raynor (2004b: 171–2) has dubbed the 'myth of nostalgia, the belief that *everything was better in the old days*, when practitioners' autonomy and "established methods" (National Association of Probation Officers 2002) provided all the guarantees of effectiveness that were needed'.

Reflective practice

Just as it is vital that all work with young people who offend should be subject to formal review processes, arguably so too must practitioners and managers evaluate their decision-making in a less formal and more introspective way. Reflective practice then is an essential part of developing an evidence-based approach.

Reflection is required in situations where the subject matter or material is unstructured or uncertain, and where there is no obvious solution or course of action. (Moon 1999)

Table 1.3 Paradigms in learning

Old	New
Knowing what you *should* know	Knowing what you *don't* know
Much learning 'complete' at the end of formal training	Able to question received wisdom
Apprenticeship, learning from accepted wisdom	Able to generate and refine a question and find, appraise, store and act on evidence to solve it
Finite amount of knowledge to be absorbed	Lifelong learner
Intuition – very powerful	Complementing experience with knowledge from research
Dominated by knowledge from experience	Problem-based learning
Knowledge-based learning	

Source: Gray (2000: 94).

> Practitioners must learn how to frame the complex, ambiguous problems they are facing and interpret and modify their practice as a result. (Schön 1983)

Applying this in the context of evidence-based public health and the need to adopt very new approaches to medical education produced a different model of learning (see Table 1.3).

Figure 1.1 shows the cycle of activity that is required for a systematic

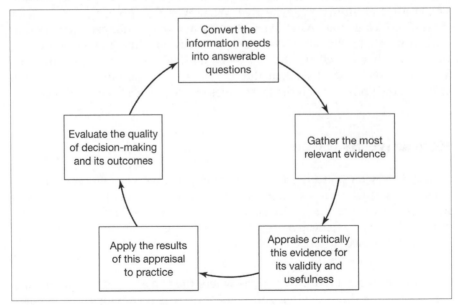

Figure 1.1   A systematic approach to reflective practice

approach to reflective practice to be adopted. Evidence-based practice can therefore be understood in terms of a different approach to learning for practitioners and managers within youth justice with more emphasis on a process of continuous self-directed learning in working to prevent offending. This generates the need for significant information to inform the key processes of assessment, planning and intervention.

Tilley has posed a series of relevant questions for policymakers, managers and practitioners to consider.

Some questions relating to evidence-based effective practice guidance:

1. **How is effective practice to be construed?**
   - Is it to be defined by method?
   - Is it to be defined by theory?
   - Is it to be defined by specific measures or tactics?
   - Is it to be consistent with specific values?

2. **What counts as research findings?**
   - Must they be 'experimental'?
   - Must they have internal and/or external validity?
   - Must the research be independent?
   - Must there have been peer review?

3. **What should be done where research findings appear to contradict one another?**
   - Should only the best or most plausible findings be drawn on?
   - Should the findings be aggregated in a meta-analysis to find net effects?
   - Should the conclusion be that patterns really vary by place, time and subgroup?
   - Should the conclusion be that the intervention differed in more or less subtle ways?

4. **What should be done where there is a shortage of research findings to draw on?**
   - Should guidance remain silent?
   - Should lack of evidence just be noted?
   - Should evidence for the underlying theory behind the practice be described?

5. **At what threshold of quality, consistency or volume of relevant research findings can policies or practices be described as good practice?**
   - Must research consistently indicate no unintended harm?
   - Must research show consistent benefits, at least for a subset of intended subjects?
   - How many studies or how many subjects are needed as a basis for establishing good practice?

---

6. **How are research findings to be applied in effective practice?**
   - How is successful work replicated?
   - How is successful work rolled out?
   - Which areas of what was done in a successful project are to be represented as effective practice?

7. **What should be included in effective practice?**
   - Should it include evidence used to identify the problem?
   - Should it include methods used to analyse the problem?
   - Should it include means by which the decisions were taken to put the measure in place?
   - Should it include results?

8. **How are research-based good practice guidance messages to be communicated?**
   - Should there be clear and specific injunctions about what to do?
   - Should there be clear injunctions about what not to do?
   - Should advice be given about what is promising?
   - Should there be discursive advice on methods of approaching crime prevention, evidence about their track record to date, and factors to be taken into account in choosing among them?
   - Should advice be pitched at specific problems or general issues?

9. **Are there aspects of good practice which lie beyond research findings?**
   - Are there ideological issues that need to be mentioned?
   - Are there tacit features of successful measures that need to be acknowledged?

(Derived from Tilley 2006: 219–20)

Conclusions

'What Works?' is a seductively simple approach to both policymaking and practice. Its appeal lies in its promise to cut through value-laden arguments, to bind different professionals and agencies together and provide *the* treatment. While it has been argued that this is a simplistic approach, neither is it as apolitical as it purports to be.

It must be emphasised that the research findings are rather cautious and incremental in nature, and build on the evolving knowledge base. This is not always echoed in the language of policymakers. Application of these findings may result in modest but significant reductions in recidivism. The systematic implementation of evidence-based practice is designed to minimise risks of offending. It offers no guarantees of success but aims to minimise the chances of failure.

It is salutary to remember that despite all the expenditure in recent years relatively little is known about *what* works, let alone *how* it works with young people who get drawn into the youth justice system.

It can be argued convincingly that work in youth justice is not always directly comparable to medicine in that a drug cannot simply be prescribed to achieve results when working with young people who offend. Despite this, it cannot be used as an excuse for not striving to develop practitioners who are qualified, research literate and evidence-based.

If the foundations of empirical evidence are to be strengthened and built upon it will be essential that not only is a reflective, evidence-based approach to practice in youth justice developed but that crucially there is an evaluation culture within teams.

Summary

- 'What Works?' is a deceptively simple and apparently apolitical concept, but it is not value-free and its applicability to youth justice has been contested. Very few interventions have been subject to the most rigorous of evaluations, and the evidence is better suited to indicating promising approaches rather than definitive prescriptions about exactly what works.

- There are inherent limitations in a simplistic 'What Works' approach, and complete reliance on RCTs and meta-analyses explains little about the mechanisms by which change occurs in an individual.

- Using a strict 'What Works' approach based on UK evidence alone means that most interventions with young people can at best be deemed promising rather than effective. Wider studies have indicated that modest but significant reductions in offending can be achieved through certain interventions.

- Risk factor research (RFR) has become even more attractive to policy-makers than 'What Works' research as through espousing a clear scientific method it has identified those aspects of the lives of young people most associated with offending. However, as with the 'What Works' evidence, practitioners need to appreciate that the findings of RFR have inherent limitations and are not free from political bias.

- 'What Works' guidance of itself appears to be a relatively weak way of transmitting research messages in order to inform practitioners and has to compete with other influences.

- The exercise of professional judgement and discretion by practitioners through casework and supervision may be undervalued by an overemphasis on accredited programmes. The effect of individual practitioner discretion and skills on outcomes has had little research attention.

- The main findings of meta-analyses may provide a useful set of guidelines for managers and practitioners to design, develop and evaluate their interventions.

Further reading

Raynor, P. (2004b) 'Seven ways to misunderstand evidence-based probation', in D. Smith (ed.), *Social Work and Evidence-Based Practice*. London: Jessica Kingsley.

Rutter, M., Giller, H. and Hagell, A. (1998) *Antisocial Behaviour by Young People*. Cambridge: Cambridge University Press.

Smith, D. (2006) 'Youth crime and justice: research, evaluation and "evidence"', in B. Goldson and J. Muncie (eds), *Youth Crime and Justice*. London: Sage.

2

Assessment, planning interventions and supervision and the scaled approach

Systematic assessment is central to work in youth justice. Currently *Asset* is the main assessment tool used in the youth justice system. *Asset* is often portrayed as emblematic of the youth justice reforms and has consequently drawn much fire from critics. Equally the Youth Justice Board has steadfastly emphasised its importance and the introduction of the scaled approach has again underlined the centrality of assessment processes. While much of the debate can seem irrelevant to the day-to-day practical realities facing practitioners, it is nevertheless essential that they appreciate the empirical basis for *Asset* and reflect on the arguments of its proponents rather than just the 'critics . . . [who] have the louder voice' (Case 2010: 91).

This chapter explores some of these issues. It also considers where *Asset* fits within the plethora of other assessment and planning systems that young people may be subject to.

The evidence base for assessment, planning interventions and supervision

There is consistent evidence (Andrews 1995; McGuire 1995; Chapman and Hough 1998; Utting and Vennard 2000) to show that interventions are more likely to be effective in preventing offending if they are characterised by:

- appropriate targeting of services to meet assessed levels of risk and need;
- work that addresses a range of offending-related problems;
- agreed objectives that are identified and adhered to.

At the heart of this process is high-quality assessment. Systematic assessment is central to the design, delivery and evaluation of both structured rehabilitative programmes and other types of intervention (for example one-to-one work with a young person that is closely tailored to his/her particular needs and capacity to respond). Assessment tools are designed to provide a common approach to the process of assessment. They can assist practitioners in planning their work, gathering appropriate and relevant information and analysing that information. This is intended to provide the basis for arriving at informed judgements and making decisions which are clearly rooted in assessment outcomes and transparent to young people, their parents/carers and professionals alike.

In the context of more recent youth justice policy, assessment has been defined to focus upon the principles of effective practice in crime prevention and rehabilitation interventions. As Utting and Vennard (2000) explain, 'prevention and rehabilitation based on the "What Works" principles requires the adoption of dependable methods for analysing the risks that individuals will continue to commit crime, and for recognising the criminogenic needs that interventions should address.'

Three types of possible risks are given priority in youth justice:

- *Reoffending* – the likelihood that the young person will commit further offences.

- *Vulnerability* – the risk that the young person might be harmed in some way by his/her own acts or omissions, or the acts or omissions of others.

- *Serious harm to others* – the risk that the young person might inflict death or injury (either physical or psychological) which is life threatening and/or traumatic and from which recovery will be difficult, incomplete or impossible.

These risk categories are not mutually exclusive; young people may experience two or more of the priority risk areas when engaging in certain risky activity. For example, a young person engaged in a high-speed chase while taking and driving away a car may be putting themselves at risk of injury as well as others who may be out on the road.

Assessment of risk

An assessment is likely to cover a wide range of issues, but within the context of youth justice, its primary focus is on risk factors relevant to offending behaviour. These are, 'factors that increase the risk of occurrence of events such as the onset, frequency, persistence or duration of offending' (Farrington 1997). A greater number of risk factors appears to increase the likelihood of offending behaviour (Farrington 2002). Broadly speaking, these fall into four main categories:

1. Family factors, for example:
   - deprivation, particularly low income, poor housing and large family size;
   - conflict within the family;

– ineffective supervision;
– passive or condoning attitudes in relation to anti-social and criminal behaviour;
– a history of criminal behaviour from parents or siblings.

2. School factors, for example:
   – low attainment from primary school onwards, particularly with respect to literacy and numeracy;
   – lack of attachment to formal schooling;
   – organisational weaknesses in the school;
   – aggressive behaviour, particularly bullying.

3. Community factors, for example:
   – a lack of attachment to the neighbourhood;
   – ready availability of drugs;
   – a disadvantaged area and neglected neighbourhood;
   – high turnover of the local population.

4. Individual/peer factors, for example:
   – hyperactivity and impulsiveness;
   – attitudes sympathetic to offending;
   – substance misuse;
   – association with delinquent peer groups.

(See pp. 3–6 for more on risk factor research and the risk society.)

An early age of onset of criminal behaviour has been shown to be associated with persistent and chronic offending (Farrington 1996). Early offending may itself produce reinforcing effects which contribute to recidivism. Once involved in offending, a young person may be more likely to associate with other young people engaged in criminal behaviour. A high number of previous convictions, a history of committing more serious offences and long periods of imprisonment have also been shown to be associated with recidivism (Cottle *et al.* 2001).

A placement away from (the parental) home may be associated with delinquency, perhaps because of the likelihood of associating with pro-criminal peers within a children's home or similar institutional environment (Moore and Arthur 1989), or the reduction of protective factors such as disruption to school placements. In the UK, evidence suggests that young people 'looked after' by local authorities are disproportionately likely to commit offences resulting in a prison sentence (Social Exclusion Unit 2001).

The evidence regarding the impact of factors such as low income and poor housing is somewhat unclear. There is much evidence to show that young people from families experiencing these problems are more likely to be involved in offending than those from affluent backgrounds (Farrington 1992). However, the connection between these factors and offending may not be straightforward. The link between social disadvantage and offending behaviour is likely to be indirect and largely mediated through family stress and poor parenting. Nevertheless, this factor still forms part of the causal chain for anti-social behaviour and provides a reasonable indicator of an increased risk of offending (Rutter *et al.* 1998).

From self-report data, Graham and Bowling (1995) identified low parental supervision as a key factor associated with the onset of offending. Having delinquent siblings was also strongly associated with offending for males, while nature/degree of attachment to family was significantly associated for females. The Dunedin study (Henry *et al.* 1996) highlighted poor parenting and adverse family situations as being associated with conduct problems persisting through childhood and into later life.

As well as being linked to early onset of offending, poor parental supervision has been shown to be associated with continuing involvement in crime (Wilson 1980). Young people from homes where parents behave aggressively are more likely to engage in violent behaviour themselves as adolescents (Farrington 1991). Clearer results have been demonstrated in relation to the link between juvenile recidivism and substance abuse and/or criminal behaviour by parents (Myner *et al.* 1998; Farrington 2000).

A history of physical or sexual abuse has been found to be associated with recidivism (Cottle *et al.* 2001). A link between abuse and loss and serious or violent offending by children and young people has also been shown (Boswell 1996).

Non-attendance at school is an important factor in relation to starting offending (Graham and Bowling 1995). Young people performing poorly at school are more likely to start offending (Maguin and Loeber 1996). Low grades and dropping out of education are associated with offending (Simourd and Andrews 1994). Being excluded from school is also strongly associated with offending (Budd *et al.* 2005). A study of the effects of permanent exclusion from school on the offending behaviour of young people (Berridge *et al.* 2001) confirmed earlier research findings of persistent offending among a high proportion of those excluded. A history of receiving special educational provision was also identified by Cottle *et al.* (2001) as a predictor of recidivism. See also Chapter 4 on education, training and employment.

This risk factor has particular implications for young African-Caribbean boys. Ofsted and the then Department for Education and Employment (Barn 2001) showed that they are four to six times more likely to be excluded than their white counterparts. At least some of this difference may be linked to teachers' responses to this group of young people. Therefore attempts to address educational requirements in this group would need to be particularly sensitive to their experience of education to date and would need to access resources directed at that experience.

'Children who grow up in economically deprived areas, with poor living conditions and high rates of unemployment, are at increased risk of involvement in crime' (Communities that Care 2001). Various other factors in neighbourhood and community life appear to be relevant to the development and persistence of offending behaviour: levels of disorganisation and neglect (Communities that Care 2001), availability of drugs and weapons (Rutter *et al.* 1998) and high levels of turnover among residents (Hope 1996).

Association with other young people who are involved in offending or anti-social behaviour is a key factor for the onset of offending (Graham and Bowling 1995; Budd *et al.* 2005), particularly for those who begin offending or engaging in anti-social behaviour during later adolescence (Fergusson *et al.* 1996). Delinquent peers and poor use of leisure time have been associated with recidivism (Cottle *et al.* 2001). Even though there are selection effects by which 'anti-social individuals tend to choose friends who are similarly anti-social', the peer group still influences the likelihood of a young person persisting with or desisting from anti-social behaviour (Rutter *et al.* 1998).

While many of the same risk factors may influence the onset of substance use and anti-social behaviour, there are additional ways in which these two types of behaviour influence each other (Rutter *et al.* 1998). Cottle *et al.* (2001) suggested that substance abuse – rather than substance use – is associated with recidivism. Associations between drug abuse and criminal behaviour are most likely to occur as a result of young people stealing to fund an addiction, or as 'an element of a deviant lifestyle in which anti-social behaviour is part of the ethos and provides some of the excitement' (Rutter *et al.* 1998). The prevalence of drug use in a cohort of young people at risk of offending or reoffending is likely to be high (Hammersley *et al.* 2003).

Rutter *et al.* (1998) summarised research concerning possible genetic and biological influences on anti-social behaviour (for example, the effects of toxins, nutrients and levels of serotonin). The influence of diet is another area receiving increasing attention (Peplow 2002). While many of these findings are still tentative, the impact of 'hyperactivity' on offending behaviour has been established (Loeber *et al.* 1993), although the attribution of hyperactivity as a label may cover a wide range of behaviours. There is evidence that many of those who display anti-social behaviour also show emotional disturbance and, in particular, that depression (and increased risk of suicide) often accompanies such behaviour (Myner *et al.* 1998). A history of non-severe pathology (defined as experiences of stress and anxiety) in young people who offend has been found to be associated with recidivism (Cottle *et al.* 2001). See Chapter 5 on mental health.

Data from the Cambridge study suggested that poor reasoning abilities contribute to criminal behaviour by limiting young people's ability to understand the consequences of their actions (Farrington 1996). Biased cognitive processing, such as misinterpreting social cues, is another factor shown to be associated with offending behaviour (Dodge and Schwartz 1997).

Studies have shown a link between high impulsiveness and criminal behaviour. Difficulty in delaying gratification when aged 12 appears to be (for boys) associated with anti-social behaviour (Krueger *et al.* 1996). Aggressiveness is another trait associated with offending behaviour (Rutter *et al.* 1998). Known school bullies have been found to be significantly more likely to be convicted of criminal offences in adolescence and early adulthood (Olweus 1991).

Young people who 'feel excluded from the mainstream and do not acknowledge responsibilities towards other people' may be at greater risk of involvement in offending behaviour (Communities that Care 2001). Those who have attitudes condoning criminal activity (and drug abuse) are more likely to get involved in such activities (Jessor and Jessor 1977). The early years of secondary school appear to be a significant turning point when young people are most likely to begin to adopt pro-criminal attitudes (Communities that Care 2001).

Protective factors and desistance from crime

The absence of risk factors may help to protect a young person from involvement in anti-social and criminal behaviour, but research has also identified other 'protective factors' which can reduce the negative impact of risk factors. These protective factors can help to explain differences in the frequency or seriousness of offending among young people exposed to similar risks (Communities that Care 2001).

There is obviously an overlap between tackling risk factors and encouraging protective developments. For example, dealing with school exclusion would both remove a risk factor and expose the young person to protective influences as a result of returning to the school community.

The number of studies focusing specifically on the concept of 'resilience' in the context of youth justice is limited. Resilience in general terms has been defined as 'positive adaptation in the face of severe adversities' (Newman 2004). Some commentators (Luthar 2003) stress that resilience is a 'process' rather than an innate character trait and that it is not limitless. In situations where adversity is persistent, extreme and unmitigated a young person is less likely to be resilient (Cicchetti and Rogosch 1997; Runyan et al. 1998). Some factors have been identified which may contribute to a young person's resilience, such as 'personal qualities that elicit positive responses from other people' (Rutter et al. 1998). Other components identified so far include a stable relationship with at least one family member (Rutter 1997) and good experiences at school as well as experiences that open up new opportunities or provide turning points (Bandura 1995; Farrington 2002). The ability to plan ahead also appears to contribute to a lower risk of anti-social behaviour (Quinton et al. 1993). In addition, the attitudes, expectations and standards of parents, teachers and communities may help to protect young people from risk (Catalano and Hawkins 1996).

A number of other studies have focused specifically on factors relating to stopping offending, although the findings of the literature on desistance are somewhat less clear than that for the onset or persistence of offending. Gaining employment has been found to be associated with desistance in some studies (Mischkowitz 1994) but not others (Rand 1987), although it should be noted that these studies focused on adults. Graham and Bowling

(1995) found differences in desistance factors between males and females. Factors such as educational achievement, avoiding heavy drinking or using drugs, and avoiding the influence of other young people were associated with desistance for males. For females, the transition to adulthood appeared more important, for example completing education or forming stable relationships.

Desistance factors are difficult to analyse in relation to the age of young people in the youth justice system (10–17) because many of the suggested factors (such as marriage or gaining employment) are not necessarily appropriate at this stage in life. Perhaps of the greatest practical relevance for youth justice staff are some of the other identified desistance factors, such as developing a sense of self-efficacy (Bandura 1995) and 'finding a sense of direction and meaning in life, realising the consequences of one's actions on others and learning that crime does not pay' (Graham and Bowling 1995).

Asset

Assessment of risk within the English and Welsh youth justice contexts has to date been by way of the *Asset* core profile, supplemented in some cases by specialist assessments relating to mental health, substance misuse or sexual offending.

Asset is the structured assessment tool used by YOTs and the juvenile secure estate in England and Wales with all young people who have offended. It examines a young person's offending and identifies the risk factors which may have contributed to it. It also highlights the young person's other needs and difficulties along with positive factors that need to be bolstered and supported. The information gathered from *Asset* informs decisions on interventions so that risks and needs may be addressed. *Asset* may be used when considering:

- bail;
- final warning;
- sentence;
- the content of programmes and interventions;
- identifying the risks of reoffending, vulnerability and serious harm to others;
- evaluating changes in needs and risk over time.

The *Asset* assessment tool has a theoretical underpinning based on examining the pattern of a young person's offending behaviour in the context of their 'life course' or 'developmental pathway' (Loeber and Le Blanc 1990; Sampson and Laub 1993). They facilitate the identification of significant life events – personal, social, situational – and ask practitioners to evaluate how they may interact to produce current behaviours (Thornberry 1996). In theory, such an analysis enables an evaluation of the different developmental pathways of young people who offend and those young people who do not. *Asset*, particularly when applied over time, may provide practitioners with an insight into a young person's 'criminal career' (Farrington 1997). Practitioners may be able to gain an understanding of what are the critical features that contribute to the different stages of offending – onset, escalation, persistence, specialisation and desistance. Although offending may be widespread among young people (Graham and Bowling 1995), there are different patterns of criminal career. A distinction is made between 'adolescence-limited' and 'life-course persistent' anti-social behaviour (Rutter *et al.* 1998; Moffitt 1993). Understanding and identifying these varying patterns is an important part of assessment and intervention.

The risk factors that *Asset* is built around are based on the likelihood of reconviction which is not the same as reoffending, as a considerable amount of crime goes unreported. It is true that this may disguise different levels of risk between those young people who have been reconvicted and those who have yet to be caught but arguably it is also acceptable to use reconviction as a proxy for reoffending given the imperfect nature of the evidence base and the discretionary nature of assessment.

With respect to serious harm to others, the *Asset* Risk of Serious Harm (ROSH) form is intended to support practitioners in making professional judgements on the level of risk and the nature and intensity of interventions needed to meet it. With respect to vulnerability, the 'indicators of vulnerability' section of the assessment documentation allows the bringing together of relevant risk factors.

Arguably the primary purpose of assessing is to prepare a plan for intervention if found necessary. This plan could include:

- the risk factors to be targeted;

- the protective factors to be bolstered;

- the role of designated staff in the risk management plan;

- the role of staff in allied organisations in managing the risk; and

- the review arrangements for the plan.

Where risks posed by young people in the community are deemed to be high or very high, local inter-agency risk management may be required either through an individually negotiated plan or through the Multi-Agency Public Protection Arrangements (MAPPA) structures. A vulnerability plan may be needed to focus on key issues such as risk of suicide, self-harm or physical/sexual abuse.

Following the introduction of *Asset*, the Youth Justice Board funded a detailed research study into the validity and reliability of its use. Two evaluations of the use of *Asset* in 39 YOTs examined the predictive validity and reliability of the assessment after 12 months (Baker *et al.* 2002) and 24 months (Baker *et al.* 2005). The research team reported that *Asset* had a predictive accuracy of 67 per cent and conclude:

> The results of the study provide further support for the . . . Youth Justice Board strategy of putting *Asset* at the centre of YOT practice. The data suggest that practitioners and managers can have confidence in using *Asset* as an indicator of risk of reoffending and also therefore of the level and intensiveness of intervention required to address offending behaviour. (2005: 7)

Criticisms of Asset

Six main criticisms have been put forward with regard to the methodology, content and practicality of *Asset*.

Factorisation

Asset is basically an actuarial form of assessment that gives rise to a series of scores for important domains of a young person's life (education, health, etc.) which indicate the likelihood of reoffending. Critics argue that reducing complex and interrelated experiences and circumstances to a score between 0 and 4 invalidates the process. Further, it is argued that the measurement of statistical relationships identified between particular risk factors and offending has been replaced by subjective judgements of practitioners.

This accusation would carry more weight if *Asset* was simply a tick-box, scoring system. However, it is made clear that scores indicate a likelihood, that evidence must be adduced to justify these assessments and that the scores reflect and guide the priorities of the practitioner in planning interventions. The practitioner is not conducting a micro research exercise to establish precise predictors of reoffending for an individual young person but rather using the risk factor evidence to provide a framework for their assessment which their professional judgement places in an appropriate context.

Marginalisation of young people's perspectives

Asset is accused of being an adult-led assessment and intervention process which is tantamount to 'a prescription without a consultation' (Case 2006: 174). As with several other criticisms of *Asset*, this is perhaps largely a failure to implement *Asset* properly rather than a function of the tool itself. The 'What do you think?' section is there to assist in the overall assessment process. Neglecting a young person's views within assessment and planning conflicts with what is likely to assist with engagement and is likely to reduce effectiveness.

Technicised practice

Rather than being an evidence-based approach that offers detailed, structured and reliable evidence of risk to inform decision-making and planning,

Asset has arguably been caricatured as a mechanistic tick-box system completed by 'zombified' practitioners (Pitts 2001a). Of course, like any system, practitioners can fail to comply with guidance but there is little evidence that *Asset* rather than the system of assessment encourages this. Rather than 'zombification' there is abundant evidence of inconsistency of practice and neglect of guidance.

Developmentalisation and psychosocial bias

One of the general criticisms of the YJB's approach is that it subscribes to theoretical views of offending such as the criminal careers model (Farrington 1997), the theory of age-graded informal social control (Sampson and Laub 1993) and interactional theory (Thornberry 1987) which tend, through their emphasis on psychosocial risk factors at different developmental stages, to focus on the individual. This is part of a wider debate which locates youth justice as part of a broader policy shift whereby the state withdraws automatic entitlement across a range of services and focuses instead on the rights and responsibilities of individuals, irrespective of broader structural circumstances and influences.

There are two issues here. In the first instance *Asset* does deal with broader more structural factors such as education, unemployment and neighbourhood. Secondly, the reality is that a practitioner deals with an individual rather than a socio-political system. While it is important to be modest about the potential that even the most skilled practitioner has for assisting change in the life of a young person, it is equally important to be realistic about the socio-structural changes that can be effected. All effective practitioners attempt to locate their intervention plans around the immediate context of the young person such as access to schools, colleges or training.

Predictive utility

Asset's predictive ability has been criticised on the grounds that about one in three young people (based on reconviction outcomes after one year) may have been predicted to offend but do not do so (false positives) or do offend when predicted not to do so (false negative). Potentially then the false positive young people could be involved in unwarranted interventions while the false negatives could miss out on possible important interventions.

Clearly it is important that practitioners do not believe that they are engaged in an exact science, and that is not how *Asset* was designed to be used. Even if the maximum score was attributed to a young person this would still only indicate a likelihood of reoffending, not a definite certainty. In relative statistical terms the prediction rate for *Asset* is good compared to other standardised tools but clearly there is a significant margin for error on an individual level.

Arguably, this and other criticisms miss the point that it is not solely the predictive validity of *Asset* that is important, but also its value as an aid to practitioners consistently and transparently identifying those domains associated most with offending in order to construct a more robust intervention plan for which they are accountable (Whyte 2009: 85).

Repressive welfarism

A more extreme criticism of *Asset* (or more accurately of the previous Labour government and the YJB's approach to youth crime) is that managerialism and a focus on risk tend to generate 'language, tools and strategies by which many "needy" young people are rendered punishable' (Phoenix 2009: 130). As the state continues to abrogate its citizenship responsibilities, YOT practitioners are driven to using increasingly punitive criminal justice interventions 'as a means to hold the state responsible for its obligations to vulnerable, marginalised and excluded young citizens' (Phoenix 2009: 130).

While these opinions are readily contestable, they do underline how perceptions of risk and need can become very blurred. This becomes even more apparent as risk of reoffending is supplemented by the more generalised notion of 'at risk' in the minds of some practitioners when using *Asset* (Phoenix 2009: 123). Clearly risk factors for reoffending can equally be construed as social welfare needs. For example, if a young person has no education or training provision available to them, then the likelihood of them becoming involved in offending through a variety of mechanisms may well increase but it is also plainly a welfare need.

Obviously allowing the concentration on risk of reoffending to become too diluted will reduce the predictive validity of *Asset* but, even within the more narrow focus, needs are not necessarily being ignored. Of course the conflict between welfare and justice approaches is nothing new in youth justice and any assessment system would have to balance these tensions.

The critics of *Asset* rarely discuss the state of assessment before the introduction of this standardised approach and instrument. Many aspects of the youth justice system operate differently whether on grounds of geography, gender or ethnic origin and assessment and planning appear to have been inconsistently applied to young people who offend. This raises important issues of accountability. Many youth justice interventions are inherently intrusive in the lives of young people and their families and significant coercive powers are used upon them. It is surely therefore a basic entitlement for young people to be subject to a consistent, evidence-based assessment process that has most chance of identifying those interventions that are more likely to reduce their chances of reoffending.

The fallibility of risk assessment processes means that there will be negative outcomes and again it is a matter of accountability that the key decisions can be seen to be reasonable. Clear accountability and defensible decision-making is important with respect to human rights legislation and principles. Used appropriately instruments like *Asset* enable more transparent professional judgements and decision-making. Whyte (2009: 83) has argued that they can assist defensibility within the principles of the United

Nations Convention on the Rights of the Child (UNCRC) by making explicit evidence of what is likely to be effective against the needs and risks identified and not simply what is available, and equally identify unmet need or the absence of early diversionary and staged intervention.

While there is a risk of focusing too much on the individual's potential for change rather than the intractable circumstances in which they find themselves, to deny agency altogether and the potential for change calls into question the effectiveness and role of practitioners. After all, if practitioners cannot be catalysts for change then this invalidates many of the arguments in favour of emphasising the importance of relationships. Most practitioners are only too well aware that many risk factors for reoffending may be beyond a particular young person's control.

Ultimately a youth justice assessment system is only as effective as the practitioners operating it. No assessment instrument can ever be perfect and practitioners are engaged in the management of uncertainty. However, the inevitable limitations are not a justification for inadequate or untimely completion of tools such as *Asset*, rather the reverse. Those limitations require *Asset* to be used in a critical and rigorous manner. Used in this way *Asset* enhances the competence of practitioners rather than supplanting their judgement.

The volume of the debate about actuarial assessment in general and *Asset* in particular can drown out the key message that assessment is simply the means to the end of effective planning and accompanying interventions. Simply focusing on the completion of the inventory and the scoring of individual risk factors can be at the expense of adducing the evidence and translating it into a well-matched plan. Unfortunately the evidence, although limited, suggests that plans often lack explicit links to assessment (YJB 2008a: 48). More generally practitioners' assessments and reports in youth justice commonly lack an analysis of the information and sometimes offer only a description or repetition of facts recorded elsewhere (YJB 2008a: 22). The failure to undertake a coherent assessment and planning process led to the findings of the Audit Commission that 'some YOTs appear to provide a standard programme for all those on their caseload, rather than tailoring interventions to particular needs' (2004: 75).

Poor communication between the different agencies involved with a young person in the care and criminal justice systems has often been cited as a cause of negative outcomes for young people. A standardised assessment instrument offers the opportunity to improve inter-agency communication. Similarly it enables the accumulation of aggregate data about the risks and needs of young people and the service gaps. This latter facility is often criticised as a feature of so-called managerialism yet this ignores the ability of individual YOTs or national bodies to advocate for young people and challenge other agencies. For example, the YJB championed the importance of education, training and employment for young people in the youth justice system. It also consistently lobbied other central government departments on their duties regarding education and training and commissioned reports that made use of *Asset* data to point out shortfalls in provision (ECOTEC 2001a, 2001b; YJB 2006). In fact it has been pointed out that the evidence from *Asset* could be used to counterbalance the more punitive approaches to youth justice by emphasising the connection between social and economic disadvantages and young people getting into trouble (Annison 2005: 124).

Practitioners are faced with apparently diametrically opposing views on the important matter of assessment. The most vociferous critics argue that: 'Risk assessment in the youth justice system (YJS) has simultaneously embodied the aggregated, deindividualised and prescriptive nature of actuarial justice and subjective and individualised nature of clinical judgements – offering an "oversimplified technical fix" to a complex social reality' (Case 2010: 98). There is an interesting lack of balance in the analysis of such critics that portrays central government as a rather malign and powerful force seizing on simplistic fixes and coercing practitioners into making 'subjective and under-informed judgements'. This of course ignores the evidence of non-compliance on assessment practice (and arguably a whole raft of government requirements) by significant numbers of practitioners where *Asset* is inadequately completed or out of date and not translated into matching action plans. This has been conveniently reframed to argue that somehow practitioners are resisting or subverting policies such as standardised assessment (Phoenix 2009: 117). A more balanced discussion would examine the role of professionals, their vested interests and why certain interventions despite evidence of ineffectiveness have been pursued. While critics urge the greater involvement of young people in the assessment process, there is relatively little criticism and discussion of why far more practitioners do not use the 'What do you think?' component of the *Asset* process as a method of formally and more systematically consulting with young people.

There is much more common ground between proponents of *Asset* and their critics than might appear (YJB 2008a). Whyte's (2009: 82–3) judicious conclusions on assessment are entirely consistent with the approach promoted by the YJB:

> It is generally recognised that a combination of professional judgement alongside and guided by appropriate actuarial data present the best available option ... Effective risk assessment requires intelligent and analytical deliberation markedly different from a sterile unreflective routinised 'tick box' approach.

Notwithstanding the above rebuttals to the criticisms of *Asset*, there is of course a case for continuing to examine the reliability and validity of the tool itself and its implementation by practitioners. Clearly there is a weight of academic pressure which should not be ignored and where criticisms have credibility, revisions to the assessment process and the tools used with young people in the youth justice system may be the most appropriate way forward in order to enhance outcomes for young people and to bring greater consistency to practice across England and Wales.

The scaled approach

In 2009 the YJB introduced the scaled approach, a model for interventions delivered by YOTs which 'aims to ensure that interventions are tailored to the individual and based on an assessment of their risks and needs' (YJB 2009c: 6). There are three intervention categories: standard, enhanced and intensive. The intervention category recommended determines the sentence proposed to the court, the proposed frequency of contact in the first three months of an order between the practitioner and the young person and the suggested content of the intervention. The YJB guidance makes it clear that the appropriate category is identified through an initial matching process with the *Asset* score but that professional judgement must be used in coming to a final recommendation. This recommendation should take into account all available information, not just *Asset* score, and vulnerability and welfare considerations must be considered with the scaled approach intervention potentially forming part of a wider overall intervention plan (YJB 2009c: 8–9). This approach is intended to help YOT practitioners to match their time, resources and interventions to assessed risks and needs.

The scaled approach has, however, been criticised on practical, method-ological and almost ideological grounds.

The overarching accusation is that the scaled approach is derived from questionable risk factor research which cannot be operationalised for individual young people. This unquestioning acceptance 'is the result of policy and strategy being politically driven and set by government, yet handed over to others for implementation, such as . . . quasi-civil servants in agencies like the YJB for example. These "half-experts" have pursued the *Scaled Approach* with an over-inflated and unjustified certainty about risk' (Case and Haines 2009: 301).

The scaled approach, it is claimed, could 'heighten deprofessionalism' (which implies that practitioners are already being 'deprofessionalised' without producing any evidence for this) as they are compelled to work in a more mechanistic and prescribed way. The chances of disproportionate intervention are increased, for example, with low-risk young people who have committed a serious offence receiving too intensive an intervention and vice versa. Finally the scaled approach assumes that dynamic risk factors are amenable to change through intervention programmes when some of the research suggests that early risk-focused intervention has little positive effect on the risk of offending and that maturation has a greater effect on desistance (Case 2010: 96–7).

In order to appreciate the significance of the scaled approach and the motives behind its introduction it is salutary to examine its origins which were in the proposals made by the Audit Commission in their report of 2004. It is worth noting that despite the assertion above, this policy was initiated by the Audit Commission which is an independent body funded by the fees it charges, although why it should be a surprise (or a criticism) that policy and strategy is set by governments and implemented by civil servants is mystifying. The proposals were put forward in a section querying the cost and effectiveness of custody and were designed to increase the use of community-based alternatives to custody (Audit Commission 2004: 44–5). The introduction of a single order (later to be known as the Youth Rehabilitation Order or YRO) to replace the nine juvenile non-custodial sentences was seen as an opportunity to shift sentencing practice away from a strictly vertical tariff to a more horizontal one. The reason behind this was that the vertical tariff was based on the notion that if a previous sentence had not worked then a more punitive one should be used, culminating in custody. In this new sentencing framework a second, third or fourth community order would not be either a repeat of an earlier sentence and intervention nor would it necessarily be an escalation in terms of intervention. This is a more dynamic, flexible approach that takes account of the changing needs and circumstances of the young person. Implicit too is the recognition that assessment is not an exact science and that practitioners need to be able to return to the court with more effective approaches in the light of experience, based on:

- a full picture of the offender's needs and circumstances and of how these may have changed;

- a detailed assessment of his or her progress on previous orders, including those elements that were working;

- a full risk assessment that shows the extent and nature of risk that the offender poses to the public and how that risk might be mitigated; and

- what combination of interventions is most likely to minimise his or her chances of reoffending.

(Audit Commission 2004: 45)

Concerns about the amount and quantity of contact time in supervision were raised by the Audit Commission report in 1996, *Misspent Youth*, and were echoed in the 2004 report. Consequently the 2004 report recommended: 'A graduated approach should be developed to the amount and quantity of contact time so that it becomes more closely tailored to the needs and risks of young offenders' (Audit Commission 2004: 51).

So rather than being about 'deprofessionalising' through this more mechanistic and prescribed model, the converse was intended – that practitioners would make more bespoke interventions that better fitted assessed needs and risks within the context of developing community-based disposals rather than custodial. If anything it was partly developed in response to the Audit Commission findings that practice was inflexible in some YOTs as they tended 'to provide a standard programme for all those on their caseload, rather than tailoring interventions to particular needs identified in the assessment' (Audit Commission 2004: 75). This finding was reiterated in 2005 when Baker *et al.* concluded that *Asset*'s role in informing planning appeared to be underdeveloped. In particular:

- Plans often did not reflect the outcome of assessments. For example, issues identified in *Asset* as being associated with a high risk of reoffending were not always incorporated into intervention plan targets.

- There appeared a tendency to create standard plans, which resulted in targets being set for areas that were not identified in *Asset* as being closely associated with reoffending;

- Intervention plans often used 'YOT jargon' and the language would have been difficult for most young people to understand.

Consequently it was argued some young people with identified problems such as substance misuse might not have had their needs met while others could be offered programmes that they did not need.

Similarly while disproportionate interventions are always a possibility (although there appears to be very little empirical evidence on this) it is as easy to argue that the likelihood of this will decrease as increase under the YRO and the scaled approach. A survey of young people and their parents found that where their needs were met by appropriate support, they were more optimistic about changing their lifestyles and reducing their offending (Audit Commission 2004: 75).

In terms of an evidence base, the scaled approach is consistent with the principle of proportionality in that properly applied it should mitigate against unnecessary interventions and avoid potentially negative consequences of undue involvement in the youth justice system (McAra and McVie 2007). Equally it has the potential to focus YOT practitioners and sentencers more on interventions that have been identified as being likely to reduce reoffending.

The history of youth justice policy is strewn with unintended consequences and the introduction of the YRO and the scaled approach may have some too. For example, one argument in favour of having a lengthy vertical tariff in sentencing was to delay the arrival of the young person at custody, to allow the effects of interventions and maturation to take hold. With fewer rungs on the sentencing ladder, young people may be propelled to the top more quickly.

The principles of effective practice and assessment, planning interventions and supervision and the scaled approach

Risk classification

At the end of each section on risk factors in *Asset*, practitioners are asked to rate the extent to which they think the issue is associated with the likelihood of further offending or serious anti-social behaviour by the young person. This assessment is not of the extent to which the practitioner believes that the risk factor is causing difficulties in the life of the young person in general; rather it is intended to be specifically focused on the risk factor in relation to offending/anti-social behaviour and the link between current risk and likely future behaviour. The following considerations might help a practitioner to establish the level of risk:

- Might this risk factor have been linked to past challenging behaviour? If 'yes', do you think the risk factor is more, less or equally significant now?

- Does there appear to be a direct or indirect link between the risk factor and the young person's behaviour?

- Does the risk factor always appear relevant to the young person's offending or serious anti-social behaviour, or only on certain occasions?

- Is the effect on future offending behaviour likely to be immediate or over a longer period?

- Does the risk factor appear to be strong enough with offending by itself, or is it only likely to contribute to offending behaviour when specific other conditions exist?

In each section, examples are given to illustrate high and low ratings. It may be beneficial for practitioners to compare assessments and the ratings that were given in order to help to create a level of local and individual consistency in assessments (see Baker *et al.* 2005 for an example of this).

The level of intervention should be related to the risk of reoffending, informed by the seriousness of the offence committed by the young person and his/her *Asset* assessment scores (see Figure 2.1). This risk evaluation is intended to be adjusted up or down, where necessary, by an evaluation of the risk of harm to others and the risk of vulnerability.

The evaluation of the level of risk can inform:

- which disposal is relevant in the case;

- the length of order required;

- any additional controls that may need to be imposed to ensure compliance with the order.[1]

59

Intervention Level	Function	Typical case management approach	Possible sentence requirement/ component (not exhaustive)
Standard	• Enabling compliance and repairing harm	• Organising interventions to meet basic requirement of order • Engaging parents in interventions and/or to support young person • Monitoring compliance • Enforcement	• Reparation • Stand-alone unpaid work • Supervision • Stand-alone attendance centre
Enhanced	• Enabling compliance and repairing harm • Enabling help/ change	• Brokering access to external interventions • Co-ordinating interventions with specialists in YOT • Providing supervision • Engaging parents in interventions and/or to support young person • Enforcement	• Supervision • Reparation • Requirement/ component to help young person to change behavior e.g. drug treatment, offending behavior programme, education programme • Combination of the above
Intensive	• Enabling compliance and repairing harm • Enabling help/ change • Ensuring control	• Extensive • Help/change management function plus additional controls, restrictions and monitoring	• Supervision • Reparation • Requirement/ component to help young person to change behavior • Requirement component to monitor or restrict movement (e.g. prohibited activity, curfew, exclusion or electronic monitoring) • Combination of the above

Figure 2.1   Indicators of level matrix
Offense seriousness (using Youth Court Bench Book guidelines, 2010).

The circumstances in which the probability of risk materialises may change rapidly. Reflection, review and reassessment of risk are thus important components of risk management. This may mean that a risk management plan developed and implemented by practitioners in the first instance may quickly be stood down (to be reassessed and reactivated should the circumstances giving rise to risk re-emerge). Alternatively, risks initially managed within the context of youth justice may be more appropriately managed by partner agencies in the medium to longer term (e.g. by social workers with respect to looked-after children).

A priority context for a change of circumstances which may give rise to risk is where a young person moves from the community into the secure estate and vice versa. An assessment of vulnerability is intended to be a routine component of case planning when a young person enters custody (via remand or sentence) and can be communicated between community-based practitioners and those within the secure estate prior to entry (young people entering custody without documentation from the community may be placed on a vulnerability alert until an appropriate assessment is made and/or the documentation arrives).

An assessment of harm to others may need to be undertaken where the young person is:

- offending persistently;

- charged with a serious specified offence under the Criminal Justice Act 2003;

- subject to a placement in the secure estate, which may contain victims of their offending.

It is a reasonable inference from this principle that the assessment of young people should be linked to a plan for working with them to reduce their likelihood of reoffending. Young people benefit most from interventions that are relevant to their assessed level of need and risk (Andrews and Bonta 1994; McGuire 1995).

Throughout interventions, practitioners may need to monitor changes in young people's levels of risk of reoffending, causing serious harm and vulnerability.

Appropriate measures may need to be put in place to manage this process, for example if there is a significant increase in the likelihood of a young person committing a particularly grave offence.

Criminogenic need

Asset is an interactional tool which is concerned with the strength of the links between risk/needs and offending behaviour, and with the links among different risks/needs. For example, acquisitive offending behaviour in a particular young person may be very strongly and directly influenced by a peer group, but the choice of peer group may be influenced for that young person by school exclusion. The school exclusion may not in itself lead directly to the offending for this young person, but is indirectly having a very significant effect. In turn, the offending peer group might be encouraging patterns of thinking and behaviour that add to the difficulty of reintegrating into the school community.

A thorough assessment also identifies practical matters that need to be considered when planning interventions (e.g. health problems, transport needs, literacy difficulties). These factors may not be directly related to the causes of young people's offending behaviour, but may need to be addressed or managed in order to give the young people a reasonable chance of completing an order successfully.

Analysis also often identifies issues which are not directly linked to young people's criminal behaviour but which, if not addressed, may prevent effective offending-related work from being undertaken. These issues could include the need for additional support with emotional, social and psychological difficulties.

Assessment, therefore, needs to gather information about individual risk factors, but to do so in a way that is also alert to connections, interrelationships and the strength of the links with offending behaviour.

Dosage

The scoring of *Asset* is important with regard to dosage. Clearly, higher scores would indicate that a more intensive intervention might be required than for those areas with lower scores.

One of the key distinctions in terms of dosage is that between what has been arranged for a young person and what they actually receive as part of an intervention. This would imply the need for careful monitoring of attendance as part of the supervision programme. One of the real challenges for practitioners supporting young people through the change process is the high rates of attrition experienced by some projects. The tension and the challenge for practitioners is how to ensure the intensity and duration of a programme is sufficient while keeping a young person motivated enough to participate fully and to maintain their attachment to it.

Although dosage is a relatively straightforward principle, little is understood about the actual volume of interventions received by young people who offend, including the amount of individual supervision received.

Responsivity

In the first instance, the principle of responsivity can be applied to the assessment process itself. Young people are unlikely to respond positively to assessment procedures that put them under pressure to perform or when they feel they are being tested in some way. This has implications for the way in which the purposes of assessments are explained to a young person, in particular in terms of explaining the benefits for them and the purposes the assessment outcomes will serve for what is to come. See Chapter 3 on engaging young people. It is clear that in the juvenile secure estate, where young people are subject to a number of assessments on entry to custody, that they do not always know what these are for and may not see the link between these and the programmes of education, training and treatment that follow (ECOTEC 2001a, 2001b).

Interventions are more likely to engage young people if they have relevance to their lives and employ methods that will motivate and interest them. Interventions are also more likely to be successful if they are delivered in ways that help young people to develop a broader range of learning strategies and are responsive to their capacity to participate (Andrews *et al.* 1990; McGuire 1995). Materials and methods should reflect the different stages of development and maturity of the young people concerned, their gender and/or sexuality, and should take account of their community, ethnic and cultural backgrounds.

Although well-designed, well-delivered interventions are critical to effective supervision, successful outcomes also depend on young people's active participation and willingness to change. The best results are achieved when young people are motivated to take up and engage with interventions (Burnett and Appleton 2002). Practitioners are more likely to actively involve and engage young people if they:

- are aware of young people's perceptions;

- communicate in a way that is appropriate to young people;

- have clear values and purpose;

- give consistent feedback;

- are solution-focused and encourage small steps towards change;

- model problem-solving;

- are open, active, optimistic and realistic.

Effective supervision with adults appears to be that which offers practical and emotional support, together with an understanding of offending, through awareness of individuals' needs and perspectives (Beaumont and Mistry 1996). A more recent survey of youth justice practitioners and young people found the following to be the hallmarks of effective engagement: the ability of staff to be 'firm but fair'; communicate clearly; demonstrate a good sense of humour; be non-judgemental; show an interest in them as individuals; show consistency; demonstrate mutual respect; and inspire trust (Ipsos MORI 2010). Addressing concerns which may be indirectly linked to young people's offending behaviour can increase participation and responsivity. For example, if there is a practical obstacle to taking part in an intervention, such as lack of transport, it is important to deal with this problem so that the intervention can take place.

Cognitive-behavioural interventions require young people and others around them to make changes in order to behave differently, in particular with regard to offending. Effective change requires active participation by young people, so they should be fully involved in the assessment and planning processes, jointly identifying problem areas in their lives and how to overcome them (Chapman 2000). In many respects, the responsivity

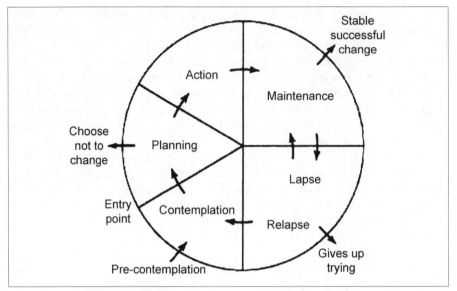

Figure 2.2   The cycle of change
Source: Prochaska and DiClemente (1982).

principle as it relates to assessment, planning interventions and supervision implies that the process must be responsive to a young person's needs, while enabling them to develop new strategies for responding to situations, in other words to change their behaviours. Drawn from the field of addiction, the cycle of change (Prochaska and DiClemente 1982) is a widely used and potentially helpful model for assessing a young person's state of readiness to change (see Figure 2.2). This model can be used to help make judgements about an individual's level of motivation and about the most appropriate interventions to develop and sustain that motivation.

The model suggests that change is a process and, because it is a cyclical model, provides a reminder that progress is always possible. It is based on the premise that practitioners cannot change young people but they can provide them with opportunities that will help them to make changes in their lives for themselves. Practitioners need to be realistic about an individual's attitude to change at a given time and in given circumstances but they should avoid labelling individuals as permanently unmotivated and therefore incapable of change because of past failures or current ambivalence.

The various stages of the cycle can be described as follows:

- *Pre-contemplation* – when individuals do not recognise the need for change. For example, they may see their offending as justifiable, inevitable or the only course of action open to them.

- *Contemplation* – when individuals are ambivalent about change. They may see some of the negatives of their current behaviours and be aware of other more positive alternatives, but be uncertain about their ability to change. One type of example might be young people who are tired of coming up against the criminal justice system, want to move on in life, but fear losing their current peers and group status if they cease offending. Another example might be young people who are unsure whether they have the skills they need to find employment or establish new and more positive friendships.

- *Planning* – the process of contemplation is uncomfortable psychologically. People tend to be unable to remain at this stage indefinitely and so move on to planning instead.

- *Action* – some young people will be at the point of taking positive action towards change. They may be ready to set goals and take concrete steps towards change, acting on the help given them.

- *Maintenance* – some will already have changed their lifestyle at the outset of involvement in an intervention or during the course of supervision. This change needs to be maintained, so resources and support should still be directed at this group.

- *Lapse and relapse* – other young people will revert to problematic behaviour. This may be a further offence or a breach in compliance during a period of genuine and significant reduction in offending behaviour and/or sustained positive attitudes (a lapse). Alternatively, it may be a rejection of the process of change and a reversion to unhelpful patterns of behaviour and thinking (a relapse).

The cycle of change brings together the tasks of assessment, planning, intervention and review. As the model's premise is that change is a process, it serves as a reminder of the importance of continuing assessment and of amending intervention plans to adapt to changes in young people's attitudes, circumstances or levels of motivation. It also highlights the importance of planning for change, supporting individuals through change and continuing to provide support beyond the initial period.

The model can be used to assist in identifying how best to target efforts to help individual young people to move through the cycle into stable, secure change. At the 'contemplation' stage, for example, the concept of the 'decisional balance' is very helpful. This is the balance between the factors that motivate young people to change and the factors that demotivate. It may also be helpful to think of this in terms of 'cost-benefit' analysis: what are the benefits for young people in changing their patterns of behaviour and how do these compare with the perceived costs of such a change? The task is to support those factors that tend to support change and to minimise those factors which militate against it. To achieve this, a clear assessment of the factors on each side of the balance is required.

Further round the cycle, in 'planning', the task is to judge whether a young person is ready to make some decisions about change. Practitioners also need to be on the alert for those young people who, perhaps because of an environmental change, have made a decision not to change. These individuals have moved out of the cycle of change and back into 'pre-contemplation'.

A review of progress during the course of an intervention may reveal difficulties at the 'maintenance' stage. Young people may face pressures which militate against the change being maintained. These pressures may come from their own deep-seated beliefs or habits of thought or from their circumstances. Situational changes may exert very significant pressure on young people to resume offending behaviour ('lapse/relapse').

Judgements about the above issues should inform the supervision process. For young people at the early stages of the cycle of change, the interventions provided should maximise their chances of beginning the process of contemplation. At the same time, it is important to be realistic and not to place young people who are at this early stage into programmes which require some degree of commitment to the process of change.

In other cases, planned interventions may need to be altered if lapse or relapse occurs and, more generally, if young people move to a different point in the cycle. As well as assessing young people, therefore, it is important to assess the services being provided and judge whether they are responsive to individual young people's current place on the cycle of change.

Community based

One of the key considerations when planning interventions is ensuring that whatever is arranged keeps young people attached to their communities and helps them to engage with them more effectively. One of the potential difficulties with this is that for those young people most at risk, the communities themselves may be operating in all sorts of ways that isolate them from the mainstream and where certain sorts of anti-social, pro-criminal behaviours are the norm. This begs a question as to how far learning can take place that will develop pro-social behaviours. Alternatively, young people may be so excluded from their communities that attempts to support their re-engagement are hindered by considerable social and structural barriers.

Some critics of the current youth justice system have criticised the design of most interventions because they place too great a responsibility on individual young people and do little to change the broader issues which have led to the social exclusion of young people at risk of offending and reoffending (Muncie 2001; Pitts 2001b). A number of studies have shown that where young people have been exposed to relatively high levels of social exclusion, interventions did little to provide them with the support they needed in order to gain stable accommodation or sustain their attachment to education, training and employment (both indicators of social inclusion) (Dignan 2000; Newburn *et al.* 2002; Gray *et al.* 2003). Gray (2005a) argues that to maximise effectiveness, those planning interventions should take more account of the structural and practical barriers to a young person's social inclusion, enabling them to overcome these. In this sense, a truly community-based intervention would take the wider social and economic circumstances into account when deciding on the best way to build the resilience of a young person in managing their own environment positively.

Gray (2005a) goes further to argue that the 'managerialist imperatives' of meeting Youth Justice Board targets and national standards has meant that the opportunities provided by YOTs for accessing the range of expertise and resources required to make changes to the social context of offending has not been maximised. The resulting emphasis, she argues, has therefore been on providing structured, time-limited, correctional programmes which focus on behaviour change by individual young people. The extent to which these two aspects of practice are polarised is debatable, although it is understandable that practitioners may not feel empowered or indeed able to challenge the fabric of a young person's community even if they wanted to. In addition, there is little in the way of hard evidence of effective practice in achieving the level of social change that this implies, while there would appear to be more to hold on to with regard to working with individual young people.

The community base principle would also suggest that, where appropriate, young people's parents/carers should also be involved in this process of identifying problems and solutions so they can provide informed support during any intervention. In some instances they themselves may need to engage in direct intervention to help meet the needs of the young person (e.g. engaging in a parenting programme). See Chapter 9 for more on offending behaviour interventions.

Intervention modality

Asset is multi-modal in the sense that it asks a number of questions across a range of important domains. The resulting plan ought, therefore, to be multi-modal, responding to the areas of risks and protection identified through the process of assessment.

The risk and protective factors identified through *Asset* also overlap and interact with each other. These interactions present a challenge for practitioners in regard to understanding causality and providing explanations for offending behaviour. It is not the number of risk or protective factors that determines the nature of an intervention, but rather the way in which they interact, reinforce or mitigate each other. An eventual intervention plan would need to take into account those interrelationships in deciding how to target and sequence interventions.

Effective assessment and planning should lead to young people being referred to appropriate interventions designed to prevent further offending and to address the identified risks and needs (Chapman and Hough 1998; Underdown 1998). Inappropriate targeting can be detrimental to individual young people, and reduces the overall effectiveness of intervention work with young people who offend.

This principle applies to the full range of interventions available for young people in community and secure settings: offending behaviour initiatives; personal development; education and training; mentoring; work with families; restorative work; drug and alcohol awareness; health advice; and artistic, dramatic or sporting activities.

Programme integrity

Aside from the issues of problems in participation, cooperation and engagement of the young person (or their parent/carer) in programme implementation, practitioners should be alert to issues of programme integrity (McGuire 2000): did the planned intervention get delivered, were there problems in staffing a programme, were sessions cancelled or otherwise interrupted? Flaws in programme integrity have diluted their potential impact (Pawson and Tilley 1997; Feilzer *et al.* 2004). Problems in this regard should be fed back to strategic managers for their action at an organisational level.

Implementing interventions successfully requires committed and effective management, trained staff who are skilled in pro-social modelling, sufficient resources for continuity, and in-built evaluation and feedback systems (McIvor 1990; Raynor 2002). Interventions are also more likely to be successful if the stated aims are linked to the methods used (Hollin 1995).

Partnership agencies can provide specialist expertise or facilities which may not otherwise be available within a team or unit. In such cases the role of practitioners may be to arrange, coordinate and monitor service delivery. It is likely that practitioners who make frequent contact with the providers and the young people will be more able to ensure that interventions are being delivered as specified in the intervention plan, and that young people are attending as required. Monitoring allows practitioners to respond effectively to changes in young people's needs by amending the delivery of services as appropriate (Chapman and Hough 1998).

The findings from Baker *et al.* (2005) (that changes in *Asset* score as a result of an intervention reflect changes in reoffending rates) has an important message for strategic and operational managers of youth justice services. Aggregated *Asset* scores tracked over time may provide the foundation for an evaluation of which programmes, or components of programmes, work. Aggregation of the findings from reviews and case closures provides vital information for the evaluation of the performance of youth justice agencies. Monitoring at a strategic level facilitates:

- building evidence as to which interventions are effective;

- improving the quality of programme interventions;

- providing feedback to practitioners on their impact;

- driving up programme integrity to deliver effective outcomes.

There is little evidence to date, however, that this data is being routinely used by YOT managers or governors in the secure estate to inform planning priorities or service developments.

The final review is very important if cases are to be closed in a positive way. It is a chance for young people to express their views on the work that has been done, and for successes (even small ones) to be celebrated and encouraged for continuation in the future. Changes in ratings are a means of assessing the success of intervention programmes and gauging the progress made by each young person since he/she began the programme. It may be that a young person's circumstances change for the worse during the course of an intervention, leading to ratings increasing rather than decreasing. Alternatively, simply knowing the young person better as a result of programme engagement may alter the scoring, reflecting an assessor's greater understanding of the dimensions of risk and need.

The challenges for practice

Assessment can mean very different things to the professionals that work in and around the youth justice arena. In educational terms, for example, assessment is often associated entirely with academic attainment whereas in social work it would be linked to the welfare of a young person and their risk of harm. This represents a significant challenge to practitioners working across agencies and organisations in relation to understanding the outcomes of different assessment systems.

The increasing range of interventions now offered by a variety of service providers (including restorative justice, mentoring, structured programmes and multi-modal interventions) present both an opportunity and a challenge. Differences in the intensity, length, structure and aims of interventions mean that careful decisions must be made about allocating young people to the interventions that are most suitable for them.

While *Asset* is the principal assessment tool it may also act as a gateway process for the identification of:

- the broader welfare needs of young people (e.g. social care, education, health);

- the need for specialist assessments and services to meet particular needs (e.g. mental health, substance misuse, sexual abuse).

The challenges for practice here are twofold. Firstly, there is a proliferation of assessment systems which a young person with multiple adversities can almost simultaneously become subject to. Secondly, the nature and purpose of assessment varies significantly between professions.

Given that these young people frequently cross the agency boundaries of health, social care, criminal justice and education, they can be subject to a barrage of multiple, uncoordinated assessments. Unsurprisingly, the result is considerable duplication of effort, and substantial gaps in the professional knowledge of the learning and other important needs of young people who are socially excluded.

Each new initiative tends to bring with it a new assessment, planning and review system for practitioners and young people and their parents/carers to participate in. Although the Connexions Service initially promised that it would 'seek to develop a common assessment tool' (DfEE 2000: 43) it ended up developing its own assessment, planning, implementation and review system (APIR) so that practitioners and young people had yet another bureaucratic system to contend with. The introduction of the Common Assessment Framework (CAF) as part of Every Child Matters in England could be viewed as another example of this tendency to proliferate assessment processes and procedures. YJB guidance does exist regarding how this should be viewed alongside the *Asset* profiling process but there has been no evaluation conducted in youth justice settings as to the efficacy of the CAF for young people at risk of offending.

Reflecting on the continued failure to gather timely and accurate information in the youth justice system (particularly that relating to education) through assessment, the Audit Commission (2004: 98) recommended that the government, 'in developing one overall assessment tool for children at risk ... should consider having a common core of questions that follow a child, supplemented by specialist sections for different agencies'. This was intended to influence the implementation of the consultation paper *Every Child Matters*, which recommended the development of a common assessment instrument for all agencies dealing with children and young people at risk. The Audit Commission report recognised that it will prove extremely difficult if not impossible to agree on a common format for all relevant agencies and professionals and to discard all existing procedures.

In fact, the problems around assessment may be far more fundamental than simply improved document design, administrative process and managerial will. Assessment processes lie at the very heart of each profession's practice. Consequently, each assessment process is guarded, as to abandon it may lead to a breach in the distinctiveness of each professional grouping and may be perceived by some as a threat to identity and status.

Given the professional cultural value of each assessment process, it is entirely predictable that a common approach that relies heavily on exhortation and goodwill will not be successful. An approach that is too discretionary may be sidelined, or worse will become yet another layer of information gathering and create further transmission problems.

Summary

- Systematic assessment is central to the design, delivery and evaluation of both structured rehabilitative programmes and other types of intervention.
- Assessment is an important opportunity to identify risks that might relate

to a young person and a management strategy that may be employed to meet those risks. It may also be useful in identifying protective factors that can reduce the negative impact of risk factors.

- *Asset* is the structured assessment tool used by YOTs and the secure estate for young people in England and Wales. It examines a young person's offending and identifies the risk factors which may have contributed to it.

- There has been considerable criticism of actuarial approaches to assessment in general and *Asset* in particular. What this debate tends to overlook is the fact that the purpose of assessment is largely to generate a plan for intervention. The evidence suggests that in current youth justice practice, plans are often not explicitly linked to assessment.

- The scaled approach is a model for interventions delivered by YOTs which 'aims to ensure that interventions are tailored to the individual and based on an assessment of their risks and needs' (YJB 2009c: 6). The scaled approach has been criticised on practical, methodological and almost ideological grounds.

Note

1 These controls may include tagging, tracking, voice verification, residence requirements, prohibited activities, exclusion requirements and curfew conditions.

Further reading

Annison, J. (2005) 'Risk and protection', in T. Bateman and J. Pitts (eds), *The RHP Companion to Youth Justice*. Lyme Regis: Russell House.

Baker, K., Jones, S., Merrington, S. and Roberts, C. (2005) *Further Development of Asset*. London: Youth Justice Board.

Case, S. (2010) 'Preventing and reducing risk', in W. Taylor, R. Earle and R. Hester (eds), *Youth Justice Handbook: Theory, Policy and Practice*. Cullompton: Willan.

Communities that Care (2001) *Risk and Protective Factors for Youth Crime – Prevalence, Salience and Reduction*, Report for the Youth Justice Board for England and Wales. London: Youth Justice Board.

3

Engaging young people

It is a paradox that perhaps the one question in youth justice work that practitioners would deem the most important, how to get young people to participate effectively in youth justice interventions, is the least researched. There has been a great upsurge in publications on youth justice and a significant rise in research projects since 1997 (Phoenix 2009) but there is little in the way of rigorous research findings that enable them to answer the most challenging questions in youth justice. These include: 'How do I enable young people, usually against their will, to become actively involved in interventions?' and 'How do I maintain this involvement and use it to facilitate change in the life of the young person?' In achieving this, 'How do I reconcile my potentially contradictory role as an enforcer of a court sentence with my pedagogic responsibilities?'

This chapter surveys the evidence that might help answer these questions. It examines the different definitions of engagement that are currently used and suggests a new one. It also looks at the practice literature from allied disciplines, particularly education. A case study is used to examine the nature of engagement within the context of a national programme and how this fits with the principles of effective practice.

The evidence base for engaging young people

Much of the research evidence on effectiveness relies on meta-analyses and their scale can provide an insight into interventions that are associated with positive or negative outcomes. This sheer mass though is a constraint as it obscures the fine detail of what happens to particular individuals in certain circumstances. These studies can tell us that offending behaviour programmes, if implemented faithfully, may be associated with, say, a 15–30 per cent reduction in reoffending but they are of little reassurance when, for example, faced with a group of teenagers who apparently have few intentions of complying with a group work activity. Such is the paucity of research in comparison with some of the other key areas of practice identified by the YJB that it was not possible to base the effective practice source document on a systematic review of research highlighting effective techniques for engaging young people who offend (Mason and Prior 2008:

8). The conclusions of Dowden and Andrews' (2004: 204) survey of meta-analyses in relation to adults who offend is equally applicable to adolescents: 'Despite these impressive findings regarding what program characteristics are most effective for offenders, very little research has focused upon the characteristics of effective staff practice to use in the delivery of these interventions.'

In these circumstances the best that can be done is to glean related knowledge from the reviews of effective practice in other youth justice interventions and to investigate the practice literature of allied fields, such as education, youth work, social work and probation. This confection may offer the practitioner a way forward.

Definitions

'Engagement' is now a term of common currency and may like others become less fashionable in time. Terms so frequently used can often become rather elastic in meaning, so it is useful to examine various definitions. Although there can be overtones of conflict in some contexts of its use, 'to engage' usefully conveys the sense of contract and mutuality that could characterise working with young people. In the context of youth justice a helpful if lengthy working definition has been proposed:

> Techniques for engaging young people who offend are concerned with the question of how to gain young people's interest and willing participation in interventions or programme of interventions intended to prevent or reduce offending. 'Engagement' suggests a set of objectives around developing young people's personal motivation and commitment to involvement in activities. It implies that passive involvement is not enough – for example, if a young person attends and takes part in a prescribed programme of activities but does not feel any commitment to the objectives of the programme and is not motivated to benefit, through learning or personal development, from the programme activities, then they are not 'engaged' and the programme is unlikely to be successful. For practitioners, the implication is that specific skills and knowledge ('techniques') are required to achieve engagement, in addition to skills and knowledge associated with the particular type of intervention. (Mason and Prior 2008: 10, 11)

This definition raises a number of key issues for the practitioner. Does it recognise sufficiently that many, perhaps most young people are only participating under duress? Is the assumption that not feeling commitment to the objectives of the programme necessarily going to preclude positive benefits? Is the implied importance of the practitioner's role warranted? After all, many people achieve success at school and in the workplace despite a lack of commitment to the stated objectives and despite a poor relationship with teachers or managers.

It is important not to allow 'motivation' and 'engagement' to be treated as synonyms. Motivation may be a necessary but is not a sufficient condition of engagement. The desire to desist from offending may exist but it does not guarantee that a young person will work effectively with a particular practitioner or that certain interventions will be right.

Engagement with education offers some interesting insights for work in youth justice. Both share significant numbers of young people who would not necessarily choose to participate in what either offers but have little choice in the matter. Helpfully far more studies of engagement have been carried out with very large samples in education compared to social work or youth work.

In an attempt to unify the diverse definitions of engagement and draw generalised findings from the varied research methodologies employed a review proposed three components of engagement: behaviour, emotion and cognition, that were all dynamically related within the individual young person (Fredericks *et al.* 2004). In considering engagement as a multidimensional construct the following definition was proposed:

> Behavioural engagement draws on the idea of participation; it includes involvement in academic and social or extra-curricular activities and is considered crucial for achieving positive academic outcomes and preventing dropping out. (p. 60)

Emotional engagement encompasses positive and negative reactions to teachers, classmates, academics and school and is presumed to create ties to an institution and influence willingness to work. Finally, cognitive engagement draws on the idea of investment; it incorporates thoughtfulness and willingness to exert the effort necessary to comprehend complex ideas and master difficult skills.

Each of these dimensions could be adapted for youth justice both by practitioners and researchers in order to build up a comparable evidence base to that which underpins these educational definitions of engagement. In youth justice terms behavioural engagement deals with compliance and participation in the supervisory process and extends to planned interventions. Emotional engagement could be developed as a concept in youth justice linked to developing pro-social values while cognitive engagement could clearly be applied to the process of facilitating change and acquiring new skills and is directly relevant to many offending behaviour programmes.

Although most of the evidence is American there were outcome correlations in relation to both attainment and detachment from education and school level effects in terms of the antecedents of engagement. Positive correlations were found in several studies between behavioural engagement and attainment across all ages. There were significant differences in behavioural engagement measures between academically successful groups, less academically successful groups but who remained within school and those who became detached. Early onset of difficulties with behavioural engagement was a predictor of later low attainment and becoming detached from school (Alexander *et al.* 1993; Alexander *et al.* 1997).

There was significantly less research information found on the relationship between emotional and cognitive engagement and attainment. This may be partly due to the fact that many different definitions of engagement often combining elements of both emotional and behavioural engagement have been used (Fredericks *et al.* 2004).

In order to simplify matters perhaps engagement could be defined as 'the positive participation and progression of a young person within a youth justice intervention'. Clearly the acceptable levels of both participation and progression will be a matter of negotiation within the requirements of the court's disposal and will usually vary according to each individual and the nature of the intervention. Whatever happens it clearly makes no sense if interventions are planned in accordance with effective practice research but few young people participate. Programmes do not simply work on individuals but rather through them. Young people will either become interested, cooperate closely, complete the intervention, learn valuable lessons and retain them or they will not. Judging which individuals are more likely to stay the course is a challenging task which is little informed by the research evidence. For example, few would deny the potential importance of basic skills to adults in the criminal justice system but a widespread failure of engagement in the Basic Skills Pathfinders programme meant that the original research intentions to judge the impact of improvements in basic skills on offending had to be abandoned (McMahon *et al.* 2004). Little work has been undertaken as to why young people or adults have not engaged and there do not appear to have been any RCTs of the same intervention with the purpose of identifying those measures, including the skills and knowledge of practitioners that are associated with different levels of engagement.

Assessment and engagement

If the assessment-plan-review process is the backbone for all interventions with young people then engagement needs to be secured both before and during assessment which, if conducted effectively, should itself be an engaging process. In turn, effective assessment starts to prepare the young person for engagement in the subsequent interventions. Clearly an assessment that consists of ticking boxes and dwells on deficits may well be unlikely to engage a young person. The approach recommended to effective assessment not only lays the foundations for the relationship with the young person but also provides pointers on to how to engage young people in other settings. Logically if the assessment process has engaged the young person, the consequent intervention plan has a greater chance of engaging the young person.

In this context an *Asset* if effectively completed both assists with and results from the interaction. As the YJB (2008a: 29) has advised, *Asset* should not be used as an interview schedule, as reading out all the questions will make it more difficult to positively engage with a young person. Instead it should be used as the framework for gathering and analysing information. It may be helpful to have a 'mental script' of what should be covered in the interview, and to keep in mind an outline of the assessment profile section that will need to be completed later.

Developing the principle of responsivity whereby interventions should be matched with the needs, circumstances and learning strategies of young people, Farrow *et al.* have applied this to the assessment process. In doing so they portray assessment as a catalogue from which a narrative develops. Accordingly the key elements upon which practitioner and young person will need to be engaged are as follows:

- *The event* – the detail of what was done (the journey to the offence).

- *The network of influences* – (positive and negative) upon the individual in relation to his/her specific offence, patterns of other behaviour and the 'shape' of his/her life experience (the holistic assessment . . .).

- *The meaning of the offending* – and how long it has been a part of his/her life. How experienced are they in their offending?

- *The individual's attitude to his/her behaviour* – why do they think that they committed the offence?

- *Any wider transitional issues.*

(Farrow *et al.* 2007: 69–70)

The practitioner has to reconcile tensions from three directions. There are the messages from the research literature about the effectiveness or otherwise of particular interventions, there is the reality of limited resources and what is actually available locally, and there is the relationship with an individual young person. Selecting the best fit between these three is often very challenging. Typically a practitioner is not faced with a comprehensive menu of programmes that are validated by vigorous research which can be offered to a willing young person. Rather there may be a patchwork of interventions that owe more to custom and practice than are carefully constructed from 'What Works' precepts. Gaps in other services, particularly in education, further limit choice. Even in the hypothetical circumstances where a youth justice practitioner is more akin to a GP and is able to dispense a series of tried and tested treatments it has been argued that this is an inadequate approach.

The focus on the characteristics of effective programmes is accused of having displaced the centrality of the relationship between practitioner and young person in promoting change (Batchelor and McNeill 2005: 26). Little of the work on effectiveness, it is argued, helps the practitioner make the intervention bespoke to the particular needs of an individual young person. There has though been a growth in studies examining the characteristics of effective working relationships between those who have offended, practitioners and those processes that may be effective. Much of this work has focused on those over 18 and has only rarely involved quasi-experimental research designs. Nevertheless there are potentially important messages for practitioners working with young people who offend. It is difficult to assess the balance of effects from the quality of relationships and the content of a programme as both are probably essential in encouraging desistance from offending. It is doubtful that a 'good' relationship lacking in structure and focus will be of any more use than referring a young person to an 'effective' programme that has no positive relational foundations.

An integral part of individualising interventions for young people is taking account of the other personal, social and health challenges in a young person's life. Offending clearly cannot be considered in isolation from the rest of their life. While their offending might be the prime concern of the court and the focus of the practitioner's work it may be well down the list of priorities for the young person. Identifying and enabling change where possible in those aspects of a young person's life that can be ameliorated and appear to directly affect their offending whether it be homelessness, substance misuse or employment are a key part of the engagement process.

Research on desistance has placed more emphasis on the how and why people stop offending rather than the characteristics of effective programmes. This approach tends to place engagement centre stage with its emphasis on the individual and relational qualities of community supervision. Six key features of desistance that are all relevant to the engagement process have been identified from this research:

- Desistance is an individualised and subjective process and therefore needs to take account of identity and diversity.

- Developing and maintaining both motivation and hope is central to enabling individual change.

- Relationships are both part of the problem and potentially part of the solution for many young people in that they are often involved in distressing relationships but, equally, other relationships can ameliorate this.

- Focusing on resilience, i.e. those personal strengths, protective factors and social networks that can help overcome adversity.

- Supporting self-determination through assisting the young person develops their capacity to govern their own life.

- Identifying the social capital, i.e. the resources within the relationships and social networks that the young person belongs to.

(McNeill 2009: 145–6)

Motivational interviewing and pro-social modelling

Two approaches have been identified from the literature that may be useful in both engaging and working effectively with young people who offend: motivational interviewing and pro-social modelling. Given that the significance of motivation is highlighted in desistance studies then techniques that can increase motivation are likely to be an integral part of engagement. Originally developed for adults with dependent behaviours with drugs and alcohol, Motivational Interviewing (MI) as a technique has been applied in other areas such as probation and social work (Miller and Rollnick 2002).

MI is a directive, client-focused method for enabling motivation to change by exploring and challenging ambivalence towards dealing with young people's behaviours. Its premise is being directive and facilitating the participant's reflection on their own behaviours where they appear ambivalent or unwilling to accept the need for change. It is intended to be a collaborative approach giving participants abundant opportunity to discuss their motivations and changing their behaviour. The techniques developed include asking open questions, affirming positives, reflecting back the meaning of what has been said and summarising statements. In many ways MI encompasses some of the features identified with effective engagement in that it encourages open, honest and supportive relationships with young people who offend in order to bring about change.

However, while there are numerous studies of MI's effectiveness in medical and treatment environments there is relatively little evidence of its effectiveness with adults who offend, let alone adolescents. One study that indicated effectiveness in changing the attitudes of probation clients with substance misuse problems compared with a control group also found that increased contact with probation officers irrespective of MI positively affected attitudes too (Harper and Hardy 2000). It may be that MI offers a framework within which to apply some of the interpersonal skills identified by other research. Clearly, as has been emphasised, there is a need for more research with young people who offend in order to be able to judge the effectiveness of MI outside of those beset with substance misuse problems (Mason and Prior 2008: 31).

An allied approach that focuses on change and motivation through the relationship between the young person and the practitioner is pro-social modelling. It has been described as both a way of thinking and behaving and a series of strategies (Cherry 2005: 4). It is more than simply acting as a positive role model and is a more or less structured approach to pro-social practice containing a series of techniques and values. They include:

- developing honest and empathetic relationships with clients, which demonstrate a genuine concern for the person, and persistence and optimism about their capacity to change;

- modelling and encouraging pro-social behaviour. This includes being clear with oneself and one's team about underlying values, and clear with the client about expectations of values and behaviour and using rewards to reinforce these;

- discouraging by challenging and confronting undesired values and behaviour, including the discouragement of pro-criminal and anti-social values and behaviour;

- the transparent, clear and appropriate use of authority, and the role of enforcement (often described as legitimacy);

- clarity and openness about the role of staff and the purpose and expectations of any interventions;

- actively working in partnership with clients to help them to change by increasing their motivation, coaching them in new skills, clear objective setting, planned and negotiated problem-solving and the monitoring of progress;

- treating the client as an individual and valuing their differences and similarities to others. This includes stereotyping and valuing diversity of ethnicity, cultural experience, gender, sexuality, differing abilities, etc. Also working at an appropriate level for the client's speaking and listening abilities, and working with different thinking and learning styles.

(Cherry 2005: 3–4)

Although, like MI, pro-social modelling has many fervent adherents, the evidence base is not yet that firm, at least in demonstrating a significant influence on reducing reoffending among young people. Most of the studies relate to adults and measured aspects other than reoffending such as improved relationships within hostel settings. Research into seven community service pathfinders in probation suggested that a focus on the accreditation of skills and pro-social modelling were promising (Rex *et al.* 2004).

Survey of youth justice practitioners and young people

One of the few large-scale studies into engagement between young people who offend and YOT practitioners produced some interesting results (Ipsos MORI 2010). In the first instance it revealed a clear distinction being made by most practitioners between 'participation' and 'engagement' and that participation is a necessary but not sufficient condition of engagement. However, there was no ready consensus on what constituted engagement. While over a quarter of practitioners did not consider turning up but having minimal input in sessions to signify either engagement or participation, a slightly higher proportion believed it did constitute engagement and over a third believed it to be indicative of participation. Part of the reason for these contrary views may lie in the fact that simply keeping appointments may represent real progress for particular young people. Equally, while engagement might generally be presumed to be an evolving process, it may on occasion appear interrupted or even reversed. External events may mean that on a particular day, while a young person may turn up for an appointment, circumstances are such that it would be counterproductive to do any serious work on changing behaviour.

Generally where behaviours were seen as more related to process such as simply turning up or completing a worksheet, they tended to be viewed only as participation. Engagement by contrast was seen to be associated with activities that had a more emotional context such as developing positive relationships, displaying an awareness of the consequences of actions and being more motivated to change behaviour.

The issue of compulsion raised some interesting questions. For most young people attendance for supervision was to avoid being breached and going back to court, yet this in the eyes of YOT practitioners did not constitute engagement. Where YOT practitioners clearly explained enforcement procedures at the initial contact and applied warnings and breaches consistently, there was the opportunity for engagement to develop. The notion of fairness which was identified as very important in developing a positive relationship with YOT practitioners by young people was connected with consistency of approach, particularly where enforcement was concerned. This survey indicated considerable variation in practice and this inconsistency could have negative effects on a young person's engagement when YOT practitioners changed during a sentence and a different approach was adopted.

There was agreement between both practitioners and young people that a 'firm but fair' approach assisted in the development of an effective relationship. One important cause of variations in practitioners being able to achieve this balance appeared to derive from their professional background. Those with a social work background appeared to adopt more of a befriending role, concentrating on issues and concerns rather than specific offending behaviour work. In contrast those from a probation background tended to have a more authoritative or directive approach, focusing on enforcement of the conditions of an order (Ipsos MORI 2010).

While there are young people who simply participate through attendance but little else there are others who may participate positively, expressing a willingness to change but yet are unable to translate this into practice. It is difficult to view this as effective engagement. Consequently the definition adopted here is that effective engagement is both the positive participation *and* progression of a young person in fulfilling their intervention plan.

Clearly this research demonstrated that there is no consensus regarding the definition of engagement with different practitioners giving more or less weight to its different aspects such as turning up and complying with an order, a readiness to participate, developing positive relationships, being motivated to change and demonstrating behaviour change.

The perception of fairness appears central to the quality of the relationship between the young person and the practitioner. Young people appeared more willing to accept enforcement procedures and their responsibilities in this process if they believed it was administered fairly. This included the clear and understood nature of the rules and boundaries at the outset and then undertaking actions that subsequently conformed to them. Reciprocity also appeared to be an important constituent of fairness in that young people felt that practitioners should also observe the same rules such as turning up for appointments and punctuality.

The conclusions from the Ipsos MORI survey (2010) of practitioners and young people found the following.

The relationship between a young person and their worker is vital to their engagement and relies on the ability of staff to be 'firm but fair' in their approach; achieving a mix of friendliness coupled with appropriate boundaries within which rules can be enforced where necessary. Where relationships are working well, it is important that there is as much consistency as possible in who is working with the young people as changes can be unsettling. For many young people, *having someone to talk to is* judged as especially positive, particularly as, in some cases, the YOT worker is one of the few people, if not the only person, the young person is able to speak with openly (p. 67).

Lessons from youth work and education

If the relational aspects of engagement are so important then the communication skills of the practitioner need to be highlighted. This is not simply a matter of transmitting information from the practitioner to the young person but how they hear and make sense of a young person's responses. Creating the right conditions to facilitate a dialogue with a young person, which could be environmental (for example ensuring there is a comfortable space and sufficient uninterrupted time) and relational (enabling a sufficiently trusting relationship with the young person so that she or he is facilitated to communicate), is also part of this process.

Communication also needs to take account of all the potential indirect and unintentional ways that can occur between the practitioner and the young person. While the basic message may be intended to be conveyed to a young person through speech, non-verbal methods can also play an important part. Some studies for example have found that as little as seven per cent of communication involved the direct words spoken between people. Paralanguage (tone of voice, speed, loudness and intonation of speech) was found to convey over a third of the meaning of a message. Similarly non-verbal signs transmitted through body language and behaviour were responsible for over half of the information communicated. Ensuring that the underlying verbal message is reinforced by a practitioner's body language, eye contact or tone of voice may well make the communication more valid and effective to a young person (Lefevre 2010).

Much of the work on engaging young people in the youth justice system is inferential in that it draws on practice evidence from other areas such as youth work. Ostensibly there are lessons to be learned in terms of both individual engagement and programmes involving groups of young people. The increasing focus on young people deemed at risk through targeted youth work may also make it more relevant. It has been argued that as effective youth work is based upon the quality of the relationship developed between youth workers and young people then the key features may provide insights for youth justice practitioners (Mason and Prior 2008: 33).

There is much discussion of the definition of youth work and one description of its key features is as follows:

> Youth work has come to mean a combination of methods or interventions (such as educational group work with), marked out by distinctive characteristics (such as voluntary engagement, active involvement, informal education and professional flexibility) and underpinned by a shared set of values ... It promotes the voice and influence of young people. Fundamentally, youth work with individuals and groups stems from negotiation and mutual agreement. It serves as a springboard for social learning – in its broadest sense – that young people can use to express and achieve their aspirations. (Merton *et al.* 2004: 29)

However, some of these key features, particularly the voluntary nature of the relationship but also the emphasis on the voice and influence of young people and their exercise of choice, are fundamentally different to the current youth justice system. Youth justice practitioners are primarily accountable to the courts. They exercise considerable power over a young person's life and have an essentially directive relationship notwithstanding the need for some measure of negotiation.

Despite a history stretching back into the nineteenth century, there has been little rigorous evaluation of the impact of youth work. Where increases in self-esteem might be a measure of youth work success, this appears of itself to have no effect on promoting desistance from offending. It may be that effective youth workers negotiate relationships with young people that share common features with those deemed to be effective in youth justice. These could include relationships based on mutual respect, characterised by honesty and trust and involving a negotiated consensus on the goals to be achieved and the means of doing this. While many of these features might be considered to be typical of most successful human relationships, there is no self-help guide for youth justice practitioners. Considerable caution should be exercised in adopting a youth work approach in that a youth justice practitioner is operating with an enormous imbalance of power in an involuntary relationship. There are risks in creating a weak form of engagement whereby a focus on criminogenic needs is lost and an emphasis on activity for activity's sake or on self-esteem is adopted, which is less likely to bring about change (Mason and Prior 2008).

While much of the literature on engaging young people in youth justice interventions tends to be inferential, drawn from work with adults or youth and social work, little use is made of research evidence from the educational world. Yet arguably there are more parallels with some aspects of a teacher's role than with that of a youth worker. Teachers, like youth justice practitioners, wield considerable potentially coercive authority over young people who would often rather be somewhere else. Both disciplines are specifically about enabling learning and change through structured programmes with very clearly defined goals based upon detailed and continuing assessment.

Obviously the comparison must not be overdone as there are fundamental differences: teachers work with relatively large groups; the immersion in the education system is hopefully for far longer than in youth justice; interaction with peers is an integral part of the process; and schools exert considerable power as a pivotal social institution. Nevertheless given the move to personalised learning, the enormous expansion in educational support roles and the importance of education in the lives of young people, there may well be useful lessons to learn for youth justice practitioners.

Certainly the evidence for positive relational effects within an involuntary context is stronger and more relevant than within youth work. Large-scale studies such as the Programme for International Student Assessment (PISA) have found that measures of engagement were correlated with school factors including high expectations by teachers of young people, a strong disciplinary culture and good student–teacher relationships (Williams 2003). The PISA findings support the argument that behaviours and attitudes can be significantly affected (both positively and negatively) by teachers and parents and moulded by individual school policies and practices (Stephenson 2007: 122).

Teachers may have other influences on change in young people. Several studies have found, for example, that schools can help young people to acquire, through positive experiences, a greater ability to plan their lives. Young people from high-risk backgrounds who were enabled to adopt this approach were less likely to join peer groups with anti-social behaviour and this had a beneficial effect on their life choices such as employment (Rutter *et al.* 1998).

Teacher attitudes and behaviour may well have a significant impact not just on educational attainment as measured by qualifications, but also on the acquisition of softer generic skills crucial for employability which is an important protective factor for offending. Analysis of the National Child Development study data has suggested that the more experienced the teacher, the more effective they were in helping young people acquire skills valued by employers (Stephenson 2007: 119).

An American study found that teachers increased the social capital of students at risk of not completing high school. In measuring social capital through the opinions of young people about how much their teachers supported their efforts to succeed, a strong relationship was found between the levels of social capital and engagement in school irrespective of risk factors (Croninger and Lee 2001).

There is abundant evidence in the research and inspection literature on the importance of positive relationships, boundaries and high expectations, again though the literature tends not to go into detail as to exactly how clear boundaries, for example, were established or how positive expectations were created. Nevertheless these are helpful insights from what is after all a much larger evidence base than in youth justice. If we replace curriculum with programmes or interventions, the parallels between the youth justice and education contexts are clear, with teachers pivotal in promoting engagement in order to facilitate learning.

Visser (2003: 39, 40) draws upon a wide range of work to identify seven characteristics that are common to successful practice in meeting the special educational needs of young people whose behaviour is challenging:

- Belief that behaviour can be changed.

- Intervening is second to preventing challenging behaviour.

- Reactions to challenging behaviour provide alternative behaviour for the young person to follow.

- Communications are honest and transparent.

- Approaches are empathetic and are underpinned by a sense of equity.

- Young people are set boundaries and are appropriately challenged about their behaviours.

- A sense of humour is apparent which supports purposeful, lively challenges.

Effective teachers tend to pay careful attention to practical issues (Daniels *et al.* 1998). Yet often the literature refers to the art or craft of teaching. In the same way those practitioners in youth justice who are particularly effective in their relationships with young people may appear to be practising an art, given how apparently effortless and natural it can seem. However, all art forms are underpinned by techniques that require analysis, practice and reflection. The conclusions from analysis of the effectiveness of teachers working with young people deemed to have emotional and behavioural difficulties could apply equally to group work in youth justice. They displayed a breadth and flexibility in their craft that contrasted with the limited repertoires of less effective teachers. This craft meant they were skilled in the use of eye contact for engaging interest or expressing disapproval and were adept at using a varying tone of voice and appropriate choice of language often blended with humour to defuse the situation.

Other evidence from the educational sector reinforces youth justice practice. For example, Ofsted's (2008) report on engaging disaffected and reluctant students found that young people consistently reported that a major contributor to their re-engagement was the way staff listened to them and consulted them wherever possible. Again they emphasised the importance of positive communication. The dangers of labelling students are emphasised as is the importance of communicating with families.

Similarly the evidence gathered by Ofsted (2007) on successful practice in pupil referral units underlined the importance of offering a 'second chance' or a 'fresh start' accompanied by high expectations, the setting of challenging tasks and anticipating the support needed. The use of skilful questioning to monitor young people's understanding and to encourage them to deepen it through reflection, discussion and justification of their answers is integral to educational engagement and is directly transferable to youth justice practice.

Frustratingly none of these studies tell us exactly how effective relationships were achieved. They do, however, provide stronger evidence that involuntary relationships with young people can have both positive and negative effects depending on the quality of the relationship. Perhaps one of the most important features is the role of expectations and their effect on engagement. This is always a challenging area for youth justice practitioners operating in a context where sanctions and punishment loom large, and most of the young people face profound barriers to achievement in many areas of their lives. Critics of the risk-based approach have argued that this is exacerbated by the emphasis on various negative aspects of a young person's life.

Sport and art

Certain activities such as sport and arts have been claimed to be especially effective at engaging young people, and in the case of the arts uniquely transformative.

The provision of sporting activities targeted at certain groups of young people has in recent years often been seen as a hook to engage young people with the aim of either crime prevention or reduction. It could be argued though that the attraction for policymakers appears to lie less in any strong empirical evidence, but rather in an echo of Victorian beliefs in the moral impact of sport (Kelly 2008: 335). While specific sports may act as a hook to engage some young people in diversionary activities or to gain involvement in long-term programmes, it is equally capable of deterring others. Attitudes towards sport are closely linked to gender stereotypes with abundant evidence of the negative effects on young women. Sport also might support a particular image of masculinity for some young men which may or may not want to be encouraged. Are the growing numbers of obese young people going to be attracted to such activities that they find very challenging? The most comprehensive survey of the evidence for sport's ability to engage young people who are at risk of offending emphasised both the potential limitations of the perceptions of sport and the crucial importance of its sensitive use by practitioners to match the needs of the young person with the potential experience sport offers (Nichols 2007: 204).

Similar claims have been made for the arts, although greater emphasis is perhaps placed on their unique power to bring about individual change rather than simply engagement. A recent review found that out of 700 projects catering for both young people and adults who had offended, 400 had used arts-based activities (Hughes 2005). A wide range of benefits is claimed, including:

- development of self-confidence and self-esteem;
- increased creativity and thinking skills;
- improved skills in planning and organising activities;
- improved communication of ideas and information;
- raised or enhanced educational attainment;
- increased appreciation of the arts;
- enhanced mental and physical health and well-being;
- increased employability of individuals;
- reduced offending behaviour.

(Jermyn 2004)

The quality of research underpinning the impressive list of claims tends not to be high. Common limitations include evaluations with small sample sizes, a lack of baseline information, lack of control groups, few appropriate measures, over-reliance on anecdotal evidence, difficulties accessing information relating to offending, and unsupported assumptions about the links between intervention and outcome (Hughes 2005). Much of the evidence relates to behavioural changes, usually of adults, within custody such as a reduction in adjudications following an arts intervention. The plethora of indirect and testimonial evidence often adduced to support the effectiveness of the arts in the criminal justice system does not come close to the rigorous methodologies required by the Home Office.

Change models

Another perspective on engagement is provided by looking at some of the change models that are commonly applied to practice.

The stages of change model developed by Prochaska and DiClemente (1982) initially for adults involved in substance misuse proposes that 'change is an evolutionary process' involving a series of distinct stages: pre-contemplation, contemplation, preparation, action and maintenance (although there is some debate as to whether preparation and maintenance are in fact distinct stages). An important aspect of this model is that it is cyclical: a person may progress through the different stages towards maintenance but may also regress to earlier stages at times. The process of behaviour change may involve several cycles until maintenance is actually achieved (see Chapter 2 for more about the change cycle described here).

Prochaska and DiClemente also identified ten distinct processes of change which are aligned with the different stages of change. This is important for practice as it suggests interventions will be most effective where 'processes of change are tailored to individuals' stage change' (Newburn *et al.* 2005). For individuals at the pre-contemplation stage (where they are yet to consider change) approaches such as motivational interviewing techniques may be most effective. For those at the contemplation stage (considering change), individuals are 'most open to information and reflection about their behaviour' and require 'increased use of cognitive, affective and evaluative processes' to move through this stage. The preparation stage is when individuals are preparing to change and this stage requires a change in attitude towards their behaviour. It has been found that 'social reinforcement and helping relations' are important in the 'translation of thought into action' (Newburn *et al.* 2005: 179). At the action stage, behavioural processes such as counter-conditioning and stimulus control become crucial for the individual to cope with external influences that may cause them to return to old behaviour patterns. It has been noted also that having significant others at different stages of change can be influential, either supporting or inhibiting progression.

As with motivational interviewing, this is a potential but unproven tool that practitioners can administer and use the results to inform their initial and continuing approaches to engaging a young person in interventions. This model illustrates both the importance of agency – a young person may simply not be ready to engage despite the best efforts of a practitioner – and provides a framework from which effective relationships can help to develop the change process. In the study by Newburn *et al.* (2005) on Mentoring PLUS, for example, they found that young people who began at the pre-contemplation stage did not engage in the programme.

Ross and Fabiano (1985, as cited in Nichols 2007: 16) proposed from their review of programmes, that criminal behaviour was 'predisposed by a set of cognitive deficiencies' in those who offend. These included:

- an inability to solve interpersonal problems and deal with social relationships;
- a lack of self control;
- a lack of the ability to reason abstractly;
- low locus of control;
- an inability to feel empathy with other people.

(Nichols 2007: 16)

The social skills development model, largely promoted by the Huskins' manual for youth work (Huskins 1998, as cited in Nichols 2007), emphasises that programmes:

must first help people develop self-esteem and a positive life attitude. This is the initial requirement for encouraging participants to benefit from activities in which they increasingly take responsibility for themselves. Through these they can develop a range of social skills:

- Recognising and managing feelings.

- Feeling empathy with others.

- Problem solving.

- Negotiation.

- Values development.

- Action planning.

- Review skills.

(Nichols 2007: 17)

The social skills development model is a progressive model. Huskins describes 'good quality' youth work as the 'progressive empowerment of the individual to take a more active and responsible part in their own development: to become more proactive' (Huskins 1996, as cited in Nichols 2007: 17).

The main criticisms of these two models of change are that they place almost complete focus on the individual, with their social environment and context largely left unaddressed. They have also been criticised for being a 'deficit model', focusing on the perceived shortcomings of the young person and proposing a 'treatment' approach which may constrain engagement.

Equally the risk and resilience model has been criticised as concentrating too much on the risks and on external factors and that not enough weight is given to agency – a young person's ability to react to their circumstances and their external pressures.

It may be that approaches that focus on strengths in the context of desistance are more likely to engage young people; for example, a relatively recent development in working with adults who have offended is the Good Lives Model (GLM) (McNeill 2009: 26–9). This is derived from the field of positive psychology and provides a strengths-based approach to rehabilitation. In addition to managing or reducing risk, the GLM assumes that interventions should aim to enable individuals to develop a life plan to secure primary human goods without damaging others. In this practice model, the practitioner balances the reduction of risk for society against the production of personal goods for the person who has offended. Motivation here is fostered by language that should be 'future-orientated, optimistic and the approach goal focused' (Ward and Maruna 2007: 127).

The principles of effective practice and engaging young people

It may be helpful to consider a case study of a programme to:

- illustrate how it was both designed and implemented using the principles of effective practice;

- examine the processes of engagement;

- assess the interplay between programmes and relationships, as it has been claimed that programmes tend to eclipse the importance of relationship.

Summer Arts Colleges are a large-scale initiative that have been running since 2007 and have involved a third of all YOTs. There is possibly more quantitative evidence available on the inputs to and outcomes from this intervention across a diverse range of environments than from any equivalent youth justice programme.

The programme objectives are to:

- increase educational engagement and facilitate transition into mainstream education, training and employment after the programme;

- provide a structured full-time arts-based project combining arts enrichment and arts appreciation activities, and to explore possible routes into employment and careers within the arts;

- reduce levels of (re)offending among participants during the project and in the following months;

- work with the arts to improve literacy and numeracy skills and to achieve an accreditation through the Arts Award.

The design of this programme was rooted in the principles of effective practice, although the design process was iterative and the model was refined each year on the basis of evaluation (Arts Council England 2007, 2008; Unitas 2009).

Risk classification

This is an intensive programme and is therefore aimed at young people on the community part of their DTO sentence or an ISS.

The rationale for reserving places for those at most risk of reoffending is partly the efficient use of resources as this is a relatively costly intervention but also because the evidence indicates more negative outcomes for those at low risk of reoffending subject to intensive interventions (Nacro 2006). This may be partly due to the effects of mixing with more delinquent peers.

Despite this some YOTs have sought to place young people on lower tariff orders on this programme. There appear to be various reasons for this. Sometimes a young person may be assessed as at significant risk of reoffending despite their current sentence being low tariff. A case is often made that the needs of a young person will be met by this programme irrespective of their risk of offending and the warnings from the evidence of net-widening. More frequently there may simply not be enough high-risk young people under supervision at that point in time, particularly at small YOTs. In this case a careful balancing act has to be undertaken to create a group that will engage taking account of potential interpersonal dynamics and the levels of risk of reoffending attributed to individual young people.

However, other influences are at work which provide insight into engagement. Characteristics of YOTs who struggle to put together groups of young people who engage effectively appear to include weaker case management processes with case workers unclear as to the need for high-risk referrals, a lack of contact and thereby engagement with parents/carers over the programme, and poor information and preparation for the young people. More insidiously and difficult to prove is that there appears to be a selection bias at work, where young people are nominated who are deemed more likely to engage but may simply be judged as 'easier to work with' and less challenging which can militate against the risk classification principle.

Criminogenic need

Clearly given the objectives of Summer Arts Colleges, the need to participate and progress in education is the priority for this programme. However, to achieve effective engagement in the programme, full account has to be taken of other challenges in a young person's life; for example, those who have unstable accommodation not surprisingly have less chance of engaging effectively so extra effort has to be made to resolve their accommodation issues both before and during the programme. Although with some young people particular challenges in their lives, for example family discord, may only be distantly related to their offending, if at all, yet may be very relevant to the practicalities of their engagement in this programme. Working with the family in this instance would therefore be key to promoting engagement and thereby enabling the area of criminogenic need – in this case education – to be focused on.

It is important when considering criminogenic need to focus on those aspects of a young person's life that are more open to change – dynamic risk factors. Increasingly, educational attainment and participation are both seen as achievable and likely to promote desistance and are therefore promising targets for intervention.

Dosage

There are two aspects to dosage: duration and intensity. Lipsey's definition of high dosage was a total contact time of 100 hours or more over more than 26 weeks (1995). In a sense this is another version of proportionality in that the more entrenched the challenges in a young person's life then the greater the professional input required to bring about change. However, Lipsey's evidence is primarily in relation to adults and few interventions with young people last longer than 26 weeks. In fact there is very little evidence at all in the UK on the volume and duration of interventions in relation to outcomes.

The Summer Arts Colleges, while they last for six weeks, are an intensive intervention with 125 hours timetabled learning time plus another 30–40 hours supervised meal and break times. The average learning hours attended has been about 20 hours per week. From an intensity point of view (and as the staff teams involved can testify) this is a highly intensive intervention which may go some way towards explaining the commensurately positive outcomes. As a measure of engagement, these levels of attendance indicate highly engaged young people with 82 per cent of young people completing the full programme in 2009. Programme completion is strongly associated with subsequent reductions in offending. It is difficult to compare these levels of engagement as no other large-scale programme appears to monitor actual attendance and completion rates in such detail.

What characterises these programmes is the high expectations of the young people in terms of participation and achievement. Each young person has to sign a contract (countersigned by parents/carers) agreeing to the terms of engagement in relation to attendance, behaviour and participation. Interestingly a small number of YOTs believe this level of engagement to be beyond the young people. The arguments used are either on the basis of how allegedly disaffected the young people are in their area or that the programme is simply too demanding for the young people who are not ready for such a challenging intervention. This rejection of one of the most important elements of the programme design either on the grounds that young people are too difficult or too damaged to engage at this level is unsupported by any empirical evidence. It also fails to recognise that full-time study, let alone employment, will require this level of engagement. Both sets of arguments could well mask the reality that constructing and running such a programme demands intensive engagement from managers and practitioners that may not be either available or forthcoming. High-intensity engagement involves a considerable amount of work, particularly over logistical matters such as transport.

Responsivity

The approach to young people on the Summer Arts Colleges programme is certainly active and participatory which is consistent with the directing principle of responsivity. Most of the young people on this programme have had poor experiences of formal education and tend not to react well to an approach that is overly didactic or too reminiscent of classroom teaching. Nevertheless the Summer Arts Colleges aim not only to increase literacy and numeracy levels, but also to prepare young people for re-engagement with formal education and training. Much of the literacy and numeracy skill acquisition is embedded within artistic and creative activities which in themselves are prepared in consultation with the young people. The three-way alliance between arts practitioners, YOT staff and educationalists seeks to construct a positive learning group but also to offer individual support to learning tailored to each young person. The challenge is for practitioners from different cultures to provide a model of authoritative but positive social relations and fostering the key aspects of engagement – motivation, participation and cooperation.

Community based

This can sometimes be one of the most difficult principles for YOTs to adhere to. This is for a number of reasons. Concern with security and risk issues sometimes leads to the suggestion that the YOT office should be used for part or all of the time as a base for a Summer Arts College. While the reduction in costs and increase in control can appear attractive, it could be seen as a breach of this principle. To link young people's learning so closely to a YOT office is to reinforce all sorts of negative connotations regarding the young people and their potential and it reinforces the spurious notion that there is a discrete category of learners known as 'offenders'.

For similar reasons (they are empty during the summer), Pupil Referral Units are often proposed as a base for Summer Arts Colleges but again there are drawbacks. The majority of the young people are over the school-leaving age and therefore receiving their educational programme in an 'under-age' setting is unlikely to be received positively. Given that young people will ultimately have to return to mainstream environments such as further education (FE) colleges then segregated educational settings may well not prepare young people adequately.

This principle often requires a great deal of logistical skill in arranging and maintaining. An FE environment is usually best for Summer Arts Colleges. It helps young people become familiar with what are usually large and potentially intimidating environments, get used to conforming to rules and modes of behaviour in the college and generally be treated more as adult students rather than offenders. These benefits will only materialise if an effective partnership is created with the host FE college. It is not unusual for there to be a degree of prejudice to be overcome within the college staff. This can lead to the allocation of unsatisfactory space or restricted access to facilities such as catering. Supervision is a real and constant challenge and in a more structurally and socially complex environment such as a large college requires a considerable amount of planning and negotiation coupled with careful deployment of staff. It is easy to see why the simplicity of cost and control issues can act against this principle.

Similarly, trips to art exhibitions are an integral part of the Summer Arts Colleges programme but can be fraught with risks. Poorly planned and supervised, such trips can increase the risks to the young people and to other members and property of the community and potentially lead to more offending. Well executed they offer tremendous learning opportunities for young people to participate in cultural experiences previously denied them, adding specifically to the learning programme and achievement of the Arts Awards and also more generally to raise their aspirations and awareness of their cultural entitlement.

Intervention modality

While the Summer Arts College programme is more akin to social education within a creative curriculum than to a cognitive-behavioural programme, it has certain common features. Both interventions have a focus on the acquisition of skills intended to enhance problem-solving, social interactions or kinds of coping skills. Arguably, an arts-based programme puts particular emphasis on increasing creativity and thinking skills and the framework of the Arts Awards reinforces the inherent need for improved skills in planning and organising activities and enhancing communication of ideas and information.

Much of the subject matter negotiated with the young people uses different art forms such as film, photography, music or theatre to explore issues pertinent to desistance such as substance misuse, violence and the effects of involvement in the criminal justice system.

Programme integrity

One of the biggest challenges to rolling out initiatives nationally is maintaining programme integrity. As programmes attempt to go to scale, their effectiveness often declines as with cognitive-behavioural skills pro-grammes. This has often been explained by implementation failures such as programme drift, reversal and non-compliance. Evidence indicates that to ensure integrity programmes should possess:

- clear and stated aims and objectives;

- links between the methods used and the stated objectives;

- staff who are trained, skilled and experienced in the intervention methods used within the programme;

- adequate resources and effective management;

- involvement of programme initiators during all stages working with those managing local delivery;

- monitoring and evaluation processes in place from the outset.

(Whyte 2009: 64)

Lipsey (1995) also found that researcher involvement in the design and implementation of an intervention made a significant difference to its effectiveness. The Summer Arts College programme has taken full account of this and there is a very detailed system monitoring the implementation of the operational specification. This coupled with independent quality audits appears to mitigate the risks of programme drift, reversal and non-compliance. There is a comprehensive online training system and access to very detailed guidance on all aspects of planning and running the pro-gramme. The researchers are closely involved throughout the programme.

It is interesting using the Summer Arts College case study to reflect on the debate between those who advocate the primacy of a strict 'What Works' programme approach and those who assert the importance of relationships in the desistance process.

There does appear to be a correspondence between the degree to which sites adhere to the operational specification and the outcomes for the young people. Each year the operational specification has been modified in the light of experience and the programme has become more rather than less prescriptive yet outcomes have improved as the scheme has rolled out in contrast to other initiatives. This is not simply a result of Summer Arts College teams accruing experience each year as the new YOTs are also achieving significantly better outcomes for young people than those for previous years.

Two modifications to the operational specification may offer insight into both general aspects of programme design and specific elements of effective engagement. Analysis of individual Summer Arts College site performances in 2008 indicated that sites that had made more intensive arrangements around transport such as a dedicated minibus or taxi service and those that had detailed incentives and sanctions schemes consistently retained more young people and thereby achieved greater gains in literacy and numeracy, achievement of the Arts Award and reductions in offending. Of course those two features may simply have been the hallmarks of effective management rather than significant causes in themselves. However, intensive transport arrangements and a detailed incentives system were introduced in 2009 and appear to be strongly related to the widespread improvement in engagement with 82 per cent of young people completing in 2009 compared to 65 per cent in 2008.

Several points emerge from this case study. It is vital to keep assessing changes in engagement levels as improvements can always be made. Despite the diversity of individuals and contexts, certain generalised ways of working can improve engagement for all. Effective programme management control is important for successful programme implementation. Practical considerations are often at the heart of engagement as in this case with transport arrangements and incentives. Certainly effective relationships are important but only if the practicalities are taken fully into account which may determine whether a young person is even able to turn up at an appointment.

The Summer Arts College case study can also be supplemented with qualitative information, particularly the views of the young people who participated. When asked how and why the programme worked for them and what kept them engaged, the diversity of answers indicated that the mechanisms differed according to the circumstances, experiences and personality of the young people. There was, though, some common ground.

Many of the young people referred were initially either reluctant or hostile to the programme with few having a choice to attend. The initial 'push' elements – court-related compulsion, parental pressure, tight transport arrangements – appear to have been superseded by a strong 'pull' from the programme that progressively engaged them.

The young people identified various aspects of the arts that proved engaging to them, although, obviously it varied considerably between individuals. For some, the newness of the art form (three art forms were undertaken per Summer Arts College) made them curious, which in turn made them want to learn more. Conversely, for others it was their existing interest in, for example, music that attracted them. The performance element was found to be helpful in developing communication skills and team working as well as providing a challenge. One particularly attractive feature of the arts was the creative licence given and that there was no pass or fail, which contrasted with their experience of formal education. Similarly the active and experiential nature of the work was appreciated. Interestingly, the fact that the arts led to a tangible product, even if only a CD or DVD, appeared to make a big difference both in terms of ownership and demonstrating achievements to others. The art form appeared to camouflage the literacy and numeracy work that was being undertaken which was recognised in retrospect by the young people but tended to go unnoticed at the time.

In addition to any intrinsically engaging features of arts and creative activities, the relationships that developed with the arts practitioners appeared to be at least as important a part of the engagement process. Being treated with parity by a professional who had non-academic but highly valued skills was very attractive to the young people. Through the relationship with the arts practitioners and partly due to the nature of the activities, the exercise of control and choice over their work was claimed by the young people to have sustained their interest and increased completion of work. The relationship with the arts practitioner was sometimes contrasted unfavourably with the role of the YOT staff who identified with compliance matters. However, some young people believed that their relationship with YOT staff was charged positively through working alongside them in these creative activities where YOT staff were not the experts and some young people consequently felt more emotionally engaged with them.

There were also some features of the Summer Arts College programme that young people identified as being relevant to their engagement, but that could apply to a wide range of non-arts interventions. The generic nature of help available to deal with a wide range of issues was contrasted with formal education and emphasises the importance of multi-modal approaches. The high ratio of staff to young people meant that they received an immediacy of attention and personal assistance that they had not received before and that they really welcomed. Consistent expectations about attendance and behaviour supported by practical measures in their full-time programme enabled the young people to develop routines. Being treated as an adult which was aided by being in an adult environment was a universal mantra.

Conclusions

Engagement is a commonly used term but despite this there is a wide variation in definitions and surprisingly little evidence on it. Engagement is clearly a prerequisite for successful interventions but there is a significant research gap in youth justice to help practitioners achieve it within the involuntary relationships they have with young people. Arguably, effective practice and engagement are symbiotic – programmes cannot function without considering their relational aspects and relationships that do not heed the messages from the evidence are unlikely to bring about desistance.

Summary

- For the term engagement to be meaningful, it needs a consistent and widely accepted definition. It is suggested that it could be defined as 'the positive participation and progression of a young person within a youth justice intervention'.

- There is a significant lack of evidence on how to engage young people in youth justice interventions and the best that can be achieved is to examine the literature in other practice settings or on adults who offend.

- The evidence base on the effects and characteristics of engagement is significantly more robust for education than, for example, for youth work. Given the involuntary nature of teacher–pupil relationships, then the practice messages may be more transferable than from other disciplines.

Further reading

Ipsos MORI (2010) *A Review of Techniques for Effective Engagement and Participation*. London: Youth Justice Board.

Lefevre, M. (2010) *Communicating with Children and Young People*. Bristol: The Policy Press.

McNeill, F. (2009) *Towards Effective Practice in Offender Supervision*. Glasgow: Scottish Centre for Crime and Justice Research.

Nichols, G. (2007) *Sport and Crime Reduction: The Role of Sports in Tackling Youth Crime*. London: Routledge.

Unitas (2010) *Summer Arts Colleges 2009: Final Outcomes Report*. London: Unitas.

4

Education, training and employment

The evidence base for education, training and employment

Detachment from education, training and employment is a significant risk factor in relation to offending behaviour. There is no single causal factor that links the two and the relationship between them is a complex one that cannot be defined in simplistic terms. The key challenge for managers and practitioners working with young people in the youth justice system is how to support young people in sustaining any attachment they have to an educational setting and how to help them to become reattached where this has broken down completely.

This chapter outlines some of the key issues with regard to young people at risk of offending or reoffending and education and employment. It highlights many of the systemic difficulties associated with detachment, particularly where young people have individual needs that impact on their capacity to learn at the same rate and in the same ways as other young people around them.

The scale of detachment

Detachment from mainstream education appears to be extensive among young people in the youth justice system. Detachment here is taken to occur through exclusion (permanent, fixed-term and informal, including not being on a school roll), non-attendance (authorised and unauthorised) and the statementing process for special educational needs (particularly for emotional and behavioural difficulties), and potentially culminates in non-participation post-16 (not in education, employment or training (NEET), or status zero).

Clearly those young people who have no educational, training or employment provision arranged for them at all can be deemed to be detached and, arguably, so too are those in segregated provision, while those on part-time programmes with mainstream schools are at least partly detached. On these definitions the great majority of those entering and leaving custody are detached from mainstream education with between one-third and a half having no provision at all (ECOTEC 2001a).

The most recent and most extensive survey (it collected information on 5,568 young people) of the scale of detachment among young people in the youth justice system found the following:

- The YOTs in the sample are struggling with very serious access issues to full-time education, training and employment.

- Under half of the young people in the sample may be in full-time provision at any point in time.

- Those young people who are older, have been in the care system, have literacy or numeracy difficulties, have previous convictions and have more serious disposals are all significantly less likely to have full-time education, training and employment provision arranged for them.

- Only around half of those in the sample of statutory school age appear to have full-time education arranged for them. This is a particularly serious issue for those in their final year of compulsory schooling.

- Dubious practices by some schools, coupled with drift and a lack of alternative educational capacity by LEAs, were revealed in the census.

- The quarterly percentage in education, training and employment figures reported to the Youth Justice Board were significantly higher than the percentages obtained in the census for all YOTs in the sample.

- Monitoring of the education and training of those young people in the custodial phase of a DTO appears to be relatively weak by some YOT staff.
(Youth Justice Board 2006)

Taking account of non-attendance as few as 35 per cent of young people in the youth justice system may actually be in full-time education, training or employment on a given day. Delay and drift appear to be relatively commonplace. Practitioners highlighted cases where young people had received no education for several years and noted the negative effects on motivation of part-time provision.

These findings are consistent with other surveys of young people in the youth justice system. For example, out of 2,211 young people engaged in the youth inclusion programme almost one-third (695) were not enrolled at a school (Burrows 2003). The extensive analysis of the *Asset* data, with a sample of 2,613, indicates that 21 per cent of young people of statutory school age had no provision arranged (Baker *et al.* 2002).

The situation for those aged 16 to 18 appears significantly worse, with 39 per cent being recorded as unemployed and a further 17 per cent having part-time or casual employment in the *Asset* sample of nearly 1,200 young people (Baker *et al.* 2002). Looking specifically at those young people who have been more persistently involved in offending and who are placed on

ISSs, even greater proportions are completely detached from mainstream education, training and employment. For those of statutory school age out of a sample of 1,640, over a quarter had no main source of educational provision and only 19 per cent were attending a mainstream school. Again the situation was significantly worse for 16–18 year-olds with 56 per cent being unemployed out of a sample of 1,150 (YJB 2006). The levels of non-participation by 16–18-year-olds is consistently high across different studies of the youth justice system. A survey of YOTs in the Greater Manchester area found only 28 per cent of this age group in college or employment, including those with only part-time provision (Youth Justice Trust 2004). Another study involving young people in an arts-based intervention revealed that of those entering the project who were above school leaving age, 47 per cent were not in education, training or employment when they reached school leaving age (Arts Council England 2008).

In 2008/2009 over 127,000 young people were involved with the youth justice system (YJB 2010). Converting these percentages on lack of access and non-attendance from the above studies means that nearly 84,000 are not in full-time education, training or employment and of these perhaps 20–25,000 have nothing arranged for them at all. Of course, given what is known about the placement instability of the wider population of those not in education, training or employment, and particularly for those in the youth justice system, then even those young people recorded as being in full-time education at any point in time are likely to have had several episodes without any education or training (ECOTEC 2001a; Hayward *et al.* 2005). Allowing for the various assumptions made it is not unreasonable to conclude that perhaps one-third of those who have become detached from mainstream education are involved in the youth justice system.

Academic failure at school is widely recognised as being endemic among the population of young people who offend. This is particularly true in the American literature: 'School failure and poor reading performance as early as the third grade, truancy, poor achievement, and misbehaviour in elementary school, and the failure to master school skills throughout schooling are among the most reliable predictors of delinquency and other adolescent "rotten outcomes"' (Schorr 1988, cited in Gemignani 1994: 16).

In terms of the wider population of young people who offend in England and Wales and are known to YOTs, *Asset* returns indicated that:

- one in two YOT clients are underachieving in school;

- one in three need help with reading and writing;

- one in five has special educational needs.

(Baker *et al.* 2002)

The charity INCLUDE (2000) carried out a small survey for the Youth Justice Board's Basic Skills Initiative of the literacy and numeracy levels of young people with whom YOTs were working. This survey revealed reading ages that were lagging several years behind chronological ages. The educational attainment levels of young people who have been involved in serious and persistent offending are even lower. The average reading age of young people starting ISS schemes is five years below their chronological age (Moore *et al.* 2004).

The levels of literacy and numeracy of 10–17-year-olds on their entry into custody is very low. For those of compulsory school age (15- and 16-year-olds in this sample) about half had literacy and numeracy levels below that expected of an 11-year-old. Almost one-third (31 per cent) had literacy levels at or below that expected of a 7-year-old, while over 40 per cent had numeracy skills at or below this level (ECOTEC 2001a). Nine out of ten young people in one STC were found to have a reading age well below their real age (Social Exclusion Unit 2002). The interim report of a study on improving literacy and numeracy (Hurry *et al.* 2005) among a group of young people aged 15 to 18 years who were all on a court order, either in the community or in custody, found that about two-thirds were at or below Level 1 (the level expected of the average 11-year-old). Over two-thirds of the respondents (69 per cent) in this study had left school without any qualifications compared with about 6 per cent in the general population (Hurry *et al.* 2005).

Interventions to prevent detachment and increase attainment

Much of the evidence for effective interventions that prevent or reverse detachment or low attainment applies to pre-school or primary-age children and often originates in the USA.

In his meta-analysis of nearly 400 studies that used control or comparison groups and representing over 40,000 young people aged 12 to 21 Lipsey (1995) detected an average overall net 10 per cent reduction in reoffending. This modest but significant effect varied significantly according to the type and amount of intervention. Both school participation and academic performance were also seen to improve on average as a result of interventions. The average effect on school participation was a 12 per cent improvement across the 93 studies reviewed. Academic performance improved by 14 per cent on average across the 42 studies reviewed. School participation outcomes were significantly and relatively highly correlated with delinquency outcomes compared to any other outcome category.

More detailed UK-based studies have proven largely unrewarding. A Home Office report that examined the findings from four studies on education and offending highlighted this problem as they 'showed the difficulties of providing robust, "evidence-based" findings to inform national policy and practice' (Home Office 2004: 19). The short duration of the programmes combined with other complexities meant that there was little insight gained into issues of causality and attribution, and other potential influencing factors could not be screened out.

When it comes to research into the effectiveness of UK interventions designed to help lower-achieving children and young people catch up there is a significant gap for those aged 12 to 18. For children at primary school there are a certain number of high-quality evaluations that have been reviewed (Brooks 2002). In the absence of specific interventions ordinary teaching did not enable children with literacy difficulties to catch up. Brooks concluded that it was reasonable to expect a doubling of the rate of progress with specific interventions and that these gains were maintained in most of the schemes where progress was followed up.

A more recent YJB funded programme, TextNow, has shown promising results in this respect however (Brooks 2009a). TextNow is a reader engagement programme that motivates young people to become more confident and able readers. The model is based on a structured programme of daily 20-minute reading sessions each weekday for a period of 10 weeks supported by trained coaches, a small library and an incentive scheme. In 2008, a national TextNow pilot ran 12 week programmes in 36 sites including 19 YOTs and two YOIs in England and Wales involving 400 young people. The evaluation demonstrated that the programme had statistically significant impacts on all aspects of reading engagement and achievement, most significantly an improvement in average reading ages of 18 months in just 12 weeks. There were also significant outcomes demonstrating that young people on the project enjoyed reading more, were reading more frequently and had branched out in terms of what they read.

A systematic review of literacy and numeracy interventions for adults 'found just enough evidence (all of it from the USA) to demonstrate rigorously in a meta-analysis that receiving adult literacy and numeracy tuition does produce more progress than not receiving it' (Torgerson et al. 2004: 13). One reading programme accompanied by a 'community-building group process' for adults in an American prison achieved positive results.

In 2008, the Bercow Report highlighted the speech, language and communication needs (SLCN) experienced by children and young people, including those who have offended. Its recommendation that the Youth Crime Action Plan (Home Office 2008) should consider how best to address the SLCN of young people in the criminal justice system, including those in custody, was acknowledged within the context of planning to meet the special educational needs of these young people. It is useful though to consider the rationale for this policy direction and also the evidence on which it is based. Brooks (2009b) explains the chain of reasoning for the pressure to assess and treat the SLCN of young people in the youth justice system as follows:

- Poor speech, language and communication (SLC) skills predispose young children to fail in acquiring early literacy and numeracy and, both indirectly as a result of that failure and directly as a result of the poor SLC skills themselves, to achieve poor results in their education.

- All these deficits in turn become risk factors for disruptive behaviour, truancy, delinquency and eventually offending.

- Early intervention to improve SLC skills may therefore protect against this trajectory.

- Later intervention to improve SLC skills may similarly protect against repetition of anti-social behaviour, including reoffending.

- Therefore measures to improve SLC skills should be introduced not only in the pre-school and school systems, but also and especially in the youth justice system.

Exploring each of these assumptions in turn, Brooks identifies some gaps in the evidence base for them. While 7–8 per cent of young people in the general population appear to have SLC difficulties, there is no national data on the prevalence of such difficulties among young people in the youth justice system. Small-scale studies, however, suggest that many may have poorer SLC than their peers in the general population (Snow and Powell 2004; Bryan 2004, 2008; Bryan et al. 2007; Gregory and Bryan 2009). While there is evidence of the benefits of speech and language (SL) therapy generally, none of it appears to be derived from RCTs. One particular approach to improving oral skills, the York Oral Language Programme, has shown benefits in two randomised controlled trials, albeit with much younger children (Bowyer-Crane et al. 2008). Three longitudinal studies have investigated whether untreated early, SLCN lead to offending (Clegg et al. 1999; Brownlie et al. 2004; Mouridsen and Hauschild 2009) but the case is not proven. There are currently no predictive measures which reliably identify which children with SLCN are at risk of later offending. To date there has been just one study of the use of SL therapy with young people who have offended the results of which seem promising, although the post-tested sample was very small – 20 out of the 49 young people in the original sample (Gregory and Bryan 2009). Brooks concludes, therefore, that there is not yet a convincing case for routine assessment of speech, language and communication skills or the widespread roll-out of SL therapy to young people in the youth justice system. A more robust evidence base needs to be established first.

Involving parents or carers in their children's education has been found to be a significant factor in strengthening attachment to school and to learning in general (Bynner 2001). A review of the research established a clear and consistent finding that spontaneous parental involvement in education has a large, positive and independent effect on the outcomes of schooling (Desforges and Abouchaar 2003). A recent DCSF study has also shown convincingly that the aspirations parents have for their children are strongly associated with their child's level of engagement at school (Ross 2009). The research base where planned parental intervention is concerned is flimsy, with findings restricted to participant satisfaction rather than increases in attainment. As with so much of the evidence of 'What Works' there is a significant gap in understanding how to make it work (Desforges and Abouchaar 2003).

Typically, most initiatives that have been relatively rigorously evaluated tend to be from the USA. The most well-known of these is perhaps the High/Scope Perry project which followed up the children involved to the age of 27. This programme was characterised by a focus on a group of families beset with high-risk factors and a relatively high dosage and length (special classes for two and a half hours daily over 30 weeks supplemented by a weekly home visit from a teacher). Considerable attention was paid to enhancing the academic performance of the children through emphasising active learning, problem-solving and concentration on task. Home–school links were emphasised. Teaching staff received specific training and dealt with small groups of children. A number of positive outcomes were found including large reductions in the numbers of lifetime arrests, lower teenage pregnancy rates and large increases in graduation rates. This programme was, however, classified as promising rather than effective (Mihalic *et al.* 2001).

The emphasis on school effectiveness in recent years has generated some relevant evidence. Many interventions that have been evaluated have not had the reduction of crime as their main aim although these interventions may directly or indirectly have reduced risk factors associated with offending (Home Office 2004). Research findings into what makes an effective school consistently emphasise the importance of leadership, systematic approaches to monitoring attendance and progress, high expectations of young people in relation to both their learning and behaviour, a balanced use of rewards and incentives, high parental involvement, opportunities for young people to exercise responsibility within the school and a positive ethos within the school (Rutter *et al.* 1998; Home Office 2004; Ofsted 2009a). This is in contrast to ineffective schools which 'tend to categorise pupils who behave poorly or persistently truant as deviants, and shift responsibility for their behaviour and welfare to other agencies or institutions' (Home Office 2004: 19).

One example of an American school-based prevention programme that focused across the school on key organisational issues and has had a relatively rigorous evaluation is the Program Development Evaluation method which is a multi-modal organisational intervention implemented by school improvement teams comprising parents, teachers and school officials. This was found to be an effective method of improving classroom management and school discipline with significant decreases in disruption in classrooms (Howell 2003).

Three US programmes for primary-age children that offer a school-based multi-modal approach, and have been evaluated and deemed to be effective, or at least to be a promising approach are: Fast Track, the Seattle Social Development Project and the Child Development Project.

The Fast Track programme targets children in their early years of schooling who are from low-income, high-crime communities and are displaying particular behavioural problems at home and school. The programme has six integrated components which match six domains of intervention. The evaluation of the programme involved the random assignment of schools to treatment and control groups. Recipients of the programme displayed decreases in aggression and disruptive behaviour at both school and home. In addition, their relationships with peers improved, as did a range of social skills.

Although the collection of robust evidence was a key objective of the Crime Reduction Initiative in Secondary Schools (CRISS) programme in the UK, methodological weaknesses meant that it was only possible to derive recommendations for promising approaches (Home Office 2004). See Chapter 1, 'Implementation', pp. 22–4.

Bullying in school has been linked to an increased risk of offending. A Norwegian programme designed to reduce bullying in schools through establishing behavioural boundaries, with the consistent application of sanctions for rule-breaking and fostering cooperative working with teachers and parents, succeeded in reducing the incidence of bullying. There were also indirect effects such as a reduction in absenteeism, vandalism and theft (Olweus 1993). This programme was also reported to have been implemented successfully in England (ECOTEC 2001a). However, both these evaluations have been criticised as not being particularly rigorous and replication in the US was reported to be unsuccessful (Howell 2003). Anti-bullying programmes operated in Sheffield across 23 primary and secondary schools. In line with evaluations of most school-based interventions greater effect was found in the reduction of bullying in primary schools with relatively small effects in secondary schools (Home Office 2004).

Individually targeted interventions tend to focus on the reduction of anger and disruptive and violent behaviour by particular individuals. The Social Competence Promotion Programme for Young Adolescents in America is a violence prevention approach that promotes a range of social competencies such as decision-making, social problem-solving, self-control, stress management and communication skills. An evaluation found that, compared to controls, the participant young people were more engaged with school and less likely to be involved in absenteeism, suspensions and minor delinquent behaviour (Weissberg and Caplan 1998).

Basing probation officers in schools has a long history in certain parts of the USA. This has become a popular approach, with officers operating in both a preventative way and also intervening directly with young people displaying delinquent behaviour. In addition to carrying out probation supervision probation staff in some instances carry out training for teachers and deliver law-related education classes. Studies indicate that attainment and attendance may be increased and anti-social behaviour in the school and also of those on probation is improved (Griffin 1999).

The Safer Schools Partnership (SSP) programme aims to promote the safety of schools and the young people attending them. They vary considerably in structure but generally have active police involvement in schools, often in collaboration with other support staff. The objectives are to improve key behavioural issues in such schools including non-attendance, bullying, anti-social behaviour and offending. The evaluation of the programme (Bhabra *et al.* 2004) was later supplemented by an extension of the study to over 1,000 schools (Bowles *et al.* 2005). They found a significant reduction in rates of absence (both authorised and unauthorised) in the SSP schools relative to those experienced in the comparison schools. GCSE performance also improved relative to the comparison schools. Difficulties with the data prevented much examination of changes in levels of bullying and anti-social behaviour in schools. Similarly the data was inadequate to support school-level analysis of convictions or arrests, making it impossible to present any robust findings of the impact of this approach on offending.

Gottfredson's comprehensive review of the evidence for effective school interventions concluded that:

> considerable evidence of positive effects for prevention programmes can be found in the available research, but that implementation, quality and quantity qualify the positive findings. Schools can be a site for effective intervention, or a site for non-intervention or ineffective intervention. Schools have the potential to contribute to the positive socialisation of youth. But the range of conditions under which they have been demonstrated to realize this potential is narrow. (2001: 258)

Further education colleges

There are a number of promising practice indicators for FE colleges planning to work with young people at risk (Utting 1999). These include:

- collaborative bridging/access programmes developed with local schools, education authorities and Learning and Skills Councils to create education and training opportunities;
- a student-centred approach with the emphasis on learning as opposed to assessment;
- sufficiently flexible curriculum and teaching methods to take account of individual student needs;
- occupational guidance and work experience as an integral part of each course;
- effective support for learning being made available, such as one-to-one tutoring and pastoral support;
- students following a curriculum that is not only relevant to their current and future needs, but also shows them how they are progressing;
- other support services such as help with transport or childcare being made available;
- joint training for school and college staff on working with young people at risk.

Employment

As being unemployed seems to be an independent risk factor, schemes that increase employment or at least employability might be thought likely to be effective but again the evidence is sparse and largely confined to adults. For young people who have completed compulsory schooling but have no or few qualifications and will thus struggle to enter the labour markets, successfully gaining post-school qualifications can have a significant impact. One study found that young people with few or no school qualifications but who went on to gain Level 2 qualifications saw a dramatic effect on employment rates. By the time they had acquired Level 3 qualifications they were on a par in terms of finding employment with those young people who went on to achieve A-Levels via the academic route (McIntosh 2003).

Previous studies into the efficacy of employment interventions with adults who offend have shown promising results although these may not always be applicable to young people. Bridges' study in 1998 found that adults who were unemployed at the beginning of their probation supervision, but who had an employment intervention while on supervision, found employment before the end of their community sentences at twice the rate of those who had no intervention. Reconviction studies suggest that employment interventions can potentially reduce reoffending rates (May 1999; Sarno et al. 2000). It is not simply having a job that is associated with reductions in offending but the quality, including the stability, of that employment coupled with levels of satisfaction (Harper and Chitty 2005).

The research challenges are highlighted by the basic skills pathfinder evaluation which sought to measure the progress of adults on basic skills programmes in terms of their basic skills improvements and increased employability, but high attrition rates made this impossible (McMahon et al. 2004).

Custodial education

Asking the bald question 'What Works?' of custodial education for young people is simplistic and arguably counter-intuitive given that the evidence suggests that for perhaps the majority of young people custody increases educational risk factors and may reduce protective factors. The best that can be done is to try to assess whether educational programmes within custody have a positive effect within that experience and whether certain approaches can be more effective than others following release.

A number of research studies have been undertaken that try to measure the effectiveness of custodial educational intervention programmes. However, these are bedevilled by relatively weak research design and are usually focused on adults.

Tolbert (2002: 19) identifies the following as being major limitations of studies investigating the relationship between educational intervention and recidivism:

- Most do not take into account other services and factors inside and outside prison that may affect recidivism rates, such as drug treatment programmes, post-release services and family support.

- Most of the results are vulnerable to self-selection bias; the methodologies do not adequately account for participant characteristics.

- Most do not follow released inmates for a long enough period of time.

- Most vary in their definitions of recidivism – a nationally (US) recognised definition of recidivism does not exist.

- Most are unable to measure various levels of improvement in inmates' behaviours.

- Most are based on correctional educational records that are often poorly kept by institutions.

A few studies, however, do provide some evidence of a positive link between educational interventions and reductions in recidivism, and provide insights into the characteristics of programmes that do seem to be effective, although the studies are North American and deal with adults.

Using three studies that employed a random or matched comparison group design, Porporino and Robinson (1992) concluded that the recidivism rate of participants in the Canadian Adult Basic Education programme was significantly lower than that of the comparison group. Other positive results were achieved in studies in the United States. One longitudinal study involving 3,400 imprisoned adults found that participation in educational programmes reduced the chances of reimprisonment by 29 per cent (Steurer et al. 2001). Similarly there was a reduction in recidivism of a third among adult prisoners who participated in vocational and apprenticeship training as part of the Post-Release Employment Project (Saylor and Gaes 1997).

According to Tolbert (2002: 1–2): 'These programmes lead to lower recidivism rates, according to advocates, because they provide inmates with the knowledge, skills, attitudes, and values needed to succeed in society and to avoid future criminal activity.'

Considerable caution should be exercised in extending these more positive findings to younger groups in the UK as they may not be applicable. Not only are they from different countries but the sentence length for adults is much greater and the effects of maturation, stable learning groups and greater dosage of education could be considerable. See also Chapter 10 on the secure estate and resettlement.

Segregated education and training

The history of the education of young people who offend is inextricably bound up with segregated educational provision. This is provided for those young people who, through their anti-social or offending behaviour, or due to perceived differences in their learning needs, are removed from mainstream school. They are seen as being more appropriately placed in 'specialist' environments. There are four broad and overlapping categories of segregated education: separate facilities on the school site, more recently termed learning support units; special schools; PRUs; and, often linked to these, a constellation of initiatives offering formal and informal learning including home tuition.

Special groups or units within schools for young people who are seen to pose behavioural problems in mainstream classes have a lengthy history but have seen a significant expansion in recent years through initiatives such as Education Action Zones and the Excellence in Cities programmes. Their main stated objectives include bringing about behavioural changes so that young people can be reintegrated into mainstream classes, thereby reducing exclusions, increasing attainment and improving attendance. Around 135,000 pupils in England spend some time in alternative provision each year.

The evaluation evidence on their effectiveness is very limited and there is very little reliable performance data available for pupils in alternative provision. What there is suggests very poor outcomes: in 2006 only 1 per cent of 15-year-olds in Pupil Referral Units achieved five GCSEs at grades A*–C or equivalent; 11.3 per cent achieved five or more grades A*–G; and 82.1 per cent achieved one or more qualifications (DCSF 2008a).

A study of seven units in Sheffield found no effect on exclusion rates or on the numbers transferred to special schools and that the focus tended to be on the perceived problems of the young person rather than the context in which they occurred – 'the half way house fallacy' (Galloway 1985: 162). Reintegration rates into mainstream classes were also found to be low in Inner London units (Mortimore et al. 1983).

There is a range of relatively systematic American studies. In reviewing these Topping (1983) found that in certain circumstances both primary and secondary age groups could show substantial academic gains and behavioural improvement, although many results were disappointing. Gains appeared to dissipate over the long term when young people were returned to mainstream classes.

The evaluation of Learning Support Units (LSUs) in the Excellence in Cities programme was largely qualitative and there was no systematic evaluation of attainment or behaviour gains (Wilkin et al. 2003). While there were abundant positive comments from staff and small samples of young people, only about 22 per cent were fully reintegrated and the majority of these were younger pupils with very few year 10 and no year 11 young people returning to mainstream classes. This provision often was not full-time for all young people.

Ofsted (2003) found that a quarter of the LSUs they inspected were not doing sufficient work to help the young people learn more effectively. Other criticisms included 'the use of units simply as "remove rooms" where disruptive pupils were sent at random, weak monitoring and evaluation and a lack of emphasis on staff training and ensuring they were an integral part of the teaching team' (Ofsted 2003: 60). A more recent Ofsted report on the impact of LSUs showed that in five out of the 11 LSUs visited, reintegration was not always successful. Reasons given for this were:

- not all teaching staff were aware of the strategies used in the LSU to manage pupils' behaviour and were unable to build on these approaches;
- not all teaching staff welcomed pupils back to their classes;
- some pupils stayed too long in the LSU and were unable to readjust to mainstream classes;
- reintegrated pupils were not effectively supported or monitored on their return to mainstream classes.

(Ofsted 2006: 8)

Pupil Referral Units

Many young people who have offended – particularly if they continue to offend – will end up being referred to off-site provision, usually a PRU. Despite the fact that the use of small segregated units for a range of young people has a long history and very high unit costs there is little evidence on its outcomes. The evidence that does exist is often limited on two counts: there is rarely follow-up data and it is characterised by differing educational expectations of the young people on, for example, curriculum, attainment and attendance. One key issue in assessing the effectiveness of PRUs is agreeing success criteria. There is a lack of clarity about whether this should be progression post-16, qualifications achieved, reintegration into mainstream schooling, desistance in offending, reductions in the behaviours that cause them to be detached from mainstream schooling and a range of softer outcomes such as increases in self-esteem.

Perhaps not surprisingly there is little reference in most studies to the impact of segregated education on offending but there are several inherent characteristics which could lead it to be less effective in terms of reducing risk factors and increasing protective factors. Given that delinquent peer groups are a significant risk factor for adolescents then a concentration in a PRU is likely to be counterproductive. In the same way that it is suggested that learning in such an abnormal environment as custody does not transfer easily to everyday life in the community, similar difficulties may be posed for young people in small units. Positive changes in behaviour or attitudes to learning may well not survive the dramatic shift from a small highly protected environment to the hurly-burly of educational life in a further education college or the workplace.

Defining successful outcomes is divided between those who argue for clear measurable outcomes (Topping 1983), those who believe this is too narrow (Munn et al. 2000) and those who recognise a progression of 'small steps' (Hustler et al. 1998; Kendall et al. 2002). Views on the measurement of effectiveness appear to lie on a continuum from a reliance on the positive attitudes of practitioners from segregated education (Kinder *et al.* 2000) through to the argument that effectiveness should be based on studies that can be generalised producing hard, objectively measurable evidence with a success rate of over 66 per cent (Topping 1983). Partly due to this lack of a consensus over the aims and purposes of segregated education very little attention has been paid to the effects, either positive or negative, on offending (Munn *et al.* 2000).

Serious weaknesses in segregated – particularly unit-based – provision have been identified:

- Reintegration is the ostensible objective of PRUs, according to guidance issued (DfEE 1999). Each pupil should have reintegration targets for a return to mainstream or special education, further education or employment. The evidence shows that this is achieved for only a minority of children and young people (Parsons and Howlett 2000).

- The curriculum tends to be narrow, and the quality of teaching can be lowered by the lack of specialist subject teachers (Ofsted 1995).

- Academic achievement and progression into further education, training and employment are often low (Ofsted 1995, 2003; Munn *et al.* 2000).

- There is often a wide range of ages in a single unit. This can mean inappropriate role models for younger pupils and a long-term exposure to an out-of-school culture that hinders their reintegration.

- The cost is at least three times that of mainstream provision (Audit Commission 1999b; Parsons and Howlett 2000).

- There are concerns over the quality of peer group relationships, particularly for the small number of young women (John 1996).

- It contributes to a 'double jeopardy' for young people in residential care, who find themselves at a crucial stage in their development outside both family and school environments. This could restrict their ability to acquire the skills to function in normal group settings.

In addition to the definition and formalisation of the status of the unit another symptom of the revitalisation of segregated education is the growth of a wide range of out-of-school educational provision, some of which is delivered by voluntary sector providers. This offers a very diverse mix of formal and informal learning, often with an emphasis on basic skills, personal and social development activities and work experience. While it very rarely ever takes place on school premises, sometimes separate centres will be used, training premises or youth centres, and there can be access to further education colleges.

A relatively large-scale evaluation was conducted for these alternative education projects (Kendall *et al.* 2002). The overall aim of the evaluation was to 'examine the effectiveness of intervention programmes for permanently excluded pupils. Effectiveness is measured in terms of their success in returning pupils to mainstream education, educational attainment, post-16 outcomes and reducing anti-social behaviour, including offending' (Kendall *et al.* 2002: 2).

Despite the fact that the six initiatives studied in this research were selected because they displayed some success in the re-engagement of young people, the findings were restricted by weaknesses in the baseline information on young people, the very diverse characteristics of the young people referred and of the projects themselves, coupled with the relatively limited nature of the evaluation.

Although there is no reference to it in the executive summary or in the key findings, the reintegration rates into mainstream appear to be low, with only eight (5 per cent) out of 162 young people in the study apparently returning to secondary school.

Analysis of educational attainment was curtailed in that there was apparently no baseline information on the young people and, in the absence of assessment of their literacy and numeracy levels on entry and exit, the evaluation provided lists of qualifications achieved as indicative of progression. There were real problems relating to the information on attendance, which effectively prevents any attempt to compare particular educational or behavioural outputs in relation to inputs.

This study is unusual in that it did look at offending. In total there was not a particularly high incidence of young people with a criminal record on referral to these projects compared to some out-of-school projects (approximately 50 per cent) but there was a total of 694 offences committed during their time on the projects. While the number of young people (for whom there was detailed information) involved in offending reduced by 11 per cent the number of offences they committed increased by 22 per cent in the intervention year. The study found that young people with undesirable destinations were 20 per cent more likely to offend and on average committed 32 per cent more crimes than those with desirable destinations.

Emotional and behavioural difficulties

Another formal route out of mainstream education is for those young people who are labelled as having 'emotional and behavioural difficulties' (EBD). For the overwhelming majority of children and young people categorised as having EBD (95 per cent), a placement in a special school is in effect permanent, whatever the intentions recorded in the individual educational planning process. Reintegration rates are very low. There are very few studies of residential special schools that can yield information on outcomes relating to attainment, detachment and offending. One study of several residential special schools for pupils with EBD found it difficult to collect data there on basic educational skills, and the outcomes in terms of progression to further education and training appear limited. Offending rates appear to have increased significantly following prolonged stays in the schools but this also may have been due to an age effect (Grimshaw and Berridge 1994). See also Chapter 5 on mental health.

Post-16 training providers

For many young people who offend and are detached from mainstream education, centre-based provision from specialist training providers is one of their main options. They tend to suffer from the same fundamental weaknesses as PRUs but have additional problems related to the length of their programmes and funding regimes. On the other hand the young people receive a training allowance.

Evidence on outcomes is very limited and, where it exists, not encouraging. The National E2E Young Offender's Pilot was an attempt to provide a route into mainstream provision for those young people on DTOs and ISS. Despite being partly funded by the Youth Justice Board its explicit aims did not include a reduction in reoffending and the evaluation consequently makes no attempt to assess this. The very limited nature of the data means that it is impossible to judge the intensity and duration of participation and educational progression. The attrition rates appear high with 41 per cent of those who commenced in custody not continuing on release, and out of the remainder 38 per cent were recorded as having a positive exit from the pilot. Although the evaluators acknowledge that the figures 'are not necessarily reliable or robust' they indicate that only 83 young people out of 340 who started this programme had a positive exit (YJB 2004b).

The bridge course – a promising approach?

This project has several unusual features: it has been replicated extensively in England and Wales with an apparently high degree of programme integrity, and has relatively comprehensive quantitative information on the antecedents of young people, their attendance, qualifications gained, changes in literacy and numeracy levels and subsequent destinations. It was evaluated as part of the Youth Justice Board's review of the education, training and employment projects that it has funded and the data has been further analysed in a later article (Hurry and Moriarty 2004; Hurry *et al.* 2006).

There were nearly 500 young people in this evaluation with an average age of 17, from 16 projects in a variety of locations. Most were completely detached from education and training, just over one-fifth were or had been looked after by the local authority. Over two-thirds had literacy and numeracy levels assessed at below Level 1 (that of the average 11 year-old) on referral. The great majority of them (83 per cent) were referred by the YOT. Nine out of 10 were repeat offenders (88 per cent) with an average of 12 previous convictions and an average gravity score of 5.3.

There appears to have been a relatively low rate of attrition with a correspondingly high dosage of received hours of education. On average young people were on the project for 17 out of the potential 24 weeks and undertook 22 hours per week of education with an average total of 370 hours received for each young person.

In terms of educational outcomes those who remained for more than 15 weeks recorded modest but highly significant gains in both literacy and numeracy. About 50 per cent gained qualifications while a significant proportion were continuing to work towards them. If those who were removed to custody (9.5 per cent) or moved out of the area (2.2 per cent) are discounted then 72 per cent of young people on the project had initial destinations of education, training or employment.

With regard to offending there was a 67 per cent reconviction rate in the year after entry to the project but this was accompanied by statistically significant reductions in offending both in terms of the number of offences and the gravity of offence. The average number of offences per young person dropped by 25 per cent from 5.1 to 3.8 comparing the year before and the year after being on the project.

In order to examine the potential effect of the programme on reoffending, three educational outcomes were assessed: positive destination; qualifications gained; and literacy and numeracy improvements. Each of these outcomes was significantly related to reductions in offending. While there was a 72 per cent reconviction rate for those who did not have a positive destination this fell to 57 per cent for those who did. There was a similar reduction for those who gained qualifications compared to those who did not. Reductions in the average number of offences per head were even greater with a fall of a half for those who gained qualifications compared to a tenth for those who did not.

A further study analysed the data using regression analysis to explore predictors of reoffending. Controlling for previous offending and background factors (gender, school leaving age, living situation, number of sessions attended and drug use) it was found that literacy and numeracy gains were significantly associated with lower rates of reoffending. The study concluded that: 'It would appear that improving participants' literacy and numeracy skills may be an effective way of reducing their offending behaviour' (Hurry et al. 2006).

The quantity and quality of data garnered by this evaluation means that there can be much closer scrutiny of the costs incurred by this programme. Instead of simply giving a per capita cost of a place, which is the normal method, costs can be calculated per contact hour. This yields interesting results. The per capita cost of the bridge course model appeared to be more than double that of similar projects funded by the Youth Justice Board, but on a cost per contact hour basis it was up to half the cost of other projects. Again, better recording practices bring benefits in that headline costs can be deceptive if the structure, intensity and duration of intervention are not sufficiently intensive to gain high rates of attendance and retention. If there is a more rigorous approach to recording what is actually received by a young person, in tandem with the collection of pre- and post-intervention assessment, then much more effective cost–benefit analysis will be possible in future.

The reasons for the apparent relative success of this project model for young people who often do not get access to or participate extensively in segregated provision may be:

- the use of mainstream environments (principally FE colleges) to dilute delinquent peer group effects and promote behaviour modification;

- intensive supervision (one-to-ten caseload over and above teaching staff);

- multi-modal – the multi-disciplinary project manager worked across social care, health, criminal justice issues;

- the high degree of programme integrity.

(Stephenson 1996; DfEE 1995)

Incentives for participation

Staying on in education has been considered to be potentially protective against delinquency. The introduction of the Education Maintenance Allowance (EMA) in selected areas enabled a quasi-experimental study to examine the impact on juvenile crime (Feinstein and Sabates 2005). The study found that there was a statistically significant decrease in convictions for burglary by 16–18-year-old males (but not for theft or violent offences) in the EMA areas compared to non-EMA areas and compared to older groups in their area. Given that areas of high deprivation tend to attract multiple initiatives from government departments, which could either individually or in concert affect the results, the study looked at the Reducing Burglary Initiative (RBI).

The main effect seemed to occur when both programmes were operated together rather than individually, giving rise to their main finding that there are 'clear grounds that introduction of the EMA together with the RBI programme had significant and substantive effects on conviction rates for burglary offences by 16 to 18 year olds' (Feinstein and Sabates 2005: 4). A further gain over time of staying on in education could potentially be lower unemployment, which is associated with decreases in offending.

Ineffective approaches

It is instructive to examine some examples of educational type projects or approaches that are still supported despite evidence of their ineffectiveness. One very well-known American project highlights this problem – Drug Abuse Resistance Education (DARE), demonstrated as ineffective but widely implemented (see Chapter 1, 'Criticisms of RCTs', p. 18).

The outcomes for those activities with a clear link to more conventional interests, such as hours spent on homework, may well be associated with less delinquency in contrast to involvement in more adult activities, such as motor projects, which are associated with increases in delinquency (Harper and Chitty 2005).

For the whole range of other activities including youth groups, volunteering, sports and individual hobbies little effect on delinquency has been observed in the American research literature (Gottfredson 2001). One study using UK data found that increased leisure activity between the ages of 8 and 10 was a predictor of both lower levels of self-control between 12 and 14 years of age and of offending between the ages of 14 and 16. It is speculated that supervision exercised in the activity settings was not as effective as that of parents, which possibly reduced self-control.

The principles of effective practice and education, training and employment

Risk classification

In the context of devising appropriate education and training programmes it should be noted that being detached from mainstream education, particularly when combined with low attainment in literacy/numeracy, is often highly associated with persistent offending. Suitable full-time education and training in order to accelerate learning are very likely to be salient features of high-level interventions.

This principle should not be taken to mean that only those young people committing the most serious offences or offending persistently should have full-time education or training. Participation in full-time education is a very significant protective factor for all young people. Those young people most at risk, however, will probably need an intensity of education such as one-to-one learning support and/or a greater volume of learning.

Risk classification is impossible without rigorous assessment of the educational status of individuals, as well as management analysis of the numbers and offending profile of those detached from mainstream education in a given YOT area. This information in tandem with aggregated risks taken from the relevant part of *Asset* will be potentially important in influencing the LEA and the local Learning and Skills Council. Developing this risk classification approach can assist with emphasising the duty of educational institutions and individual teachers in preventing offending.

Criminogenic need

Programmes must focus on those factors that contribute most directly to offending as opposed to more distantly related causes. For obvious reasons, managers and practitioners in education may not willingly accept that their actions, such as a permanent exclusion or part-time provision in a PRU, could actually be directly contributing to offending. Similarly staff who are not teachers, feeling that access to education and training is outside their authority, may pay less attention to this area than it merits in terms of its contribution to offending behaviour. This may be compounded by the feeling among some practitioners that education is 'best left to teachers', which can lead to an underestimation of risk factors. For instance, there is evidence from the *Asset* data that both practitioners and, to a lesser extent, young people themselves are understating just how low the literacy and numeracy attainment levels are for many individuals (Baker *et al.* 2002).

In this area, as in most areas of youth justice, the evidence base does not allow us to give unequivocal answers as to direct causes or to the detailed transmission mechanisms that turn risk factors into offending behaviour.

Individual practitioners could argue strongly that being detached from suitable full-time education is much more likely to lead a young person into associating with delinquent peer groups or reducing their employability significantly. Similarly, the fact that over half of young people leaving custody have no education or training immediately available on release is probably a powerful contributory factor to the very high and fairly immediate reoffending rates of many of these young people. This would indicate that ensuring that such provision is available ought to be a priority for practitioners.

In terms of associated need, there is evidence demonstrating that young people with mental health problems have significantly higher rates of school non-attendance (Green *et al.* 2005; see also Chapter 5). The use of illegal drugs and underage drinking is also significantly higher among young people who are not attending school or have been excluded (McAra 2004; see also Chapter 6).

Dosage

While programmes as noted above must have sufficient 'breadth' to match the range of needs of individual young people, they must also have the 'depth' and be of sufficient intensity and duration to achieve programme aims.

While YOT practitioners always have to be concerned with the impact of the totality of interventions, education, training and employment should be considered often the most important single component. 'Sufficient duration' needs to be interpreted as commencing from the moment of sentence and for the full duration of the order. Similarly, 'sufficient intensity' means suitable full-time education, training or employment.

There is no statutory number of hours that represent full-time education for those of compulsory school age, but this is deemed by the Youth Justice Board to be 25 hours per week (30 hours when in custody). For those over compulsory school age it is deemed to be 20 hours per week.

'Intensity' also relates to the quality of the educational experience. Several hours each day simply occupying a young person's time in leisure activities may not be challenging enough, nor fitting within an appropriate curriculum to be deemed of sufficient intensity. If, for example, a young person of school age has had the national curriculum disapplied, the local education authority must still be ensuring a broad, balanced curriculum.

Given that a high proportion of young people who encounter the youth justice system also have difficulties with literacy and numeracy, it is interesting to consider the recommendations with regard to dosage for making progress in these areas. Findings of literacy interventions and youth justice interventions suggest that learners usually need to attend at least 100 hours of instruction to make progress equivalent to one grade level (Torgerson *et al.* 2004). Interestingly, a high dosage in youth justice for any intervention is also deemed to be more than 100 hours (Lipsey 1995).

It is essential that YOT staff distinguish between what is arranged (in volume and quality terms) and what a young person actually receives. The dosage is not synonymous with the timetable. The clear implication is that YOT staff need to ensure effective monitoring of attendance and participation.

Responsivity

It used to be claimed that the learning styles of most young people at risk of offending require active, participatory methods of working (McGuire 1995) but the latest research commissioned by the Youth Justice Board (YJB 2005a) has found little evidence for this (see Chapter 1, pp. 30–2). This claim may be related to the more pervasive belief that, as many of these young people have not succeeded in mainstream school (or that mainstream school has not met their needs appropriately), then they will usually require learning in more active settings, probably vocational.

It is striking that many discussions by educationalists or non-educationalists turn to the need for more vocational training for young people who offend or are seen to be academically underachieving. This may be derived from observations of other countries whose education systems place more emphasis on a vocational education and appear to have fewer problems with engagement and possibly higher-skilled workforces. It can also be driven by a belief that traditional 'chalk and talk' teaching methods have alienated these young people. This issue has been thrown into relief as the virtually automatic transition from school to labour market has withered away. The UK, unlike countries such as Germany and Denmark, does not offer a high-status vocational training route as an alternative to continuing with academic studies. Given the popularity of the vocational remedy reiterated recently by the Audit Commission (2004) and by the Tomlinson review of 14–19 education (DfES 2004b), it is worth examining the evidence base.

The underlying hypothesis is that learning that is more obviously associated with the world of work will provide much greater motivation to young people with low attainment and limited or no attachment to school. Vocational subjects could also offer greater opportunities to link to their out-of-school interests and hobbies than academic subjects. Accordingly, there has been a range of experimental educational programmes from the early 1990s onwards targeted at 14–16-year-olds attempting to improve motivation and engagement through an emphasis on work-related learning. The evaluations of these initiatives have lacked RCTs, had limited comparison groups and struggled to find an appropriate and consistent approach to measuring progress (Steedman and Stoney 2004).

A review of evaluations of a range of initiatives, including those arising from the disapplication of the national curriculum at Key Stage 4, GNVQs, vocational GCSEs, the Connexions Service, the Increased Flexibilities Programme and other work-related initiatives, found that for those who were disengaged:

- there was little effect on attainment;

- motivation may have increased but was not necessarily translated into greater attainment;

- careers guidance and information appear to be a major weakness;

- contact with the workplace could sometimes reduce the likelihood of remaining in education and training.

(Steedman and Stoney 2004)

Drawing on extensive Labour Force Survey data, McIntosh (2003: 14) came to the conclusion that 'it does not appear that post-school vocational qualifications have been at all successful in raising those who failed at school to the generally accepted desirable level (Level 3), or even, for that matter, to Level 2.'

Emerging evidence from the implementation of 14–19 reforms, including the 14–19 diplomas which are vocationally orientated, is having some impact on the numbers of young people not in education, employment or training (Ofsted 2009c). It is not clear, however, whether this can be attributed to increased access to more vocationally orientated accreditation routes alone. In the 19 out of 23 areas visited by Ofsted where the number of young people not in education, employment or training (NEETs) had been reduced, other strategies had also been used typically involving a range of providers and agencies.

The latest research findings advise youth justice practitioners to take full account of the specific learning environment and the considerable variation in preferred approaches to learning between individual young people in tailoring how they facilitate learning and in ensuring there are sufficient support structures in place to prevent detachment.

While this has specific implications for teachers who will usually be aware of the need to differentiate their teaching according to the needs of individual young people, it is equally important for non-educational practitioners.

The effectiveness of offending behaviour interventions, for example, is likely to be increased if YOT staff ensure that attention is paid to the individual levels of literacy and numeracy attainment, the nature of the learning environment and their own approach in terms of the structure, content and resources used in each session.

There is abundant evidence that the educational expectations of young people in both the care and criminal justice systems are often very low and therefore may be self-fulfilling. The evidence also suggests that this is often compounded by the low expectations of professionals and parents/carers in relation to what these young people can achieve in educational terms (DfES/DoH 2000). For example, Ofsted (2009a) has found evidence in some children's homes that insufficient priority is given to education with some young people not attending school regularly and staff taking little action to rectify this. High expectations of learners, by the setting of demanding and progressively more difficult challenges, is extremely important and is substantiated by evidence of the strong links between expectations and attainment.

Community based

It is the transfer and subsequent application of learning that is the crucial test in youth justice of behavioural change having occurred. Many programmes are deemed by research evidence to be ineffective as they have little impact on offending, even though the deliverers feel that the young people were engaged and had benefited.

Evidence suggests that behaviour is very specific to contexts. Therefore, when programmes are delivered in settings that are radically different from the normal experience and everyday challenges, then they are less likely to work. This applies to both the methods of delivering a programme and the resources used. For example, using literacy/numeracy materials that young people find too childish, old-fashioned or not relevant to their experiences is unlikely to stimulate their interest and encourage optimal learning. Custody is perhaps the most extreme example of an abnormal context. It is therefore not surprising that the evidence suggests approaches that emulate certain features of community orders make for a more successful custodial experience in terms of changing behaviours (Tolbert 2002).

Much of the criminal justice approach and sentencing is, by definition, inimical to learning and behaviour change. Custody tends to inhibit the development of the essential planning and decision-making skills that are fundamental to changing behaviour back in the community. Evidence from the US indicates that where young people serving custodial sentences experience their education in the community, attainment is higher than in control groups (Coffey and Gemignani 1994).

The practical implications are that YOT supervising officers might be pushing for release on temporary licence (RoTL) to involve young people in mainstream education and training. The continuity of courses and teaching and learning materials between custody and community is of paramount importance. Similarly, home visits to the actual or potential host education institution could be useful in securing immediate placements post-custody and smoothing the transition to the community.

It would be a misinterpretation of this principle to argue for the placement of young people in segregated educational settings on the grounds of common experience, for example in PRUs. There is evidence that the significant protective factor of resilience, i.e. the ability to surmount adversity, is fostered by the diversity of normal experiences inherent in participation in mainstream school life. Young people themselves express a desire to engage with mainstream settings (ECOTEC 2001b).

Intervention modality

One of the challenges with wide-ranging programmes is enabling the young person and the allied professionals to appreciate how joined up the approach should be. Most teachers will not know what 'intervention modality' is, let alone accept that their curriculum is part of it.

There are three main threats, particularly where intensive packages are concerned, in relation to education and training:

1. A range of programme interventions may compete with each other and crowd out education as a priority (Ofsted 2009b). For instance, in YOIs in particular, education is continually interrupted and is not treated as an absolute priority.

2. There are very real dangers where extensive daytime programmes are arranged by YOTs that schools will be happy for young people to attend these activities rather than being a potentially disruptive influence within the school. The evaluation of youth inclusion programmes found a very significant deterioration in attendance at school, which may be partly explained by the pull of these activities and possibly the push of the school (Burrows 2003).

3. YOTs will be tempted into establishing their own education programmes. While this may keep young people occupied, the track record of such activities is very poor, particularly in terms of progression into further education or full-time training.

Even if some elements are skills-based and with a cognitive-behavioural approach, learning can still be inhibited if there are inadequate linkages or continuity of experience with the opportunities to apply the learning. For example, outward bound type courses may appear to fit this definition but their outcomes in terms of preventing offending tend to be limited as there is considerable difficulty transferring the learning to meaningful everyday contexts for young people (Lipsey and Wilson 1998).

YOT practitioners need to be working with young people to instil and develop a theory of action to underpin all their learning and give shape to the interventions. For example, Offending Behaviour Programmes with their emphasis on actions and consequences and the need to develop decision-making skills can be placed within the wider context of improving attainment (particularly in relation to literacy and numeracy). Improving attainment enables young people to achieve qualifications which in turn may lead to sustained employment and the cessation of offending.

Although the jargon is particularly opaque for teaching professionals, the approach is directly applicable in terms of effective teaching. The main challenge is cultural: gaining the trust and understanding of education practitioners so that they see themselves as part of a much wider programme.

Programme integrity

As has already been shown, it is not known what makes effective education and training programmes. Knowledge in this field, as in others, is still so limited as to prevent the adoption of a prescribed programme approach.

One of the advantages of education and training is that it tends to have clear objectives and it is possible to measure progress towards them through educational assessment and accreditation of learning outcomes. This rigour is useful and adaptable to the youth justice approach.

One of the key challenges for YOT staff is ensuring programme integrity where others deliver it. Protocols with local education authorities, schools, Connexions and training providers will all help but will also depend heavily on the skills and knowledge of individual YOT practitioners and recognition of these by teaching staff. Boundaries of professional specialism can be fiercely guarded but this must not put off attempts at brokering or identifying where the staff of provider agencies are not adequately trained and/or supported. Ensuring programme integrity indirectly through other professionals suggests that monitoring and evaluation become even more important, as it is often a matter of quality assuring others rather than delivering directly.

Clearly, one of the keys to ensuring programme integrity is the collation and monitoring of data about how far young people at risk of offending and reoffending are accessing, participating in and progressing within education, training and employment. Yet paradoxically very little is known about this. Ofsted, for example, was withering in its criticisms in relation to young people detached from mainstream school: 'Most significantly, schools and LEAs are not tracking pupils and do not have a comprehensive view of their whereabouts, achievements or destinations. There is insufficient monitoring of the quality and range of alternative provision' (Ofsted 2004: 5). More recently, the DCSF acknowledged there are limitations to the performance data available on young people in PRUs (2008a). These weaknesses directly affect those young people of most concern to YOTs 'indicating a high potential for pupils to be lost to the system, to be accessing minimal education and training opportunities, and to be out of school for a large proportion of the school week without the knowledge of the LEA' (Ofsted 2004: 25).

Within custodial education the paucity of management information, particularly with regard to outcomes, may even be preventing recognition of some progress. A Youth Justice Board review of the implementation of its education reforms in YOIs concluded:

Despite the increased inputs particularly through new posts and increased expenditure on resources the fundamental weakness in monitoring and reporting systems effectively prevent this review from establishing equivalent improvements in either outputs (e.g. number of educational hours received by individual young people) or outcomes such as learning gains. (YJB 2005c: 7)

The challenges for practice

It is recognised that education, training and employment issues pose very different problems for managers and practitioners in the youth justice system than other areas identified by the Youth Justice Board as priorities for guidance on effective practice. Important areas such as final warning interventions or remand management are specific to those working in youth justice and have a statutory basis. Other interventions such as mentoring or parenting programmes, although used by other agencies, are often provided directly by YOTs.

Education and training, in contrast, is delivered by separately constituted agencies. The challenge is therefore that an area containing such important risk factors for the onset and continuation of offending behaviour, and that also provides powerful protective factors, is not under the direct control of managers or practitioners in YOTs.

Consequently, managers and practitioners may well feel even more frustrated with regard to education and training issues, feeling they have relatively little effect due to the responses of institutions and professionals beyond their control.

Challenges may also arise as a result of contradictory tensions. Many teachers may feel that colleagues from social work and youth justice do not understand school cultures and their everyday pressures. Equally youth justice or social work practitioners may, all too often, defer to the assumptions and practices of teachers.

Being able to describe what is effective practice in a successful school is, however, some way from being able to prescribe how to achieve this with all schools. Changing the culture within any institution remains one of the stiffest management challenges, even if systematic evaluations had made clear exactly how this can be achieved – which they have not. The matter is not simply one of the discrete reorganisation of a given school, as – particularly where young people at high risk are concerned – there are all the variable relationships with the other agencies and their professionals to be considered as well as the resources available to the community.

Summary

- Detachment from mainstream education appears to be extensive among young people in the youth justice system. It is estimated that the great majority of those entering and leaving custody are detached from mainstream education.

- Despite the prevalence of and persistent use of segregated educational provision for young people who offend, there is little evidence of its success in terms of key indicators such as reintegration or positive progression.

- Interventions which have been evaluated to a relatively high standard and have been shown to be promising in preventing detachment are the same as for tackling low attainment and include pre-school education, family literacy, intensive reading schemes, reasoning and social skills education, and organisational change in schools.

- There is some evidence of a relationship between attendance, attainment (particularly in literacy and numeracy) and lower offending rates.

- Most studies that try to measure the effectiveness of custodial educational intervention or resettlement programmes have been compromised by weak research design but do provide some evidence of a link between educational intervention and reduction in recidivism, although this tends to be for adults.

- There is no evidence that young people in the youth justice system require active or vocational learning any more than other young people.

- Maintaining programme integrity is a key challenge for YOT staff due to a lack of useful management information about the educational status of young people and because they are not directly responsible for service delivery.

Further reading

Stephenson, M. (2007) *Young People and Offending: Education, Youth Justice and Social Inclusion*. Cullompton: Willan.
Youth Justice Board (2006) *Barriers to Engagement in Education, Training and Employment for Young People in the Youth Justice System*. London: Youth Justice Board.

5

Mental health

Introduction

> We are all mental ... mental health is fundamental to us all. (Mental Health Foundation 1999)

Mental health issues are relatively common among children and young people. They are even more common among young people who offend; may be associated with self-harm and suicidal behaviour; may be a manifestation of serious physical or sexual abuse, neglect, or of poverty and deprivation; and may lead to self-medication with illicit drugs. This chapter explores what is meant by 'mental health' within the context of adolescence in particular; outlines the prevalence of mental health problems for this age group and specifically for young people in the youth justice system; and looks at some of the theoretical explanations of the relationship between mental health and offending behaviour by children and young people. While the evidence base for mental health interventions is not well established, compounded by what appear to be endemic systemic issues in providing timely and appropriate services for this highly vulnerable group of young people, the chapter attempts to identify some implications for practice from what research there is.

The evidence base for mental health

Definitions

> 'Mental' is a word which has for too long been seen almost exclusively in negative terms – as a term of abuse within the playground, the workplace or even the family – and when mental is linked to health, the result is often confusion. (Mental Health Foundation 1999)

Many attempts have been made to define mental health in a single sentence or statement. Perhaps the most well known definition of health, both mental and physical, is that of the World Health Organisation (WHO). The WHO

124

defined health as a 'complete state of physical, mental and social well being, and not merely the absence of disease or infirmity'. More recently, and in light of the difficulty of achieving short definitions that are clear and meaningful, contemporary definitions have suggested a range of elements or descriptions that constitute the concept of mental health (Weare 2000).

In practice, the term 'mental health' is often synonymous with 'mental health problems'. Training courses and materials which are described as being about mental health or mental health awareness, for example, often turn out to be almost exclusively concerned with mental disorders and mental health problems.

Different professions and agencies working in the field of mental health use different terms to describe the range of emotional and behavioural difficulties in children and young people. The language used in the mental health field tends to have a medical bias, 'perhaps because of the rapid advances in research in this area – but this is by no means a complete picture' (National Assembly for Wales 2000). Other sectors and professions use different terminology which youth justice practitioners are likely to come across in their practice.

Some people use broader phrases when referring to this area of young people's lives, such as 'mental, emotional and social health'. These terms, familiar to educators, community workers and others, reflect work with children and young people known as emotional, social or personal education. They are seen as less narrowing and negative than 'mental health' on its own (Weare 2000). Educationalists tend to use the term 'emotional and behavioural difficulties' (EBD) to describe the difficulties children and young people face. The definition of EBD is so broad that it embraces a large number of young people facing multiple difficulties (Stephenson 2007) and refers to a continuum of behaviours from 'behaviour which challenges teachers but is within normal, albeit unacceptable, bands and that which is indicative of serious mental illness' (DfEE 1994: 7). 'Special educational needs' (SEN) is also commonly used as a label within educational spheres. This can apply to problems with learning as well as to mental health and behavioural difficulties. Given the multiple difficulties that young people who encounter the youth justice system often face, and the strong likelihood that they may have detached from education or are at risk of doing so, it is likely that many will already have acquired such labels. The label itself tells us nothing about the nature of their difficulties nor how severe they are.

In this chapter 'mental health' is used as an umbrella term embracing concepts of mental well-being, mental health problems, mental disorder and mental illness. These terms are used to refer to and describe specific experiences and problems as follows:

- *Mental well-being* – the positive capacities and qualities that enable young people to deal with the ups and downs of life, experience emotions appropriately, make friends and have a sense of identity.

- *Mental health problems* – a broad range of emotional or behavioural difficulties that may cause concern to parents and carers and/or distress to the young person. These difficulties may be short or long term. Although they affect a young person's day-to-day life, they may not be diagnosable as a mental disorder.

- *Mental disorder* – those problems that meet the requirements of ICD-10 (*International Statistical Classification of Disease and Related Health Problems*, 10th Revision, World Health Organisation 1994), an internationally recognised classification system for mental and behavioural disorders, usually associated with considerable distress and substantial interference in a young person's everyday life. The distinction between a *problem* and a *disorder* is not always exact but depends on the severity, persistence, effects and combination of difficulties experienced by the young person and those around them.

- *Mental illness* – sometimes used in the mental health sector to refer to the most severe types of mental disorder: 'for example, more severe cases of depressive illness, psychotic disorders and severe cases of anorexia nervosa could be described in this way' (National Assembly for Wales 2000). Practitioners may come across this term in their practice, but it is only referred to in this chapter where it has been used by other authors.

These definitions are underpinned by the assumption that mental health affects all of us in one way or another, and that the mental health of children and young people is an issue that concerns all staff who come into contact with young people in the youth justice system.

These broad definitions mask a range of distinct difficulties young people are experiencing. They describe a continuum of behaviours from those that simply challenge societal norms and authority figures in some way to those that are severe and potentially life threatening at the other end.

The situation is further complicated by the fact that different services each have their own conceptual framework and language for understanding disturbed and disturbing behaviour in children and young people. This means that:

> A YOT team member may talk about a young person engaged in antisocial activity, a teacher about poor concentration and aggressive behaviour, and a social worker or youth worker may perceive a needy, anxious, abused child – all are describing the same child. (Walker 2003)

Different agency responses to a specific difficulty may therefore be the consequence of different theoretical models of understanding, working cultures and practices.

Table 5.1 shows how youth justice, social services, education and psychiatry respond differently to the same presenting problem. Increasingly, however, there is recognition that 'no one agency has the monopoly of

Table 5.1 Different agency responses to the same presenting problem

Problem: aggression

Juvenile justice	Social services	Education	Psychiatry
Referral to police: decision to charge	Referral to social services	Referral to education department	Referral to child psychiatrist
Pre-sentence report completed	Social work assessment conducted	Educational psychology assessment	Psychiatric assessment
Sentenced to custody	Decision to accommodate	Placed in residential school	Admitted to regional in-patient unit
Labelled as young person who offends	Labelled as beyond parental control	Labelled as having learning difficulty	Labelled as mentally ill

Source: Walker (2003), adapted from Malek (1993).

understanding and capability when trying to help troubled young people' (National Assembly for Wales 2000).

Given the multiplicity of specific difficulties and behaviours subsumed under the various mental health labels and definitions, it is hard to see how a large proportion of young people who encounter the youth justice system could not be described as having a mental health problem of some kind. As Liabø and Richardson (2007) point out, the diagnostic criteria for conduct disorder set out in the ICD-10 and DSM-IV (*Diagnostic and Statistical Manual of Mental Disorders*, American Psychiatric Association 1994) classifications include offending behaviours such as stealing, fire-setting and physical cruelty towards others. There is also a danger in attributing medical labels to young people's behaviours in that it locates the difficulty within the young person and may lead professionals to reach for a medical response. An example of this is the relatively recent phenomenon of Attention Deficit Hyperactivity Disorder (ADHD), a label attached to many young people at risk of offending or reoffending. The bundling together of challenging or 'difficult' behaviours and defining them as a 'disorder' clearly puts the onus on the young person as the one with the problem and not, for example, on the way the school curriculum is organised or the behaviours of others around them, parents/carers for example. There is also the risk that work within this area could become dominated by biogenetic theories of crime that characterised the late nineteenth century in particular whereby delinquent behaviour could be attributed to a particular genetic 'type' (Whyte 2009), ignoring the socio-economic and psychosocial aspects of mental health and crime.

It is also important to consider mental health within a cultural context, as each culture has its own ideas about well-being and what promotes it:

Different cultures have varying views about the roles and responsibilities of children within the wider family as well as society – what is seen as 'mentally healthy' behaviour may well differ, therefore, from one culture to another. Some stress the importance of children acquiring independence from the family, for example, whereas others encourage dependence. (Mental Health Foundation 1999)

The scope and scale of the problem

In 2005, the Office for National Statistics (ONS) (Green *et al.* 2005) reported on the findings of a 2004 survey into the mental health of children and adolescents in Great Britain. The survey looked at children and adolescents aged 5–16 living in private households in Scotland, England and Wales. Using the criteria that the mental disorder should 'cause distress to the child' or have a 'considerable impact on the child's day-to-day life', the report concluded that 10 per cent of children aged 5–16 had a mental disorder. Thirteen per cent of boys and 10 per cent of girls aged between 11 and 16 had a mental disorder. Other socio-demographic variations were identified in the prevalence of mental disorders, including higher incidence among children in lone parent or reconstituted families, among those whose parents had no educational qualifications, in families where neither parent was working, and those who were living in areas classed as 'hard pressed'.

In terms of the type of disorder young people were experiencing:

- 6 per cent had conduct disorders;

- 4 per cent were assessed as having emotional disorders (anxiety or depression);

- 6 per cent had a hyperkinetic disorder;

- less common disorders, such as autism, tics and eating disorders, affected 0.5 per cent of the sampled population.

To put these figures into perspective, it might be useful to consider a secondary school with 1,000 pupils. What these statistics suggest is that 60 of them will have some kind of conduct disorder, 40 some kind of emotional disorder and 60 a hyperkinetic disorder. This in itself represents a significant challenge in terms of meeting the needs of young people in the general population.

Research from the USA and the UK suggests that the prevalence of mental health problems and disorders is even higher among young people who offend. In a sample of 1,829 juveniles in a detention centre in America assessed using the Diagnostic Interview Schedule for Children, results showed that nearly two-thirds of young men and three-quarters of young women met the diagnostic criteria for one or more psychiatric disorders (Teplin *et al.* 2002). Research on behalf of the ONS (Lader *et al.* 1997) involving 600 young people, both on remand and convicted, concluded that 'a high proportion of all young offenders had evidence of several mental disorders. In all sample groups, at least 95 per cent were assessed as having one or more disorders and a very large proportion, about 80 per cent, were assessed as having more than one' (Lader *et al.* 1997).

More recently, Harrington and Bailey (2005) interviewed 300 people in the youth justice system (50 per cent in the community and 50 per cent in the secure estate) using assessments for demographics, mental health and social needs. They found a third of young people had mental health needs, a fifth with depression, a tenth reporting self-harm in the past month and a tenth suffering anxiety and post-traumatic stress symptoms. Hyperactivity was reported in 7 per cent of the young people and psychotic-like symptoms in 5 per cent. Almost a quarter had learning difficulties and a further third borderline learning difficulties.

Bearing in mind the difficulties of comparing studies in this area and the different definitions being used, Hagell's conclusion is perhaps the most useful for youth justice practitioners. Making extensive use of a range of research projects she concluded that in relation to young people and young adults:

> The rates of mental health problems are at least three times as high for those within the criminal justice system as within the general population, if not higher. (Hagell 2002)

There also appears to be a high correlation between mental health and substance misuse. The ONS survey of young people in the general population (Green *et al.* 2005) also showed that those with mental health disorders were much more likely to smoke, drink alcohol and take drugs. For example, 23 per cent of young people with emotional disorders were smokers and 20 per cent had taken drugs compared with 8 per cent for both among other young people. The figures were even higher for young people experiencing conduct disorders, where 34 per cent were smokers and 28 per cent had taken drugs.

Hagell also reported very high incidence of mental health problems among young people referred from court for possible alcohol and drug issues. For example:

> . . . 91 per cent were shown to also have conduct disorder, 58 per cent oppositional disorder, 33 per cent aggressive conduct disorder, 32 per cent depression and 23 per cent attention deficit disorder . . . Riggs et al. (1995) assessed levels of depression in a sample of 90 young offenders who had both conduct disorder and substance use disorders. A fifth had major depression. (Hagell 2002: 19)

Similarly, YJB research into the substance misuse of young people in custody found that:

- 30 per cent said they had taken drugs not to get high but just to feel 'normal';
- 38 per cent had taken a drug to 'forget everything or to blot everything out';
- 56 per cent were identified as being eligible for a mental health screening interview using the *Asset* mental health screening tool.

(Galahad SMS 2004)

Suicide and self-harm in young people – and indeed across the whole of the general population – may be related to mental health problems and mental disorders. The rate of self-inflicted death among young people who offend, particularly young men aged between 15 and 17, is significantly higher than for this age group within the general population (Safer Custody Group 2003).

The link between education and mental health may also be significant. Among children and young people generally, young people with mental disorders were found to be much more likely than other children to have special educational needs and have more time off school (Green *et al.* 2005). Young people with conduct disorders in particular had very high levels of unauthorised absences. Young people with hyperkinetic disorders were found to be four times as likely as other children to have an officially recognised special need (71 per cent compared with 16 per cent). Rates of non-attendance are also high for young people in the youth justice system and they are also more likely to experience low attainment and/or have a recognised special educational need (Stephenson 2007).

It is perhaps sobering to note also that the operation of the criminal justice system itself, may contribute to or exacerbate a mental health problem or disorder. Whether or not young people are experiencing mental health problems before contact with the youth justice system, it is reasonable to assume that they will be affected by their interactions with it and that for some this may have a considerable impact on their mental health and well-being. The experience of attending court can be intimidating and place young people under considerable stress, for example. The experience of custody may also be highly unsettling, particularly for those who are already vulnerable (Hagell 2002). Remand can be a highly stressful experience for young people, especially where they are expecting to be bailed and/or are remanded away from their home area. It is likely that the uncertainty of remand may increase the risk of suicide (Howard League website 2005 press releases). The question here is whether this can be attributed to a mental 'disorder' or mental health problem of some kind or the additional stress experienced by the young person as a result of the experience. Attributing a mental health label to young people in these circumstances, however, places more emphasis on the problem being theirs rather than the system that may be contributing to it significantly.

Mental health services

The pressures young people and their families experience both as a result of a mental health difficulty and involvement in the youth justice system are often compounded by the capacity of the system to respond to their needs, particularly with regard to more serious and pressing mental health disorders.

This has also led to frustrations by staff in YOTs. Studies by both Pitcher *et al.* (2004) and Harrington and Bailey (2005) indicated that at the community-level Child and Adolescent Mental Health Services (CAMHS) for young people were patchy. Of health workers seconded to YOTs some 40 per cent were seconded by CAMHS, but most of these were not formally members of the service, so did not receive clinical supervision by this route. Few opportunities were found in the studies for formal and regular consultation between YOTs and CAMHS. Mental health resources within YOTs were often stretched and some tensions arose with respect to confidentiality, time-limited working and the extent to which mental health workers should engage in core YOT activities discharging youth justice processes.

In the juvenile secure estate Harrington and Bailey (2005) found that there was no routine mental health assessment of young people on admission, with *Asset* not specifically highlighting this issue. Frequently, mental health services were provided on a sessional basis with a lack of appropriate intervention packages available. See also Chapter 10 on the secure estate and resettlement.

Support to secure estate staff to enable them to meet the mental health needs of young people was in short supply. Multidisciplinary approaches to service provision were uncommon. While there was some evidence that the mental health needs of young people were lower in custody due to the levels of supervision provided, these needs often increased on discharge. Continuity of care between custody and community was poor. In addition there was little coordination of interventions between youth justice, mental health, education and social services.

This evidence was corroborated by the Annual Inspection Report for YOTs 2005–6 which summarises the current challenges for mental health services as follows:

- One in five health workers was not able to access the services they required if they were to meet the health needs of the YOT population.

- Access to CAMHS for support, advice and appropriate supervision remained difficult in some YOTs. There was limited provision of tier 3/4 CAMHS in some areas, with long waiting times experienced by the young people. Some groups of children and young people, particularly 16- and 17-year-olds and those with dual substance misuse and mental health needs, found it especially difficult to access services.

(HM Inspectorate of Probation 2006: 41)

The research

Research into specialist interventions with children and young people with mental health problems is less well developed than that relating to young people who offend (Perry *et al.* 2008). This may be because of the wide range of factors impacting on young people's mental health at any one time and the difficulties of isolating a specific intervention as having a demonstrable impact on the outcome for the young person (Walker 2003). In addition, 'the wide range of professionals from many agencies having some impact on child mental health is so diverse as to make it unrealistic to identify a linear sequence of causality from intervention through to outcome' (Mental Health Foundation 1999).

In 1999, an Audit Commission report into specialist Child and Adolescent Mental Health Services (CAMHS) in England and Wales identified a gap in knowledge and understanding about emerging effective practice in mental health interventions. The report concluded: 'There is limited evidence about the efficacy of CAMHS interventions' (Audit Commission 1999a). Efficacy is defined as the ability of a medical or surgical intervention to produce the desired outcome in a defined population under particular conditions. The report concludes that although some findings are beginning to emerge, 'It is difficult to demonstrate conclusively a cause and effect relationship between interventions and changes, particularly with children and families who have severe and longstanding difficulties' (Wallace *et al.* 1997).

One of the most comprehensive pieces of research into specialist interventions is by Fonagy *et al.* (2002), reviewing the existing evidence for the range of treatments used in child and adolescent psychiatry. With the aim of informing clinical decision-making, Fonagy *et al.* appraised the findings of hundreds of studies into treatments for specific mental disorders. Owing to the lack of existing research in key areas, the small sample size of most studies, and the inconsistency of outcome measurement and child age ranges across the studies, they conclude that the available evidence is insufficient to identify effective interventions.

While acknowledging these limitations Fonagy *et al.* did, nonetheless, identify several common features that emerge from the research on treatments for individual mental disorders. These include:

- the importance of early intervention;

- the need to use a range of methods, and combinations of methods, within individual treatment plans;

- the key role of the relationship between therapist and client in treatments;

- the importance of the family context, both in the assessment process and in supporting or thwarting treatment efforts.

(Fonagy *et al.* 2002)

A more recent systematic review of the evidence base in this area (Perry *et al.* 2008) also acknowledged that while research has helped to record the prevalence of mental health problems among young people in the youth justice system, there have been few systematic reviews which identify the impact of mental health care provision on young people in general as well as on young people who offend.

Nonetheless, there are some interventions which can be deemed to be promising, both with regard to offending behaviour and mental health outcomes. Some of these are detailed below in the context of the principles of effective practice.

The principles of effective practice and mental health

Risk classification

High levels of mental health problems have been detected in cohorts of young people identified as being at risk of offending or reoffending, particularly when screened using assessment tools specifically developed to ascertain these needs (Audit Commission 2004; Arnull *et al.* 2005). Harrington and Bailey (2005), for example, found 31 per cent of young people to have mental health problems in a national cross-sectional study using the Salford Needs Assessment Schedule for Adolescents (SNASA). This compared with only 15 per cent of young people identified with mental health problems from a cross-sectional study of 600 *Asset* forms sampled from six YOT areas. On this basis, Harrington and Bailey (2005) concluded that 'Asset is not sufficiently sensitive in identifying mental health needs in young offenders' (see Chapter 2).

The response to this was the development of a screening tool specifically used with young people in the youth justice system and a screening pathway to improve the identification of mental health needs. Where a young person scores two or more in the emotional and mental health section of *Asset*, a Screening Questionnaire Interview for Adolescents (SQIfA) is completed. This consists of a screen for eight common mental health problems in adolescence, including substance use, depression, traumatic experiences, anxiety and stress, self-harm, hyperactivity and psychotic symptoms. If the SQIfA scores three or four, a full Screening Interview for Adolescents (SIfA) is undertaken by an appropriately trained youth justice worker. The SIfA was developed from a modified version of the Salford Needs Assessment Schedule for Adolescents (Kroll *et al.* 1999) which follows the design of the Cardinal Needs Schedule (Marshall *et al.* 1995) which has established reliability and validity. It should be noted, however, that the validity and reliability of the Cardinal Needs Schedule was established using adult populations and not adolescents. It should not, therefore, be assumed that the reliability or validity of SIfA has been established – there are no studies in this area to date and it is not included in the list of largely American tools identified as having 'promising' psychometric properties in Perry *et al.*'s systematic review of mental health research for the Youth Justice Board (2008). Further, in research carried out among 11 YOTs in the North East of England (Wade 2006), SQIfA was widely criticised as being overly mechanistic, omitting some common mental health problems that ironically are covered in section eight of *Asset*, and then repeating issues that are covered in other sections of *Asset* (substance misuse, for example). With regard to SIfA, Wade reports that the majority of YOT health workers used either an adaptation of SIfA or had abandoned it entirely, using assessment forms from CAMHS on the basis that SIfA was 'narrow and unimaginative' and because it was felt that the CAMHS-type forms would be more readily accepted when seeking referrals to specialist services.

One of the benefits of this staged approach, regardless of which tools are used, is that it links very closely with the CAMHS four-tier framework (see Table 5.2), which is similar to the HAS four-tier model of care for substance misuse services described in Chapter 6. Each tier of the framework describes an increased level of provision of care which will be determined by the level of risk or need identified in the assessment process.

Criminogenic need

While the statistics point to a strong association between mental health and young people in the youth justice system, the relationship between mental health problems or mental disorders and offending behaviour is by no means clear-cut. The key question for youth justice workers in determining criminogenic need though is to decide how salient they are with regard to a young person's offending behaviour.

It could be suggested that mental health problems and offending behaviour have similar causes. There is a high degree of overlap between the risk factors for developing mental health problems and disorders and for engaging with offending behaviour. Factors associated with both include:

- physical, sexual and/or emotional abuse and neglect;
- poverty and deprivation;
- family dysfunction and discord;
- school exclusion, poor academic attainment and high levels of unemployment;
- individual characteristics, including learning difficulties and hyperactivity.

It could also be argued, that broadly speaking, they are related in the following ways:

- The behaviours associated with a particular mental health problem or disorder lead to a criminal act and/or make a young person more conspicuous to the criminal justice agencies.

Table 5.2 The CAMHS four-tier framework

Tier	Kinds of provision include	Professionals providing the service include
Tier 1 A primary level of care	Non-specialist staff identify mental health problems early in their development; offer general advice; pursue opportunities for promoting mental health and well-being; and, where appropriate, provide treatment for less severe mental health problems.	GPs, health visitors, school nurses, social workers, teachers, **youth justice workers**, voluntary agencies.
Tier 2 A service provided by a professional relating to workers in primary care	A professional working on their own who relates to others through a network rather than a team, offering training and consultation for other professionals and families; identifying severe or complex needs; and providing assessment that may trigger treatment at this level or in a different tier.	Clinical child psychologists, paediatricians, community child psychiatric nurses, child and adolescent psychiatrists and **YOT mental health workers.**
Tier 3 A specialist service for more severe, complex or persistent disorders	Usually involves a multidisciplinary team or service working in a community child mental health clinic or child psychiatry outpatient service providing assessment and treatment of child mental health disorders; assessment for referral to tier 4; contributions to the services and consultation and training at tiers 1 and 2; and participation in research and development projects.	Child and adolescent psychiatrists, clinical child psychologists, nurses (community or inpatient), occupational therapists, speech and language therapists, art, music and drama therapists, family therapy.
Tier 4 Essential tertiary level services such as day units, highly specialised outpatient teams and inpatient units	A specialist working at this level might expect to provide services for adolescent inpatient units, specialist services for young people with learning difficulties, outpatient teams for risk assessment, offence-specific treatments and specialist teams for neuro-psychiatric problems and specialist teams for children with sensory impairments.	Child and adolescent psychiatrists, clinical child psychologists, nurses (community or inpatient), occupational therapists, speech and language therapists, art, music and drama therapists, family therapy.

Adapted from DoH and DfES (2004) and Perry *et al.* (2008).

135

- Criminal activity contributes to a young person's mental health problems (as in post-traumatic stress disorders, for example).

- There is an overlap between other risk factors for mental health difficulties and offending behaviour, substance misuse for example (often referred to as 'co-morbidity').

These relationships are explored in more detail below.

Some theorists suggest that as well as low mood, feelings of irritability, hostility and anger can result when depression occurs in adolescence, which in turn can lead to a young person interpreting annoying behaviour in others as a direct threat, leading in some cases to defensive aggression (Dubicka and Harrington 2004, cited in Bailey and Kerslake 2008). In the more severe types of mental disorder such as bipolar disorder and psychosis, offending behaviour may be a symptom of the mental disorder. Young people who are experiencing delusions (false beliefs) or visual hallucinations, for example, may behave in bizarre or manic ways that bring them into contact with the police. Others have suggested reasons why young people with learning disabilities or autistic spectrum disorders may become involved in offending or display aggression, including social naivety making them more prone to being led into criminal acts by others; aggression arising from disruption to routines; anti-social behaviour stemming from a lack of understanding or misinterpretation of social cues; or obsessive behaviour, particularly when linked to fascinations with violence (O'Brien 1996 and Howlin 1997, cited in Bailey and Kerslake 2008).

Witnessing or being the victim of extreme forms of criminal behaviour (violence or sexual abuse, for example) may trigger violent or destructive episodes. It has been argued that post-traumatic stress disorder (PSTD), an anxiety disorder often following a terrifying physical or emotional event causing the person who survived, or witnessed, the event to have persistent, frightening thoughts and memories, or flashbacks, of the ordeal, can lead in some cases to aggressive behaviour as a protective fear response when exposed to reminders of earlier trauma (Fletcher 2003). In Hagell's study of the mental health of young people who offend (2002), she found that some young people attribute their mental health symptoms to 'witnessing violence as part of their criminal lifestyles' (2002: 11).

The statistical association between mental health problems and substance misuse has been shown above. The relationship between the two is, however, more complex than the statistics suggest and the two are often difficult to disentangle. Mental health problems may, on the one hand, be a contributory factor in substance misuse.

A young person may try to manage symptoms of a mental health problem such as depression, for example, by self-medicating with alcohol or drugs and become dependent upon them. This in turn can lead to criminal behaviour for the purpose of obtaining more drugs. On the other hand, substance misuse may accelerate or trigger a predisposition to a mental health problem. Research linking substance use with violent or aggressive behaviour shows a clear link between alcohol use and aggression, but is more equivocal with regard to other drugs (Hoaken and Stewart 2003).

Dosage

Programmes must be of sufficient intensity and duration to achieve their aims, especially with respect to high-risk young people. Several impediments to the delivery of appropriate intensity of support to offending young people with mental health needs have been identified in the research, including inadequacy of resources for intervention, expectation of time-limited work from health staff, the pressures associated with waiting lists, poor coordination of support across sectors (custody/community, youth justice/CAMHS) and the non-engagement of young people.

The need for a local mental health strategy engaging YOTs, secure establishments, CAMHS, education and social care has been widely canvassed as a vehicle to improve multidisciplinary service delivery. In line with this, a strategy is proposed to respond to young people who do not attend for intervention. This requires:

- clearly defined procedures for monitoring attendance and engagement in programme elements;

- tight, but supportive, supervision of the young person; clear lines of communication between relevant professionals providing the various elements of the intervention;

- support of parents/carers in encouraging the young person to attend and participate;

- a focus on attendance and participation in sentence management review meetings.

Responsivity

As has been demonstrated, there are many different types of mental health problems and disorders. It is important therefore to understand the likely behaviours and responses associated with different problems and disorders when considering the most appropriate treatment modality for a mental health intervention. Broadly speaking though, a distinction can be made between those with 'internalising' problems, such as anxiety or depression, and those with 'externalising' problems such as hyperactivity and opposition defiant disorder.

A key indicator of effective responsivity for a particular intervention is the degree to which young people engage with a programme which can be measured through things like attendance and dropout rates. What the research shows is that young people with internalising problems are likely to attend more regularly and stay for longer periods of time in treatment

(Pagnin *et al.* 2005). Young people with more externalising problems tend to drop out earlier. In terms of general YOT practice, this would suggest that different approaches to the way interventions are delivered will be needed for young people in each of these two groups. In terms of treating the particular mental health disorder, Perry *et al.* (2008) suggest that interventions for those with internalising disorders might focus on the development of coping strategies for anxiety and stress, whereas those with externalising problems might focus on parental strategies for structuring, monitoring and supervising the young person.

Given the prevalence of learning difficulties and disabilities within the youth justice population, the responsivity principle would also suggest that particular care should be taken over the way in which treatment programmes are introduced and delivered. Low cognitive ability is clearly an impediment to understanding, which in turn has implications for the way that key concepts are communicated to young people (Perry *et al.* 2008).

Some young people are likely to respond better to treatment in group settings whereas others may respond better with more one-to-one approaches. One study which used an RCT design to compare psychodynamic group work programmes for young people who have offended (Viney and Henry 2002) has shown greater gains for those involved in the group work sessions, including greater self-reliance and sense of enterprise, more confidence in moving into new social groups, and reduced frustration at lack of achievement.

Community based

Applying the principle of community based would suggest that it might be better to treat young people with mental health problems on an outpatient rather than an inpatient basis on the premise that they would be learning to manage their difficulties in settings that are meaningful to them. To date, however, there is no real evidence of the effectiveness of one over the other, with some evaluations showing equally positive outcomes from both settings (Dowden and Latimer 2006, cited in Perry *et al.* 2008).

The principle would also suggest that outcomes from community rather than custodial settings might be more effective. There is some evidence from evaluation of diversion schemes in the USA which supports this. The Texas Special Needs Diversion Program diverted young people assessed as having a mental health disorder at the point of arrest to a community-based mental health programme. They found that young people who had received the treatment had a lower probability of being rearrested for any offence (Cuellar *et al.* 2006).

One of the issues with research relating to young people in secure settings is that it sometimes focuses on behaviours exhibited within that setting. For example, one RCT involving young women with serious mental health problems in a juvenile secure establishment in the USA showed that dialectical behavioural therapy (DBT – an approach using a combination of skills training, problem-solving and validation to reduce self-destructive, impulsive and aggressive behaviours) showed a reduction in the number of behavioural problems and use of punitive staff responses (Trupin *et al.* 2002). While changes in behaviour within a secure setting are useful, the question remains as to how far these behavioural changes are maintained on return to a community setting.

Another study, identified by Perry *et al.* (2008) as promising, looked at the impact of time spent in a 'Youthful Offender Unit' in which the environment was changed so that opportunities and support were provided for self-improvement, change and planning for the future. While there were improvements in this group over longer time periods as compared to a control group, the measure used was disciplinary violations within the institution itself. It can be concluded, therefore, that this approach provides some indication as to how behaviour might be modified within a custodial setting to encourage compliance with its particular rules and regulations. The research design, however, does not provide any evidence as to the extent to which it can bring about lasting behavioural change for individual young people.

One of the difficulties in supporting young people with mental health problems who are subject to a custodial confinement is ensuring continuity of care and approach on release from the secure establishment. Difficulties in maintaining continuity of care may arise from a number of issues such as:

- poor information accompanying young people on entry into the secure estate from the community;

- repeated assessments of the young person as they move through different settings;

- lack of appropriate services in the community to ensure continuity;

- young people refusing to engage.

Many resettlement programmes stress the importance of 'wraparound' services and care in order to achieve this transition effectively. The evidence for wraparound services within the context of mental health is equivocal with one RCT utilising specially trained staff to provide support showing better outcomes for those receiving the service than those receiving conventional services, including fewer assaults on other people, fewer incidents of being picked up by the police and increased school attendance (Carney and Buttell 2003). Another study, using wraparound teams comprising non-professional, informal support such as family and neighbours did not show this kind of association (Pullman *et al.* 2006). While the Pullman *et al.* study was based on a larger sample, the difference in methodology may also have been significant, suggesting that the support network for such wraparound services should be largely managed by suitably trained professionals. It should be noted also that both these studies were conducted in the USA.

These studies did highlight some factors that are likely to contribute to more successful transitions, including:

- helping the young person to plan and practise new behaviours in increasingly challenging and realistic situations before release;
- developing a multidisciplinary transition plan involving the young person, his/her family and relevant service providers;
- monitoring and anticipating difficulties that could arise after release;
- awareness raising for significant others (family and friends, for example) and other relevant staff regarding relapse risks and risk situations and training in how to reinforce pro-social behaviours;
- ensuring there is a clear chain of command within the transition period to ensure emergencies are dealt with efficiently;
- making sure professionals know who to contact if they have a concern about a young person's welfare.

Another study from the USA evaluated the impact of Family Integrated Transitions (FIT), a family and community-based treatment for young people with co-occurring mental health and substance abuse diagnoses, on a group of 11–16-year-olds being released from secure institutions in Washington State's Juvenile Rehabilitation Administration (Washington State Institute for Public Policy 2004). The study showed a 34 per cent reduction in serious crime rates for the FIT group (41 per cent) compared with a control group (27 per cent). The approach utilised a combination of therapies, including:

- Multi-systemic Therapy (MST) to change the systems that create the reinforcement contingencies for behaviour;
- DBT to promote emotional and behavioural regulation;
- Motivational Enhancement Therapy (MET) to promote engagement in treatment;
- relapse prevention to give young people skills to promote sustained abstinence.

See also Chapter 10 on the secure estate and resettlement and Chapter 9 on offending behaviour interventions.

Intervention modality

What the FIT approach, described above, suggests is that interventions for mental health that are effective or promising tend to conform to the principle of intervention modality, that is that they are multi-modal, skills based and focused on problem-solving with a cognitive behavioural approach.

From their review of four different approaches to the treatment of mental health disorders (psychological, pharmacotherapy, systemic/family therapy and multi-modal treatments) Harrington and Bailey (2005) conclude that interventions should seek adaptation of a young person's circumstances using cognitive behavioural and problem-solving skills; adopt multi-modal approaches which simultaneously focus on the involvement of the young person, his/her family and their peer group; and assist young people to engage with interventions using motivational approaches such as motivational interviewing. Similarly, among the characteristics of empirically supported treatments with young people in the juvenile justice system, Trupin (2005) identifies a focus on the development of skills (rather than catharsis or insight) and a focus on problems and solutions (rather than changing personality) as keys to achieving reductions in offending behaviour.

Cognitive behavioural and problem-solving based packages for offence reduction and mental health may be more effective if they share common principles. Interventions, for example, that improve self-esteem may also have an effect on depressive symptoms.

Programme integrity

Analyses of recent and past intervention programmes have commented upon the uneven and poor quality of implementation, the ambiguity of the theoretical underpinning of programmes, and poor or flawed evaluation initiatives. In the arena of mental health interventions, a number of recurrent impediments to the integrity of programme delivery can be identified:

- poorly defined referral pathways: 'Even where Asset identified a mental health/substance misuse need associated with offending behaviour, a quarter of these children and young people were still not referred on for specialist assessment and/or treatment' (HM Inspectorate of Probation 2006);

- long waiting times;

- failure to define responsibility for service provision for 16- and 17-year-olds;

- absence of provision for those with dual diagnosis (mental health and substance misuse needs);

- shortage of trained staff;

- requirements of discipline and control in secure environment taking precedence over therapeutic requirements.

Clear case management standards within the context of a local mental health strategy for young people who offend may need to focus considerations on these key impediments to programme integrity.

Young people and their families are often reluctant to engage with mental health services and quickly cease to be engaged (Audit Commission 1999a; Mental Health Foundation 1999). It is self-evident that where young people withdraw from interventions these are unlikely to be effective. It is therefore important that monitoring and review of interventions are not simply carried out by practitioners and professionals, but include the views of young people and their families about the services they have received (or not for those who have dropped out of treatment).

The challenges for practice

Given the complexity of the relationship between mental health and offending behaviour, a challenge for youth justice workers will be in making decisions about the extent to which a mental health problem is a risk factor for offending behaviour. The introduction of the Scaled Approach (see Chapter 2) throws this issue even further into relief. Where there are issues identified but these are not directly related to offending, then referral to other services might be a more appropriate response rather than dealing with them within the YOT.

The proliferation of labels within the discourse of mental health also represents a considerable challenge for young people, their parents/carers and the professionals working with them both in terms of basic understanding but also with regard to providing an individualised and personal response which also takes account of the socio-economic and other external factors that may be impacting on the mental health of a young person.

Given the specialist nature of much mental health work, it is clear that in many cases a multidisciplinary response will be required:

> In the history of child and adolescent mental health services there has always been a recognition that multi-disciplinary effort needs to be brought to bear on the difficulties of troubled children. (Walker 2003)

Working effectively with other agencies appears to be pivotal to the early detection and treatment of mental health problems and disorders: 'A system of care made up of multiple agencies working together acknowledges that troubled children have multiple needs which require, at different times, different combinations of a broad range of health and social care agencies' (Walker 2003).

Several researchers have, however, described a range of barriers that stand in the way of different practitioners and agencies working together in the interests of prevention, early detection and treatment for young people with mental health problems or disorders.

The Mental Health Foundation (1999) found that while it is clear that 'effective multi-agency working within child and adolescent services, and between child and adolescent mental health services and other services is key to effective service delivery', a number of factors were working against this:

- the fragmentation of services, both within and between agencies;
- the lack of priority accorded to children's mental health services in health, social services and education;
- different approaches and lines of accountability across disciplines;
- different conceptual frameworks and language;
- issues of status, salary and training.

(Mental Health Foundation 1999)

Multidisciplinary training is one of the approaches suggested to overcome these barriers, along with the development of multi-agency screening and assessment tools. A degree of cultural change may also be required, with a commitment from everyone concerned to develop a common language by building on the broad areas of agreement that can be found.

In the interests of better inter-professional relationships, Walker (2003) argues for:

- shared training across disciplines;
- more integrated provision at tier 1, with staff receiving support to intervene in ways that meet the needs of the local community;
- a community-work dimension to mobilise individuals and groups who can act as grass-roots facilitators to help create preventive resources when and where they are needed.

Hagell (2002) reports that while the 'criminal justice system is notoriously bad at detecting (mental health) needs, the NHS is also not good at meeting them even once the right people have been referred'. Hagell urges the need for 'improvement in inter-agency communication, understanding and delivery that is tailored to the stage in the criminal justice system at which the young person is engaged' and an 'end to the confusion about which agency should provide services'.

In summary, the nature of the relationship between mental health and offending is not fully understood. More specifically, there is no clear understanding of the impact that mental health interventions will have on a young person's offending behaviour. This is compounded by the lack of specialist CAMHS to meet the level of mental health needs among children and young people in England and Wales. In addition, many young people with mental health problems and mental health disorders are not in contact with CAMHS. Clearly, this highlights a need to continue to expand the evidence base through rigorous research and evaluation to determine the most effective approaches to the assessment and treatment of young people in the youth justice system with mental health difficulties in the most cost-effective way.

Summary

- Research indicates that the incidence of mental health problems among young people and young adults in the criminal justice system is at least three times as high as in the general population.

- There is a high degree of overlap between the risk factors for developing mental health problems and disorders and for engaging with offending behaviour.

- While the statistics point to a strong association between mental health and young people in the youth justice system, the relationship between mental health problems or mental disorders and offending behaviour is by no means clear-cut. A challenge for youth justice workers will be in making decisions about the extent to which a mental health problem is a risk factor for offending behaviour.

- It is important to understand the likely behaviours and responses associated with different problems and disorders when considering the most appropriate treatment modality for a mental health intervention.

- Research conducted in the USA suggests that interventions for mental health that are effective or promising tend to conform to the principle of intervention modality, that is that they are multi-modal, skills based and focused on problem-solving with a cognitive behavioural approach.

- The pressures young people and their families experience as a result of both a mental health difficulty and involvement in the youth justice system are often compounded by the capacity of the system to respond to their needs, particularly with regard to more serious and pressing mental health disorders.

Further reading

Bailey, S. and Kerslake, B. (2008) 'The process and systems for juveniles and young persons', in K. Soothill, P. Rogers and M. Dolan (eds), *Handbook of Forensic Mental Health*. Cullompton: Willan.

Hagell, A. (2002) *The Mental Health of Young Offenders*. London: Mental Health Foundation.

Harrington, D. and Bailey, S. (2005) *Mental Health Needs and Effectiveness of Provision for Young Offenders in Custody and in the Community*. London: Youth Justice Board.

6

Substance misuse

There is a high prevalence of substance use among children and young people in the UK. While for the majority this is largely experimental, a significant minority will develop substance misuse problems. Substance misuse problems are correlated with young people who might be described as vulnerable or, put another way, are exposed to a number of other risk factors associated with offending behaviour and social exclusion. For this reason, it is hard to isolate the independent impact of substance misuse on offending behaviour.

While the scope and scale of substance misuse among children and young people is well documented, there is little definitive evidence relating to effective interventions for preventing substance misuse in the first place and with regard to providing programmes for the treatment of substance misuse difficulties. This chapter explores what evidence has emerged to date and its implications for practice in working with young people in the youth justice system who are experiencing substance misuse problems.

The evidence base for substance misuse

Studies of the prevalence of drug use among young people consistently demonstrate that a significant minority engage in such behaviours over time (MORI 2004). Statistics on drug use, smoking and drinking among young people aged 11–15 in 2008 (NTA 2009a) show:

- 6 per cent regularly smoked;

- 18 per cent had consumed alcohol in the last week;

- 8 per cent had taken drugs in the last month and 15 per cent in the last year.

The prevalence of taking drugs and other substances increases with age. Males are more likely to drink or take drugs regularly, although the opposite is true for regular smoking. The most commonly used drug is cannabis, with only 3.6 per cent of 11–15-year-olds having taken a Class A drug in the last year. For those who report using drugs, the most frequent age of onset is between 10 and 15 years.

It should be noted, however, that there are a number of methodological issues with self-report studies such as the NTA annual study where young people may be frightened to reveal the extent of their substance use, fearing punishment or labelling. Additionally, where surveys are conducted at school, this inevitably excludes a number of young people who are not attending (a particular risk group for substance misuse).

Frequent substance use may be associated particularly with young people in vulnerable groups. These include:

- young people not attending school;

- young people at risk of offending and reoffending;

- homeless young people and runaways;

- young people living in drug-using families;

- 'looked after' young people;

- some black or minority ethnic groups;

- young people involved in commercial sex work or sexual exploitation;

- those with behavioural, mental health or social problems.
  (Goulden and Sondhi 2001; Edmonds *et al.* 2005; NICE 2007; NTA 2009a)

For 10–16-year-olds the following factors are associated with increased risk of taking drugs:

- serious anti-social behaviour;

- weak parental attitude towards negative behaviour;

- being in trouble at school (including non-attendance and exclusion);

- friends in trouble;

- early smoking.
                                        (Dillon *et al.* 2007; Frisher *et al.* 2007)

A key characteristic of the group of young people at risk of offending studied by Hammersley *et al.* (2003) was that many had been excluded or had dropped out from school before age 16, most left school without qualifications and a considerable proportion were not in education, training or employment. In addition, the earlier young people begin using substances, the greater the negative effects are likely to be in later adolescence and into adulthood, in particular with respect to education, making and sustaining relationships and physical and mental health (Kibblewhite 2002, cited in Keeling *et al.* 2004).

Research shows consistently that substance use is more prevalent among young people who offend (Hammersley *et al.* 2003; Galahad SMS 2004;

Matrix Research and Consultancy and ICPR 2007). The OCJR household survey reported that just over two-thirds (66 per cent) of 10–17-year-olds who had taken a drug in the last year had also committed an offence, compared with 23 per cent who had not taken a drug. In their survey of 15- and 16-year-olds in England and Wales who had been referred to YOTs, Hammersley et al. (2003) found that the levels of self-reported substance use were much higher than those in the Youth Lifestyles Survey and the British Crime Survey for the same year. The cohort they studied contained relatively few heroin or crack cocaine users: alcohol, cannabis and tobacco were by far the most frequently used. Frequent drug users were more likely to offend than occasional drug users, although there was no strong association between frequency of drug use and seriousness of offending (Hammersley et al. 2003; Budd et al. 2005). Among young people known to YOTs, some 86 per cent reported to have used a drug (usually cannabis) (Hammersley et al. 2003). It should be noted, however, that the sample in the cohort here were mainly 15- and 16-year-olds and those with longer offending histories and/or those who had greater involvement with the YOT were over-represented. To this extent, the findings from this study may exaggerate the severity of substance misuse and offending among the general YOT population.

Young people in contact with arrest referral through a police custody suite reported using a range of substances: cannabis (30 per cent), tobacco (30 per cent) and alcohol (23 per cent). By comparison, the reported use of cocaine (4 per cent), crack (1 per cent) and heroin (1 per cent) was low. The frequency of reported use of alcohol, tobacco and cannabis was high with over half reporting using each of these substances either daily or weekly (Matrix Research and Consultancy and ICPR 2007).

Over half of 16–20-year-olds in custody reported dependence on a drug in the year prior to imprisonment. Over half the young women and two-thirds of the young men had a hazardous drinking habit prior to entering custody (HMIP 2008). Young people in custody are more likely than young people in general and in the youth justice population overall to be using a mixture of substances at one time (Galahad SMS 2004).

> The evidence points to associations between a diverse group of risk factors for drug use. These factors include parental discipline, family cohesion, parental monitoring, peer drug use, drug availability, genetic profile, self-esteem, hedonistic attitudes, reasons for drug use, and the rate of risk/protective factors. (Frisher et al. 2007: 19)

While there are clear links between crime and substance use – possessing or selling illicit drugs is a crime in itself, for example – any association between drug use and crime does not necessarily imply causality (Seddon 2006). The risk factors associated with drug use problems among young people are very similar to those with offending careers (Lloyd 1998; Hammersley et al. 2003). Typically these include:

- disrupted family backgrounds;

- poor supervision;

- delinquent peer groups;

- poor social skills;

- low psychological well-being;

- non-attendance at school;

- having been in care.

When these factors are present then substance misuse and crime tend to develop together, at the same age and within the same peer group. Given the 'normalisation' of drug use among young people (Parker *et al.* 1998) – that is that they now culturally accommodate the availability of drugs even if they do not engage themselves – some form of substance misuse among young people who offend should be expected, unrelated to the presence of classic 'risk factors'. Another way of considering substance misuse problems among children and young people is to consider the issue of vulnerability, defined by Drugscope and DPAS (2001) as 'the presence in an individual of one or more factors which may have an influence on them developing a drug problem'.

Hammersley *et al.* (2003) identified three factors for substance use frequency: stimulant and poly-drug; addictive type; and socially acceptable. The last of these categories included the use of alcohol, cannabis and tobacco. The study showed that particular types of offending behaviour were predicted by each factor. Shoplifting was more associated with addictive type substance use, for example, whereas stealing from cars and violent assault was more associated with stimulant and poly-drug use.

A number of theories have been advanced to propose reasons why drug use occurs and escalates in some people and not in others, including the 'gateway' and 'stepping-stone' theories (Witton 2001).

The stepping-stone theory argues that cannabis use leads inevitably to the use of harder drugs, culminating with heroin or crack. This is based on predominantly physiological explanations: that cannabis use unleashes chemicals in the brain which desire new drugs, or that cannabis users, after experiencing and getting used to the mild high of cannabis, begin to crave a more intense high and thus move on to other drugs. The stepping-stone theory has proved unsustainable and lacking any evidence base. The 'evidence' – that most heroin users started with cannabis – is hardly surprising, but demonstrably fails to account for the overwhelmingly vast majority of cannabis users who do not progress to drugs like crack and heroin. In respect of young people at risk of offending and reoffending specifically, Hammersley *et al.* (2003) found no evidence of a funnelling towards heroin and crack cocaine, rather that heavy users tended to use alcohol and cannabis frequently and other drugs occasionally.

The gateway hypothesis takes as its starting point the user's environment and behaviour rather than the drug itself. The gateway theory suggests that drug-using careers follow a generally predictable progression in which the individual moves from using legitimate drugs, including alcohol and tobacco, to various forms of illicit drug use. This is different from the stepping-stone theory in that there is no inevitable direction to the drug user's choices. The gateway theory is a metaphor: the individual has access to new gates after entering the first gate or field, but may or may not choose to open those new gates. Individuals may go back to where they started, may stay in the first field, or may decide to open further gates and move on to using other drugs. The gateway theory does not try to determine drug progression; it is simply about access to choices and proximity to drugs.

The weight of empirical evidence suggests that a link between cannabis and more harmful drugs like heroin and crack may exist. The reason for this is not, as the stepping-stone theory suggests, a cause or a chemical process started by cannabis. More likely explanations are as follows:

- Some cannabis users have personality profiles or environmental conditions that are in common with those of the users of more harmful drugs.

- Once drugs (be they cannabis, alcohol or tobacco) are used, if the harm ascribed to them is overstated or false, individuals using them will dismiss this information and are less likely to be concerned about moving to more 'harmful' drugs.

- Cannabis use puts individuals in social situations and supply transactions where they are more likely to experience people using, accepting and supplying more harmful drugs than are others in the population.

The gateway theory does not suggest that cannabis use leads to the use of other, harder drugs. It does stress the relevance of common profiles, environment, experience and access (Home Office Research, Development and Statistics Directorate 2002).

Tackling substance misuse is a priority for work with young people at risk of offending and reoffending. All YOTs are required to have a dedicated substance misuse worker and the YJB and National Treatment Agency for Substance Misuse (NTA) have published guidance on integrating substance misuse provision (2006). Overall, positive messages have emerged in respect of the role and deployment of substance misuse workers in YOTs (Pitcher *et al.* 2004). The majority of such workers (90 per cent) are physically located within the YOTs, providing post-screening assessment of young people and substance misuse interventions both within the YOT and within community settings. High proportions (60 per cent) of young people supervised by the YOT were considered by substance misuse workers to have a substance misuse problem. Many of these issues can be addressed within the YOT by the substance misuse worker themselves providing tier 1 or tier 2 services (see section on 'risk classification' below).

Historically, the response to the substance misuse needs of young people entering custody or those seeking continuity of support at discharge has not been a positive one. The Youth Justice Board's research on substance misuse and young people in custody (Galahad SMS 2004) identified a range of systemic difficulties and inconsistencies in the delivery of substance misuse services at all levels and stages. Specifically, it identified:

- failures to recognise substance misuse needs on entry to custody;

- limited options for substance misuse treatments within the establishment or insufficient resources to access external programme providers;

- a lack of structured interventions for alcohol misuse or smoking cessation;

- a lack of standardisation coupled with variable delivery of prevention services through personal, social and health education (PSHE); and

- a tendency to treat psychiatric problems in isolation from substance misuse issues.

In response to this report, the YJB produced its National Specification for Substance Misuse which has recently been revised (YJB 2009b). A study evaluating the extent to which the implementation of the National Specification for Substance Misuse had improved services for young people showed progress in all areas, although there remained gaps in provision, particularly concerning those young people on remain, highly mobile populations, females, black and minority ethnic young people and those on longer sentences. Issues still remained regarding continuity of care between custody and the community and between establishments, meaning that care plans tended to be determined by what was available rather than the needs of individual young people (Galahad SMS Ltd 2009).

There is no hard and fast evidence that substance misuse treatment reduces the number of criminal convictions for young people (Britton 2009). However, there are some promising studies that suggest reduction in offending behaviour can be achieved as a result of involvement in substance misuse treatment programmes (Farabee et al. 2001; Henggeler et al. 2002; Jainchill et al. 2005). Research by Farabee et al. (2001) suggests a positive association between being supervised by a criminal justice agency and reductions in offending compared with young people who were not supervised in this context, regardless of the fact that the criminal justice supervised group were more likely to have committed more crimes, come from families where other members were involved in crime and to have met the criteria for having a conduct disorder. Henggeler et al. (2002) found that multi-systemic therapy (MST) seemed to be associated with reductions in violent crime but not property crime. It should be noted, however, that all these studies are from the USA and are based on self-report data.

Given the paucity of research evidence on what interventions for substance misuse work or might be promising in terms of reducing crime, it would seem logical to look at the evidence base for programmes that reduce substance misuse by young people in general on the basis that they may have the potential to minimise a significant risk factor associated with offending behaviour. While there is a growing body of evidence about interventions for reducing substance misuse for young people under the age of 18, there are limitations to it with regard to making definite treatment decisions (Britton 2009). For example, the majority of evidence comes from the USA, so should be regarded with caution in relation to its application in England and Wales. There is also no strong evidence regarding which particular programmes might achieve greatest change or which are best suited to particular individuals or groups (Britton and Farrant 2008).

The evidence as it exists for these various treatment approaches in relation to young people is explored further within the context of applying the principles of effective practice below.

The principles of effective practice and substance misuse

Risk classification

Given the 'normalisation' of substance use among young people (Parker *et al.* 1998) it is important to be able to identify where it is a significant risk factor for a young person's offending. This may be a stand-alone risk factor or more usually a factor interrelated with others. For example, persistent substance misuse may cause depression and volatility. This, in turn, may produce low self-efficacy and a failure to engage in academic learning.

The *Asset* core profile specifically explores the nature and extent of young people's substance use (tobacco, alcohol, solvents and drugs) and its links to offending behaviour, including:

- practices which put young people at particular risk (e.g. injecting, sharing equipment, poly-drug use);
- seeing substance use as a positive and/or essential to life;
- noticeably detrimental effect on education, relationships, daily functioning;
- offending to obtain money for substances;
- offending while under the influence, or possessing/supplying illegal drugs.

The challenge for practitioners in completing *Asset*, therefore, is making the judgement about the extent to which substance use by a young person is a significant risk factor in their offending behaviour and determining a plan accordingly (see section on 'intervention modality' below). The key question

151

would seem to be the extent to which current substance use is likely to contribute to the risk of further offending by the young person.

This principle also states that the level and intensity of an intervention should be linked to the seriousness of offending. With regard to substance misuse, this would suggest that a graded approach is taken linked to the *Asset* scores in this area. The HAS four-tier model of care for substance misuse services (see Table 6.1) provides a framework for ensuring young people receive the type of service that most closely matches their level of need, while avoiding the labelling of young people without serious problems (Keeling *et al.* 2004).

Criminogenic need

As has been shown from the research on the prevalence of substance misuse and young people at risk of offending and reoffending, YOTs can expect substantial numbers of the young people they engage with to screen positive on this measure. The key issue will be the need to assess and analyse whether the presence of substance misuse is a key contributor to the young person's current offence and/or their offending career. Substance misuse issues which primarily provide a lifestyle context for the young person's offending behaviour may require lower tiers of preventive intervention whereas misuse which has a causal contribution may need a more intensive and extensive response.

Dosage

Clearly, the intensity and regularity of a substance misuse element within a wider programme of intervention should be determined by the risk this issue presents with regard to reoffending. Key to maintaining the required regularity and intensity is ensuring engagement and retention in substance misuse programmes. Research has shown that weekly case management focusing on removing barriers that may inhibit active participation delivered using CBT techniques can be effective in achieving this (Noel 2006). In Noel's study, specific weekly sessions were arranged in places that were accessible for the young person, focusing on such issues as planning and coordinating other interventions, ensuring young people attended their treatment sessions, acting as an advocate and helping with practical things such as transport to venues or with housing difficulties.

When a programme is to be delivered by the YOT substance misuse worker it may be directly monitored for attendance, punctuality, participation and impact. Where the sentence plan is multi-modal, the worker responsible for the substance misuse element needs to communicate with the case manager and other providers with regard to the young person's participation (and vice versa).

In custodial settings the unavailability of certain kinds of provision may mean that assessed need cannot immediately be met. It may be advisable in sentence planning to consider whether substance misuse

Table 6.1   HAS four-tier framework

Tier 1: Universal services

Interventions	Practice/Agencies
• Information/education concerning tobacco, alcohol and drugs within the education curriculum • Educational assessment and support to maintain in school • Identification of risk issues • General medical services/routine health screening and advice on health risks/Hep B vaccination/referral/parental support and service	Teacher Youth worker Connexions staff School health

Tier 2: Services offered by practitioners with some specialist knowledge

Interventions	Practice/Agencies
• Programme of activities and education to address offending • Family support regarding parenting and general management issues • Assessment of risk and protection issues • Counselling addressing lifestyle issues • Educational assessment	YOT/bail support Mentor Social services Counselling One-stop shop service Educational psychology

Tier 3: Services provided by specialist teams

Interventions	Practice/Agencies
• Specialist assessment leading to a planned package of care and treatment augmenting that already provided by tiers 1 and 2 and integrated with them • Specialist substance-specific interventions including mental health issues • Family assessment and involvement • Inter-agency planning and communication	Specialist young people's drug and alcohol services integrated with CAMHS or 'one-stop shops' combined with child mental health, educational assessment and support, statement of special educational needs

Tier 4: Very specialist services

Interventions	Practice/Agencies
• Short period of accommodation in crises • Inpatient/day psychiatric or secure unit to assist detoxification if required • Continued tier 3 and multi-agency involvement alongside tier 1 and tier 2	Forensic child and adolescent psychiatry Social services Continued involvement from young people's substance misuse services Substantial support for education

services unavailable within the secure estate can be quickly assessed once the community part of the sentence is started. Throughcare workers may need to prioritise these elements within cases.

Specific considerations about the delivery of services arise where a young person has a dual diagnosis – substance misuse needs and mental health problems. In these circumstances it may be more effective for drugs workers and CAMHS workers to collaborate to ensure the appropriate sequencing of their respective service inputs. See Chapter 5 on mental health.

Even though substance misuse might have been identified as a significant risk factor in relation to a young person's offending behaviour and an appropriate intervention begun, the length of their order may well jeopardise its completion and chances of long-term success. Ensuring longer-term interventions may entail coordination with specialist substance misuse services beyond the young person's involvement with the youth justice system (NTA 2005).

Responsivity

The responsivity principle would suggest that for substance misuse interventions to be relevant they must engage young people in such a way that meets their particular needs and circumstances. At the same time, interventions should provide them with a range of strategies to enable them to learn safer ways of responding to situations in which they may be tempted to engage in risky behaviours. This implies that to be responsive, therefore, interventions might need to be:

- structured;

- motivational;

- relevant to the lives of young people;

- providing them with skills to manage challenges;

- presented by staff with a common purpose and approach.

Approaches that hector, patronise, label or stigmatise young people are unlikely to generate a positive response. Initiatives that motivate, foster better understanding and develop skills, confidence and strategies in how to manage, reduce or stop the use of substances (particularly those taken to harmful levels) are likely to have an impact.

A key consideration in this respect would be whether a group or individual approach might be more appropriate. Waldron and Kaminer (2004) found two studies of group CBT which showed similarly effective results to individual CBT. They suggest that there may be something specific to group work that can help to facilitate change, including realising that others share similar problems and the development of social skills, modelling, rehearsal and peer feedback. In particular, they posit that the opportunity for role-play within a group setting may enable young people to practise coping with high-risk situations within a safe and supportive environment.

Not all young people will necessarily respond well to a group situation, however. In one study, young people in a custodial setting felt unsafe disclosing personal information with others for fear that they would not maintain confidentiality or use the information to manipulate (Stathis *et al.* 2006). In their evaluation of the YJB's drug and alcohol projects, Hammersley *et al.* (2004) identified some organisational difficulties in implementing group work approaches. Specifically, the time-limited nature of disposals meant that, at any one time, there were relatively few eligible young people with relevant substance use problems and it was difficult to collect a group in one place. They recommend, therefore, that incorporating substance misuse work into generic group work to tackle offending behaviour might be an easier option.

Studies have also shown that the relationship between the person delivering the intervention and the young person and/or his/her parents can impact on the outcome. Sometimes called a 'therapeutic' or working alliance, this relationship could be described as a collaborative and affective bond between a practitioner and those involved in the intervention (Britton and Farrant 2008). Failure to develop an affective alliance can lead to early dropout from family programmes (Robbins *et al.* 2006). Research would indicate that it is the alliance with the parent/carer that has the greatest impact on engaging a young person with an intervention at the start of a programme, but thereafter the alliance with the young person becomes more important (Shelef *et al.* 2005; Hogue *et al.* 2006).

Dillon *et al.* (2007) suggest that a strategy of providing accurate and credible information, using appropriate language helps provide young people with the facts necessary to develop a collection of beliefs and attitudes that develops a resilience to drug use. While there is no adequate evidence base establishing the effectiveness of drug and alcohol education per se, Dillon *et al.* (2007) suggest that an education strategy needs to be accompanied by help for young people to develop realistic and achievable life goals (e.g. future career) and to develop and maintain strong self-efficacy so that they may resist drug use.

The responsivity principle suggests that substance-related advice and information should be culturally and age appropriate for children, young people, parents and carers. The principle also raises the question about how to ensure that young people and/or parents/carers who have low levels of literacy, or for whom English is a second language, can be best catered for across the full range of interventions.

Community based

Research on the impact of multi-systemic therapy (MST) which focuses on the individual young person within the context of their family, peer, school and social networks has shown to be effective in reducing substance misuse among young people with both short and more established patterns of criminal activity (Liddle *et al.* 2004; Henggeler *et al.* 2006). While the precise reasons behind this are not well-established, it is likely that helping young people and others around them to consider substance misuse within the context of their communities is more likely to result in the development of meaningful and relevant strategies for minimising harm or abstaining.

Involving parents and carers in substance misuse interventions, in particular in being proactive in helping a young person stay drug and alcohol fee and attend treatment after care meetings, has also been shown to improve an intervention's capacity to respond to the young person's needs (Whitney *et al.* 2002). Parents/carers can be viewed as a resource to the young person and staff, but are likely to need support or information in relation to the impact of substance misuse, their own attitudes and patterns of substance misuse and their role in supporting their child. Hammersley *et al.* (2003) suggest parental engagement might be easier to achieve with regard to alcohol, cannabis and tobacco rather than for drugs which are perceived to be harder and have more stigma attached to them. Difficulties are likely to emerge where parents/carers of young people themselves misuse substances, and it may therefore be useful to signpost them into adult provision.

It would seem logical to assume that the community-based principle could also be applied to schools and other educational establishments within a particular community. Education-based programmes though have not been shown to have a particular impact on reducing or preventing substance misuse (Frisher *et al.* 2007). The reasons for this are unclear and deserve further exploration. Additionally, Hammersley *et al.* (2003) argue that the zero tolerance policies within some community settings towards substance use may not be helpful as they encourage young people to conceal rather than deal with their substance use. Ironically, such a policy is also likely to lead to exclusions from school which further place a young person at risk both of substance misuse and offending.

Long-term outcome studies of residential treatment models compared with non-residential models show no significant differences: both have the potential to reduce substance misuse (Spooner *et al.* 2001; Dennis et *al.* 2004). One particular residential model, residential therapeutic community-based treatment, however, has been shown to have no impact on reducing substance misuse (Jainchill *et al.* 2005). Young people also express negative feelings towards residential treatment which suggests their capacity to participate effectively may be compromised. Retention on these kinds of programmes can, therefore, be a problem (Currie 2003).

Transitions within the context of substance misuse could be as a result of the move from residential to community-based services, from high-intensity to low-intensity interventions or from custodial settings where a young person has received substance misuse treatment to their communities. Evidence suggests that young people can find these transitions highly stressful. Young people returning to their communities from residential treatment programmes have reported particular concerns about going back into a difficult family situation, losing the support of the residential service and meeting with peers who are still using substances (Duroy *et al.* 2003). What evidence there is from research seems to reinforce the principles of early planning for departure, including the young person, his/her family and health and education services, with a strong case management support function (Wood *et al.* 2002; Godley *et al.* 2007).

Within the YOT, the presence of the substance misuse worker may facilitate direct access to services, either from within the YOT or via protocols to access community-based substance misuse provision. The Annual Inspection Report for YOTs 2005–6 indicates that 'substance misuse workers usually had good access to their parent service for more specialist tier 3 support' (HM Inspectorate of Probation 2006). Issues may arise where support and intervention is required that is beyond the remit of the YOT worker. In those circumstances it may be important to ensure that local protocols specify the extent to which young people concluding orders are a priority for ongoing intervention, and that the needs of the young person with respect to substance misuse are effectively communicated to those who will have continuing contact with them.

Intervention modality

As has been established earlier, there is a wide diversity in the substance use of young people at risk of offending and reoffending. For this reason, it would seem obvious that responses might need to be tailored to the individual and that funnelling these young people into generic programmes may be detrimental. This implies that substance misuse treatment might include a range of interventions provided within the context of an overall plan that is focused on addressing the young person's substance misuse.

There are a number of interventions designed for young people who are using substances either experimentally or regularly which are provided in both community and residential (including secure) settings. These have a number of different intended outcomes, ranging from the reduction of harm (needle exchange, for example) to complete abstinence such as 12-step programmes. The ways in which they seek to achieve these outcomes are many and varied, including pharmacological treatment, cognitive-behavioural therapy (CBT), counselling, family therapy, therapeutic communities and motivational interviewing.

Pharmacological interventions are used to treat withdrawal symptoms, to substitute for substances and/or to reduce craving and block effects of substances. Pharmacological responses are widely used in adult settings and there is evidence of their effectiveness for treating drug and alcohol dependency in that context. Indeed, one study shows a marked reduction in crime among adult drug users following the prescribing of treatment for drug use (NTA 2008). There is very little evidence on its potential for treating young people due to the very small numbers of young people with serious dependencies that would warrant such an intervention (NTA 2009b) and ethical considerations regarding drug trials with those under the age of 18 (Britton 2009). There are other issues to consider in transferring this model to young people. There may be physical and mental health dangers associated with using strong drugs with young people whose bodies are not fully developed. The medicines used are themselves strong drugs and can be misused with potentially fatal consequences.

The research suggests that a more behavioural approach, in particular a cognitive behavioural one, can achieve promising results (Elliot *et al.* 2001; Waldron and Kaminer 2004; NICE 2007). Kaminer *et al.* (2002) compared young people who received CBT rather than psycho-educational therapy among 16–18-year-old males and found that short-term outcomes were better for young people who had received CBT. There was no significant difference between the two approaches over a nine-month period, however, where they produced similarly effective outcomes. Waldron and Kaminer's (2004) systematic review of the research relating to CBT approaches to treating substance misuse concluded that it was effective and had a positive impact on other related problems.

Brief interventions (single sessions lasting no more than an hour) are used to encourage self-reflection and can be a one-off intervention in its own right for a young person whose needs are not that great, for example, or as an engagement tool to encourage young people with more entrenched issues onto more specialist programmes. Brief interventions usually employ motivational interviewing techniques (see Chapter 3) which aim to encourage reflection on the risks involved in substance misuse in relation to personal values and goals (Britton 2009). Brief interventions with young people have been shown to reduce alcohol misuse and cigarette smoking (Tevyaw and Monti 2004; Gray, McCambridge *et al.* 2005). Improvements in attendance at community treatment services have also been demonstrated (Tait *et al.* 2004, 2005) as well as the capacity to produce a more meaningful therapeutic relationship and enhanced treatment engagement as a result (Stein *et al.* 2006).

One of the most publicised interventions related to the reduction of substance misuse by young people who offend has been the Drug Treatment and Testing Requirements. However, the report from Matrix Research and Consultancy and the ICPR (2007) reached inconclusive findings on the impact of these requirements. Specifically, they found that with regard to arrest referral, which is designed to reduce young people's offending through improving their access to relevant support services, there was no change in offending, there was no change in the services young people accessed after arrest referral, and there was no discernible difference between patterns of substance misuse and offending risk in the pilot group as compared to the comparator group. In the case of drug testing, analysis of data from *Asset* showed that very few young people used Class A drugs in either the pilot or comparator areas, and the drug use pattern after drug testing in the pilot area did not vary significantly from that observed in the comparator areas.

Programme integrity

The lack of a completely robust or credible evidence base for the efficacy of the range of substance misuse programmes available presents a challenge in determining what intervention is best for a young person where substance use is identified as a problem. This would imply the need for strict monitoring and evaluation of the outcomes from substance misuse interventions provided directly by a YOT or a secure establishment, and from programmes delivered by third parties. In this respect, Hammersley *et al.* (2003) suggest that specific consideration needs to be given to the impact of intervention on the substance misuse needs of the young person and the impact of changes in the substance misuse needs of the young person on their offending behaviour.

The prevalence of substance use among young people at risk of offending and reoffending also has implications for the staff who work with them. While the substance misuse worker will take a strategic lead in this area of practice, the prevalence of substance misuse among young people at risk of offending and reoffending indicates that all staff will require a reasonable awareness of these issues in order to make sensible decisions and to refer appropriately.

The challenges for practice

While considerable change has taken place over the last five years in the recognition and response to the substance misuse needs of young people at risk of offending and reoffending, a number of outstanding challenges remain.

While there is a growing evidence base for what effective or promising approaches might look like in general, there are still significant gaps in terms of identifying specific groups with whom particular approaches are likely to be most effective. This presents challenges for practitioners in terms of putting together intervention plans that are most likely to reduce substance misuse on the basis of the outcomes from assessment.

Keeling *et al.* (2004) argue that substance misuse interventions in the past were based on the idea that young people did not want to experiment with drugs and alcohol, and those that were doing so wanted to stop. In the light of more recent evidence, services need to recognise the fact that young people do want to experiment with and regularly use drugs and alcohol. This makes the provision of appropriate services and interventions much more challenging. In addition, the 'normalisation' of substance use and its apparent prevalence in the lives of children and young people means that the task of discriminating between what is 'normal' experimentation and what is likely to be deleterious use, particularly in relation to the risk of further offending, is more difficult to determine. In addition, this process of normalisation may also make it much more difficult to get young people to see the need for them to reduce their consumption of drugs, alcohol or tobacco.

Summary

- Research shows consistently that substance use is more prevalent among young people who offend.

- There is little definitive evidence relating to effective interventions for preventing substance misuse in the first place and with regard to providing programmes for the treatment of substance misuse difficulties.

- While there are clear links between crime and substance use, any association between drug use and crime does not necessarily imply causality. The risk factors associated with drug use problems among young people are very similar to those with offending careers and include disrupted family backgrounds, poor supervision, delinquent peer groups, poor social skills, low psychological well-being, non-attendance at school and having been in care. When these factors are present then substance misuse and crime tend to develop together, at the same age and within the same peer group.

- There is no conclusive evidence that substance misuse treatment reduces the number of criminal convictions for young people. However, there are some promising studies that suggest reduction in offending behaviour can be achieved as a result of involvement in substance misuse treatment programmes.

- Research on the impact of multi-systemic therapy (MST) which focuses on the individual young person within the context of their family, peer, school and social networks has shown to be effective in reducing substance misuse among young people with both short and more established patterns of criminal activity. Research also indicates that cognitive-behavioural therapeutic approaches can achieve promising re-sults. Brief interventions (single sessions lasting no more than an hour) have been shown to reduce alcohol misuse and cigarette smoking.

- While there is a growing evidence base for what effective or promising approaches might look like in general, there are still significant gaps in terms of identifying specific groups with whom particular approaches are likely to be most effective. This presents challenges for practitioners in terms of putting together intervention plans that are most likely to reduce substance misuse on the basis of the outcomes from assessment.

Further reading

Britton, J. (2009) *Young People's Specialist Substance Misuse Treatment: Exploring the Evidence*. London: National Treatment Agency for Substance Misuse.

Frisher, M., Crome, I., Macleod, J., Bloor, R. and Hickman, N. (2007) *Predictive Factors for Illicit Drug Use among Young People: A Literature Review*, Home Office Online Report 05/07. London: Home Office RDS.

Keeling, P., Kibblewhite, K. and Smith, Z. (2004) 'Evidence-based practice in young people's substance misuse services', in D. White (ed.), *Social Work and Evidence-based Practice*. London: Jessica Kingsley.

7

Parenting

When their children become teenagers, parents may experience demands that they can feel ill-equipped to deal with. Young people themselves are responding to physical, emotional and lifestyle changes that can have a profound impact on them. These challenges, for both parents and young people, have to be faced in the context of major shifts in the last decade in social structures, as well as in political responses to parenting, teenagers and the family (Coleman and Roker 2001). These external factors can exacerbate the internal challenges families are facing. This chapter explores some of these tensions as well as some of the issues resulting from the evaluation of parenting programmes in the UK and in other countries.

Throughout this chapter, the term parent is used to include birth parents (whether married or unmarried) and guardians or other carers, including step-parents, adoptive parents, foster parents, grandparents, older siblings or other relatives who may undertake a parenting role. Parenting in the youth justice context therefore relates to the parenting support needs of anyone who is involved in the care of a young person, whether they live within the same household or not, as in the case of a non-resident parent.

The evidence base for parenting

There are four major features of family life associated with the offending behaviour of young people (Loeber and Stouthamer-Loeber 1986). These risk factors are:

1. parental and sibling criminality;

2. parental neglect, including lack of supervision;

3. chronic family conflict, either between partners or between parent and young person;

4. harsh or erratic discipline.

The first two of these – the criminal behaviour of parents or other family members and neglect – appear to be the most powerful variables which link

162

with the offending behaviour of young people. In considering interventions with parents, therefore, it may be necessary to recognise that not all risk factors are equally amenable to change. A parenting intervention is more likely to impact on parenting styles, communication, ways in which conflict is handled or types of discipline than on parental criminality, for example.

Rutter *et al.* (1998) identify a number of needs that should be met in order for parenting to be successful in preventing anti-social behaviour. These are:

- effective monitoring or supervision so the parent knows which behaviours are likely to lead to trouble;
- clear setting of standards with explicit and unambiguous feedback;
- skilled diversion or distraction to avoid the development of confrontation and crises;
- responsivity to the child's sensitivities and needs;
- fostering of pro-social behaviour, self-efficacy and social problem-solving;
- encouraging the development of internal controls through open communication;
- recognition of the child's rights and the taking of responsibility.

Parents of 'anti-social children', they argue, fall down on all of these, failing to monitor their child's activities, providing instructions that are often ambiguous and using discipline methods that result more from their own moods, for example.

Kumpfer and Alvarado (1998) have identified the following parenting behaviours as protective factors against young people becoming involved in offending:

- the use of positive discipline methods;
- active monitoring and supervision;
- supportive parent–child relationships;
- families who advocate for their children;
- parents who seek information and support.

Desforges and Abouchaar (2003) have shown that parental involvement in the form of 'at-home good parenting' has a significant positive effect on children's achievement and adjustment, even after all other factors shaping attainment (the quality of schools, for example) have been taken out of the equation. This can be shown to be the case across all classes and all ethnic groups. Given the negative impact low attainment and lack of achievement have on young people, particularly in respect of increased risk of offending, this is a significant finding.

These parenting risk and protective factors need to be seen within the context of other challenges that families face that may also impact on parenting and family functioning. That is, families may be experiencing stress at a community level, for example living in an impoverished neighbourhood; at a family level, such as family poverty and poor housing; and at an individual level, such as social isolation or depression (Ghate and Hazel 2002). Further, families may have experienced long-term frustration, sometimes beginning in their own childhoods, where multiple contact with agencies has not resulted in the kind of support they felt they needed or requests for help have not been heard (Ghate *et al.* 2007, 2008).

Parenting and family support programmes have become an increasingly important plank of government responses to reducing social exclusion, anti-social behaviour and youth offending in particular. As such, they form key elements within the raft of recent policy initiatives for improving outcomes for children and young people spanning the areas of health, education, youth justice and safeguarding, including Every Child Matters (DfES 2004a), Youth Matters (DfES 2005) and Every Parent Matters (DfES 2007). These have been accompanied by the establishment of a wide range of services for parents, such as Sure Start Projects, children's centres, On Track Projects and Family Intervention Projects introduced as part of the 1997–2010 Labour government's anti-social behaviour strategy. To support those who work within this expanding 'family support industry' (Moran *et al.* 2004: 14), a National Academy of Parenting Practitioners has been established whose remit is to link research, training, practical support and information.

In the specific context of youth justice, the Crime and Disorder Act 1998 established 'reinforcing the responsibilities of parents' to exercise control over their children as a main objective of work to prevent youth offending. It enshrined in law the principle that a young person's behaviour could be affected by the nature of the parenting they received. Introduced in 2000, the Parenting Order place a mandatory requirement on parents of young people who offend and young people not attending school to participate in parenting education and support. In 2003, Parenting Contracts were introduced. These are voluntary agreements made between YOTs and parents providing an opportunity for YOTs to engage with parents on a voluntary basis before a Parenting Order is applied.

There were 1,034 Crime Parenting Orders and 230 Education Parenting Orders recorded across all YOTs in 2007–8 (YJB 2009a). There is, however, a widely uneven distribution of Parenting Orders among the 157 YOT areas. Analysis of data provided by the YJB for 2005/6 shows that nearly one in eight YOTs obtained no Crime Parenting Orders and over a third only obtained between one and five. A small number of YOTs obtain relatively large numbers (Burney and Gelsthorpe 2008). The reasons for this disparity in the use of Parenting Orders is not entirely clear, although some critics have suggested that it may reflect the extent to which a YOT engages with parents in general and how well they brief magistrates about the needs of parents (Burney and Gelsthorpe 2008).

The introduction of the Parenting Order has been controversial and there are a number of arguments that can be cited against holding a parent responsible for a young person's behaviour.

From a human rights perspective, the Parenting Order has been challenged on the basis that it criminalises a parent when they haven't actually committed a crime (Henricson 2003). Concerns have been expressed about the specific requirements component of the Parenting Order, as Article 7 of the Human Rights Act (no punishment without law) may be violated by the use of broad and general requirements specified under section 8(4)(a) of the Crime and Disorder Act 1998. If a parent cannot 'reasonably foresee' what they should do or not do to avoid incurring a criminal sanction through breach of the Parenting Order, then Article 7 might be contravened (Lindfield 2001).

A review by Narain in 2001 suggested, however, that they were likely to be compatible on the basis that the rights to privacy and family life enshrined in the Act must be balanced against the legitimate interests of the state in preventing a young person's future offending or anti-social behaviour. A test case in 2003 exonerated the Parenting Order in the light of the European Convention on Human Rights (*R(M)* v. *Inner London Crown Court* (EWHC 301 Admin)) ruling that, although the Parenting Order is an infringement of family life (Article 8), it was justified as necessary but must be proportionate. It also ruled that a Parenting Order does not breach Article 6 (right to a fair trial) as it is based on evaluation rather than a particular standard of proof (Burney and Gelsthorpe 2008).

It could also be argued that the approach places total responsibility for a young person's behaviour with the parent and ignores the wider community while undermining a young person's agency (Morrow 1999).

The majority of Parenting Orders are made against mothers rather than fathers, as it is mothers who are more likely to attend court and receive the order. This has implications for equal opportunities and equality under the law (Morrow 1999; Ghate and Ramella 2002; Burney and Gelsthorpe 2008).

Some critics have also argued that compulsion to attend and the stigma associated with a court order may make it less likely that parents will engage fully in the programme (Henricson *et al.* 2000; Holt 2010). In her qualitative study of the experiences of a small number of parents (17) who had been made subject to a Parenting Order by the courts, Holt (2010) identifies a range of emotions felt by these parents, including anger towards their own sentences which they felt were more severe than their child's; humiliation that they had been publicly branded as a 'bad parent'; confusion as to why 'support' was being administered through the courts when they had been asking for help for a number of years; injustice that this support was being issued by magistrates who did not understand their circumstances and appeared to be letting other parents 'get away with it'; and frustration that as parents they had no involvement in judicial decision-making relating to their child. These findings would seem to reinforce the observation from the evaluation of YJB-sponsored parenting programmes that parents subject to a

Parenting Order experienced uncertainty at the start of programmes (Ghate and Ramella 2002).

While providing an interesting insight into the views of a small group of parents, Holt's findings regarding the failure of the subsequent parenting interventions to have any long-term impact on these parents' lives should be treated with caution for a number of reasons. A sample of 17 from across only four YOTs is simply not large enough to be representative. In addition, they appear to be founded on self-report data from the parents only. These findings would also seem to be at odds with those of the YJB evaluation which found no difference between the level of benefit reported by parents who had come via the Parenting Order and those who had not (it was generally positive), even when they had experienced uncertainty at the start of the programme (Ghate and Ramella 2002). The YJB evaluation was based on a much larger sample of parents who had been referred to programmes as a result of a Parenting Order (178 in total). While there are methodological weaknesses in the YJB evaluation as well, it is clear that more robust research needs to be focused on the impact of parenting interventions on parents who have received Parenting Orders. Research will need to rely on more than the perceptions of parents before the legislation is rejected out of hand as a response to the challenges faced by families.

Whatever ethical, practical and legal issues surround this legislation, it is clear that the introduction of the Parenting Order and the Parenting Contract has meant that YOTs have been important contributors to the development of parenting services aimed at the most 'at risk' families and young people (Ghate et al. 2008). It is also the case that proportionately, very few referrals to YOT parenting interventions are as a result of either Parenting Orders or Parenting Contracts. In 2005/6 only 12 per cent of interventions were through Parenting Orders and 7 per cent through Parenting Contracts, as compared with 81 per cent of voluntary referrals (Burney and Gelsthorpe 2008).

Parenting support provided in the youth justice context is a relatively new development in the UK, although there has for years been a well-established body of knowledge and expertise in supporting parents of younger children. Increasingly, more is being learnt about potentially promising approaches for parents of teenagers, including parents of young people who offend. When focusing on promising practice in working with parents in the youth justice context, it is important to acknowledge the process of building on a range of existing research and practice-based findings, from other areas of parenting support work and from other countries, to inform the development of work in this field.

The YJB Source Document for Parenting (Ghate et al. 2008) provides an overview of a range of parenting interventions, the majority having originated and been evaluated in the USA, and provides ratings for their effectiveness according to the Maryland Scientific Methods Scale. Two reviews of practice from the USA are particularly significant in that they rate programmes in relation to the strength of their research design and the evidence of effectiveness produced. The Strengthening America's Families programme identified exemplary, model and promising programmes by reviewing each programme on a number of criteria including sampling strategy, data analysis and programme integrity (Kumpfer 1993). The focus was on individual, group and family-based parenting programmes. The Blueprints programme for violence prevention selected 11 model programmes on a number of effectiveness criteria, of which the three given the greatest weight were evidence of deterrent effect with a strong research design sustained effect and multiple site replication. Three programmes were listed in both reviews as achieving the highest rating for effectiveness for programmes designed for parents and families of teenagers who offend. They are Functional Family Therapy (FFT), Multi-systemic Therapy and Multidimensional Treatment Foster Care.

Studies of FFT in America show that when compared with no treatment, other family therapy interventions and traditional juvenile court services (e.g. probation), it can reduce rearrests by 20–60 per cent (Sexton and Alexander 2000). One trial of FFT with young people committing serious or persistent offences showed that compared with a control group young people receiving the treatment were six times as likely to avoid arrest (Barton et al. 1985, cited in Whyte 2009). Underpinned by a multi-systemic approach, FFT is based on three phases:

1. Engagement and motivation where – families are helped to respect individual differences and values, develop a trusting relationship with the therapist, reduce resistance and negativity, and raise expectations that change is possible.

2. Behaviour change – where the therapist works with each family member to enhance skills in communication, problem-solving, contingency management and contracting, limit setting and reinforcement.

3. Generalisation – whereby the therapist helps families to apply the techniques and skills they have learned in a range of settings and situations and encourages the maintenance of changes through linking participants with relevant community resources and services.

The National Academy for Parenting Practitioners is conducting its own randomised control trial of the effectiveness of this approach in the UK, including Youth Offending Teams.

The Parenting Early Intervention Pathfinder (PEIP) tested three of these more promising models in England with families of 8–13-year-olds. Incredible Years, Triple P and Strengthening Families, Strengthening Communities were selected as having a sound evidence base to start with (DCSF 2008b). The courses were deemed to be a success as measured by completion rates and measures of parents' mental well-being, their parenting skills, their sense of being a parent and also in the behaviour of the child about whom they were concerned. While the outcomes from this study seem to suggest that these approaches have promise for work with this age group, the implications for youth justice are not clear. The average age of the children of the parents targeted was just over nine, i.e. younger than the YOT age range. This low average is accounted for by the fact that, despite the target age group, over a quarter of the sample was in fact in the 0–7 bracket and 8 per cent were older than 13. What the study did show is that these programmes appear to be less effective with the older age range, i.e. the 14–20-year-olds with regard to reducing parental laxness and over-reactivity than it is for the 8–13-year-olds. A weakness of the study is that it provides no empirical data about the impact on the young people's behaviour, relying on parental perception instead. It is perhaps interesting to note in this respect that the Triple P programme for the younger age group has shown a high level of success through evaluation whereas there is much less robust evidence for 'Teen Triple P' (Ghate *et al.* 2008).

There have been a number of research reviews that have helped to identify a range of promising parenting interventions in the UK as well as in other countries (Smith 1996; Barlow 1997; Lloyd 1999; Communities that Care 2001; Sutton *et al.* 2004). These include pre-natal services, home visiting services and group-based parenting programmes. They have tended to focus either on parents of younger children or parents of children with special needs such as learning disabilities. In 2004, the Home Office and DfES published a review of the international evidence of emerging effectiveness in parenting support (Moran *et al.*). This identified promising approaches in parenting support, what is still not known about effectiveness in this field and the implications these findings have for policy. In respect of promising approaches in practice, they identified the following:

- Both early and later interventions may produce positive outcomes.
- Interventions should have a strong theoretical base.
- Interventions should have measurable objectives and defined mechanisms of change.
- Universal interventions (primary prevention at the community level) should be used for less severe parenting problems.
- Targeted interventions should be used for more complex parenting difficulties.
- Programmes should pay close attention to getting, keeping and engaging parents.
- Programmes should use multi-methods of service delivery.
- Interventions should be delivered by appropriately trained staff, backed by good management and support.
- Behavioural interventions are helpful for changing complex parenting behaviours and impacting on child behaviours.

- Cognitive interventions may help in changing beliefs, attitudes and self-perceptions as to parenting.

- Interventions should work in parallel (though not necessarily at the same time) with parents, families and children.

With regard to reconviction rates among children and young people whose parents have attended a parenting programme, evaluation of YJB-sponsored programmes found that during the year after parents had left the programme, reconviction rates had dropped to 61.5 per cent (a reduction of nearly one-third), offending had dropped to 56 per cent and the average number of offences per young person had dropped to 2.1 (a 50 per cent reduction). While these look promising on the surface, caution should be exercised. The evaluators themselves acknowledge that it is hard to say whether the programme alone was responsible for this as the intervention was only a part of a range of interventions. Furthermore, there was no control group to provide comparative data for the group studied.

Evaluation of the impact of Family Intervention Programmes (FIPs) shows positive improvements across a wide range of dimensions, including reducing anti-social behaviour and the number of juvenile-specific orders and pre-court juvenile-specific actions (DCSF 2009). FIPs work with the most challenging families and tackle issues such as anti-social behaviour, youth crime, school non-attendance, drug and alcohol misuse, domestic violence, mental health difficulties and inter-generational disadvantage. Families are supported by a dedicated 'key worker' who coordinates a multi-agency package of support and works directly with family members to help them overcome problems. The evaluation shows that the proportion of families not involved in anti-social behaviour had increased to 66 per cent compared with 10 per cent at the start; juvenile-specific orders were reported for 10 per cent compared with 12 per cent at the start; and the number of juvenile-specific actions had reduced from 6 per cent of families at the beginning to 3 per cent at the end.

This study focused on information provided about 699 families who had completed a programme. It should be noted that it does not include data from the 367 families (16 per cent of all those offered an intervention) who refused to engage at different stages of the FIP intervention. The study states that these families left 'because they had achieved positive outcomes or because changes in family circumstances meant that the FIP could no longer work with the family (e.g. because they had moved from the area, because it was decided that the family were too high-risk for FIP workers to continue working with them, because the family were no longer living together as a family unit or because children had been taken into care' (p. 8). Further investigation of this group would be useful in terms of learning more about whom this kind of intervention works with and, importantly those with whom it does not work in order to establish whether this is an approach that has promise for the work YOTs do with families.

The evaluation of YJB-sponsored parenting programmes did provide information about project implementation issues, about who received services, their level of need, their satisfaction with the services provided and their perception of the changes that had taken place as a result of participating in the programme. On exit from the projects, parents reported positive changes in parenting skills and competencies, including:

- improved communication with their child;

- improved supervision and monitoring of young people's activities;

- reduction in the frequency of conflict with young people and better approaches to handling conflict when it arose;

- better relationships, including more praise and approval of their child and less criticism and loss of temper;

- feeling better able to influence young people's behaviour;

- feeling better able to cope with parenting in general.

(Ghate and Ramella 2002)

The nature of parenting support provided by YOTs varies considerably. Pickburn et al. (2005) identify the following broad types of support:

- Service delivery – a programme of activities which address areas of the parent–child relationship that are causing difficulty (dealing with conflict and challenging behaviour, constructive supervision and monitoring, and boundary setting, for example).

- Family therapy.

- Group work programmes – where groups of parents come together to participate in a programme of activity.

- Multi-media cognitive-behavioural programmes – where a range of media is used.

- Parent adviser – where an adviser offers counselling and guidance in the home.

- Parent mentor – which involves the linking of a parent with a volunteer mentor.

Some of these interventions may be delivered directly by practitioners in the YOT, although some of them are likely to be services offered through external agencies or the voluntary sector.

Moran et al.'s (2004) assessment of the available research into parenting programmes highlighted a number of significant gaps in the research literature. In terms of types of intervention, less is known about the impact of some types of open access or universal services than those that target a specific type of user. They also report a significant lack of research that is focused on the views of children and young people, which is ironic given that the ultimate aim of parenting programmes is to effect change that impacts on them. A notable exception to this is the evaluation of the YJB-sponsored parenting programmes where 300 young people were interviewed, reporting slight but statistically insignificant improvements in communication with and mutual understanding, supervision and monitoring by their parents, a reduction in frequency of conflict and better relationships (Ghate and Ramella 2002).

Overall, much less is known about the medium- to long-term impact of parenting interventions, with research tending to focus on the short-term outcomes and outputs. In addition, while there is a substantial focus on parenting support that identifies risk factors, there is much less on support services that focus on building protective factors.

Further, Moran et al. (2004) highlight some issues relating to diversity in relation to the available evidence base. All the research about who attends parenting programmes indicates that the overwhelming majority of interventions primarily serve white women (Ghate and Ramella 2002; Asmussen et al. 2007). The reasons for this are likely to be complex and reflect certain societal and cultural perceptions about who does the parenting in a family. The impact on the available evidence base is significant as it means that most evaluation samples contain too few men to be able to draw any conclusions about promising approaches for fathers and whether these are different from promising approaches for mothers.

The same is therefore true of ethnically diverse groups of parents. The evaluation of the YJB-sponsored parenting programmes showed that most of the parents who attended the services were white British (96 per cent). Butt and Box (1998) found a low rate of participation by black families in parenting services offered at family centres that seemed to result from the inability of the services to engage with them. A number of reviews also identify a lack of materials and culturally sensitive programmes (Roker and Coleman 1998; Butt and Box 1998).

There is very little available research on what works with regard to parents of young people in custody. None of the studies in the YJB's systematic review of parenting interventions shows outcomes for this group (Ghate et al. 2008).

There is some evidence about the cost-effectiveness of parenting interventions, although it should be noted that most of it is from the USA. Two studies focusing on the effects of targeting anti-social behaviour highlight the cost-effectiveness of multidimensional treatment foster care (Moore et al. 2001) and multi-systemic treatment (Borduin et al. 2000). A more recent American study looked specifically at the cost of crime to the taxpayer and victims of crime in Washington and established that functional family therapy (shown to achieve a recidivism rate of 18.1 per cent) could achieve a cost saving of nearly $50,000 per young person (Drake et al. 2009). Evaluation of six Anti-social Behaviour Intensive Family Support Projects reported considerable cost savings by comparing the average annual cost of delivering a project of between £8,000 and £20,000 with the estimated annual cost to the taxpayer for those families who did not participate of £250,000 to £350,000 (DCLG 2006).

The principles of effective practice and parenting

Risk classification

It is likely that higher levels of parental stress are experienced by the parents of young people who are committing crimes more persistently or who commit more serious crimes, although this may not be true in all cases. Where it is, it could imply that the more intensive responses to parenting are likely to be required by those parents.

Families of young people with long histories of challenging behaviour, starting in early childhood, may need different interventions from those whose young people commence offending during their teenage years. In practice, the longer the history of difficulty, the more intensive the intervention may need to be and the more it could be necessary to involve the wider family.

Parent assessment and referral are crucial elements in the success of parenting interventions. In particular, the existence of clear and rigorous protocols, which are understood by all agencies involved in the assessment and referral process, may be important for the success of parenting interventions. All involved agencies may need to have a stake in producing, communicating and updating assessment and referral systems (Ghate and Ramella 2002).

As has already been identified, there is a range of risk and protective factors that are specific to parenting. It would seem sensible, therefore, to ensure that these underpin the assessment process for parents about to embark on some kind of parenting programme. While the identification of risk factors is important for establishing the areas where a parent might require specific input, so are the protective factors. Identifying protective factors could help to build parents' confidence and reveal the areas on which parenting support can focus.

The levels and types of stress that families are experiencing at a community, family and individual level could also influence the type of support that parents will find most helpful. Practitioners have reported that they have found that they may need to work with a parent individually, for example on strategies to address a housing crisis, before a parenting programme can be considered (Ghate and Ramella 2002).

Criminogenic need

While criminogenic need focuses on young people at risk of offending or reoffending, it can also be applied to the parents of these young people. The issue here would seem to be about the extent to which difficulties with parenting are directly associated with or contribute to the offending behaviour of a young person. The most obvious example here would be where parents or other family members themselves are offending, which can be assessed as having a direct impact on young people.

Where parenting can be seen to be an issue but is more distantly related to the offending behaviour of a young person, there may be a need to refer parents to another agency or organisation for support. This could help to ensure that interventions ultimately aimed at preventing offending are properly targeted and focused.

While this principle as applied within the context of youth justice would suggest that the content of a parenting intervention should focus on the reduction of risk factors for offending behaviour as identified through *Asset*, it does not necessarily mean that the content of programmes should focus entirely on what is going wrong. The YJB source document for parenting highlights the fact that some of the most successful work in the area of parenting as identified from the wider literature on parenting support utilises a strengths based approach, which would suggest that such interventions are more likely to be successful if they also focus on a family's strengths and positive aspects of family life (Ghate *et al.* 2008). This is further reinforced by Asmussen *et al.*'s (2007) finding that parents will not attend services that they perceive as judgemental or stigmatising, which suggests that the content and approach to parenting interventions should aim to validate parents' experiences rather than focus on their inadequacies.

Dosage

As with any intervention, the intensity and duration of a parenting intervention needs to reflect the seriousness of the difficulty being experienced. Families experiencing high levels of stress are likely to require more support over longer periods of time (Asmussen *et al.* 2007). Programmes that are too short in these cases may simply open up issues and difficulties and leave parents feeling they know or can do even less than at the start of it. Conversely, there is a risk that drawing parents into the youth justice system as part of inappropriately lengthy programmes may create dependency by the parent on practitioners within it. In addition, it may result in the labelling of whole families, making them the target of more scrutiny than other families.

It is interesting to note that parents taking part in the YJB-sponsored parenting programmes (Ghate and Ramella 2002) felt that the eight-week courses they were attending were on the whole too short. While this is self-report information, it would indicate the need to consider both the exit strategies utilised at the end of programmes and, in some cases, referral to further support, possibly separate from the YOT.

One of the issues for ensuring that parents get the appropriate dosage (i.e. the intensity and regularity of inputs required to meet the identified need) may be ensuring they attend in the first place and then helping them to maintain their attendance at sessions or appointments. The following have been found to be promising in these respects:

- At least one initial home visit, even where services are to be delivered entirely in another location, was found to be effective within the 'Strong African American Families Programme' (Brody *et al.* 2006).

- Follow-up reminders by phone or letter can reduce the likelihood of parents not attending a first appointment (Staudt 2003).

- Telephone calls to clarify what is going to happen and to discuss concerns both prior to and after an initial visit to a service (Forehand and Kotchick 2002).

- Requiring some parents to invest time in completing various forms and assessment questionnaires before a first visit (although, conversely, for a minority of parents this may also be a barrier to engagement) (Staudt 2003).

- Warning parents that they may be demoted to the bottom of a waiting list for services if they miss a specified number of appointments. It is interesting to note that rewards for attendance were less effective in encouraging attendance (Parrish *et al.* 1986).

- Making attendance mandatory through, for example, a Parenting Order.
  (Ghate and Ramella 2002)

Responsivity

The primary purpose of a parenting intervention is to enable parents to learn new skills and strategies for approaching their relationships with children and, in some cases, others around them. Interventions may also simply reassure parents that they are doing the best they can. Engaging parents and families in any intervention may be regarded as the key to successful outcomes. If parents are not engaged they are unlikely to participate fully in any change process. See Chapter 3 on engagement.

Barriers to engagement identified by parents include:

- negative experiences of 'helping agencies'/holding low expectations with respect to the help on offer;

- negative experiences of education and fear that parenting support will involve 'classes' and being taught 'how to be a good parent' (sometimes fed by media messages);

- the preconceptions or lack of understanding among other agencies/ referrers about the nature of parenting education and support so that an unclear picture is given;

- anger at 'being punished' or blamed for the young person's behaviour, in particular for those parents on Parenting Orders;

- being ashamed or feeling stigmatised by the requirement to attend parenting interventions;

- reluctance to share sensitive experiences with others/confidentiality/privacy issues;

- programme/facilitator insensitivity to cultural diversity;

- language, literacy, disability issues not addressed;

- lack of clear information about the service, i.e. how to get to the venue, the availability of childcare, transport and so on.

(Elliott *et al.* 2002)

Just as young people present with a wide range of existing skills and needs, so do parents. In addition to a menu of support options available, the responsivity principle would imply that further flexibility is likely to be required in three main areas.

Firstly, the mode of delivery may be important in responding to the needs of parents at particular points in an intervention. Some parents are likely to benefit from working with a group of parents. The added value of such a group approach might be the mutual support of other parents who are experiencing difficulties with their children. For some parents this group approach may well be threatening. This is more likely to be the case where parents are insecure about their own learning skills, in particular where reading and writing are concerned. For some one-to-one work, particularly to start with, might be more appropriate in terms of building confidence and responding to significant need.

Secondly, the medium of delivery would seem to be important in terms of ensuring parents can access the programme and have the opportunity to develop a range of new strategies. Evaluation of YJB-sponsored programmes suggested that parents on the whole preferred approaches that:

- avoided formal, classroom-style delivery;

- avoided over-reliance on written materials;

- used interactive methods such as audio-visual material, role-play, discussion and debate.

(Ghate and Ramella 2002)

Variation in presentational style may be important in maximising the opportunity for behavioural change. 'Information alone has not been found to have an impact on behaviour unless combined with discussion time, experiential practice, role-playing and homework to solidify behavioural changes' (Kumpfer 1993). Varying learning methods also helps to reflect the diversity of participants and their life experiences. Whatever the content of the programme, it may be important to note that 'the factor that is likely to make the programme most effective is the skill of the facilitator in understanding group needs and process and being able to use groupwork skills to provide an optimum environment for learning and change to take place' (Howell and Montuschi 2002).

A significant number of adults experience difficulties with literacy and numeracy (Williams *et al.* 2003). Given the high proportion of young people in the youth justice system who experience such difficulties and the established correlation with parents who struggle with basic skills, it is likely that the need may well be more widespread and entrenched than in the general population. Careful attention may therefore need to be given to the way in which materials are presented (Moran *et al.* 2004; Asmussen *et al.* 2007). This extends beyond written materials to the presentational style of practitioners.

Thirdly, the content of support is likely to be an important consideration in terms of responding appropriately to parents' needs. The core elements of many parenting programmes could be categorised under the headings shown in Figure 7.1.

Some of the parents involved in the YJB-sponsored parenting programmes requested additional topics that it was not possible to cover in the courses they attended. These core elements may, therefore, be supplemented with additional topics relevant to the parents, such as alcohol and other drug misuse, step-parenting issues, divorce and separation.

A Parentline Plus (2006) consultation concluded that minority ethnic parents do not wish to be treated differently from other parents seeking support but would like services to show an understanding and respect for their culture and value-system. This suggests that group workers may need to consider how their programme will reflect participants' different cultural backgrounds and ethnicity in the way that the programme is structured, in its content and in the materials used. It may also be helpful to provide culturally or ethnically specific groups to engage parents. Establishing links with different community groups and services may help to extend the range of programmes that can be provided for different groups within a locality. Another issue to consider is how to make programmes accessible and engaging for parents whose first language is not English.

Many evaluations of parenting programmes highlight the difficulties they experience in recruiting and retaining fathers (Ghate and Ramella 2002; Asmussen *et al.* 2007). This means consideration will need to be given to fathers, both in terms of attracting them into programmes and also being responsive to them when they do attend. One promising model funded by the Home Office sought to engage fathers through providing sporting activities for fathers and their children. The project provided formal or informal parenting support to the fathers. The evaluation of the project concluded that 'Using sport and recreational activities as a strategy to engage fathers was a successful approach with fathers from different ethnic and class backgrounds' (Richardson and Roker 2002). A note of caution should be sounded here with regard to stereotyping fathers and sons as all being motivated by sport and projects may wish to look more closely at the ways in which fathers would like to learn. See Chapter 3, pp. 85–6 on sport and engagement.

Knowledge:	Skills:
Adolescent behaviour – child development	Communication – active listening
Parenting styles – authoritarian, permissive, authoritative	Conflict resolution – assertiveness, negotiation
Cultural background – influence on parenting role	Boundary setting – 'I' statements, behaviour charts
Resources – accessing all sorts of support, friends, specialist agencies	Problem-solving – family meetings, generating options
Attitudes:	**Experience:**
Discipline methods – alternatives to use of physical punishment	Own adolescence – how past impacts on present and connecting up
Being a parent – responsibilities and rights and social context	Sharing own experience of promising approaches – why, what, when, who, where and how
Being a teenager – responsibilities and rights and social context	
Potential for change – belief and indicators that change is possible	

Figure 7.1 Core elements of parenting programmes
Source: Lindfield and Cusick (2001).

Community based

In the same way as learning is likely to take place in contexts that are meaningful to a young person, the same is likely to be true for their parents. Parenting programmes are intended to promote behaviour change and it may be advisable for them to be rooted in the experiences and life contexts of the parents taking part and those of the young people they care for. On one level it would imply that how, where and when parenting programmes are offered could be important, particularly with regard to ensuring that parents will turn up in the first place, but also that they will maintain their attendance for the duration of the programme. The evaluation of the YJB-sponsored parenting programmes also found that a home visit prior to starting work with a parent was felt to be important in terms of dispelling hostility and any anxieties parents were experiencing about attending a programme (Ghate and Ramella 2002).

The other issue that arises from the community-based principle is the potential for focusing too heavily on parenting and family interventions. This may serve to place a burden of responsibility on a family that ignores the impact and influence of the wider community on a young person's offending behaviour and any difficulties families may be experiencing (Morrow 1999).

The principle of community base may pose particular difficulties when applying it to young people who are in custody, where ties with home are fractured, often physically (young people are removed from the home), geographically (many young people are in facilities a long way from home which militates against regular family visits) and emotionally (the stigma and shock of a young person going to prison provides added stress to many parents/carers). In addition, parents may have high expectations that things will have changed when a young person returns from custody, which is contrary to available evidence about the impact of a custodial intervention on a young person after they have returned to their communities (ECOTEC 2001b; Hazel *et al.* 2002).

As has already been established, there are no robust studies that focus on parenting interventions with this group (Ghate *et al.* 2008). There is also little evidence that parenting support is deeply rooted in secure estate culture, where the focus is mainly on dealing with young people and not their parents. An analysis of the experiences of 15–18-year-olds in prison (Tye 2009) reveals that only 35 per cent of young men and 31 per cent of young women felt that it was easy or very easy for their family or friends to visit them. Fifty-six per cent of young men said that they and their family/friends were treated well by visits staff. One study has shown that prisoners who received at least one visit from a family member or partner during custody were statistically significantly more likely to have education, training and accommodation arranged on release (Niven and Stewart 2005). This research also showed that where positive destinations were in place, families or friends were instrumental in organising it in the majority of cases. The researchers point out that family and/or partner visits should be seen here as a proxy measure of strong family ties rather than a factor which directly caused improved outcomes and that other forms of contact may be equally effective in facilitating effective resettlement on release.

Given the significance of consistent and robust family support as a protective factor for offending behaviour and other forms of social exclusion such as homelessness (Thomas 2008), it would seem that the active involvement of parents in planning and review meetings held in the secure estate could go some way towards ameliorating this. Where geographical distance is a significant issue, videoconferencing services may provide an opportunity for parents and young people to communicate and for joint planning sessions to take place. The YJB Source Document for Accommodation (Thomas 2008) also suggests that family mediation might help with regard to rebuilding family relationships and increasing the likelihood of young people returning to the family home.

Intervention modality

Findings from research suggest that 'multidimensional' or 'multi-modal' approaches and styles of delivery are likely to be more effective (Utting *et al.* 2007).

It could be argued that there is no one 'correct' model of parenting programme that will address all parents' diverse needs. This suggests that a menu of possible intervention options could be made available to which parents and families can be referred as a result of a thorough assessment of need.

In the early stages of parenting work YOTs tended towards the delivery of group programmes for all parents, but over time an array of services has emerged including:

- individual structured programmes;
- systemic family therapy;
- parallel group work with parents and young people;
- groups working with a specific ethnic minority;
- interactive CD-ROM programme;
- telephone support programme;
- parent advisers;
- parent mentors;
- information sessions on drugs and legal issues;
- fathers' groups;
- parent-led support groups.

It may be advisable for projects to clarify parents' expectations with them, so that it is clear what they can reasonably expect to be achieved. In addition, parents may need to be informed of the full range of services that are available to them to facilitate their informed participation. They could also be given the opportunity to identify helpful programme content as this may give parents more of a sense of ownership of the programme.

Projects are likely to encounter a variety of family structures, with parenting roles provided by one or two parental figures, step-parents, adoptive parents, non-resident parents, foster carers, grandparents and same-sex parents.

Knowing about the way in which a family is structured may be crucial to providing support, since the strengths the family has, as well as the tensions experienced and related needs, may be directly related to its structure. The effectiveness of the support provided to families is likely to be influenced by the ability of the practitioner to work with the strengths of their family structure and to acknowledge and help the family to address the tensions.

There are social, psychological, emotional and relationship pressures that may be linked to the way in which a family has been created and is structured. Understanding the key relationships within families will help parents and practitioners to identify the most appropriate services to provide, as well as who should be involved in any programme.

Programme integrity

Many of the parenting programmes sponsored by the Youth Justice Board appeared to experience difficulties in recruiting and training sufficiently skilled staff to work directly with parents (Ghate and Ramella 2002). The evaluation also found that practitioners working on parenting programmes had most success when they were freed from other responsibilities and when there was strong support from the YOT managers. This may be a consideration with regard to ensuring programme integrity is maintained for parenting interventions offered directly by a YOT.

With regard to monitoring parenting interventions effectively, the evidence from the USA indicates that there should be procedures for the systematic gathering and analysis of throughput, output and outcome data (Brody *et al.* 2006). This is particularly important for YOTs where parenting services are commissioned or brokered through other agencies or organisations. Careful monitoring of inputs, processes and outcomes of these interventions for the parents and families of young people at risk of offending and reoffending would seem important here. In addition, clear protocols and agreements about what these services will provide are likely to be important, particularly with regard to assessment and referral systems.

Once the parenting project has established aims and objectives, a steering group, clear protocols and agreements on working with other agencies' assessment and referral systems, and a range of services for parents and families, it needs to be publicised in order to reach parents and colleagues who will refer to the service.

The lack of promotion of a project may result in:

- too few parents being referred;

- group programmes having insufficient numbers to run effectively;

- ultimately parents not benefiting from support when they need it.

This has happened in some areas where YOTs have been in partnership with a voluntary agency to provide parenting services. Without sufficient knowledge or ownership of the parenting project within the YOT, workers have not regularly assessed parents' needs and referred them on to the voluntary agency. Alternatively, they may have referred parents but not known enough about what is on offer to sufficiently motivate and engage the parent to keep appointments with the provider agency. This appears to have resulted in partnership projects breaking down and parents not gaining access to the services that they require (Ghate and Ramella 2002).

At the end of any programme of intervention, it is important to review the progress made and to identify any unmet needs that parent(s) and other family members may have. A final review might involve practitioners who have worked with the family (whether from the YOT or partner agency) and the parent(s) and other family members who have been involved in the programme. As has already been established, reviews and evaluations sometimes ignore the views of young people. It may be appropriate to carry out one review with a young person and another with their parents plus a joint review involving both parents and young people. This may be necessary when confidential issues that are not shared between parent and child need to be discussed. In summary, evaluation of outcomes need to be 'parent-focused, child-focused and parent and child focused' (Ghate *et al.* 2008: 4).

Parents' own views, in terms of what has happened as a result of participating in a programme contribute to decisions about whether change is necessary to achieve the objectives which have been set. Dissatisfaction with service provision could indicate that change is necessary, and responding to views expressed by parents could lead to a more effective delivery of support. Parents participating in a consultation process identified some changes they felt were necessary in order to meet their needs:

- Increase numbers in the group as not enough participants.

- Facilitators should explore their own values and beliefs with regard to parental responsibility so that their values don't clash with ours as parents.

- Programme not to focus on being too educational.

- Need for variety in group, i.e. others experiencing similar problems.

- Programmes need to be longer and follow-up programmes should be available.

(Elliott *et al.* 2002)

This is also an issue shared with wider parenting services. Some of the reasons identified for the low levels of engagement of fathers are the lack of father-friendly services (Lloyd 2001), undervaluing of the role of fathers (Burgess 2002), and the focus on mothers in assessment of parental need (Cusick 2001).

There is not enough data to be clear about the over- or under-representation of black and minority ethnic parents in Parenting Order figures and in voluntary involvement in parenting programmes provided by YOTs. It appears from a survey conducted by the Trust for the Study of Adolescents (TSA) that the proportion of black mothers receiving parenting services reflects the over-representation of young black people in the youth justice system. The lack of comprehensive ethnicity monitoring by YOTs and their parenting service is an issue that appears to need addressing.

The challenges for practice

A challenge that faces projects at the outset, and in terms of sustaining them, is how to ensure maximum awareness of services to those making referrals to them (Ghate and Ramella 2002). Without such awareness, referrals are likely to be low and may ultimately jeopardise the sustainability of a parenting programme. This would imply that projects need to be proactive in advertising and readvertising the service. A number of successful strategies have been identified, including practitioners who are working on parenting projects talking directly with court and YOT staff, leafleting and getting the project featured in the local media (Ghate and Ramella 2002).

For parents who are referred to programmes as a result of a Parenting Order, there may well be additional work to be done at the outset to get their commitment to engage with it fully. This is likely to need to focus on reducing their anger, humiliation, confusion or frustration regarding the court process itself and decoupling this from the potential of the intervention being offered to support them in ways that recognise their strengths and the positive aspects of family life.

Another significant challenge is the low numbers of fathers attending parenting programmes. Over the last few years, though, there has been an increasing recognition of the positive role that fathers can have in parenting and in family life. Parenting support services have begun to reflect this wider societal change and increasingly to work on engaging fathers in parenting programmes. The challenge for practice remains with regard to finding innovative ways of attracting fathers to programmes and to ensuring their full participation over time.

The challenge relating to accessibility also includes parents from black and ethnic minority groups. Staff working in rural areas may find that resources that are specifically geared to black and minority ethnic groups are harder to access. In this case, it may be important to address the realities and effects of racism and cultural isolation for black and minority ethnic families who may be isolated in a majority white environment.

The concept of providing a menu of options for parents may also have significant resource implications for YOTs. Further, the monitoring and evaluation of programmes brokered or commissioned from other agencies/ organisations as part of that menu will be a challenge for youth justice practitioners, particularly in ensuring that they are achieving the desired outcomes for parents and ultimately for the young people themselves. Linked to this is the inherent difficulty of how to measure the impact of a parenting programme on a young person.

Summary

- Parenting and family support programmes have become an increasingly important plank of government responses to reducing social exclusion, anti-social behaviour and youth offending in particular.

- Research has highlighted four major features of family life associated with the offending behaviour of young people: parental and sibling criminality;

parental neglect, including lack of supervision; chronic family conflict, either between partners or between parent and young person; and harsh or erratic discipline.

- A number of parenting behaviours have been identified as protective factors against young people becoming involved in offending. These are the use of positive discipline methods, active monitoring and supervision, supportive parent–child relationships, families who advocate for their children, and parents who seek information and support.

- There are two routes into a parenting programme. One is voluntary referral and the other a requirement of the court to attend through a Parenting Order. The introduction of the Parenting Order has been controversial and there are arguments against it.

- Evaluation has shown that there appear to be promising outcomes with regard to reconviction as a result of the parents attending programmes, although it is hard to say whether the programme alone was responsible for this.

- Research reviews have helped to identify a range of promising parenting interventions in the UK as well as in other countries which include pre-natal services, home visiting services and group-based parenting programmes, although these have tended to focus either on parents of younger children or parents of children with special needs.

- Significant gaps in the available research have been identified, including a failure to consider the views or impact of parenting interventions on young people, the impact of more open-access services, the impact of parenting interventions over the medium and long term, and the efficacy of programmes that focus on protective rather than risk factors.

- More robust research needs to be focused on the impact of parenting interventions on parents who have received Parenting Orders. Research will need to rely on more than the perceptions of parents before the legislation is rejected out of hand as a response to the challenges faced by families.

Further reading

Asmussen, K., Corlyon, J., Hauari, H. and La Placa, V. (2007) *Supporting Parents of Teenagers*. London: DfES.

Ghate, D. and Ramella, M. (2002) *Positive Parenting: The National Evaluation of the Youth Justice Board's Parenting Programme*. London: Youth Justice Board.

Moran, P., Ghate, D. and van der Merwe, A. (2004) *What Works in Parenting Support? A Review of the International Evidence*, Research Report 574. London: DfES.

8

Restorative justice

Restorative justice has received much interest and publicity as an intervention for young people who have offended and is often an integral part of a number of specific youth justice orders and programmes. Its widespread appeal politically both in the UK and other countries, it has been suggested, is that it combines both welfarist principles (through the restorative aspect) and justice (Haines and O'Mahony 2006; Hazel 2008). There is, however, emerging reliable evidence for its effectiveness as a useful approach to preventing offending.

This chapter considers the evidence base for restorative justice from England and Wales and from other countries (most notably Australia and America). It further asks questions about where and when restorative justice approaches might be most useful in relation to the prevention of offending. It also considers the tension inherent in restorative justice interventions with regard to who they are for – the young person or the victim of crime?

The evidence base for restorative justice

What is restorative justice?

There is no single definition of restorative justice. There are a number of programmes and practices that could be described as restorative, from conferencing and mediation to court-ordered reparation, victim-impact statements and victim-awareness programmes. In some ways, these programmes are so diverse, it is difficult to identify what each of them has in common that can be called restorative (Roche 2001).

Perhaps the most useful definition of restorative justice is that suggested by Marshall (1999: 5): 'Restorative justice is a process whereby parties with a stake in a specific offence resolve collectively how to deal with the aftermath of the offence and its implications for the future.'

In broad terms, restorative justice processes bring victims and young people who have committed offences into contact, whether directly or indirectly, so that victims can receive answers to their questions, tell the young person what the impact of their offending was and receive an apology. Restorative justice gives young people the chance to take responsibility and make amends for their crime through apologising and making reparation either to the victim or to the community.

Sherman *et al.* (2008) make a distinction between 'restorative justice' and 'restorative practices'. Restorative justice in this sense is a subset of restorative practices which are more generally the attempts that are made to enhance a young person's awareness of the harm they have caused or encourage them to make reparation for that harm. For a restorative practice to be described as 'restorative justice', the victim must have a direct role in deciding how to deal with the consequences of an offence and the young person must agree to trying to 'restore' the victim to the state they were in prior to the offence.

The aim of restorative justice is to repair the harm caused by crime. The most obvious harm is that suffered by victims of crime. Restorative justice also recognises that crime harms society as a whole, and brings the wider community into decision-making to find a way to repair the harm caused by crime.

Restorative justice has been developing in this country and abroad since the mid-1970s. Restorative justice has been a key objective of the youth justice system since 1998, because the evidence suggests that this process can meet the needs of victims in a way that traditional justice processes on their own cannot. The Victims Code of Practice also places a statutory requirement on YOTs to take the needs of victims into account as part of service delivery and restorative justice has a key role to play in this respect. Statutory guidance for the implementation of Referral Orders also requires Youth Offender Panels (YOPs) to operate on restorative justice principles.

The Youth Justice Board has defined the key aims and outcomes of restorative justice as:

- victim satisfaction – reducing victims' fear and ensuring that they feel 'paid back' for the harm done to them;

- engagement with the young person – to ensure that they are aware of the consequences of their actions, have the opportunity to make reparation and agree a plan for their restoration in the community;

- creation of community capital – increasing confidence in the criminal justice system among the public.

The Youth Justice Board has further defined the basic principles of restorative justice as including the following:

- The main objective is to put things right and heal relationships, thereby giving high satisfaction to victims and reducing reoffending.

- Those directly affected by crime are to be involved in the process and their wishes given careful consideration.

- Positive outcomes for the victim and community to be valid objectives alongside change in the behaviour and attitudes of the young person.

185

In 2005/6, YOTs offered victims the opportunity to take part in a restorative justice process in 87 per cent of the 46,000 cases for which victims were identified. Of those, 48 per cent accepted the opportunity.

The Youth Justice Board's evaluation of restorative justice programmes offered by YOTs (Wilcox and Hoyle 2002) identified that restorative practices are used mostly as part of Final Warnings (33 per cent) or Reparation Orders (30 per cent). The Joint Inspection of Youth Offending Teams Annual Report 2005/06 (HMIP 2006) suggests that this is still the case, although the Report also notes that YJB standards require that attention to victims is paid in most other orders as well. This would seem to indicate that restorative interventions tend to be focused on those in the early stages of a criminal career. Wilcox and Hoyle also showed that theft and violent offences (including robbery) accounted for over half of all offences leading to referral and that very few referrals were made for fraud, drugs or sexual offences.

How does it work?

Within youth justice, there are three broad areas where restorative justice work is intended to make a difference through:

- providing benefits to the victims of crime through repairing harm;

- reducing reoffending by individual young people;

- reducing crime in institutional and community settings.

(Sherman *et al.* 2008)

There are a number of ways in which restorative justice might have an impact on reoffending. The restorative process might induce empathy for the victim and counteract any techniques that young people who have offended might use for neutralising feelings of guilt or shame, such as a belief that the victim was not affected by the offence or that the losses were covered by insurance, for example.

The restorative process may also result in young people coming to a better understanding of how their behaviour is upsetting those whom they care about (such as parents/carers) and a strengthening of their resolve to avoid causing such harm in future. It may also result in an agreement which might make offending less likely (where the terms include regular school attendance or the avoidance of risky situations or people).

Where the offending has arisen out of a conflict or where there is a prospect of retaliation, the restorative process may result in defused tension and reduced likelihood of the matter flaring up again. Finally, many see it as crucial that restorative justice insists on treating young people fairly and respectfully. They feel that this makes it more likely that young people who have offended in the past will treat others with fairness and respect in the future. However, much more research is needed before firm conclusions can be drawn concerning the relative importance of these mechanisms in practice.

Models of restorative justice

Restorative justice is founded on a philosophy about how individuals, societies and criminal justice systems can respond to crime and other issues of conflict. The majority of restorative justice theory has been developed to explain the successful outcomes of various models of practice devised in different countries. Restorative justice is a field largely grounded in practice, although research supporting the effectiveness of that practice is emerging.

The most well-known practice models are:

- victim–offender mediation (direct or indirect);
- restorative conferencing;
- community panel meetings.

All these models have a common aim of repairing the harm caused by the crime through balancing the interests of young people who have offended with those of victims and communities.

Whichever model is used, evidence suggests, restorative approaches are appreciated by the majority of those who take part. There is no strong research evidence at present to suggest that any one model of restorative justice is more effective than another in general or in particular circumstances. There is some evidence to suggest that only face-to-face contact with a victim leads to reductions in reoffending. But it is also known that indirect contact through a mediator or facilitator is the only form of restorative justice that is effective for many victims. Examining the benefits of different models of restorative practice is something that needs further research.

There are potential strengths in having a range of models available to meet the needs of particular victims and young people who have offended. All the models of restorative practice appear to be effective in meeting the needs of victims who choose to participate. They are also useful in producing agreements, supported by all of the participants, for reparation work to be undertaken for the community or victims. Agreements made following restorative justice processes are more likely to be completed, and in less time, than those simply ordered by the court.

Victim–offender mediation

Also called 'victim–offender dialogue' and historically called 'victim–offender reconciliation', victim–offender mediation was the first restorative justice model to develop in England and Wales. It is a process whereby a neutral or impartial person assists a victim of crime and the young person who has committed that crime to communicate with each other in the hope of reaching some degree of reconciliation. A face-to-face meeting may take place between the parties, but most cases result in indirect mediation, which may provide victims with answers to their questions and give them reassurance about their safety.

In some countries, it is undertaken as a voluntary addition to the formal response of the criminal justice system. In others (England and Wales among them), it occurs as the response of the criminal justice system. In the latter case, it sometimes constitutes all or part of a sentence, or results in the case being diverted from the system.

In this model, the actual focus of any indirect or direct mediation session is driven primarily by the parties involved, not the mediators. The mediator's role is to prepare the parties so that they are clear about what it is they wish to discuss, and are able to do so in as productive a manner as possible.

Restorative conferencing

Restorative conferencing was initially developed to provide a more effective cautioning experience for young people in New South Wales, Australia. Conferences tend to follow a similar structure to that suggested for panel meetings and the facilitator often has a 'script' of questions to follow to guide the discussion. The main differences between this model and victim–offender mediation relate to the role of the facilitator, the use of a set structure or script, and the number of people who are involved in a conference.

Whereas victim–offender mediation tends to focus on the interaction between the primary victim and the young person who has offended only, the conferencing model generally involves more people. This is based on the view that young people need to understand the wider impact of their offence (for example on a victim's family and on their own family), and that these 'secondary victims' also need restoration and can benefit from the restorative process.

Developed initially in New Zealand, family group conferencing allows the family (on the basis of information from the victim, young person and professionals at the conference) to create an action plan intended to address the consequences of past offending and prevent further offending. In New Zealand, family group conferences are also used to form the core contents of sentences or as a means of diverting young people from the criminal justice system. A key distinguishing feature of family group conferencing is the use of private family time to develop plans which are then brought to the wider conference.

At a restorative family group conference, the victim is a key participant and contributor. They must be given advice and support, and helped to attend and present their 'story'. The victim is present during the first stage of the family group conference and withdraws, together with the profes-sionals, to leave the family to plan in private. The family has responsibility for determining the most appropriate responses to offending by a young person and for making proposals for reparation. The victim rejoins the conference, with the professionals, to hear the family's plans. In this sense, this model could not be seen to be a form of restorative justice in that the victim is not directly involved in making decisions about how the issues will be resolved.

Community panel meetings

A community panel meeting is a legislative requirement following a Referral Order. A young person is required to attend a panel meeting composed of at least two community volunteers, a member of the YOT and a parent/carer (if the young person is under the age of 16). Victims may also be invited to attend or be asked to contribute in other ways if they want to. An agreement or contract is drawn up and it is an expectation that the agreement will contain an element of reparation.

Indirect mediation

Some victims may be interested in communicating with the young person who committed the offence against them but may not want to meet them face to face. In these cases indirect communication is facilitated, usually in writing, through third parties.

Reparation

Reparation refers to those general processes whereby young people undertake activities which 'repair harm' which may or may not involve a direct victim. Exclusion of the victim from a reparation process, however, means that it cannot be classed as restorative justice.

While these broad distinctions between different restorative approaches are useful, the reality is that programmes offered across the youth justice system in England and Wales vary widely in terms of what is offered and the level to which they might be described as restorative.

It can be seen from Table 8.1 that, unlike some other interventions within youth justice, the prevention of offending is not the only aim of restorative justice. The repair of harm, including harm to relationships, is also important. Restorative justice entails a different way of working, with a different focus to other interventions, whereby the measures of effectiveness comprise measures of victim satisfaction as well as measures of recidivism.

Restorative justice and reducing reoffending

Internationally, a number of evaluations have now been conducted of different schemes for restorative justice (see McCold and Wachtel (2002) and Sherman et al. (2008) for a comprehensive review).

In Canberra, Australia, young people who had offended were randomly assigned to court or to a restorative justice conference. Sherman et al. (2000)

Table 8.1 Types and degrees of restorative justice practice

Fully restorative	Mostly restorative	Partly restorative
Family group conference	Victim–offender mediation	Compensation
Community conferencing	Victim support circles	Victim services
Peace circles	Victimless conferences	Offender family services
Restorative conference	Therapeutic communities	Family-centred social work
	Direct reparation to victim	Victim awareness
		Community reparation

Source: McCold and Wachtel (2002).

concluded that the effect of diversionary conferences was to cause a significant drop in offending rates by young people who had committed violent crimes (by 38 crimes per 100 young people per year), a small increase in drink-driving offences (by six crimes per 100 young people per year) and no difference in repeat offending by young people committing offences against property or shoplifting. These findings have been treated by some as justification for 'targeting' restorative justice at young people who commit violent crimes. However, it should not be assumed that findings from one jurisdiction (whether positive or negative) will hold good elsewhere.

Evaluations of family group conferences in New Zealand have shown a positive impact in terms of reducing reoffending, with some areas showing a reduction of a third annually (cited in Masters 2005). There have not been many attempts at family group conferencing in England and Wales, although one project in Essex which mimics the New Zealand model in working with the 20 per cent of young people committing the most serious of offences, has shown reductions in reoffending (Masters 2005).

McGarrell *et al.* (2000) studied an Indianapolis experiment in which young people who had committed only one offence were randomly assigned to either a restorative justice conference or to the normal range of diversion programmes. Rearrest was 40 per cent lower in the conference group than in the control group after six months, an effect that declined to a 25 per cent reduction after 12 months.

Studies of various restorative justice programmes in the UK are less conclusive in relation to the impact on reducing offending. In a UK study of restorative cautioning,[1] Hoyle *et al.* (2002) went further than most in that they studied rates of self-reported offending rather than relying on the usual proxy measure for reoffending of reconviction or rearrest. They found a substantial aggregate move towards desistance, calculating that young people who went through a restorative caution were half as likely as those experiencing the traditional police caution to be re-sanctioned within a one-year follow-up period. This study did not involve random assignment and the sample size was small, i.e. below significant levels.

Overall, while reviewers of the available evidence differ in their precise conclusions, they are in agreement that restorative justice programmes rarely make reoffending worse and often achieve more positive results than other types of intervention (Latimer *et al.* 2001; Umbreit *et al.* 2001; Braithwaite 2002; McCold and Wachtel 2002).

In the UK, Wilcox and Hoyle (2002) evaluated 46 restorative justice projects funded by the Youth Justice Board. Here they found a reconviction rate over 12 months of 31.4 per cent for those undergoing restorative justice programmes compared to 33.3 per cent for a comparator sample. While there was no statistically significant difference in outcome between the samples, young people who had met the victim of their offence were the least likely to be reconvicted, as were those who had victim awareness intervention.

A further 12-month follow-up of the cohorts (Wilcox *et al.* 2004) found the size of the effect much reduced. No statistically significant difference in outcome was found between the two approaches. Moreover, the style of caution used had no impact on seriousness or frequency of subsequent reoffending. Restorative approaches, however, did have substantial benefits for victims and young people who had offended in terms of raising awareness and 'closing' the issue.

A recent study of restorative justice interventions suggests that in general they seem to reduce crime more effectively with more, rather than fewer, serious crimes, in particular with crimes involving personal victims and with violent crimes as opposed to property crimes (Sherman and Strang 2007). Their conclusions though are drawn from a mixed sample of adult, youth and international studies. Only one of the examples relating to violent crime featured young people from the UK (young women from Northumbria) and similarly, out of the four RCTs relating to property crime, only one referred to young people under the age of 18 in the UK (Shapland *et al.* 2004, 2006, 2007, 2008). It is the studies included in Sherman and Strang's 2007 report which largely form the background of analysis for the YJB's 2008 Source Document on Restorative Justice, although this looks exclusively at the data on young people and young adults.

While it is difficult to draw absolute conclusions as to the efficacy of restorative justice in reducing offending or reoffending by young people in England and Wales, the emerging evidence would tend to suggest that it is more likely to be effective where crimes are more violent and serious in nature. Given the current emphasis on certain forms of restorative justice as part of very early interventions for less serious crimes, this begs a question as to how useful this approach is.

Although considerable emphasis is given in guidance to restorative approaches to delivering Final Warning interventions, the available evidence as to the superiority of its impact remains equivocal. Wilcox *et al.*'s (2004) two-year study, following up the work of Hoyle *et al.* (2002) comparing the performance of restorative and traditional cautions, found no statistically significant difference on re-sanctioning outcomes between three police forces. Moreover, the style of caution used had no impact on the seriousness and frequency of subsequent offending:

Taking the results of these analyses together, there was no evidence to suggest that the restorative cautioning[1] initiative had resulted in a statistically significant reduction in resanctioning. Importantly, neither was there evidence that restorative cautioning had increased resanctioning rates. (Wilcox *et al.* 2004: vi)

Again, it should be noted that the sample in this study was combined adults and young people with just over one-third being 17 and under. Analysis of the data by age showed no statistically significant benefit of one type of caution over another for this age group.

There is some evidence that the use of restorative approaches in schools can have a positive impact on the levels of bullying behaviour reported in student surveys. Three schools using restorative approaches for three full years as part of the YJB's Restorative Justice in Schools Programme (YJB 2004a) reported lower rates than those in three comparison schools not implementing the principles. However, this finding was not replicated in the 23 schools that only ran the programme for 18 months and represents a very small sample of schools.

There is very little evidence of what constitutes effective practice with regard to the processes involved in restorative justice, for example what works in engaging young people in face-to-face restorative justice or on how to encourage victims to participate in a YOP (Sherman *et al.* 2008). While the available studies from the UK and abroad provide interesting descriptions of the characteristics of cases or the manner in which interventions were delivered, few make comparisons between different approaches. Additionally, there is virtually no reliable evidence on the best methods of implementing indirect mediation in ways that can show effects on recidivism or repairing harm to victims. Similarly, there is little research relating to the effects of reparation schemes, including the implementation of the Reparation Order, for example (Sherman *et al.* 2008).

It is not clear, however, that restorative approaches in England and Wales are always being implemented in ways that capture and reflect the 'spirit' of restorative justice (Crawford and Newburn 2002; Morris 2002). The involvement of victims in the restorative process remains relatively low across the full range of orders that contain an element of reparation, although this appears to be changing. In Dignan's evaluation of four pilot reparation areas in 2002, direct reparation to a victim occurred in only 12 per cent of cases with just 9 per cent resulting in mediation. In 2002, Newburn *et al.* also showed that victim involvement in the Referral Order process was low (Newburn *et al.* 2002) and the Wilcox and Hoyle evaluation (2002) pointed to a reliance on indirect community reparation as opposed to the direct involvement of victims in the restorative process. This balance seems to be shifting, although it is still largely in favour of indirect approaches. In 2005/6, for example, YOT quarterly returns showed that out of all the cases where a victim agreed to participate, just under one-third took part in face-to-face interventions, the remaining two-thirds being involved in indirect restorative practices (Sherman *et al.* 2008).

Some critics also argue that when emphasis is placed on 'the respon-sibilisation of young offenders', the principles of restorative justice will always be derogated (Gray 2005b). It has been argued that in the current climate of youth justice policy, greater priority is placed on getting young people to accept responsibility for their criminal and anti-social behaviour than on seeking to make good the loss and injury to the victims or on seeking a restorative resolution to any conflict. In particular, research which has focused upon discourse analysis of restorative justice conferences and Referral Order panels (Crawford and Newburn 2002; Gray 2005b; Haines and O'Mahony 2006) has highlighted a number of tensions between the spirit of restorative justice and the practice of youth justice decision-making. These tensions include:

- coercive and confrontational approaches used in decision-making forums;

- police-led resolution of the conflict (not victim and young person working out their own resolutions);

- low levels of victim involvement in restorative justice processes;

- lack of resources to deliver effective restorative justice solutions;

- predominant use of community-based reparative schemes rather than individually tailored restorative justice solutions.

Haines and O'Mahony comment:

> The growth in popularity and spread of restorative justice precisely at a time when attitudes towards young people find expression in generally more controlling and/or punitive measures (especially in England and Wales) both rest in, and at the same time expose, the crucial tension within restorative justice to be simultaneously both positive and punitive. In practice, the positive elements are more rhetorical while the punitive expressions are more materially apparent. (2006: 119)

Restorative justice and benefits to victims

Many victims of crime would like an acknowledgement from the young person that they have been wronged, combined with steps to put that wrong right (Strang 2001). These steps might include offers of financial or practical reparation, but more usually an apology is sought, coupled with reassurance that the offence will not be repeated. Victims also often value the chance to hear the young person's explanation of the offence, to voice their own questions, views and feelings about the matter, and to be listened to with respect. This can also be true of others affected by the offence, such as people who are close to the young person or victim, and other members of the community who were affected by the offence. Some models of restorative justice seek to involve these wider 'stakeholders'.

An essential feature of restorative justice programmes is to consider and meet the needs of victims, and possibly to bring about some 'closure' for them regarding the incident. International research has firmly established that such effects are regularly achieved (Marshall and Merry 1990; Maxwell and Morris 1993; Strang 2002; Umbreit 1994; and acknowledged by Utting and Vennard 2000). Victims consistently report that a strong feeling of justice has been delivered to them, and that their levels of anger and distress are often greatly reduced.

In the UK, Hoyle *et al.*'s (2002) in-depth study of 31 victims who participated in a restorative conference found that 68 per cent felt the process had helped the young person to understand the effects of the offence; 71 per cent said they felt better as a result of the meeting and only 3 per cent said that they felt worse. When asked for their overall assessment of the meeting, 97 per cent considered that it had been a good idea. Most of the victims who provided follow-up data in the year following the conference reported a long-term positive (and sometimes substantial) impact on themselves, with none reporting any long-term significant negative feelings. Other participants, including young people who have offended, reported in similarly positive terms, thus indicating that restorative justice can be successful in giving equal weight to the interests of young people who have offended, victims and other participants.

The Oxford University report on the 46 YJB-funded restorative justice projects (Wilcox and Hoyle 2002) found that 79 per cent of victims had been able to put the offence behind them and that seven out of 10 thought that the young person better understood the impact of the offence on the victim. The expectations and orientations of victims prior to conferences vary and there is similar variation in the extent to which they derive benefits from the experience, but few consider it a waste of time (Daly 2003).

Studies also show that there are some kinds of activity that are not valued by victims, in particular apologies that are made under pressure from facilitators (or courts) or that otherwise appear lacking in sincerity (Maxwell and Morris 1993; Strang 2002; Crawford and Newburn 2003).

Restorative justice in the juvenile secure estate

The Youth Justice Board has funded research to establish the scope of restorative work being undertaken within secure establishments (Curry *et al.* 2004). The main finding was that there was little restorative justice intervention of any kind taking place. Some projects, which had previously flourished, were in decline. This was largely due to the pressure of numbers of young people sentenced to custody and secure conditions, and the resulting inability to allocate places within a reasonable distance of the home area. Staff in these settings, however, were broadly sympathetic to the notion of experimenting with restorative approaches to working with young people, especially in relation to tasks such as dealing with bullying and disciplinary matters and in order to bring home to young people the impact of their behaviour on the victims of crime. Questions remain therefore regarding the mechanisms whereby young people would agree to restorative justice before transition into or out of custody, who would be the best person to deliver an intervention (custodial staff or someone from the YOT), and whether and how victims would agree to meet with a young person in secure settings (Sherman *et al.* 2008).

The principles of effective practice and restorative justice

Risk classification

One of the criticisms levelled at the use of a restorative approach has been the extent to which it may draw young people prematurely into the youth justice system. In their review of Police-led Restorative Cautioning Pilots in Northern Ireland, O'Mahony and Doak (2004) report that 80 per cent of cases they examined were for incidents involving property loss of less than £15.00, many of which would normally be dealt with by a simple caution. As has already been shown, restorative justice interventions are more likely to be effective with young people who have committed more serious offences (Sherman and Strang 2007; Sherman *et al.* 2008), which calls into question its use as part of Final Warnings or Referral Orders, notwithstanding some encouraging results from trials in Northumbria (Shapland *et al.* 2006). An implication of this for YOTs might be to suggest using restorative justice in court cases resulting in disposals other than Referral Orders (Sherman *et al.* 2008). The implementation of the scaled approach and the YRO should facilitate this more readily, although it will clearly rely on practitioners making appropriate assessments of risk and considering individualised and evidence-based responses to those risks.

Risk assessment is also relevant when working with the victim and young person and in considering the appropriate type of restorative justice intervention in a case. Even where a young person accepts responsibility for having harmed the victim, there may be other factors that would constitute a risk in promoting communication between them and the victim of crime (where a young person is unable to control their anger or ready to blame the victim for having provoked their behaviour, for example). Risk assessment factors determine whether it is advisable for the victim and young person to meet face to face, or whether a more indirect form of restorative practice would be suitable.

The principle of risk classification highlights one of the tensions inherent in restorative justice already discussed in this chapter, i.e. are the needs of the young person or the victim of crime to take priority when making decisions about whether or not to instigate a restorative process? Taking into consideration the needs of the victim may argue in favour of a restorative process between victim and young person, even if this is not indicated as necessary to reduce reoffending by the young person. An assessment of both parties may determine that a young person who poses very little risk of reoffending might nonetheless be encouraged to participate in a restorative justice intervention because a victim has been significantly affected by the young person's behaviour. It may be harmful to the process if, for example, a person who has been a victim of crime several times over were to blame a young person responsible for only one of those offences for all the harm they have suffered.

Criminogenic need

Again, the contracts made at YOP meetings with young people who have offended should include programmes identified to address the factors most closely linked to their offending. A key aim of the subsequent panel meetings during the course of the Referral Order is to monitor young people's completion of these programmes as agreed in their contract with the panel.

Similarly, this principle again relates directly to the choice of restorative justice programme and the need to remain flexible over a period of time. A complexity of criminogenic issues in a case might, for example, favour the use of a family group conference or a YOP, which would allow criminogenic factors to be looked at alongside, or as part of, the communication with the victim.

The principle of focusing on programmes to address young people's criminogenic needs must be balanced with a key tenet of restorative justice, which is that participants play an active role in determining how to respond to an offence. The outcomes from research would suggest that restorative justice practitioners should be wary of taking over the process or setting the agenda. Creative ways of dealing with the risk of reoffending often emerge from interaction among the participants if they are given the space and time to discuss these matters, and 'professional interventions' are not always necessary. At panel meetings this can best be allowed to take place by enabling victim and young person to first suggest what should be in the contract, before contributing the advice from the YOT based on assessment.

From the victim's perspective, there is a danger that focusing on criminogenic needs gives the appearance that the restorative process is weighted too much towards the young person's interests. It may, therefore, be important that a restorative process begins with a clear focus on the victim's needs rather than on the young person's criminogenic needs. It may be much easier for victims to show concern for a young person's future once their own sense of harm and injustice has been acknowledged and addressed. Once this has been achieved, many victims appear keen to help to minimise the risk of reoffending. The structure of restorative conferencing, and the suggested structure for mediation and YOPs, recognises this need to deal with the effect of the crime, thus meeting the victim's needs, before going on to consider the future.

Dosage

A restorative justice approach should not be considered as a one-off intervention but as a flexible process which adapts to changing situations and need. The Referral Order allows for this in follow-up meetings to review the contract. Restorative justice processes should in part be selected based on an understanding of what type of process is most likely to bring about change in the young person (as long as the victim also sees this process as meeting their own needs). It is worth noting that young people who have offended very often voluntarily agree to comply with restorative justice agreements and interventions for longer than a court sentence may require them to.

The dosage principle could also be applied to victims. Where a victim has suffered only minor inconvenience as the result of an offence, a simple letter of apology may be all that is needed for the young person to repair the harm caused. Victims who suffer greatly as a result of the offence may require much more by way of support, preparation and reparation if their needs are to be met through restorative justice.

Responsivity

Restorative justice approaches are suitably flexible that they can be tailored to meet the needs of young people and victims of crime while helping them to develop new strategies for learning and new ways of perceiving things.

A conference with a victim, for example, provides opportunities for young people to consider a range of strategies for effective oral communication. Writing a letter of apology can also be a valuable activity if used as an opportunity to develop new ways for young people to express themselves in writing. In order to maximise the learning from these experiences, practitioners will need to prepare young people effectively and to support them without imposing so much support that it makes the restorative aspect of the activity meaningless.

Notwithstanding the warning against relying too much on community reparation schemes as the main restorative justice response provided, such programmes may provide all kinds of opportunities for incidental learning for young people. Programmes might involve, for example, producing a piece of art to enhance the local area, where the learning outcomes are both directly related to making reparation and to learning a range of skills related to the arts.

Many advocates of restorative justice see one of the key benefits as helping victims to see that young people who have offended rarely live up to the media stereotype of the unfeeling, calculating 'yob'. Related benefits for victims may include reduced fear that they will be victimised again by the same young person, coming to terms with the experience of victimisation and increased confidence in their ability to deal with the aftermath of crime.

Whereas all young people involved within the youth justice system are by definition non-adult, victims may be young children, teenagers, young adults, the middle-aged or the elderly. Allowing victims to negotiate the restorative process in their own way, for example by allowing them to say as little or as much as they want at the point and in the manner they choose, would seem to enhance the prospects that victims will take positive lessons away from the process.

Clearly, being responsive to issues of diversity are pertinent here. While there is no evidence of differential effects for restorative justice for particular ethnic groups in the UK, there is an interesting finding from a study which used face-to-face restorative justice with Australian Aboriginal young people who had been involved in property crime (Sherman *et al.* 2000) where there was a significant *increase* in offending. Sherman *et al.* (2008) posit the theory that 'victim illegitimacy' on the grounds of race could have played a part. It is also noted that the facilitators in the experiment were all white police officers. The sample is too small and the findings unreplicated to draw any hard and fast conclusions from this, but it does suggest that practitioners need to be mindful of the potential effects of these issues when considering appropriate responses to black and minority ethnic young people in England and Wales. The concept of victim legitimacy is a particularly challenging one when considering cases in which there may be issues relating to race, religion, ethnicity or gender.

Community based

Restorative justice processes hold unique potential for involving the wider community as a support for both young person and victim. For example, the YOP brings in community members as part of the restorative process. Restorative conferencing and family group conferencing also involve the wider community. All these forms of restorative practice recognise that the long-term healing or repair of harm for both the victim and the young person may rely on their being supported in their own social and community context in order to move on from the crime.

The use of restorative justice approaches is minimal in the juvenile secure estate. Despite the logistical difficulties involved in this, restorative justice where young people are encouraged to engage with and make reparation in some way to their communities may have the potential to enable secure establishments to better implement the community-based principle in their work with individual young people. This might be achieved through letters of apology, through arranging face-to-face conferencing between young people, victims and families during the custodial phase of a DTO and continuing such work during the community phase or, where facilities exist, through videoconferencing. Victims might also be encouraged to communicate with young people who have committed crimes through similar channels, giving them the same rights and access to restorative justice as victims of young people who remain in their communities.

At the point of release, restorative processes have also been used as forums to make plans addressing the future needs of young people who have offended in the community. Consideration could be given to inviting victims to participate in such forums (whether directly or indirectly), so that any remaining victimisation needs can be addressed alongside criminogenic needs. See also Chapter 10 on the secure estate and resettlement.

Intervention modality

In relation to restorative practice, processes can be both an intervention in their own right *and* a planning tool for further interventions. For example, the YOP could be seen as a restorative process; it is also a planning tool for further interventions as the contract can include a commitment to a further restorative justice process with the victim. As indicated above, the implication for effective restorative practice is that the most appropriate restorative process should be deployed in individual cases.

The multi-modal principle can also be applied to victims. Responses to victimisation are complex and vary from victim to victim. Restorative processes should allow for such complexity and be flexible enough to meet as many of the victim's needs as possible. At the same time, it should not be assumed that a victim–young person encounter could possibly satisfy all of a victim's needs. Victim Support has argued that victims are entitled to: compensation; protection from intimidation or harassment; respect and support from criminal justice professionals; clear information about the progress of their case, the procedures being followed, their role in the process and any rights they may have; the opportunity to give a statement about the full consequences of the offence which is then taken into consideration whenever decisions are made about their case; and to be free of the burden of deciding what should happen to a young person. This list makes it clear that while restorative justice may have an important part to play in meeting the multiple legitimate expectations of victims, it is unrealistic to expect young people who have offended to repair all the harm suffered by victims.

In some respects, it could be argued that the processes involved in a fully restorative process fit a cognitive-behavioural model. The process is designed to get a young person to confront the consequences of their offending behaviour and change their behaviour accordingly. The reliance on practices that can only be described as 'partly restorative' according to the distinctions made by Wilcox and Hoyle (2002) – community reparation, for example – may call into question the extent to which cognitive-behavioural approaches are being fully utilised as part of restorative justice interventions. Interestingly, Wilcox and Hoyle's research also indicated that it was the cognitive-behavioural elements of victim awareness training that had the most lasting impact and not the increased sensitivity to the victim's point of view.

Programme integrity

A key element of programme integrity in relation to restorative justice is ensuring that restorative justice practitioners, including community panel members, are trained to deliver restorative justice to an appropriate standard and that some kind of quality assurance is in place. At the same time, an important part of restorative justice is its flexibility to meet the needs of particular victims and young people who have offended. Each panel contract should be unique, reflecting the decision-making process at that particular panel meeting. This presents a challenge in relation to programme integrity, although, with appropriate recording of key data regarding both outcomes for young people and victims involved in the process, this might be overcome. This would provide youth justice staff with a clearer picture of what kinds of approaches are working, with whom and in what circumstances.

As indicated earlier, low levels of victim involvement in restorative justice to date may be seen to have compromised the integrity of programmes. The research indicates that better outcomes can be achieved from programmes where victims are directly involved, and yet more indirect methods of reparation are routinely used.

Integrity in restorative justice is also about monitoring and supporting young people who have offended to complete the action points agreed in their panel contract, or in an outcome agreement with the victim if the restorative process takes place separately to a panel meeting (for example, as part of a Reprimand or Final Warning). Completing the contract or agreement may be regarded as essential, both for meeting the young person's criminogenic needs and, as indicated above, for meeting the needs of the victim.

For managers, the integrity principle implies that adequate resources and monitoring are crucial to successful restorative justice. This suggests that programmes need to be sufficiently resourced to prepare all participants for the process and have access to adequate interventions to implement the plans drawn up.

The challenges for practice

One challenge for practice is how to increase the level of involvement of victims in restorative justice interventions. This may involve practitioners in looking critically at some of the community reparation schemes they routinely use and asking, in the first instance, whether these are achieving positive outcomes in terms of reducing reoffending and, significantly, whether these are actually helping the victims of crime and the local community in ways that reduce their fear of crime and resentment towards young people.

The research would indicate that the low level of victim participation is not related to an unwillingness on the part of victims to become involved. Where particular effort has been made to involve victims, 60 per cent participation levels have been shown both in this country and in New Zealand (Masters 2005). What studies have shown, however, is a 'cultural resistance' among some youth justice staff who do not see it as a priority in their work and so fail even to contact the victims (Newburn *et al.* 2001; Dignan 2002). This would imply that a shift is required in some areas of organisational culture in order to raise the importance of giving victims the opportunity to participate in some kind of restorative process, both for their own benefit and also to strengthen the potential impact of the experience for young people who have committed crimes.

What the research on what is promising indicates in practical process terms is that victim agreement to participate can be increased if a trained facilitator meets with them face to face to explain how the process works; they are allowed to choose a date or a time for a meeting; they are assured that the facilitator will convene the process and remain present throughout; they think it will help the young person to stop offending; they receive follow-up reminders of meetings; and transport and/or childcare is provided (Wilcox *et al.* 2004; Shapland *et al.* 2004; Sherman *et al.* 2008).

What this 'cultural resistance' might indicate is a lack of appropriate training for staff from both YOTs and the juvenile secure estate in restorative justice. In their evaluation of referral orders, Newburn *et al.* (2001) found that less than a quarter of YOT staff involved in contacting victims and preparing them for community panel meetings considered that they had had adequate training.

Further systemic challenges for practice stem from the speeding up of youth justice processes, which may conflict with the time required to adequately prepare a victim, young people and their parents/carers/other supporters for a meaningful restorative intervention. There is also some evidence that police forces may withhold contact information about victims in the spirit of data protection unless they have had informed consent from the victim themselves, although the *Code of Practice for Victims* (Office for Criminal Justice Reform 2005) attempts to circumvent this.

While restorative justice has underpinned much recent work in youth justice and remains set to do so, the evidence for the efficacy of such approaches in England and Wales (while well received by victims, young people, parents/carers and professionals) with regard to reoffending is uncertain, particularly with regard to ascertaining which processes are most effective, with whom and in what circumstances.

Summary

- Restorative justice is promoted as a core element of youth justice interventions at all stages within the youth justice system.

- The most well-known practice models of restorative justice are victim–offender mediation, restorative conferencing and community panel meetings.

- Studies of restorative justice approaches in other jurisdictions, primarily in Australia and New Zealand, have shown promising outcomes with regard to reducing likelihood of reoffending.

- Studies conducted in England and Wales of restorative justice projects and Referral Orders have shown little impact with regard to recidivism, although evaluations show that they do have a positive impact on and are well regarded by victims of crime.

- There is an inherent tension between the reparative elements of restorative justice approaches and the more punitive elements of the youth justice system which is seen to impose reparation as part of an order rather than a voluntary scheme.

- Despite evidence that suggests approaches that directly involve victims are more promising, levels of victim involvement remain low across the range of restorative interventions.

- Restorative justice interventions seem to reduce crime more effectively when applied to young people who have committed more serious and violent crimes and those involving personal victims.

Note

1   A restorative caution is 'a meeting facilitated by a trained police officer, based around a structured dialogue about the offence and its implications (with active involvement from the offender and the victim, if present)' (Wilcox *et al.* 2004: 1).

Further reading

Crawford, A. and Newburn, T. (2003) *Youth Offending and Restorative Justice: Implementing Reform in Youth Justice*. Cullompton: Willan.

Sherman, L. and Strang, H. (2007) *Restorative Justice: The Evidence*. London: Smith Institute.

9

Offending behaviour interventions

Offending behaviour interventions are designed to prevent (or at least reduce) offending and reoffending by children and young people. Meta-analyses have determined a number of core principles that may make such programmes more effective. They suggest in particular that interventions that contain elements of cognitive behavioural and multi-systemic approaches can achieve significant effect sizes for recidivism. In addition, they highlight a number of interventions that are less likely to work overall.

This chapter provides an overview of cognitive behaviourism and multi-systemic techniques but also urges caution in relying too heavily on these meta-analytical outcomes to provide blanket approaches for young people, on the basis that there are things that are effective for some young people in some circumstances which may not be effective for others in different circumstances.

The evidence base for offending behaviour programmes

In discussing offending behaviour interventions, it is helpful to distinguish three forms of prevention:

- *Primary prevention* – planning and delivery of developmental services to improve the overall life opportunities of disadvantaged communities as a mechanism for long-term crime prevention.

- *Secondary prevention* – intervention with children and families who are considered to be at risk of involvement in offending on the basis of factors associated with the onset of criminal activity.

- *Tertiary prevention* – intervention with those who have already been involved in offending.

Offending behaviour interventions are directed primarily at those young people whose behaviour has brought them to the attention of the youth justice system. Accordingly, they will have received a reprimand or warning as an alternative to prosecution, or will have been convicted by the criminal courts. Offending behaviour work is thus focused at the level of tertiary prevention; that is, it aims to prevent or reduce the seriousness or frequency of further offending by that group of young people who have already been in trouble.

Such interventions are designed to influence the behaviour of young people in a manner that makes it less likely to give rise to further offending. In this respect, the design of an offending behaviour intervention will need to be capable of responding to:

- a broad array of behaviour from the Final Warning stage, where the offending is relatively minor and the young person may not previously have come to police attention, to those young people whose offending is sufficiently serious or persistent to warrant custody or the highest levels of intervention available in a community setting;

- the nature of the offences (e.g. acquisitive, violent or sexual);

- the context in which offending occurs (e.g. premeditated or planned, committed in groups or alone, committed at particular times of the day, under the influence of alcohol or drugs, targeted or random victimisation, motivated by material gain or excitement);

- patterns of offending (e.g. one-off, out of character delinquent act, occasional minor offending, persistent criminality, infrequent serious offences).

Interventions to address offending behaviour therefore vary significantly according to the local offending profile, the category and particular circumstances of the young people for whom the intervention is intended. On this basis, offending behaviour interventions have usefully been defined, in broad terms, as structured, prearranged sequences of opportunities for learning and change designed specifically to have a positive impact on the subsequent recidivism of those young people who take part (McGuire *et al.* 2002).

It is also necessary to stress the breadth of such interventions. In particular, many offending behaviour interventions include elements of cognitive-behavioural and/or multi-systemic approaches and, towards the upper end of the offending scale, may be closely associated with a particular cognitive-behavioural or multi-systemic programme. It is important, however, not to equate offending behaviour interventions with cognitive-behavioural programmes or multi-systemic therapy, since the former describe a much wider range of services.

Effective interventions, particularly for those young people whose offending is more serious or persistent, tend to have a core content, which targets or includes key components addressing young people's ways of thinking and the moral content of their thinking. This training is designed to enhance skills and improve problem-solving capacity, and has a cognitive element. Cognitive-behavioural approaches have become increasingly identified with effective practice in youth justice and are based on the premise that if you can change the way a young person perceives and thinks about his/her social context and his/her actions, then behavioural change is possible. Reported recidivism rates as a result of cognitive-behavioural interventions is between 20 and 30 per cent (Lipsey *et al.* 2000; Landenberger and Lipsey 2005; MacKenzie 2006). More specifically, cognitive-behavioural approaches have been shown to be most effective with young people aged between 13 and 18. Other approaches focusing on parenting may be more likely to have an impact for the younger age group (McCart *et al.* 2006).

As the term suggests, the cognitive-behavioural model derives from a synthesis of two traditions within psychology: behaviourism and cognitive theory. In the former tradition, human behaviour is considered to be a product of learning through interaction with the environment. To explain human behaviour is thus to explain how that learning takes place in interaction with the external world. The model is often described in terms of antecedents, behaviour and consequences: ABCs. In this model, behaviour is influenced by an initial environmental stimulus and previous experiences of the consequences that follow from responding to that stimulus in different ways. Cognitive theory, on the other hand, focuses on the importance of the individual's thought processes, attitudes and beliefs in determining behaviour.

From the mid-1970s onwards, a number of writers began to synthesise the two approaches. This synthesis was supplemented with references to social learning theory, which is concerned with the possibility of learning through observation of others' behaviour. As a consequence, the relationship between individuals' environment, previous experiences and behaviour is understood as being mediated by their thoughts, emotions and beliefs. Before individuals can change their behavioural reactions they need to understand their thought processes and the factors that affect their perceptions and emotions.

It is erroneous to conceive of cognitive behaviourism as a single, unified, theoretical approach. It is best understood as describing a range of methods of intervention. Indeed, McGuire (2000) identified seven different theoretical currents along a spectrum running from behaviour modification (using techniques such as aversion therapy) at one end to cognitive therapy (which aims to correct cognitive distortions or dysfunctional beliefs) at the other. Some of the more commonly used approaches with young people who offend include training in (often in combination):

- anger management;
- behaviour modification;
- cognitive restructuring;
- cognitive skills training;

- moral reasoning;

- relapse prevention;

- social skills training;

- victim impact.

(Wikstrom and Treiber 2008)

The Youth Justice Board's evaluation of cognitive-behaviour projects (Feilzer *et al.* 2004) reported some reduction in reconviction rates for young people who participated. However, it should be noted that the sample of young people followed up for reconviction data was relatively small and there was no control group for comparison. The study also showed that there were lower reconviction rates for those who completed programmes. Completion rates across the project were low at 59 per cent overall. Completion rates for young people who committed crimes more persistently were lower still and significantly higher completion rates were found for the younger age group (63 per cent for those aged 15 compared with 41 per cent for those aged 17). Reasons given for non-completion were related to the length and intensiveness of the projects, which young people found difficult to sustain.

Some critics argue that there has been an overdependence on cognitive behavioural approaches in youth justice interventions when none of the research shows that they can lead to reduced offending when used in isolation (Pitts 2001c; Gray 2005a). This is the result, it has been argued, of a narrow definition of risk which places all the responsibility on the young person – it supposes that it is their attitudes and lifestyles that are the problem and that should be the primary focus of change (Muncie 2001). Consequently, the principle of reintegration or 'social inclusion' is neglected (Gray 2005a) and few interventions go far enough in addressing the broader social issues that have excluded young people who offend from the mainstream (Muncie 2002).

By contrast, multi-systemic approaches focus on the need for changes in a young person's social networks, in particular with regard to family, peer and school contexts, in order to help modify behaviours. This approach recognises that young people do not offend in a vacuum and for many their offending behaviour may be caused by their social environment.

Multi-systemic therapy (MST) draws on two theoretical traditions: human ecology theory and family systems theory. Human ecology theory deals with the relationship between humans, human societies and their natural, social and created environments. Bronfenbrenner (1979), one of the leading proponents of human ecology theory, argues that the way a child develops will be determined by a combination of genetic attributes, the immediate family and eventually the wider social systems in which they operate. Family systems theory suggests that families are systems of interconnected and interdependent individuals, none of whom can be understood in isolation from the system. MST brings these two theoretical traditions together by working for behavioural change through providing support, skills training and behavioural therapy within a young person's natural settings (home, school or neighbourhood, for example) rather than in a residential or correctional setting, and by targeting the multiple systems in his/her social network and the barriers to service access that may exist within them.

There have been a number of meta-analyses of randomised experimental evaluations of MST (Farrington and Welsh 2002; Curtis *et al.* 2004; Littell *et al.* 2005; MacKenzie 2006). Three of these conclude that MST is a potentially effective programme that can reduce recidivism among young people at serious risk of reoffending. Littell *et al.* (2005), however, are more circumspect about its overall effectiveness, concluding that the evidence is inconclusive and that it is possible that MST is no more effective than other services. They point to the problem of small sample sizes in the programmes they evaluated, which is a more general issue across all these meta-analyses and which weaken their statistical power. It should also be noted that none of the programmes evaluated was in England or Wales.

The principles of effective practice and offending behaviour interventions

Risk classification

Intervention is more effective where there is a relationship between the risk of further offending and the intensity of the offending behaviour work being undertaken. In particular, total contact time ought to be higher for young people whose offending is most persistent or serious. Conversely, over-intrusive intervention with young people who represent a lower level of risk can be counterproductive, and may on occasion lead to an increase in offending (McIvor 1990). See Chapter 2.

On the face of it, this particular message from research appears to be counter-intuitive, since it might reasonably be assumed that young people who are more entrenched in an offending lifestyle would also be more resistant to change. On the other hand, it seems plausible that interventions that focus on offending behaviour may have a labelling effect where participants' offending is at a low level. In other words, such interventions may be more likely to consolidate and confirm delinquent identities which, once established, tend to lead to further offending (Goldson 2000). In addition, where groups bring together young people with a range of offending histories, it is possible that 'contamination' may serve to increase the anti-social behaviour of the least criminal in the group.

There is also the question of how young people perceive the intervention. If punitive approaches are ineffective, it might be anticipated that outcomes would be influenced according to whether participants regard the intervention as a 'fair response' to their behaviour. An intensive intervention following on from a relatively low level of minor offending is more likely to be experienced as excessive, unjust or perhaps punitive. The research evidence on this point appears to have similar practical implications to the statutory requirement that interventions should be proportionate to the seriousness of the offending. In practical terms, it follows that planning should allow for a range of available programmes with an incremental increase in intensity. More specifically, offending behaviour interventions at the Final Warning stage, for example, should be limited in both duration and intensity.

Interventions should be planned on the basis of an assessment of those static and dynamic risk factors that are pertinent to the young person's current offending behaviour and likely future potential to reoffend. In classifying risk, therefore, it is important to distinguish between those static and dynamic factors. Around 80 per cent of young people who offend are young men, so being male is a characteristic that may be associated with a risk of becoming involved in criminal activity. Similarly, a history of persistent delinquency in the recent past is a relatively strong indicator that a young person will commit further offences. It is clear, however, that in both cases, these identified risk factors could not be altered by any form of intervention. A young person's previous offending record is a historical fact, unaffected by subsequent developments. These are static factors. The process cannot, however, afford to ignore static variables since these may frequently offer 'clues' to modifiable areas of risk. For instance, examination of a young person's criminal history may provide indicators that the young person tends to associate with an offending peer group, evinces an anti-social outlook, suffers from lack of victim empathy, or has problems with temper control.

Dynamic factors, by contrast, are those that are in principle modifiable and might be successfully influenced by an offending behaviour intervention. For example, substance misuse or difficulties with anger management might, in some individuals, increase the risk of offending behaviour. Criminogenic needs of this sort are amenable to change through planned intervention and are thus described as dynamic. See Chapter 2.

Criminogenic need

Offending behaviour interventions ought, by definition, to focus on criminogenic needs, that is those that are more directly related to risk factors for offending as identified through assessment. One of the tensions here is how to provide bespoke interventions that meet the individual criminogenic needs of each young person while providing a range of programmes for groups of young people. The most recent research into the reliability and validity of *Asset* (Baker *et al.* 2005) studied a number of intervention plans and found that they often did not reflect the outcome of assessments and that issues identified as being associated with a high risk of reoffending were not always incorporated into intervention plan targets. Attitudes to offending, substance use and education were the areas with the highest proportion of relevant targets. Some areas were unexpectedly low – family and personal relationships, and lifestyle, for example. Baker *et al.* (2005) suggest that this may be because practitioners find it more difficult to think of appropriate targets for working with a young person when the problems identified involve other people (e.g. parents/carers or friends and peer groups).

Conversely, this research showed that in some plans intervention targets were often given for areas that had a low *Asset* score. Education, training and employment, thinking and behaviour, and attitudes to offending were areas with particularly high instances of intervention plan targets being set where the *Asset* score for these areas was 0 or 1. One conclusion that can be drawn from this is that some plans for tackling offending behaviour may be conforming to a stock response where interventions such as victim empathy, community reparation and referral to Connexions/Careers Wales, for example, are included as standard, regardless of any link with the *Asset* profile (Baker *et al.* 2005). See Chapter 2.

Research into young people and offending behaviour has focused on identifying risk and protective factors for offending (Communities that Care 2001, for example). Establishing direct causality between risk factors and offending is notoriously difficult (see Chapters 1 and 2). In terms of ensuring offending behaviour programmes tackle criminogenic need as a priority, therefore, thorough analysis of the risk factors identified may be required in order to establish the most appropriate response. If detachment from education, training and employment was deemed to be a significant risk factor for a young person, for example, further analysis of the reasons for that detachment may be required in order to provide the most appropriate response. Is it, for example, that the young person does not have the literacy skills to manage the curriculum effectively that is the main barrier to attachment, or is detachment more closely related to bullying? The response required to address detachment as a criminogenic need in each case will be different.

Another challenge for practitioners when working with young people with multiple difficulties and barriers to social inclusion is to distinguish which needs are most salient in terms of the risk of further offending and which are less directly related to an individual's offending behaviour. Where a need exists that is serious but less directly related to the offence a young person has committed, referral to other agencies may be the most appropriate response.

Conversely, where certain behaviours are highly prevalent in a particular area, substance misuse for example, there is a risk that this is given too high a priority in responses to young people in that area. The behaviour, although causing some problems, may not be as closely related to a young person's offending as other risk factors. Where certain risk behaviours are prevalent in a population, the ready availability of programmes to tackle that issue may also influence responses to young people at the expense of providing fully individualised interventions.

Dosage

To date, one of the most intractable problems associated with offending behaviour work has been that significant numbers of those who are referred fail to complete the programmes. Evidence from the adult arena indicates that dropout rates for the one-to-one programme range from 25 per cent to 40 per cent in some areas. For others, the equivalent figure is closer to 80 per cent (Hollin *et al.* 2002). Evidence from the Youth Justice Board's evaluation of cognitive-behaviour projects (Feilzer *et al.* 2004) would suggest that similar rates of attrition are endemic for programmes offered to young people, particularly those who are older and those who are more persistently involved in offending behaviour. Indeed, one might be led to expect higher rates of attrition for young people than for adults because of adolescents' impulsiveness and inability in some cases to appreciate fully the consequences of their actions (particularly those who are most at risk of offending) (Grisso and Schwartz 2000).

One of the dangers with consistently high levels of attrition is that it might lead some services to be withdrawn regardless of their potential for effectiveness. Some evidence to support this expectation derives from London, where the Probation Service decided to close a day centre running a 'Reasoning and Rehabilitation' programme for young people. This decision has been made on the basis that completion rates of between 15 and 24 per cent were not cost-effective (National Probation Service 2003).

Effectiveness in relation to offending behaviour interventions relates, therefore, to what inputs are received by young people, not just what is arranged for them. This would suggest that programmes should have clear strategies in place for fostering participation and engagement. This might include:

- clearly defined procedures for monitoring attendance and punctuality in all programme elements and across all phases of a sentence;

- tight, supportive supervision;

- clear lines of communication among relevant staff members;

- enlisting the support of parents/carers in encouraging regular and sustained attendance and punctuality;

- discussion about attendance and punctuality at all review meetings.

Programme providers might also employ mechanisms which encourage or facilitate attendance. As a minimum, young people's fares may be reimbursed or, given the financial circumstances of many families, could be advanced where this is feasible. Where transport can be arranged for participants, attendance at the right time can be maximised. Encouragement might also be provided through inducements, such as linking attendance to leisure activities or other rewards. Providing refreshments or building in an element of recreation as part of the session can also act as a motivator.

It may be important to address potential barriers to attendance. Where young people are parents or have responsibility for dependants in other ways, allowance should be made for this fact and facilities provided so that they are not disadvantaged. In rural areas, where distance is a significant issue, it might mean delivering programmes on a one-to-one basis in the young person's home.

To reinforce the importance of compliance, information should be provided to young people and their families in a variety of forms and at regular intervals. The information provided should spell out the expectations of staff, participants and participants' carers during the life of the programme. Information given might include oral and written explanations at the outset of the intervention, reminders by telephone and letter in advance of any appointment, and diaries for the young people showing where they are expected to be on a day-to-day basis.

Particular care should be taken to ensure that information is given in a form that young people can readily understand. Where literacy is an issue, consideration should be given to how diaries might be used to provide a visual representation of appointments. As a matter of course, all information provided for young people should also be explained and provided in writing to parents and carers.

Programmes are very likely to be disrupted by the impact of young people's lifestyles. Participation in a group might be interrupted by court appearances, breach action, the impact of subsequent orders, attending under the influence of drugs or alcohol, late arrival and simple non-attendance. Wherever possible, programmes may attempt to anticipate and allow for such difficulties without suspending the service. This might mean providing 'catch-up' sessions, repeating modules, covering the same learning points at a variety of stages in the programme, or using one-to-one work at certain stages during the life of a group.

While it is appropriate to focus on expectations and the consequences of non-compliance, it is also important that information giving should be experienced as motivational rather than threatening (Morgan 2006).

Responsivity

The principle of responsivity suggests that the content of offending behaviour interventions should be structured into discernible units appropriate to the conceptual level and concentration span of participants. Material should be sequential, building on what participants have already learned, with elements of reinforcement to sustain what has been achieved to date.

In order to succeed in challenging deeply held attitudes, which may give rise to anti-social behaviour, programme deliverers also need to give guidance on what would be appropriate, pro-social responses in particular circumstances. The extent to which the young people accept such guidance depends in large part on the quality of programme delivery and the relationship between participants and practitioners. See Chapter 3 on engaging young people.

A wide-ranging approach to understanding and attempting to tackle offending behaviour is likely to be more successful. Measures focusing directly on the offences may be appropriate in some circumstances. In others, a more indirect approach dealing with environmental issues and improving problem-solving skills or empathy for others may be more useful. In particular, any intervention needs to take account of:

- the age, maturity and level of understanding of the young person;

- the nature and extent of any previous intervention – there is little point in delivering the same programme to a young person within a short space of time;

- the level of engagement and motivation to change;

- broader environmental factors which are likely to have an impact on the young person's behaviour and response to any form of work to address offending.

One of the key issues in ensuring the responsivity principle is achieved is the literacy level at which particular offending behaviour programmes are pitched. Home Office research into the accessibility of general offending behaviour programmes delivered through probation services to adults found that the literacy demands of the programmes offered was in advance of the literacy skills of a large number of participants (Davies *et al.* 2004). While 57 per cent of those taking part had reading skills well below what is expected of an 11-year-old (Level 1), the reading demands of the programmes were often at or above this level. Things were even more extreme with regard to speaking and listening, with the programme demands at Level 2 (GCSE A*–C equivalent) or Level 3 (A Level equivalent) in some cases while 37 per cent of participants were assessed to have speaking and listening skills below Level 1. While this was an adult-focused study, it is well known that a considerable number of young people in the youth justice system have literacy levels well below what is expected of them (see Chapter 4). This has considerable implications for the way in which practitioners present materials as part of offending behaviour interventions, but also, and perhaps more significantly, the way in which they deliver the interventions to young people.

In addition, consideration might be given to whether it is feasible to run a programme on a rolling basis as opposed to a closed-entry basis. Closed programmes have a single entry point and exit point. Accordingly, they have (at least in principle) a stable group of participants and sequential programme design. Building learning experiences onto what has been tackled in previous sessions is therefore facilitated. Rolling groups, on the other hand, may allow entry at any point or, perhaps more practically, at a number of predetermined points in the life of the programme. This arrangement lends itself more readily to reintegrating young people who have, for whatever reason, missed one or more sessions (Merrington 1998).

More generally, group work offers certain advantages – and not simply in terms of resource management. Many of the problems common to young people who offend are experienced in the community in a group setting. Learning solutions may therefore be more effectively developed in the company of others. Young people with similar needs can provide mutual support in the problem-solving process and may increase each other's motivation to change. Group dynamics are powerful, and emotions, beliefs and attitudes may be more amenable to change in a group setting.

At the same time, there are individuals for whom group work is difficult or inappropriate. Accordingly provision should be made to ensure that materials, which would generally be used within a group setting, can also be delivered on a one-to-one basis where the characteristics of particular young people or the details of their offending behaviour make this desirable. It must be borne in mind though that grouping deliquent young people may actually increase the risks of offending (Stephenson 2007).

Community based

Attention has already been drawn to research which suggests that offending behaviour interventions delivered within the community are likely to have greater success than those provided in a custodial setting. This should not, however, be taken to imply that effective practice is not possible within secure settings. But it suggests that 'boot camp' approaches or regimes associated with 'short, sharp shocks', physical drilling and training are unlikely to prevent offending behaviour (Farrington *et al.* 2002).

The limited research available on this topic suggests that, for young people serving custodial sentences, similar principles of effectiveness apply as those that ought to govern community interventions. However, within a custodial setting, intervention characteristics and design appear to play a greater role in influencing outcomes. Conversely, young people's individual attributes have rather less impact than they do where the intervention is delivered in the community (Hobbs and Hook Consulting 2001).

In some respects, this is unsurprising since choice as to whether to attend sessions is more tightly circumscribed in custody. Moreover, given the limited activities frequently available within an institution, offending behaviour interventions are more likely to be seen as a welcome diversion. The value of pro-social modelling as an approach is again emphasised in the literature (see Chapter 3). One recent review suggests that this approach is currently more highly developed in secure training centres and local authority secure units than within Prison Service establishments (Hobbs and Hook Consulting 2001).

To a considerable extent, long-term success depends on any positive learning experiences being carried over into the community. In this context, it is clearly important to have effective sentence planning in order to establish an integrated intervention where the community supervision part of the sentence builds on what has gone before. Cooperation and exchange of information between staff in the secure estate and responsible officers working within YOTs is a prerequisite of such continuity.

Even where this is achieved, however, major obstacles remain. Almost 30 per cent of those released from custody do not return to the parental home, and many of them will have problems with accommodation. Similarly, there are frequently substantial delays in arranging and starting education and training.

In a very real sense, effective work within a custodial setting depends on the YOT and the secure estate being able to access services through interaction with other parts of the criminal justice system and beyond (Hazel *et al.* 2002). See Chapter 10 on the secure estate and resettlement.

Intervention modality

A fully multi-modal approach requires that YOTs and secure facilities have access to a wide range of interventions to address the variety of risk as reflected in individual need. Service managers should therefore aim to develop a portfolio of services, which can be combined to create tailor-made programmes for the assessed needs of their target population.

It should be acknowledged that this is by no means an easy task. There is an obvious risk of building up costly services which prove to be unsustainable. Conversely, there may be a temptation to rely on a small number of proven projects into which a wide variety of need must then be channelled. The most promising strategy for avoiding both pitfalls might be to develop services on the basis of an audit of local need. Such an audit would build on information derived from assessment to provide an aggregate picture of the needs of young people to whom offending behaviour programmes are to be offered. The data derived in this manner needs to be updated on a regular basis to ensure a continuous match of service provision with the local needs profile.

Evidence would suggest that despite the significant advances made with the introduction of multi-agency YOTs and the concomitant revisions to the youth justice system, engaging service partners to provide for the full range of the needs of young people who offend continues to present significant problems (Audit Commission 2004; Arnull *et al.* 2005; Gray, Taylor *et al.* 2005; Stephenson 2007).

Clearly, a multi-modal approach to offending behaviour requires planning derived from the assessment of need previously undertaken when considering the young person's eligibility for engagement. However, research suggests that:

- there should be more consistency in linking assessed needs to planned interventions (Baker *et al.* 2005);

- interventions do not routinely focus on common criminogenic needs or risk factors (Arnull *et al.* 2005);

- recording of anticipated outcomes and delivered outcome from interventions are not robustly documented (Arnull *et al.* 2005).

Programme integrity

Programmes of intervention should be informed by a clear theoretical base which spells out the relationship between the methods employed, the objectives set and the ultimate aim of reducing or preventing offending. Clarity in this respect:

- assists in developing appropriate referral criteria for particular offending behaviour programmes;
- ensures that programme design is internally consistent;
- assists staff in the delivery of material;
- allows proper evaluation of outcomes.

The largest effect sizes for recidivism will be achieved in interventions where integrity is maintained. Research shows that the effect sizes for CBT, for example, are much higher in demonstration projects involving researchers and evaluators than in routine practice (average recidivism of 11 per cent in practice projects compared with 49 per cent in demonstration projects (Lipsey and Landenberger 2006)). The challenge for practitioners, therefore, is how to achieve the same degree of rigour applied to the demonstration projects in their day-to-day practice. Landenberger and Lipsey identify the following as key characteristics of effective CBT research and demonstration projects:

> ... high quality implementation as represented by low proportions of treatment dropouts, close monitoring of the quality and fidelity of the treatment implementation, and adequate CBT training for the providers. (2005: 471)

As Wikstrom and Treiber point out (2008), research and demonstration projects often only involve participants who have agreed to take part. This luxury is not available in routine practice which would suggest that attention may need to be given to methods for engaging young people in the first place and motivating them to remain engaged, particularly with those who may be reluctant to participate. See Chapter 3 on engaging young people.

Programme integrity has been interpreted quite rigidly by some to mean that the complete content of each session should be scripted, that every module of the programme should be undertaken in a pre-ordained order, and that staff should follow the manual without deviation. Given the disorganisation and chaos in the lives of many young people who offend and the multiplicity and depth of their welfare needs, 'integrity' understood in this rigid manner may well contribute to the failure of those at the highest risk to complete the programme. Flexibility to deal with crisis or other pressing matters which young people bring with them to the programme is a prerequisite of successful work with young people who offend.

Of course, this is not to deny the validity of integrity where it is construed as the design of interventions to meet stated aims with a clear methodology. There should, however, be room within the intervention to allow practitioners an element of flexibility so that they can depart from the script where circumstances make it necessary within an overall framework of standards for delivery. Ultimately, it is a question of staff exercising discretion in a skilled manner. Achieving the right balance depends on proper planning and review, proper management supervision and the quality of practitioners.

It is important for the development of evidence-based practice to ensure that evaluation of interventions is an integral and ongoing aspect of programme delivery. An integrated model of evaluation would be multidimensional, looking at both quantitative and qualitative aspects of performance, including:

- programme conceptualisation;

- programme delivery;

- cost-effectiveness;

- outcomes.

The challenges for practice

In recent years, there has been a considerable literature on the nature of effective interventions. However, less attention has been paid to the importance of skilled staff for effective delivery of offending behaviour interventions. In many ways, that oversight is regrettable, since it encourages a tendency to see programme content as the defining feature of effective practice. In reality content without the human resources to ensure skilful delivery is unlikely to maximise the potential for a positive impact on recidivism. (See Chapter 3 on engaging young people.)

But the issue of relationship appears to go deeper than this. Cognitive approaches may only carry conviction with the young people to whom they are addressed if they feel some form of obligation or loyalty to staff who seem committed and whose ideas make sense. Motivation is thus in part a consequence of what those who are supervised consider to be a display of interest in them as autonomous individuals (Rex 1999). This provides echoes of some rather older research in a therapeutic setting, which suggested that 'people variables' might be as important as 'method variables' in determining success or failure. In this context, people variables were defined as empathy, genuineness and 'non-possessive warmth' (Truax and Carkhuff 1967). In practice, this means that young people whose offending is persistent may need to be won over by persistent workers (McNeill and Batchelor 2002; Gray, Taylor et al. 2005).

The success of the Freagarrach project in Scotland for young people who offend persistently is testimony to the importance of such an approach. The evaluation pointed out that what set this project apart from others which were less effective was the high quality of work delivered by staff. This was in terms of both the content and (importantly in the current context) the style of what was delivered:

> A vital stage ... was the initial process of engagement. The staff succeeded in conveying to the majority of young people that it was worth making a commitment to the project and what it had to offer. They communicated an attitude of respect and care, which many young people – and their parents – contrasted favourably with their experience of other adults in positions of authority. (Lobley *et al.* 2001)

From a slightly different perspective, it has been noted that young people generally enter offending behaviour interventions for *extrinsic* reasons. That is, they attend in the initial stages because they are subject to a court order. Failure to comply can result in breach action, return to court and, frequently, a custodial sentence.

Lasting behavioural change, however, is more likely where there is an *intrinsic* motivation to engage in the process for reasons that are not related to compulsion, such as the potential for an improved quality of life (Williams and Strean 2002). Thus the court order might be regarded as providing a window of opportunity; it requires certain actions of the young people, irrespective of their disposition, but those actions are not in themselves guaranteed to produce the desired change. It is the intervention of the practitioner, and the way in which he or she is able to engage a young person (rather than the programme's content *per se*), which is crucial to effecting the shift from extrinsic to intrinsic motivation. That shift is required if the programme is to maximise the opportunity for change offered by the judicial process.

Reference has also been made already to the importance of staff having some scope to exercise discretion to depart from the programme. Staff should be empowered to adopt a flexible approach which makes the best use of the issues that young people bring to sessions, and which can respond to crises. The absence of such discretion discourages initiative and creativity, and is unlikely to engender the required degree of 'responsivity' to programme participants. At the same time, limits of discretion should be clear.

A useful model, developed in a slightly different context by Eadie and Canton (2002), proposes that the tension between discretion and accountability should be understood in terms of four ideal types of practice (see Figure 9.1).

Quadrant C is easily dispensed with. Nobody would seriously suggest that practitioners should be unaccountable for what they do and simultaneously exercise no professional discretion. Effective structured programmes would clearly be impossible in such a context.

Quadrant D 'Constrained practice' High accountability and low discretion	*Quadrant A* 'Best practice' High accountability and high discretion
Quadrant C 'Worst of all worlds' Low accountability and low discretion	*Quadrant B* 'The bad old days' Low accountability and high discretion

Figure 9.1 Discretion versus accountability

Quadrant B, it is suggested, represents the early days of youth justice service delivery in which quality standards, programme content and casework decisions were the preserve of professional judgement. Monitoring of outcomes was minimal and consistency a matter of chance. While the delivery of effective offending behaviour programmes would be possible within this quadrant, this would depend on the quality of the practitioner and could not be guaranteed. Moreover, in a climate of limited agreement about what, if anything, might constitute an effective intervention, the likelihood of achieving positive outcomes is further reduced.

Quadrant D, on the other hand, represents the converse problem, where innovation and flexibility are stifled. But a degree of creativity and use of discretion is essential for delivering a sensitive response to the problems presented by young people who persistently offend. In many cases, the engagement of difficult young people depends on it. The low discretion found in this quadrant is accordingly likely to inhibit effective practitioners.

The model suggests that the most effective practice is located within quadrant A, where there is a combination of high accountability and high discretion. This would work by allowing a certain discretion to staff delivering offending behaviour interventions. Any departure from the programme should be within agreed permissible parameters of variability and would have to be justified (and justifiable) by the practitioner concerned.

Another significant challenge for practice is the potential for differential treatment and outcomes for particular groups. Monitoring of gender and ethnicity is key to ensuring that offending behaviour interventions are delivered to all potential participants within an anti-discriminatory frame-work. In practice, girls and young women are frequently excluded from certain types of programme, thereby limiting the range of court disposals available to them relative to those used for boys and young men. There is also sometimes a tendency to require relatively higher levels of intervention with females, on the basis of perceived welfare need, in circumstances where this is not warranted by considerations relevant to their offending behaviour (Gelsthorpe and Sharpe 2006).

It is well established that black young people are over-represented at every stage of the youth justice system, and this is especially marked among those who are sent to custody (Feilzer and Hood 2004). Well-delivered and targeted offending behaviour interventions have the potential to divert some of those young people from custody. In these circumstances, the importance of monitoring referral and completion rates by ethnicity is patent.

Summary

- Offending behaviour interventions can be characterised as being designed to influence the behaviour of young people in a manner that makes it less likely to give rise to offending. They vary significantly according to the local offending profile and the category and particular circumstances of the young people for whom the intervention is intended.

- There are three forms of prevention – primary prevention (designed to improve overall opportunities in communities); secondary prevention (intervention with children and families deemed to be 'at risk'); and tertiary prevention (intervention with those who have been offending).

- Effective interventions, particularly for those young people whose offending is more serious or persistent, tend to have a core content which targets or includes key components addressing young people's ways of thinking and the moral content of their thinking.

- Multi-systemic approaches focus on the need for changes in a young person's social networks, in particular with regard to family, peer and school contexts, in order to help modify behaviours. This approach recognises that young people do not offend in a vacuum and for many their offending behaviour may be caused by their social environment.

- High-quality offending behaviour interventions are likely to be characterised by a combination of full accountability and discretion on the part of the practitioners involved to depart from the programme within agreed, permissible parameters.

Further reading

Feilzer, M., Appleton, C., Roberts, C. and Hoyle, C. (2004) *Cognitive Behaviour Projects: The National Evaluation of the Youth Justice Board's Cognitive Behaviour Projects.* London: Youth Justice Board.

Roberts, C. (2004) 'Offending behaviour programmes: emerging evidence and implications for practice', in R. Burnett and C. Roberts (eds), *What Works in Probation and Youth Justice: Developing Evidence-based Practice.* Cullompton: Willan.

10

The secure estate and resettlement

This chapter mainly focuses on resettlement in its own right, although it begins with a consideration of custody as a response to young people who have offended. The issue of custody raises some important questions in relation to evidence-based and effective practice as reconviction rates for young people who have experienced a custodial intervention are high. With regard to resettlement, it explores some of the models that have been proposed, all of which stress the importance of continuity of care, smooth transitions between custodial and community-based interventions and maintenance of strong links between a young person and their communities while they are removed from them. It also highlights the consistent failure as shown by evaluation in achieving such continuity through the fracturing that continues to occur for young people when they enter and leave custodial establishments and/or are moved between them.

The evidence base for the secure estate

In August 2010, there were 2,156 young people under the age of 18 held in custodial establishments within the secure estate for young people. Of these, 2,050 were young men and 106 were young women. While this is a relatively small number, compared with the total number of young people in the youth justice system overall, the cost of custody is very high both literally – the average bed in a Young Offender Institution (YOI) costs £53,112, £172,260 in a Secure Training Centre (STC) and £185,532 in a Secure Children's Home (SCH) (figures from the YJB, cited in Morgan 2010) – and, some would argue, in terms of the relatively poor outcomes achieved for young people for this significant investment of public money, accounting for two-thirds of the youth justice budget (YJB 2007).

Custody occupies a particular and highly political place in the youth justice system and its attraction for the public may be little influenced by discussions of effectiveness (although it should be noted that the custody figures for young people under the age of 18 have reduced by almost a third in the last two years). Judging effectiveness is also complicated by the range of outcomes that custody is expected to achieve:

220

For those whose offending is serious or persistent, custody may, however, be the only way of protecting the public from further offending. It may be the best way of bringing home to the young person the seriousness of his or her behaviour and the best way of preventing the young person from continuing to offend. Placing a young person in a secure environment that provides discipline, structure, education and training, as well as programmes to tackle offending behaviour, may provide a vital opportunity for the young person to break out of a pattern of offending and regain control of his or her behaviour. (Home Office 1998: para. 9)

This list of intended outcomes has a notable omission – punishment.

There are generally four justifications for the use of custody for young people: incapacitation, deterrence, rehabilitation and punishment. There is little convincing evidence to support all or any of these justifications. In relation to the American evidence Howell concluded that:

Large, congregate, custodial juvenile corrections facilities are not effective in rehabilitating juvenile offenders . . . Post release recidivism rates for correctional populations range from about 55% to 90% and prior placement in a juvenile correctional facility is one of the strongest predictors of returning. It is clear that housing juvenile offenders in large reformatories is not an effective way to prevent or reduce juvenile offending. (2003: 134)

Data for young people discharged from custody shows that 75 per cent of those released from custody in 2007 reoffended within a year (Ministry of Justice 2009). A Youth Justice Board study showed that 27 per cent had offended in the first month of release (ECOTEC 2001b). Young people with seven or more previous convictions are even more likely to be reconvicted (96 per cent) and most return to custody (83 per cent) within two years of release (Home Office 2003). There is emerging evidence to suggest that higher reconviction rates are associated with younger children. A third of the children aged 12 to 14 leaving Medway STC in 1998/9 were reported by their supervising officers to have committed criminal offences leading to rearrest within a month of release, and 67 per cent were said to have committed offences before the expiry of their sentence (Hagell et al. 2000).

Incapacitation is effective in the sense that it prevents the young person from committing crime in their communities while they are detained in custody. In relation to a dangerous individual there is certainly a high degree of effectiveness at least in the short-term. Where the argument weakens is that to have an effect on offending of even a few per cent would necessitate locking up very large numbers of young people (Tarling 1993; Greenwood et al. 1994). Even at the level of the individual there may be intrinsic aspects of custody that increase risks of reoffending.

Deterrent effects appear to be weak at both general and individual levels. Experience of custody might even lead some young people to regard it as a badge of honour (Hagell 2005). While punishment has a powerful resonance with the public and incarceration is seen as valuable in achieving this, studies suggest that such an approach is likely not only to be ineffective but may be counterproductive (Lipsey 1995; Goldson and Peters 2000).

Rehabilitation in the sense of improved behaviour and attitudes may occur within a custodial institution but there is limited evidence of their continuation upon release into the community (Hagell *et al.* 2000; Hobbs and Hook Consulting 2001; ECOTEC 2001a).

The secure estate for young people comprises three different types of institution – YOIs, STCs and SCHs. The majority of young people are held in YOIs (just over 80 per cent of under 18 year olds in August 2010). There has been some systematic comparison work carried out for institutions providing custody for young people who offend. One such study compared the reconviction outcomes for young people who had committed grave crimes and who were accommodated in YOIs compared to SCHs (Ditchfield and Catan 1992). Reconviction rates were significantly higher after two years for those leaving YOIs (53 per cent) compared to those leaving SCHs (40 per cent); there was also a much higher incidence of reconviction for violent offences for those in YOIs. The main differences between the approaches in each type of establishment were that SCHs ensured stronger ties with the families (39 per cent received family visits at least three times a month compared with 1 per cent of those in YOIs), more contact with the external community (over two-thirds of those in SCHs had weekly trips away from the institution compared to 1 per cent of those in YOIs) and a wider range and higher volume of education and training. The emphasis on education was highlighted by the fact that a much higher proportion attained educational qualifications in SCHs. While these young people form a small minority of even the custodial population, let alone the wider population of young people who offend, these findings do suggest that an approach that maintains ties with family, community and education and training can have a positive effect on later outcomes (Ditchfield and Catan 1992).

Removing young people by force or circumstance from their immediate communities appears to have a significant negative impact on young people's education, training and employment prospects. Custody means that the most delinquent and damaged peer groups live together. Institutional life may lessen the resilience of a young person by weakening or preventing the growth of those protective factors that enable some young people to surmount adversities that defeat others. The stifling of autonomy in custodial institutions could have such an effect.

Custody appears to have three innate weaknesses that weaken protective factors and increase risks. First, it curtails decision-making and planning skills in those who require them the most. Second, learning is provided in such an abnormal environment that the subsequent application of this learning in the community is extremely limited. This has long been recognised. The Reverend J. Turner, who established the Philanthropic

Society, in his evidence to the Parliamentary Committee in 1850 asserted that 'the best prisoner makes the worst free boy ... because he has been so accustomed to depend upon the mere mechanical arrangements about him, that he finds self-action almost impossible' (Carpenter 1968: 339). Finally, by removing young people who have only a tenuous attachment to formal education (even if only a PRU with part-time provision), further dislocation is caused for a young person, their parents/carers and the relevant professionals.

While custody cannot be deemed effective and is probably in many cases ineffective in promoting desistance from offending, this does not mean that its negative aspects cannot, to an extent, be ameliorated by practitioners. The evidence suggests that placements in smaller establishments, maintaining links with significant adults in the community, full-time high-quality education and training that links to their reintegration in the community, assistance with resisting drugs and an overall pro-social ethos may in some cases limit the negative effects (Ditchfield and Catan 1992; Hazel *et al.* 2002).

What is unclear is whether it is custody itself that impacts so negatively with regard to recidivism and other outcomes for individual young people or whether it is the fractured structures and systems that characterise the operation of custodial regimes that are to blame. Stephenson (2007) has identified a number of significant institutional issues relating to the operation of secure facilities themselves and the weaknesses of multi-agency working, including:

- weak case management and supervision structures;
- the lack of integration between separate planning systems and the wider sentence planning process coupled with the poor transmission of key information relating to need and progress made by young people between custodial and community providers;
- difficulties in establishing stable learning groups within custodial establishments due to population churn resulting from a large number of short sentences and the transfer of young people between establishments;
- the high turnover rate of staff working in custodial establishments;
- lack of continuity between custodial-based services and those provided (if at all) in the community;
- overcrowding in large secure establishments. The impact of large numbers of young people in confined spaces coupled with low staffing levels is likely to result in an overemphasis on regime security and the greater use of punitive sanctions, overriding the effective delivery of services.

(Howell 2003)

The net result of this is to make regimes more akin to boot camps, shown in research to have no impact on recidivism (Lipsey *et al.* 2000; ECOTEC 2001a; Howell 2003).

The evidence base for resettlement

'Resettlement' is the term currently used within youth justice to describe the process relating to young people who have been held in custody and who will be returning to the community. Nearly half of young people in custody at any one time are on Detention and Training Orders (DTOs), where half their sentence is served in a YOI, STC or SCH, and the other half is served in the community. The remainder of the sentenced population are serving sentences for 'grave crimes' under sections 90 or 91 of the Powers of Criminal Courts (Sentencing) Act 2000. About a quarter of this total population are on remand.

In August 2010, 1,225 young people were serving the custodial part of a DTO. Based on an assumption that there will be approximately the same number serving the community part of their sentence, this means that there are around 2,450 young people requiring supervision.

The majority of young people serving DTOs are aged 16 or 17. Around 78 per cent are above the statutory school-leaving age. The majority are white, although a disproportionate number are non-white (27 per cent in 2006/7), with black and mixed race being the largest minority ethnic groups (YJB 2008b).

What the available research tells us about the profile of these young people indicates that they are highly likely to:

- *have received little or no education or training for some time prior to their admission to custody.* The *Review of the Pre- and Post-custodial Education and Training Experiences of Young People* (ECOTEC 2001b) showed that between a quarter and a third of young people had no education or training available to them immediately prior to release;

- *have low levels of literacy and numeracy.* Nearly half of young people in custody have literacy and numeracy levels below those expected nationally of an 11-year-old and over a quarter have literacy and numeracy levels at or below what is expected nationally of a seven-year-old (ECOTEC 2001b);

- *have some kind of special educational need.* Figures from *Asset* suggest this might be around 35 per cent, although this is likely to be an underestimate given the numbers of young people who have not been accessing any formal education prior to custody;

- *experience some kind of mental health difficulty.* Harrington and Bailey (2005) found a third of young people had mental health needs, a fifth with depression, a tenth reporting self-harm in the past month and a tenth suffering anxiety and post-traumatic stress symptoms. Hyperactivity was reported in 7 per cent of the young people and psychotic-like symptoms in 5 per cent. Almost a quarter had learning difficulties and a further third borderline learning difficulties (see Chapter 5);

- *experience issues related to substance misuse.* A YJB-commissioned study of the substance use of young people subject to custodial sentences in the juvenile secure estate (Galahad SMS 2004) showed that by the age of 15, 76 per cent had become regular smokers (nearly 3.5 times the national average according to the Department of Health), 74 per cent had drunk alcohol more than once a week, 72 per cent had used cannabis on a daily basis in the 12 months before their arrest, 26 per cent had used ecstasy more than a few times a week, and 10 per cent had used heroin on a daily basis (see Chapter 6);

- *be homeless or in housing need.* Where young people have been living with a parent prior to custody, there may be reluctance to take them back afterwards. Those who had problematic living arrangements prior to custody tend to continue to do so afterwards. Those in temporary accommodation before custody are likely to lose their accommodation on entry to custody and to experience significant difficulty in finding somewhere to live on release (Niven and Stewart 2005; Nacro Cymru 2006). Indeed, there is some evidence to suggest that young people with unstable or temporary living arrangements are more likely to be sentenced or remanded to custody (Nacro 2005; Thomas 2008);

- *come from chaotic and disrupted family backgrounds.* Various studies have found that: two out of five young women and one in four young men report having suffered violence at home; one in three young women and one in 20 young men report sexual abuse; 17 per cent are on the child protection register; 41 per cent have been in the care of the local authority at some point in their lives, with a significant proportion of these still being looked after at the point of sentence (Hazel *et al.* 2002).

Definitions of resettlement

Resettlement is a relatively new term for processes that have historically been referred to as 'aftercare' (also used widely in the USA, though lately superseded by 're-entry') and 'throughcare' (current until the late 1990s). Throughcare refers to a single rehabilitative process, which starts with sentence planning and continues into the community: the 'seamless approach' as envisaged in the 1991 Criminal Justice Act (Raynor 2004b). Aftercare implies that the process is only relevant once a young person has been released into the community (Gies 2003).

The term resettlement was introduced by the Home Office in 1998 as an alternative to the use of throughcare. The change in terminology was justified on the basis that throughcare was a term 'unlikely to be properly understood outside of prison and probation worlds', and that 'public and sentencer confidence would be enhanced if the focus was on the ultimate goals of "throughcare" – high-quality sentence planning and successful resettlement in the community' (Home Office 1998). In this sense, resettlement refers to the outcomes of a throughcare process.

225

Raynor (2004b) points out that some possible concepts of resettlement may be contradictory. For example, does resettlement mean:

- restoration to a condition and social environment roughly corresponding to that existing before imprisonment (in which case, is this the correct term when so many young people who enter custody have been living in conditions that could hardly be described as 'settled')?

- attempted establishment of a basic adequate standard of living and opportunity, which may not have been experienced before?

- re-establishment of social contacts, links or relationships with family/ carers and/or peers?

- establishment of new links and connections with pro-social influences and resources?

- action to identify and address defined needs?

In addition, resettlement as defined in national policy terms may be largely an adult concept which makes generalisation to the juvenile context difficult. The state has additional responsibilities for young people (particularly those below statutory school-leaving age) in terms of providing education, and for those young people who are looked after. This also means that the support provided for young people in custody carries similar obligations to those that exist in the care system. The sentencing framework is also different for juveniles.

In some respects, resettlement can be seen as an umbrella term for a range of interventions and approaches which are subsumed within other areas of practice such as mental health, substance misuse and education, training and employment. Constructing effective resettlement programmes for young people therefore requires practitioners to consider the range of other areas of practice in developing interventions based on the best evidence of promising approaches. (See Chapters 4, 5 and 6.)

Dimensions and models of resettlement

Raynor (2004b) defines the difficulties for people experiencing custody for relatively short periods of time as falling into two categories:

1. Access to opportunities and resources.

2. Individuals' attitudes, beliefs and habitual responses.

These categories are not distinct and they may interact to reinforce each other in complex ways. For example, practical or situational difficulties in accessing services (for example, education, training, accommodation or substance misuse services) may lead to negative emotions such as anger or depression, and difficulties in seeing ways of dealing with the problem other than by offending (Zambe and Quinsey 1997, cited by Raynor 2004b).

It could also be argued that assumptions about young people's offending lie along a continuum of responsibility on the part of the young person, with young people assuming they are victims of circumstance at one end of the continuum and exercising choice about how they respond to circumstances at the other (Raynor 2004b).

Raynor also defines the relevant methods or approaches that are likely to be most appropriate at either end of the spectrum in terms of intervention. Advice, support, sympathy, advocacy and referral are linked to those with no confidence in their capacity to initiate change and cognitive challenge, and motivational and pro-social input for those with high levels of self-efficacy. A combination of these methods leads to effective programme design for resettlement. The implication is that services address not only the difficulties relating to the situations that young people experience, but also young people's personal resources, strategies and motivations for responding to these difficulties.

This view is borne out by research related to youth transitions more generally. Coles (2000) suggests that the development of a youth transition model should include balancing 'the two sides of the careers equation'. On one side, this equation has young people's behaviour and the decisions they make. On the other side, it has the decisions made by those in social and statutory institutions and agencies which impact on young people's lives. This equation is linked to the concept of providing young people with more control over decision-making. One of the key challenges with regard to custody is its capacity to remove the need for independent decision-making by young people.

A core principle underpinning most resettlement models is the dimension of continuity ('continuity of care' in the USA). The whole DTO structure and the Youth Justice Board's *Youth Resettlement: A Framework for Action* (2005d) are based on the principle that a seamless approach to resettlement is likely to yield better outcomes. It should be noted, however, that there is no real evidence for these models that can be shown from research or evaluation of specific resettlement programmes.

The concept of continuity is deceptively simple and appears very hard to achieve in reality. This is because the context of resettlement necessarily implies time spent in two different places, with one (custody) often providing a fundamentally different social environment, level of control and range of services and programmes to that experienced in the community. The difficulty is compounded by the lack of continuity when young people are moved between custodial establishments.

Much of the work relating to aftercare in the USA has focused on developing a model based on the broad principles of effective practice emphasising the importance of:

- assessment and planning from the earliest stages;

- custodial programmes that focus on developing skills that will have application in the community;

- community programmes that build on the work done in the custodial phase;

- an overarching case management system providing direct supervision and brokering access to relevant services.

The Intensive Aftercare Programme (IAP) model is theory-driven, risk and needs assessment-based and empirically grounded (Altschuler and Armstrong 1994a, 1994b; Altschuler et al. 1999; Gies 2003). It proposes an intensive, fully integrated mix of support for young people at 'high risk' of reoffending, with an overarching case management process incorporating:

- substantial control over young people once they are released to the community;

- enhanced service delivery that focuses on recognised risk and protective factors.

The principles for programme design underpinning the IAP model are based on the best evidence of emerging effectiveness in terms of preventing offending:

- preparing young people for progressively increased responsibility and freedom in the community;

- facilitating involvement and interaction between young people and their communities;

- working with young people and targeted community support systems (families, peers, schools, colleges, employers) on the qualities needed by all for constructive interactions that advance young people's integration into the community;

- developing new resources, support services and opportunities as required;

- monitoring and testing young people's capacity to receive (and the community's capacity to provide) services and support.

The intent is to have community-based aftercare services parallel those that are first initiated in the institution, and institutional services geared to achieve essentially the same purposes as those that will be achieved in the community (Altschuler et al. 1999).

Clearly, there are similarities here with the principles applied to interventions for young people at serious risk of offending or reoffending in England

and Wales. The DTO as a framework for resettlement, for example, emphasises the significance of a supported transition through consistent case management by a YOT practitioner from the pre-sentence stage through to the end of the sentence.

Based on continuity of care and some features of the IAP model, Rees and Conalty (2004) have defined a four-phase approach, which reflects the DTO framework. In this approach, a comprehensive resettlement process begins at the pre-sentence stage, continues through the defined custodial and community phases of the sentence, and carries on beyond the end of the sentence.

The four-phase model emphasises the point that there is no real end to resettlement, and that being genuinely 'settled' is a longer-term process than relatively short sentences allow for. This approach also emphasises the importance of the intensity and quality of case management by the YOT supervising officer in ensuring continuity across the phases.

Current resettlement models are underpinned by three straightforward principles:

- All plans for resettlement should be based on a rigorous assessment of individual risk and need.

- Planning for resettlement should begin at the earliest opportunity (pre-sentence).

- Seamless provision of services (education, health, etc.) across the custodial and community phases should be supported by the timely transmission of information to ensure that continuity of approach, content and materials is maintained.

One difficulty in defining what is effective in relation to resettlement is that there is little in the way of specific programme evaluation (Howell 2003). Attempts at evaluating the models proposed above have been undermined by a range of issues largely relating to maintaining programme integrity. What little research exists focuses solely on custodial interventions, is based on outcomes for adults rather than young people, or is methodologically flawed (Altschuler and Armstrong 2002; Howell 2003).

Research which focuses only on custodial interventions often overemphasises the positive change in young people's attitudes within institutions without considering the impact on recidivism in the community (Hobbs and Hook Consulting 2001). Furthermore, research looking at resettlement processes is often bedevilled by issues relating to research methodology (small sample sizes and poorly matched control groups, for example) and/or focuses on programmes that are poorly designed or not implemented faithfully according to their principles:

> Flawed implementation is a substantial limitation, because, from an evidence-based and research-driven perspective, it is only when

continuity of care is reflected in practice ... that it becomes possible to determine whether and in what ways continuity of care contributes to success. (Altschuler and Armstrong 2002)

For example, recent interim evaluation of the IAP programme in the USA has shown less than promising results in relation to recidivism (Weibush 2001, cited by Howell 2003). But the significance of this finding is called into question because sample sizes were small and the control group at one of the sites received some aspects of the intervention which should have been received only by the treatment group.

One aftercare programme in the US has produced positive short-term effects (Josi and Sechrest 1999, cited by Howell 2003). The Lifeskills '95 programme was designed to reinforce progress made while helping young people to confront the fears of the communities to which they were returning. The programme was based on six principles:

1. Improving the social skills necessary for successful reintegration.

2. Reducing criminal activity in terms of both amount and severity.

3. Reducing the need for, or dependence on, drugs and alcohol.

4. Improving lifestyle choices (e.g. social, and education, training and employment).

5. Reducing the need for participation in delinquent peer groups and gangs as a support mechanism.

6. Reducing the rate of short-term reconvictions.

Researchers found that individuals assigned to the control group were twice as likely as those in the experimental group to have been arrested, to be unemployed, to find it difficult to gain and maintain employment, and to have abused drugs and alcohol frequently after release.

It should be noted that much of the available evaluation and research specifically related to juveniles comes from the US. The extent to which this can be applied to young people in England and Wales, where the social and legal context is different, should be considered. Research conducted in this country, largely driven by the Youth Justice Board, has focused on implementation of the DTO (Hagell *et al.* 2000; ECOTEC 2001a, 2001b; Hazel *et al.* 2002; Youth Justice Board 2003, 2004d, 2005c; Curry *et al.* 2004; Galahad SMS 2004). Whether concentrating on education, training and employment or on substance misuse, this research describes a system that is fractured and beleaguered by difficulties in inter-agency cooperation, leading to a breakdown of continuity between community and custodial-based services.

In many respects, more is known about what does not appear to be effective in this country with regard to resettlement than about what is effective. Examples include the poor transmission of information between establishments and from custody to the community, and the associated failure to provide continuity of approaches, materials and courses across key transition points.

Given the paucity of positive evidence of effectiveness in relation to resettlement from custody, the most helpful approach for devising programmes is likely to be through extracting principles and guidelines for effective interventions as revealed by meta-analysis (McGuire 1995; Howell 2003).

Lipsey and Wilson (1998) conducted a systematic review of the evidence for effective intervention with young people whose offending behaviour was deemed to be serious. They reviewed around 200 studies relating mostly to young men aged between 14 and 17, and looked at the evidence in relation to non-institutionalised and institutionalised young people. A summary of their findings on the most and least effective types of treatment is given in Table 10.1.

Lipsey and Wilson (1998) went on to draw separate conclusions about the effectiveness of interventions with both groups of young people. With regard to institutionalised young people, effectiveness was increased if interventions were of longer duration, if the level of monitoring was high, or if the programme was well established. The duration factor was also important for non-institutionalised young people, but interventions were more effective with fewer contact hours.

Lipsey and Wilson also found that for non-institutionalised young people the programme's characteristics were less important than offence-related characteristics, especially previous offences. The opposite effect was the case for institutionalised young people, with programme type and length being particularly important. For the institutionalised young people, offence-related characteristics appeared insignificant.

While there is still a gap between research and practice in relation to promising approaches in resettlement, it should be possible, by applying the principles of effective practice, to improve the outcomes for young people who are subject to custodial sentences.

The principles of effective practice and resettlement

Risk classification

Young people with experience of custody are likely to be the most at risk of reoffending. This is because they are often the most detached from education, training and employment, and are more likely to misuse drugs and alcohol and have mental health issues, which are all known risk factors.

Enhanced risk might be where:

- a young person is returning to changed, less stable or no accommodation – one study has shown that 30 per cent of young people had a different

Table 10.1 Summary of the most and least effective types of treatment regarding recidivism rates

Types of treatment used with non-institutionalised* young people	Types of treatment used with institutionalised** young people
Positive effects, consistent evidence	
Individual counselling	Interpersonal skills
Interpersonal skills	Teaching in family homes
Positive effects, less consistent evidence	
Multiple services	Behavioural programmes
Restitution, probation/parole	Community residential
	Multiple services
Mixed but generally positive effects, inconsistent evidence	
Employment related	Individual counselling
Academic programmes	Guided group counseling
Advocacy casework	Group counselling
Family counselling	
Group counselling	
Weak or no effects, inconsistent evidence	
Reduced caseload, probation/parole	Employment related
	Drug abstinence
	Wilderness/challenge
Weak or no effects, consistent evidence	
Wilderness/challenge	Milieu therapy
Early release, probation/parole	
Deterrence programmes	
Vocational programmes	

*'Non-institutionalised young people' refers to young people under the authority of the juvenile justice system at the time of treatment, supervised through probation.
**'Institutionalised young people' refers to those in custody at the time of treatment. Of the studies focusing on institutionalised young people, 74 related to juvenile justice institutions and the other nine to residential facilities under private or mental health administration.

place of accommodation on release than they had before entering custody (ECOTEC 2001b);

- a school has taken the young person off its roll, there is no mainstream, full-time equivalent placement arranged immediately on return to the community and the young person is pessimistic about his/her chances of not reoffending. This may be a particular issue for young people suffering from depression or other mental health issues, which may have been exacerbated by the experience of custody.

It is also likely that risk factors may change over the course of a sentence.

For example, a young person's participation in a substance misuse programme in custody may have reduced the risk this represented at the start of the sentence. If no support is available to continue this work or help the young person to transfer positive learning to their community setting, the risk factor remains. Indeed, the risk may be increased in some cases as a result of disappointment or a sense of frustration on the part of the young person when that support is removed abruptly or without warning. The risk relating to substance misuse is particularly relevant as access to alcohol and drugs is severely limited while a young person is in custody but becomes readily available immediately on release. Use of these substances when tolerance levels may have decreased may represent a significant and immediate danger to young people leaving custody. See Chapter 6 on substance misuse.

The pre-sentence stage can supply important information about what young people need in an appropriate intervention to reduce the risk of reoffending. Pre-sentence reports should specify the elements of a programme's design that reflect the young person's risk factors, without necessarily assuming that custody will be the outcome of sentencing. This can also provide a useful starting point for practitioners in secure establishments in terms of:

- providing custody-based interventions that emulate as far as possible what happens in the community relevant to individual young people;
- ensuring that young people develop the specific skills they will need in order to gain access, participate and make progress when they return to their communities.

Criminogenic need

In working with young people who have multiple barriers to effective participation and are high-risk in relation to offending behaviour, there may be a danger of developing programmes that try to tackle all their difficulties, regardless of how salient they are to the risk of reoffending. This can lead to a confused programme of support that is unfocused and lacks a clear sense of priority.

This may be a particular issue in relation to short sentences where decisions have to be made about what can be done within the time available, focusing on those risks that are most salient and susceptible to being changed. This should not though be a justification for not providing the appropriate volume of learning and skills for young people, particularly those on short sentences. Detachment from the learning process has been identified as one of the most significant risk factors for offending behaviour (Communities that Care 2001). This suggests that the immediate provision of appropriate education, training and employment should always remain a priority. (See Chapter 4.)

The YOT supervising officer (as the case manager) also has a duty to ensure that referrals are made to appropriate agencies and follow-up action is monitored if young people have needs that are not currently being met but are not necessarily criminogenic in nature.

Providing relevant assessments is important for planning and delivering appropriate interventions. Young people experiencing custody are often subjected to multiple and often repeat assessments as they move between custody and community and between different custodial establishments. This would suggest that all assessment information should travel with young people when they make such transitions.

Also significant are the records of action taken in starting the resettlement process and progress made to date. If continuity of care is to be achieved, these records would seem to be key in terms of a young person's progression over the course of his/her sentence, and as a tool for disseminating information to the various agencies and service providers who work with young people in the community. These include Connexions/Careers Wales, drug action teams, LEAs, schools, colleges, training providers, accommodation services, leaving care teams, social services and health services.

Dosage

It appears that the most promising programmes for young people who are most at risk of offending provide larger amounts of meaningful contact over longer periods (Lipsey and Wilson 1998). This suggests that frequent, high-quality interaction between practitioners and young people, both in custody and in the community, is more likely to ensure successful resettlement.

The dosage is specified in terms of educational programmes: 30 hours per week in custody and 25 hours per week in the community. However, this intensity of provision relies on planning being started very quickly on entry to custody, both for the custodial-based component and in arranging provision to be available immediately on release.

It should be noted that levels of effectiveness relate to what provision is *received* by a young person, not just what is *arranged*. The evaluation of YJB-funded education, training and employment (ETE) interventions showed a direct correlation between attendance and lower offending rates (Hurry and Moriarty 2004). Evidence from schools shows that a same-day response to absence has proved effective in preventing further non-attendance (DfEE 1995). While most of the evidence relates to education and training, it has implications for attendance and punctuality in any element of a resettlement programme, for example offence-related and substance misuse work. A prompt response to non-attendance or poor punctuality implies the need for:

- clearly defined procedures for monitoring attendance and punctuality in all programme elements and across all phases of the sentence;
- tight, supportive supervision, particularly in the community phase of the sentence;

- clear lines of communication among relevant staff members;

- the support of parents/carers in encouraging regular attendance and punctuality;

- discussion about attendance and punctuality at all review meetings.

Close monitoring of young people once they return to their communities is likely to be a critical factor in the success of programmes, for example monitoring their attendance at school/college and ensuring that they are attending appointments.

Evidence shows that over-reliance on surveillance in the absence of other programme components is likely to be ineffective (Raynor 2004a). In addition, technology (such as tagging) used in the surveillance of young people in the community may reduce the amount of active involvement of YOT supervising officers and other practitioners with young people and their parents/carers which, in turn, may compromise the outcomes of the intervention with regard to repeat offending (Altschuler and Armstrong 1994b).

Responsivity

While there does not appear to be sufficient evidence to support the notion that all young people at risk of offending/reoffending are 'active' learners, the focus instead could be on helping young people develop a range of strategies for managing their lives, particularly important when considering the structure of the DTO. This implies that work done while in custody might focus less on giving young people practical 'things to do' and more on helping them develop a broader range of strategies for managing tasks and solving problems.

Young people who have had negative experiences of the education system may have developed a range of inappropriate responses to certain situations in which they are asked to undertake new challenges and take risks. In addition, the custodial context is likely to create more situations in which young people feel exposed in front of their peers. They may also have developed a range of strategies for avoiding tasks and/or a number of useful strategies that have only been employed in the exercise of anti-social behaviours. Young people are unlikely to see the transferability of these strategies to more pro-social activities, such as work, learning and community life generally.

In relation to resettlement, it is likely to be important then that the learning strategies young people develop while in custody are those that will help them to function more effectively in the community. If new strategies learned in the context of a secure setting only have meaning in relation to surviving in a custodial environment, they may not easily survive transfer to the community (Stephenson 2000). To this end, information on learning strategies should be passed between key agencies and service providers so that these strategies can be enhanced and developed further in the new context. Integration of the individual learning plan with the sentence plan may be critical in this respect. It could also be important in terms of ensuring that all those who deliver programmes (including health, offence-related and other programmes) understand the wider implications for the work they carry out with young people.

Community based

Current evidence suggests that programmes in the community have more effective outcomes than those in custody or other segregated settings. The reason for this is probably that the learning is more likely to occur in a context that is meaningful to the young person and can be readily transferred to his/her everyday experiences. The implication for practice is that approaches which emulate certain features of community orders may make for a more successful custodial experience in terms of changing behaviours (Tolbert 2002).

One of the practical implications of the community-based principle might be that secure establishments and YOTs should look for opportunities to provide release on temporary licence (RoTL). Visits to arrange housing can be particularly useful in preparing for release. Similarly, home visits to the actual or potential host education institution have proved effective in securing immediate placements post-custody and smoothing the transition to the community.

Benefits may also be accrued from RoTL in terms of fostering greater independence and graduated autonomy. For example, the use of town visits local to the establishment to practise life skills such as shopping, engaging in leisure activities and using community facilities could help to reinforce skills and minimise the shock of returning to relative freedom in the community.

In addition to RoTL, wider use of videoconferencing could serve to bring young people closer to their communities. YOTs and secure establishments can, for example, use videoconferencing to hold case meetings at a distance involving the YOT supervising manager, other key agency representatives from the community base and parents/carers.

While the family circumstances of young people subject to custodial sentences may be difficult in many ways, parents/carers (and other family members and significant others) also provide a bridge to the community. Research has shown that young people who maintain contact and receive regular visits from their family and friends are more likely to have accommodation and education, training or employment arranged on release from custody (Niven and Stewart 2005). Parental involvement in planning and review meetings, from pre-sentence through to the end of the sentence, may provide an important forum for understanding what the young person is trying to achieve. It could indicate to parents/carers what kind of support they might provide in order to facilitate positive change.

A number of young people in custody will be parents themselves. Maintaining links between young parents and their children might also be considered, both to help the young people in custody to maintain ties, where this is appropriate, and for the sake of their children.

Intervention modality

It is likely that programmes for working with young people at risk of offending are most promising when skills-based and when they emphasise problem-solving within a cognitive-behavioural framework. In relation to resettlement, this would indicate that whatever methods are used reflect community-based situations. Those that focus solely on behaviours that enable young people to cope within a secure environment are unlikely to have relevance when a young person returns to his/her community.

Young people who end up in custody are likely to have complex, multiple needs that place them at risk of further offending. Programmes to meet those needs will usually comprise a range of different and often complex interventions: education and training, offence-related work, healthcare and work with parents/carers, families and peer groups, for example.

The implication of this would seem to be that resettlement programmes need to comprise a degree of direct input by youth justice practitioners and, particularly in the community phase of the sentence, services brokered from a range of providers and other agencies. As with any complex multi-modal intervention, the intensity and quality of consistent case management (the responsibility of the YOT supervising officer) would seem to be key to ensuring continuity of care.

It is important not to prolong a young person's connection with the YOT unnecessarily. However, support is likely to be needed beyond the end of the statutory sentence. Connexions in England and Careers Wales might have a role to play in this respect.

While the networks required are inevitably complex, it would seem important that these are drawn up and understood between staff in custody, YOTs and other agencies/service providers.

It is possible that there may be a level of resistance from some service providers and employers to engaging with young people returning from custody. It may therefore be important for the YOT supervising officer to establish good relationships with existing service providers and develop new ones with those prepared to work with this group of young people. Practitioners may need to beware of relying entirely on those service providers and agencies that work exclusively with groups on the margins. This may simply result in replicating the deviant and delinquent peer groups that place young people at further risk.

Although service provision is fundamentally important, so is preparation of the young person's immediate community, parents/carers and peers. Everyone involved with the young person has the potential to encourage and reinforce pro-social behaviour. Research on risk factors shows that family, peers and social networks may not be in a position to provide this support without specific input to improve the situation and strengthen their capacity to provide support. See Chapter 9 for more on offending behaviour interventions.

Programme integrity

Critiques of recent and past intervention programmes for young people at risk of offending have repeatedly commented on the uneven and poor quality of implementation, the ambiguity or absence of a theoretical rationale and conceptual base, and flawed evaluations. This is an even greater problem when programmes are complex and the more components they comprise, as is inevitably the case with resettlement programmes.

The lack of a clear rationale makes it likely that a programme will become a disconnected set of activities, with problems such as:

• services provided, sanctions and incentives used, and community resources and social networks tapped, all determined in an ad hoc and fragmented fashion;

• individual staff pursuing their own direction and inclinations;

• target-group criteria, referrals and selection not matched to the most appropriate programme or person;

• a lack of coherence and continuity between programme components, features and processes;

• young people's major difficulties or needs not being met, leaving gaps in service or wasted opportunities.

When case-managing complex resettlement programmes, therefore, the challenge for YOT supervising officers is to ensure that all stakeholders are clear about the programme's overall rationale and their role/responsibility within it, and that they are implementing the programme in ways which are faithful to the overall design. The full range of stakeholders includes the young people themselves, their parents/carers, teachers, health workers and Connexions/Careers Wales advisers.

As recidivism rates for young people who have experienced custody are so high, it is vital for managers and strategic partnerships to monitor and evaluate the elements of programme design that contribute to positive outcomes at the four stages of implementation:

1. Pre-sentence;

2. Custody under sentence;

3. Community under sentence;

4. Community post-sentence.

Evaluation of a resettlement programme requires objective data collection and analysis of the type of young people, the nature and amount of intervention and supervision, and how the programme is implemented and with what input. Specifically, this entails systems for collecting data on outcomes for young people reintegrating from custody and for documenting the processes involved in providing the resettlement programme within three broad areas:

1. The extent to which programme elements, services and activities provided, and the population served, reflect the philosophy and principles of effective practice.

2. The quality and nature of implementation, including:
   - staffing policies, patterns, roles and responsibilities;
   - management structure and lines of authority;
   - incorporation of services into programme components, features and
   - processes;
   - the number and type of young people being resettled;
   - the services they receive and from whom;
   - the length of services and their results.

3. The problems, obstacles and difficulties encountered, for example:
   - funding and community resources;
   - cooperation from secure establishments, magistrates and other public and private agencies;
   - community relations.

The challenges for practice

A conceptual difficulty for staff working in the youth justice system, particularly in the juvenile secure estate, is that custody appears to weaken protective factors and increase risk factors in relation to offending behaviour (Stephenson 2007). In this respect, preventing young people from entering custody in the first place may be the most effective in terms of preventing further offending.

Furthermore, the experience of custody means that young people are forced to live, learn and socialise entirely with a peer group whose common characteristic is their offending behaviour, which is another well-attested risk factor (Communities that Care 2001).

For some young people, incarceration may be another stage in what Fleisher (1995, cited in Howell 2003) calls the 'street life cycle', where custody represents a safe haven from the chaos of young people's lives and the pull toward anti-social behaviours exerted by their communities. Custody may provide not only a safe haven for some young people, but also a highly structured environment where there is limited choice and which is governed by strict rules and relatively simplistic systems of reward and sanction, again in contrast to their experiences in their communities.

239

But custody also has an immediate labelling effect, branding a young person in the eyes of the public, professionals and employers as not only an 'offender', but a 'dangerous' one at that. Ironically, this in itself is likely to present a further barrier to maximising mainstream opportunities (school, college, employment, housing) in addition to any other barriers experienced by the young person prior to custody.

These difficulties may be further compounded by institutional issues relating to the operation of secure facilities and the failure of multi-agency working, including the following:

- weak case-management and supervision structures – support from the YOT supervising officer appears to drop off while the young person is in custody, and planning for release happens too late and too slowly;

- lack of integration between separate planning systems and the wider sentence planning process, coupled with poor transmission of key information (on young people's needs and progress made) between custodial establishment and the community;

- difficulties in establishing stable learning groups within secure establish-ments because of population turnover resulting from a large number of short sentences and the transfer of young people between establishments;

- the high turnover rate of staff working in secure establishments;

- lack of continuity between custodial-based services and those provided (if at all) in the community;

- community-based services shutting down for some young people while they are in custody, making seamless reintegration when they return to their communities that much harder.

The geographical distance between young people in secure establishments and their home communities is another significant barrier to resettlement. As there are relatively few secure establishments for juveniles, this means that young people are often placed far from home. In 2005/6, about one-third of young men and half of young women were held in establishments more than 50 miles from home (YJB 2007). This reduces the capacity for contact with family members and carers. Research from social care indicates that where looked-after young people lack positive family support, they are more likely to have poor post-care outcomes and experience greater difficulty in making and sustaining relationships with others (Biehal et al. 1995, cited in DoH 2003). The same is also likely to be the case for young people who are removed very suddenly from their communities and then return fairly abruptly with little interim support or contact.

Geographical distance also appears to exacerbate difficulties of communi-cation between YOTs and secure establishments. Practitioners continue to highlight this issue as a barrier to effective case management and cooperative working to ensure seamless resettlement from custody (Galahad SMS 2004; Morgan 2010).

It is generally argued that programmes delivered in the community are more likely to be effective. The legitimacy of this argument may need testing by further research, particularly if programme integrity is so threatened by the organisational and structural weaknesses of custodial care identified above. Sanctions such as the loss of liberty provide only the context for service delivery; it is the intervention within that setting that may have the capacity to initiate change in young people.

In many respects, resettlement from custody resembles the experience of young people leaving care. The evidence suggests that looked-after young people make better educational progress, for instance, if they have had relatively stable care careers and proactive support from carers, social workers and teachers (Biehal *et al.* 1995, cited in DoH 2003). There appears to be a tendency for support from these sources to fall away soon after a young person leaves care. This experience seems to mirror that of most young people subject to DTOs, where the level of support provided when they leave custody diminishes considerably and very suddenly.

In addition, the complete withdrawal of support at the end of the sentence when the statutory component has been fulfilled may be too sudden and too soon to enable young people to sustain any positive progress. The post-sentence support needs of young people should be considered carefully; the involvement of agencies such as Connexions/Young People's Partnerships (Wales) is key to this.

Young people's perceptions

The full participation of young people and their parents/carers is seen as vital for effective resettlement. It is also generally accepted that the process of resettlement should be 'seamless', with continuity of approaches and services between custody and the community across all specific elements of a programme. This concept of 'seamlessness' may not accord with young people's perceptions. The contrast between custody and their community lives is inevitably very stark and the capacity of young people to perceive seamlessness therefore may be very limited in this context.

The concept of a 'resettlement programme' may also have limited currency in young people's eyes. It may require the knowledge and skill of relevant professionals (particularly the case manager based in the home YOT) and other supportive adults or peers to help young people to make the links between different areas of service delivery.

The timeliness and speed at which things need to happen to facilitate seamlessness, particularly in arranging accommodation or suitable ETE for example, can be a further challenge, especially where young people are on short sentences. Even very short time lapses during which nothing is arranged or available can have a profound impact on increasing the likelihood of reoffending. What might seem like a short space of time to a professional could feel like a long time in a young person's life.

The challenge for managers and practitioners is, therefore, to use evidence of any promising approaches to develop interventions for preventing reoffending that:

- start at the pre-court stage and continue beyond the official end of the sentence;
- minimise the negative impact of custody;
- reduce the organisational and systemic barriers to providing timely, consistent and coherent interventions across secure and community settings.

Summary

- Custody is associated with high levels of reconviction and other poor outcomes, although the evidence is unclear as to whether this is to do with custody itself or how custody is currently configured, with its emphasis on punishment and the smooth operation of the regime as opposed to focusing more on rehabilitation and meeting the individual needs of young people.

- Resettlement is a relatively new term which is hard to define. Further, it implies young people were 'settled' prior to entry to custody which is far from the case for many.

- It is difficult to establish what is effective in relation to resettlement as there is little in the way of specific programme evaluation, and what little research does exist focuses solely on custodial interventions, is based on outcomes for adults rather than young people or is methodologically flawed.

- A core principle underpinning most resettlement models is the dimension of continuity: the DTO as a framework for resettlement emphasises the significance of a supported transition through consistent case management by a YOT practitioner from pre-sentence stage through to the end of the sentence.

Further reading

Hagell, A., Hazel, N. and Shaw, K. (2000) *Evaluation of Medway Secure Training Centre,* Occasional Paper. London: Home Office.

Hazel, N., Magell, A., Liddle, M., Archer, D., Grimshaw, R. and King, J. (2002) *Detention and Training: Assessment of the DTO and Its Impact on the Secure Estate across England and Wales.* London: Policy Research Bureau.

Stewart, G. and Tutt, N. (1987) *Children in Custody.* Aldershot: Avebury.

References

Adey, P., Fairbrother, R. and William, D. (1999) A *Review of Research on Learning Strategies and Learning Styles*. King's College: London School of Education.

Alexander, K., Entwisle, D. and Dauber, S. (1993) *On the Success of Failure – A Reassessment of the Effects of Retention in the Primary Grades*. Cambridge: Cambridge University Press.

Alexander, K., Entwisle, D. and Horsey, C. (1997) 'From the first grade forward: early foundations of high school drop out', *Sociology of Education*, 70: 87–107.

Altschuler, D. (1998) 'Intermediate sanctions and community treatment for serious and violent juvenile offenders', in R. Loeber and D. Farrington (eds), *Serious and Violent Juvenile Offenders: Risk Factors and Successful Interventions*. Thousand Oaks, CA: Sage.

Altschuler, D. and Armstrong, T. (1994a) *Intensive Aftercare for High-risk Juveniles: A Community Care Model. Program Summary*. Washington, DC: Office of Juvenile Justice and Delinquency Prevention.

Altschuler, D. and Armstrong, T. (1994b) *Intensive Aftercare for High-risk Juveniles: Policies and Procedures. Program Summary*. Washington, DC: Office of Juvenile Justice and Delinquency Prevention.

Altschuler, D. and Armstrong, T. (2002) 'Juvenile corrections and continuity of care in a community context – the evidence and promising directions', *Federal Patrol: A Journal of Correctional Philosophy and Practice*, Special Issue, 'What Works' in Corrections, September.

Altschuler, D., Armstrong, T. and Layton MacKenzie, D. (1999) *Reintegration, Supervised Release and Intensive Aftercare*, Juvenile Justice Bulletin, July 1999. Washington, DC: Office of Juvenile Justice and Delinquency Prevention.

American Psychiatric Association (1994) *Diagnostic and Statistical Manual of Mental Disorders*. American Psychiatric Association.

Andrews, D. (1995) 'The psychology of criminal conduct and effective treatment', in J. McGuire (ed.), *What Works: Reducing Re-offending: Guidelines from Research and Practice*. Chichester: John Wiley & Sons.

Andrews, D. and Bonta, J. (1994) *The Psychology of Criminal Conduct*. Cincinnati, OH: Anderson.

Andrews, D., Zinger, I., Hoge, R., Bonta, J., Gendreau, P. and Cullen, F. (1990) 'Does correctional treatment work? A clinically relevant and psychologically informed meta-analysis', *Criminology*, 28: 369–404.

Annison, J. (2005) 'Risk and protection', in T. Bateman and J. Pitts (eds), *The RHP Companion to Youth Justice*. Lyme Regis: Russell House.

Arnull, E., Eagle, S., Gammampila, A., Archer, D., Johnson, V., Miller, K. and Pitcher, J. (2005) *Persistent Young Offenders. A Retrospective Study*. London: Youth Justice Board.

Arts Council England (2007) *Summer Arts Colleges 2006: Evaluation Report.* London: Arts Council England.

Arts Council England (2008) *Summer Arts Colleges 2007: Evaluation Report.* London: Arts Council England.

Asmussen, K., Corlyon, J., Hauari, H. and La Placa, V. (2007) *Supporting Parents of Teenagers.* London: DfES.

Audit Commission (1996) *Misspent Youth: Young People and Crime.* London: Audit Commission.

Audit Commission (1999a) *Children in Mind – Child and Adolescent Mental Health Services.* London: Audit Commission.

Audit Commission (1999b) *Missing Out: LEA Management of School Attendance and Inclusion.* London: Audit Commission.

Audit Commission (2004) *Youth Justice 2004. A Review of the Referred Youth Justice System.* London: Audit Commission.

Bailey, S. and Kerslake, B. (2008) 'The process and systems for juveniles and young persons', in K. Soothill, P. Rogers and M. Dolan (eds), *Handbook of Forensic Mental Health.* Cullompton: Willan.

Baker, K., Jones, S., Roberts, C. and Merrington, S. (2002) *The Evaluation of the Validity and Reliability of the Youth Justice Board's Assessment for Young Offenders: Findings from the First Two Years of the Use of ASSET.* Oxford: Centre for Criminological Research, University of Oxford.

Baker, K., Jones, S., Merrington, S. and Roberts, C. (2005) *Further Development of Asset.* London: Youth Justice Board.

Bandura, A. (1995) *Self-efficacy in Changing Societies.* Cambridge: Cambridge University Press.

Barlow, J. (1997) *Systematic Review of the Effectiveness of Parent-Training Programmes in Improving Behaviour Problems in Children Aged 3–10 years.* Oxford: Health Services Research Unit, Department of Public Health.

Barn, R. (2001) *Black Youth on the Margins.* London: York Publishing Services for the Joseph Rowntree Foundation.

Batchelor, S. and McNeill, F. (2005) 'The young person–worker relationship', in T. Bateman and J . Pitts (eds), *The RHP Companion to Youth Justice.* Lyme Regis: Russell House.

Bateman, T. and Pitts, J. (eds) (2005) *The RHP Companion to Youth Justice.* Lyme Regis: Russell House.

Beaumont, B. and Mistry, T. (1996) 'Doing a good job under duress', *Probation Journal,* 43 (4): 200–4.

Bercow, J. (2008) *The Bercow Report: A Review of Services for Children and Young People (0–19) with Speech, Language and Communication Needs.* London: DCSF.

Berridge, D., Brodie, I., Pitts, J., Porteous, D. and Tarling, R. (2001) *The Independent Effects of Permanent Exclusion from School on the Offending Careers of Young People.* London: Home Office.

Bhabra, S., Hill, E. and Ghate, D. (2004) *Safer Schools Partnerships: National Evaluation of the Safer Schools Partnership Programme.* London: Youth Justice Board.

Bonta, J. (1996) 'Risk-needs assessment and treatment', in A. Harland (ed.), *Choosing Correctional Options that Work.* Thousand Oaks, CA: Sage.

Borduin, C., Heiblum, N., Jones, M. and Grabe, S. (2000) 'Community-based treatments of serious anti-social behavior in adolescents', in W. E. Martin and J. L. Swartz-Kulstad (eds), *Person-Environment Psychology and Mental Health: Assessment and Intervention.* Hillsdale, NJ: Erlbaum.

Boswell, G. (1996) *Young and Dangerous: The Backgrounds and Careers of Section 53 Offenders.* Aldershot: Avebury.

Bottoms, A. (2005) 'Methodology matters', *Safer Society*, 25: 10–12.

Bowles, R., Pradiptyo, R. and Garcia Reyes, M. (2006) *Estimating the Impact of the Safer Schools Partnerships Programme*. York: University of York.

Bowles, R., Reyes, M. G. and Pradiptyo, R (2005) *Safer Schools Partnerships*. London: Youth Justice Board.

Bowyer-Crane, C., Snowling, M. J., Duff, F. J., Carroll, J. M., Miles, J., Götz, K. and Hulme, C. (2008) 'Improving early language and literacy skills: differential effects of an oral language versus a phonology with reading intervention', *Journal of Child Psychology and Psychiatry*, 49 (4): 422–32.

Box, L. (2001) 'Supporting black and minority ethnic teenagers and their parents', in J. Coleman and D. Roker (eds), *Supporting Parents of Teenagers: A Handbook for Professionals*. London: Jessica Kingsley.

Braithwaite, J. (2002) *Restorative Justice and Responsive Regulation*. Oxford: Oxford University Press.

Bridges, A. (1998) *Increasing the Employability of Offenders: An Inquiry into Probation Service Effectiveness*, Probation Studies Unit Report No. 5. Oxford.

Brindle, D. (6 January 2010) 'Season of good cheer for advocates of targets in public services'. *The Guardian Society*. Retrieved from http://www.guardian.co.uk.

Britton, J. (2009) *Young People's Specialist Substance Misuse Treatment: Exploring the Evidence*. London: National Treatment Agency for Substance Misuse.

Britton, J. and Farrant, F. (2008) *Substance Misuse Source Document*. London: Youth Justice Board.

Brody, G. H., Murrey, V. M., Spoth, R. L., Luo, Z. and Chen, Y. (2006) 'The Strong African American Families Program: prevention of youths' high-risk behavior and a test model of changes', *Journal of Family Psychology*, 20 (1): 1–11.

Bronfenbrenner, U. (1979) *The Ecology of Human Development: Experiments by Nature and Design*. Cambridge, MA: Harvard University Press.

Brooks, G. (2002) *What Works for Children with Literacy Difficulties? The Effectiveness of Intervention Schemes*, Research Report RR380. London: DfES.

Brooks, G. (2009a) *Evaluation of TextNow 2008*. London: Unitas.

Brooks, G. (2009b) 'Speech, Language and Communication Provision for Children and Young People, Especially Those Who Have Offended'. London: ECOTEC (unpublished).

Brownlie, E. B., Beitchman, J. H., Escobar, M., Young, A., Atkinson, L., Johnson, C., Wilson, B. and Douglas, L. (2004) 'Early language impairment and young adult delinquent and aggressive behavior', *Journal of Abnormal Child Psychology*, 32: 453–67.

Bryan, K. (2004) 'Preliminary study of the prevalence of speech and language difficulties in young offenders', *International Journal of Language and Communication Disorders*, 39: 391–400.

Bryan, K. (2008) 'Speech, language and communication skills in juvenile offenders', in C. Hudson (ed.), *The Sound and the Silence: Key Perspectives on Speaking and Listening and Skills for Life*. Coventry: Quality Improvement Agency, pp. 52–60.

Bryan, K., Freer, J. and Furlong, C. (2007) 'Language and communication difficulties in juvenile offenders', *International Journal of Language and Communication Disorders*, 42 (5): 505–20.

Budd, T., Sharp, C., Weir, G., Wilson, D. and Owen, N. (2005) *Young People and Crime: Findings from the 2004 Offending Crime and Justice Survey*, Home Office Statistical Bulletin 20/05. London: Home Office, RDS.

Burgess, A. (2002) *Fathers and Families*. London: Parent Education and Support Forum.

Burnett, R. and Appleton, C. (2002) *Teaming Up to Reduce Youth Crime: A Study of the Oxfordshire YOT*. Oxford: Centre for Criminological Research.

Burnett, R. and Appleton, C. (2004) *Joined-up Youth Justice: Tackling Youth Crime in Partnership*. Lyme Regis: Russell House.

Burney, E. and Gelsthorpe, L. (2008) 'Do we need a "naughty step"? Rethinking the Parenting Order after ten years', *Howard Journal*, 47 (5): 470–85.

Burrows, M. H. (2003) *Evaluation of the Youth Inclusion Programme*. London: Youth Justice Board.

Butt, J. and Box, L. (1998) *Family Centred: A Study of the Use of Family Centres by Black Families*. London: Race Equality Unit.

Bynner, J. (2001) 'Childhood risks and protective factors in social exclusion', *Children and Society*, 15: 285–301.

Cabinet Office (1999) *Modernising Government*. London: Stationery Office.

Carney, M. M. and Buttell, F. (2003) 'Reducing juvenile recidivism: evaluating the Wraparound Services Model', *Research on Social Work Practice*, 13 (5): 551–68.

Carpenter, M. (1968) *Reformatory Schools for the Children of the Perishing and Dangerous Classes, and for Juvenile Offenders*. London: Woburn Press.

Case, S. (2006) 'Young people at risk of what? Challenging risk focussed early intervention as crime prevention', *Youth Justice*, 6: 171–9.

Case, S. (2010) 'Preventing and reducing risk', in W. Taylor, R. Earle and R. Hester (eds), *Youth Justice Handbook: Theory, Policy and Practice*. Cullompton: Willan.

Case, S. P. and Haines, K. R. (2009) *Understanding Youth Offending: Risk Factor Research, Policy and Practice*. Cullompton: Willan.

Catalano, R. and Hawkins, J. (1996) 'The social development model: a theory of antisocial behaviour', in J. Hawkins (ed.), *Delinquency and Crime: Current Theories*. Cambridge: Cambridge University Press.

Chapman, T. (2000) *Time to Grow*. Lyme Regis: Russell House.

Chapman, T. and Hough, M. (1998) *Evidence Based Practice: A Guide to Effective Practice*. London: HM Inspectorate of Probation/Home Office.

Cherry, S. (2005) *Transforming Behaviour Pro-social Modelling in Practice*. Cullompton: Willan.

Chitty, C. (2005) 'The impact of corrections on re-offending: conclusions and the way forward', in G. Harper and C. Chitty (eds), *The Impact of Corrections on Re-offending: A Review of 'What Works'*, Home Office Research Study 291. London: Home Office Research, Development and Statistics Directorate.

Cicchetti, D. and Rogosch, F. (1997) 'The role of self-organisation in the promotion of resilience in maltreated children', *Development and Psychopathology*, 9: 797–815.

Clegg, J., Hollis, C. and Rutter, M. (1999) *Life Sentence*, Royal College of Speech and Language Therapists Bulletin 571, pp. 16–18.

Coffey, D. and Gemignani, M. (1994) *Effective Practices in Juvenile Correctional Education: A Study of the Literature and Research 1980–1992*. Washington, DC: Office of Juvenile Justice and Delinquency.

Coffield, F., Mosely, D., Hall, E. and Ecclestone, K. (2004) *Learning Styles for Post-16 Learners: What Do We Know?* London: Learning and Skills Research Centre.

Coleman, J. and Roker, D. (2001) 'Setting the scene: parenting and public policy', in J. Coleman and D. Roker (eds), *Supporting Parents of Teenagers: A Handbook for Professionals*. London: Jessica Kingsley.

Coles, B. (2000) *Joined-up Youth Research, Policy and Practice: A New Agenda for Change?* Leicester: Youth Work Press.

Communities that Care (2001) *Risk and Protective Factors Associated with Youth Crime and Effective Interventions to Prevent It*. London: Youth Justice Board.

Cottle, C., Lee, R. and Heilbrun, K. (2001) 'The prediction of criminal recidivism in juveniles', *Criminal Justice and Behaviour*, 28 (3): 367–94.

Crawford, A. and Newburn, T. (2002) 'Recent developments in restorative justice for young people in England and Wales: community participation and representation', *British Journal of Criminology*, 42: 476–95.

Crawford, A. and Newburn, T. (2003) *Youth Offending and Restorative Justice: Implementing Reform in Youth Justice*. Cullompton: Willan.

Croninger, R. and Lee, V. (2001) 'Social capital and dropping out of school: benefits to at-risk students of teachers' support and guidance', *Teachers College Record*, 103: 548–81.

Cuellar, A. E., McReynolds, L. S. and Wasserman, G. A. (2006) 'A cure for crime: can mental health treatment diversion reduce crime among youth?', *Journal of Policy Analysis and Management*, 25 (1): 197–214.

Currie, E. (2003) '"It's our lives they're dealing with here": some adolescent views of residential treatment', *Journal of Drug Issues*, 33 (4): 833–64.

Curry, D., Knight, V., Owens-Rawle, D., Patel, S., Semenchuk, M. and Williams, B. (2004) *Restorative Justice in the Juvenile Secure Estate*. London: Youth Justice Board.

Curtis, N., Ronan, K. and Borduin, C. (2004) 'Multi-systemic treatment: a meta-analysis of outcome studies', *Journal of Family Psychology*, 18 (3): 411–19.

Cusick, J. (2001) *Working with Fathers*. Brighton: Trust for the Study of Adolescence.

Daly, K. (2003) 'Making variation a virtue: evaluating the potential and limits of restorative justice', in E. Weitekamp and H. J. Kerner (eds), *Restorative Justice in Context*. Cullompton: Willan.

Daniels, H., Visser, J., Cole, T. and de Reybekill, N. (1998) *Emotional and Behavioural Difficulties in Mainstream Schools*, Research Report RR90. London: DfEE.

Davies, K., Lewis, J., Byatt, J., Purvis, E. and Cole, B. (2004) *An Evaluation of the Literacy Requirements of General Offending Behaviour Programmes*, Home Office Findings 233. London: Home Office.

Dennis, M., Godley, S. H., Diamond, G., Tims, F. M., Babor, T., Donaldson, J., Liddle, H., Titus, J. C., Kaminer, Y., Webb, C., Hamilton, N. and Funk, R. (2004) 'The Cannabis Youth Treatment (CYT) study: main findings from two randomized trials', *Journal of Substance Abuse Treatment*, 27 (3): 197–213.

Department for Children, Schools and Families (2008a) *Back on Track: A Strategy for Modernising Alternative Provision for Young People*, White Paper. London: DCSF.

Department for Children, Schools and Families (2008b) *Parenting Early Intervention Pathfinder Evaluation*. London: DCSF.

Department for Children, Schools and Families (2009) *Anti-Social Behaviour Family Intervention Projects Monitoring and Evaluation*. London: DCSF.

Department for Communities and Local Government (2006) *Anti-social Behaviour Intensive Family Support Projects: An Evaluation of Six Pioneering Projects*. London: DCLG.

Department for Education and Employment (1994) *The Education of Children with Emotional and Behavioural Difficulties*, Circular 9/94. London: DfEE.

Department for Education and Employment (1995) *More Willingly to School? An Independent Evaluation of the DfEE's Truancy and Disaffected Pupils (TDP) GEST Programme*. London: DfEE.

Department for Education and Employment (1999) *Social Inclusion: Pupil Support Truancy and School Exclusion*, Circular 10/99. London: DfEE.

Department for Education and Employment (2000) *Connexions: The Best Start in Life for Every Young Person*. London: DfEE.

Department for Education and Skills (2004a) *Every Child Matters: Change for Children*. London: DfES.

Department for Education and Skills (2004b) *14–19 Curriculum and Qualifications Reform: Final Report of the Working Group on 14–19 Reform*. London: DfES.

Department for Education and Skills (2005) *Youth Matters*. London: DfES.

Department for Education and Skills (2007) *Every Parent Matters*. London: DfES.

Department for Education and Skills/Department of Health (2000) *Guidance on the Education of Children and Young People in Public Care*. London: DfES.

Department of Health (2003) *Leaving Care*, Research Briefing No. 6. London: DoH.

Department of Health and Department for Education and Skills (2004) *CAMHS Standard, NSF for Children, Young People and Maternity Services*. London: DoH.

Desforges, C. and Abouchaar, A. (2003) *The Impact of Parental Involvement, Parental Support and Family Education on Pupil Achievement and Adjustment: A Literature Review*, DfES Research Report No. 433. London: Queen's Printer.

Dignan, J. (2000) *Youth Justice Pilots Evaluation: Interim Report on Reparative Work and Youth Offending Teams*. London: Home Office.

Dignan, J. (2002) 'Reparation orders', in B. Williams (ed.), *Reparation and Victim-Focused Social Work*. London: Jessica Kingsley.

Dillon, L., Chivite-Matthews, N., Grewal, I., Brown, R., Webster, S., Weddell, E., Brown, G. and Smith, N. (2007) *Risk, Protective Factors and Resilience to Drug Use: Identifying Resilient Young People and Learning from their Experiences*, Home Office Online Report 04/07. London: Home Office RDS.

Ditchfield, J. and Catan, L. (1992) *Juveniles Sentenced for Serious Offences: A Comparison of Regimes in Young Offender Institutions and Local Authority Community Homes*. London: Home Office.

Dixon, M. and Margo, J. with Pearce, N. and Reed, H. (2006) *Freedom's Orphan: Raising Youth in a Changing World*. London: Institute of Public Policy Research.

Dodge, K. and Schwartz, D. (1997) 'Social information processing mechanisms in aggressive behaviour', in D. M. Stoff (ed.), *Handbook of Antisocial Behaviour*. New York: Wiley.

Dowden, C. and Andrews, D. A. (2004) 'The importance of staff practice in delivering effective correctional treatment: a meta-analytic review of core correctional practice', *International Journal of Offender Therapy and Comparative Criminology*, 48 (2): 203–14.

Downes, D. and Morgan, R. (2002) 'The skeletons in the cupboard: the politics of law and order at the turn of the millennium', in M. Maguire, R. Morgan and R. Reiner (eds), *The Oxford Handbook of Criminology*. Oxford: Oxford University Press.

Drake, K., Aos, S. and Miller, M. G. (2009) 'Evidence-based public policy options to reduce crime and criminal justice costs: implications in Washington State', *Victims and Offenders*, 4: 170–96.

Drugscope and DPAS (2001) *Assessing Local Need: Planning Services for Young People*. Drug Prevention Advisory Service.

Duroy, T. H., Schmidt, S. L. and Perry, P. D. (2003) 'Adolescents' and young adults' perspectives on a continuum of care in a three-year drug treatment program', *Journal of Drug Issues*, 34 (4): 801–32.

Eadie, T. and Canton, R. (2002) 'Practising in a context of ambivalence: the challenge for youth justice workers', *Youth Justice*, 2 (1): 14–26.

ECOTEC (2001a) *An Audit of Education and Training Provision within the Youth Justice System*. London: Youth Justice Board.

ECOTEC (2001b) *Review of the Pre- and Post-custodial Education and Training Experiences of Young People*. London: Youth Justice Board.

Edmonds, K., Sumnall, H., McVeigh, J. and Bellis, M. (2005) *Drug Prevention among Vulnerable Young People*. Liverpool: National Collaborating Centre for Drug Prevention.

Elliot, L., Orr, L., Watson, L. and Jackson, A. (2001) *Drug Treatment Services for Young People: A Systematic Review of Effectiveness and Legal Framework*. Edinburgh: Scottish Executive Effective Interventions Unit.

Elliott, A., Lindfield, S. and Cusick, J. (2002) *Parents' Views*. Brighton: Trust for the Study of Adolescence.

Farabee, D., Shen, H., Hser, Y., Grella, C. E. and Anglin, M. D. (2001) 'The effect of drug treatment on criminal behavior among adolescents in DATOS-A', *Journal of Adolescent Research*, 16 (6): 679–96.

Farrington, D. (1991) 'Childhood aggression and adult violence', in D. Pepler and K. Rubin (eds), *The Development and Treatment of Childhood Aggression*. Hillsdale, NJ: Lawrence Erlbaum.

Farrington, D. (1992) 'Explaining the beginning, progress and ending of antisocial behaviour from birth to adulthood', in J. McCord (ed.), *Facts, Frameworks and Forecasts: Advances in Criminological Theory*, Vol. 3. New Brunswick, NJ: Transaction.

Farrington, D. (1996) *Understanding and Preventing Youth Crime*. York: Joseph Rowntree Foundation.

Farrington, D. (1997) 'Human development and criminal careers', in M. Maguire, R. Morgan and R. Reiner (eds), *The Oxford Handbook of Criminology*, 2nd edn. Oxford: Oxford University Press.

Farrington, D. (2000) 'Psychosocial predictors of adult anti-social personality and adult convictions', *Behavioural Science and the Law*, 18: 605–22.

Farrington, D. (2002) 'Developmental criminology and risk-focused prevention', in M. Maguire, R. Morgan and R. Reiner (eds), *The Oxford Handbook of Criminology*, 3rd edn. Oxford: Oxford University Press.

Farrington, D. and Welsh, B. (2002) 'Developmental prevention programmes: effectiveness and benefit-cost analysis', in J. McGuire (ed.), *Offender Rehabilitation and Treatment: Effective Programmes and Policies to Reduce Reoffending*. Chichester: John Wiley & Sons.

Farrington, D., Ditchfield, J., Hancock, G., Howard, P., Jolliffe, D., Livingston, M. and Painter, K. (2002) *Evaluation of Two Intensive Regimes for Young Offenders*, Home Office Research Study 239. London: Home Office.

Farrow, K., Kelly, G. and Wilkinson, B. (2007) *Offenders in Focus*. Bristol: Policy Press.

Feilzer, M. and Hood, R. (2004) *Differences or Discrimination? Minority Ethnic People in the Youth Justice System*. London: Youth Justice Board.

Feilzer, M., Appleton, C., Roberts, C. and Hoyle, C. (2004) *Cognitive Behaviour Projects: The National Evaluation of the Youth Justice Board's Cognitive Behaviour Projects*. London: Youth Justice Board.

Feinstein, L. and Sabates, R. (2005) *Education and Youth Crime: Effects of Introducing the Education Maintenance Allowance Programme*, DfES Research Brief No. RCB01–05.

Fergusson, D., Lynskey, M. and Horwood, J. (1996) 'Factors associated with continuity and changes in disruptive behaviour patterns between childhood and adolescence', *Journal of Abnormal Child Psychology*, 24: 533–54.

Fletcher, K. E. (2003) 'Childhood post-traumatic stress disorder', in E. J. Mash and R. A. Berkley (eds), *Child Psychopathology*. New York: Guilford Press.

Fonagy, P., Target, M., Cottrell, D. and Phillips, J. (2002) *What Works for Whom? A Critical Review of Treatments for Children and Adolescents*. New York and London: Guilford Press.

Forehand, R. and Kotchick, B. (2002) 'Behavioral parent training: current challenges and potential solutions', *Journal of Child and Family Studies*, 11: 377–84.

Fredericks, J., Blumenfeld, P. and Paris, A. (2004) 'School engagement: potential of the concept, state of the evidence', *Review of Educational Research*, 74 (1): 59–109.

Frisher, M., Crome, I., Macleod, J., Bloor, R. and Hickman, N. (2007) *Predictive Factors for Illicit Drug Use among Young People: A Literature Review*, Home Office Online Report 05/07. London: Home Office RDS.

Fullwood, C. and Powell, H. (2004) 'Towards effective practice in the Youth Justice System', in R. Burnett and C. Roberts (eds), *What Works in Probation and Youth Justice: Developing Evidence-based Practice*. Cullompton: Willan.

Galahad SMS Ltd (2004) *Substance Misuse and the Juvenile Secure Estate*. London: Youth Justice Board.

Galahad SMS Ltd (2009) *Substance Misuse Services in the Secure Estate*. London: Youth Justice Board.

Galloway, D. (1985) *Schools and Persistent Absentees*. Oxford: Pergamon.

Gelsthorpe, L. and Sharpe, G. (2006) 'Gender, youth crime and justice', in B. Goldson and J. Muncie (eds), *Youth Crime and Justice*. London: Sage.

Gemignani, R. (1994) *Juvenile Correctional Education: A Time for Change*. Washington, DC: Office of Juvenile Justice and Delinquency Prevention.

Ghate, D. and Hazel, N. (2002) *Parenting in Poor Environments: Stress, Support and Coping*. London: Jessica Kingsley.

Ghate, D. and Ramella, M. (2002) *Positive Parenting: The National Evaluation of the Youth Justice Board's Parenting Programme*. London: Youth Justice Board.

Ghate, D., Hauari, H. and Hollingworth, K. (2007) *Qualitative Research Amongst At Risk Families*. London: Social Exclusion Task Force.

Ghate, D., Hauari, H., Hollingworth, K. and Lindfield, S. (2008) *Parenting Source Document*. London: Youth Justice Board.

Gies, S. (2003) *Aftercare Services*, Juvenile Justice Bulletin. Washington, DC: Office of Juvenile Justice and Delinquency Prevention.

Godley, M. D., Godley, S. H., Dennis, M. L., Funk, R. R. and Passetti, L. L. (2007) 'The effect of assertive continuing care on continuing care linkage, adherence and abstinence following residential treatment for adolescents with substance use disorders', *Addiction*, 102 (1): 81–93.

Goldson, B. (2000) 'Whither diversion? Interventionism and the new youth justice', in B. Goldson (ed.), *The New Youth Justice*. Lyme Regis: Russell House.

Goldson, B. and Muncie, J. (eds) (2006) *Youth Crime and Justice*. London: Sage.

Goldson, B. and Peters, E. (2000) *Tough Justice: Responding to Children in Trouble*. London: Children's Society.

Gottfredson, D. (2001) *Schools and Delinquency*. Cambridge: Cambridge University Press.

Goulden, C. and Sondhi, A. (2001) *At the Margins: Drug Use by Vulnerable Young People in the 1998/99 Youth Lifestyles Survey*, Home Office Research Study 228. London: Home Office.

Graham, J. and Bowling, B. (1995) *Young People and Crime*, Home Office Research Study 145. London: Home Office.

Gray, E., McCambridge, J. and Strang, J. (2005) 'The effectiveness of motivational interviewing delivered by youth workers in reducing drinking, cigarette and cannabis smoking among young people: quasi-experimental pilot study', *Alcohol and Alcoholism*, 40 (6): 535–9.

Gray, E., Taylor, E., Roberts, C., Merrington, S., Fernandez, R. and Moore, R. (2005) *Intensive Supervision and Surveillance Programme. The Final Report*. London: Youth Justice Board.

Gray, J. A. M. (2000) 'Evidence-based public health', in L. Trinder and S. Reynolds (eds), *Evidence-Based Practice: A Critical Appraisal*. Oxford: Blackwell Science.

Gray, P. (2005a) 'Community interventions', in T. Bateman and J. Pitts (eds), *The RHP Companion to Youth Justice*. Lyme Regis: Russell House.

Gray, P. (2005b) 'The politics of risk and young offenders' experience of social exclusion and restorative justice', *British Journal of Criminology*, 45: 938–57.

Gray, P., Mosely, J. and Browning, S. (2003) *An Evaluation of the Plymouth Restorative Justice Programme*. Plymouth: University of Plymouth.

Green, H., McGinnity, A., Meltzer, H., Ford, T. and Goodman, R. (2005) *Mental Health of Children and Young People in Great Britain, 2004*. London: Office of National Statistics.

Greenwood, P., Rydell, P., Abrahamse, A., Caulkins, J., Model, K. and Kelin, S. (1994) *Three Strikes and You're Out: Estimated Benefits and Costs of California's New Mandatory Sentencing Laws*. Santa Monica, CA: Rand.

Gregory, J. and Bryan, K. (2009) *Evaluation of the Leeds Speech and Language Therapy Service Provision within the Intensive Supervision and Surveillance Programme provided by the Leeds Youth Offending Team*. Leeds: Youth Offending Service and Guildford: University of Surrey (mimeograph).

Griffin, P. (1999) 'Juvenile probation in the schools', *NCJJ in Focus*, 1 (1): 1–10.

Grimshaw, R. and Berridge, D. (1994) *Educating Disruptive Children: Placement and Progress in Residential Special Schools for Pupils with Emotional and Behavioural Difficulties*. London: National Children's Bureau.

Grisso, T. and Schwartz, R. (eds) (2000) *Youth on Trial: A Developmental Perspective on Juvenile Justice*. London: University of Chicago Press.

Hagell, A. (2002) *The Mental Health of Young Offenders*. London: Mental Health Foundation.

Hagell, A. (2005) 'The use of custody for children and young people', in T. Bateman and J. Pitts (eds), *The RHP Companion to Youth Justice*. Lyme Regis: Russell House.

Hagell, A., Hazel, N. and Shaw, K. (2000) *Evaluation of Medway Secure Training Centre*, Occasional Paper. London: Home Office.

Haines, K. and O'Mahony, D. (2006) 'Restorative approaches, young people and youth justice', in B. Goldstein and J. Muncie (eds), *Youth Crime and Justice*. London: Sage.

Hammersley, R., Marsland, L. and Reid, M. (2003) *Substance Use by Young Offenders: The Impact of the Normalisation of Drug Use in the Early Years of the 21st Century*, Home Office Research Study 261. London: Home Office.

Hammersley, R., Reid, M., Oliver, A., Genova, A., Raynor P., Minkes, J. and Morgan, M. (2004) *The National Evaluation of the Youth Justice Board's Drug and Alcohol Projects*. London: Youth Justice Board.

Harper, G. and Chitty, C. (2005) *The Impact of Corrections on Re-offending: A Review of 'What Works'*, Home Office Research Study 291. London: Home Office Research, Development and Statistics Directorate.

Harper, R. and Hardy, S. (2000) 'An evaluation of motivational interviewing as a method of intervention with clients in a probation setting', *British Journal of Social Work*, 30: 393–400.

Harrington, D. and Bailey, S. (2005) *Mental Health Needs and Effectiveness of Provision for Young Offenders in Custody and in the Community*. London: Youth Justice Board.

Hayward, G., Hodgson, A., Johnson, J., Oancea, A., Pring, R., Spours, K., Wilde, S. and Wright, S. (2005) *The Nuffield Review of 14–19 Education and Training Annual Report 2004–05*. Oxford: University of Oxford Department of Educational Studies.

Hazel, N. (2008) *Cross-National Comparison of Youth Justice*. London: Youth Justice Board.

Hazel, N., Hagell, A., Liddle, M., Archer, D., Grimshaw, R. and King, J. (2002) *Detention and Training: Assessment of the Detention and Training Order and Its Impact on the Secure Estate Across England and Wales*. London: Youth Justice Board.

Hendrick, H. (2006) 'Histories of youth crime and justice', in B. Goldson and J. Muncie (eds), *Youth Crime and Justice*. London: Sage.

Henggeler, S. W., Clingempeel, W. G., Brondino, M. J. and Pickrel, S. G. (2002) 'Four-year follow-up of multisystemic therapy with substance-abusing and substance dependent juvenile offenders', *Journal of American Academy of Child and Adolescent Psychiatry*, 41 (7): 868–74.

Henggeler, S. W., Halliday-Boykins, C. A., Cunningham, P. B., Randall, J., Shapiro, S. B. and Chapman, J. E. (2006) 'Juvenile drug court: enhancing outcomes by integrating evidence-based treatments', *Journal of Consulting and Clinical Psychology*, 74: 42–54.

Henricson, C. (2003) *Government and Parenting: Is There a Case for a Policy Review and a Parents' Code?* York: Joseph Rowntree Foundation.

Henricson, C., Coleman, J. and Roker, D. (2000) 'Parenting in the youth justice context', *Howard Journal*, 39 (4): 325–8.

Henry, B., Caspi, A., Moffitt, T. and Silva, P. (1996) 'Temperamental and familial predictors of violent and non-violent criminal convictions: age 3 to age 18', *Developmental Psychology*, 32: 614–23.

HM Inspectorate of Prisons (2006) *Annual Report of HM Chief Inspector of Prisons for England and Wales 2004–2005*. London: Stationery Office.

HM Inspectorate of Prisons (2008) *Annual Report 2006/2007*. London: HMIP.

HM Inspectorate of Probation (2002) *Annual Report 2001–2002*. London: Home Office.

HM Inspectorate of Probation (2004) *Joint Inspection of Youth Offending Teams First Phase: Annual Report*. London: Home Office.

HM Inspectorate of Probation (2006) *Joint Inspection of Youth Offending Teams Annual Report 2005/2006*. London: HM Inspectorate of Probation.

Hoaken, P. and Stewart, S. (2003) 'Drugs of abuse and the elicitation of human aggressive behavior', *Addictive Behaviours*, 28: 1533–54.

Hobbs and Hook Consulting (2001) *Research into Effective Practice with Young People in Secure Facilities*, Youth Justice Board Research Note No. 3.

Hodges, H. (1982) 'Madison prep – alternatives through learning styles', in W. Keefe (ed.), *Student Learning Styles and Brain Behaviour Progress, Instrumentation, Research*. Reston VA: National Association of Secondary School Principals (28: 31).

Hogue, A., Dauber, S., Stambaugh, L. F., Cecero, J. J. and Liddle, H. A. (2006) 'Early therapeutic alliance and treatment outcome in individual and family therapy for adolescent behavior problems', *Journal of Consulting and Clinical Psychology*, 74 (1): 121–9.

Hollin, C. (1995) 'The meaning and implications of programme integrity', in J. McGuire (ed.), *What Works: Reducing Re-offending: Guidelines from Research and Practice*. Chichester: John Wiley & Sons.

Hollin, C., McGuire, J., Palmer, E., Bilby, C., Hatcher, R. and Holmes, A. (2002) *Introducing Pathfinder Programmes into the Probation Service: An Interim Report*, Home Office Research Study 247. London: Home Office.

Holt, A. (2010) 'Parenting and youth justice: policy and practice', in W. Taylor, R. Earle and R. Hester (eds), *Youth Justice Handbook: Policy and Practice*. Cullompton: Willan.

Home Office (1998) *Joining Forces to Protect the Public: Prisons-Probation*. London: Home Office.

Home Office (2003) *Prison Statistics, England and Wales 2002*. London: Stationery Office.

Home Office (2004) *The Role of Education in Enhancing Life Chances and Preventing Offending*, Home Office Development and Practice Report 19. London: Home Office.

Home Office (2008) *Youth Crime Action Plan 2008*. London: Home Office.

Home Office Research, Development and Statistics Directorate (2002) *The Road to Ruin? Sequences of Initiation into Drug Use and Offending by Young People in Britain*, Home Office Research Study 253. London: Stationery Office.

Hope, T. (1996) 'Communities, crime and inequality in England and Wales', in T. Bennett (ed.), *Preventing Crime and Disorder. Targeting Strategies and Responsibilities* (Cropwood Series). Cambridge: Institute of Criminology.

Howell, E. and Montuschi, O. (2002) *Groupwork with Parents of Adolescents*. London: Parenting Education and Support Forum.

Howell, J. (2003) *Preventing and Reducing Juvenile Delinquency: A Comprehensive Framework*. London: Sage.

Hoyle, C., Young, R. and Hill, R. (2002) *Proceed with Caution – An Evaluation of the Thames Valley Initiative in Restorative Cautioning*. York: York Publishing Services.

Hughes, J. (2005) *Doing the Arts Justice: A Review of Research Literature, Practice and Theory*. Canterbury: Unit for the Arts and Offenders, Centre for Applied Theatre Research.

Hurry, J. and Moriarty, V. (2004) *The National Evaluation of the Youth Justice Board's Education, Training and Employment Projects*. London: Youth Justice Board.

Hurry, J., Brazier, L. and Moriarty, V. (2006) 'Improving the literacy and numeracy skills of young people who offend: can it be done and what are the consequences?', *Numeracy and Literacy Studies*, v. 14, n. 2, pp. 47–60.

Hurry, J., Brazier, L., Snapes, K. and Wilson, A. (2005) *Improving the Literacy and Numeracy of Disaffected Young People in Custody and in the Community: Summary Interim Report of the First Eighteen Months of Study*. London: National Research and Development Centre.

Hustler, D., Callaghan, J., Cockett, M. and McNeill, J. (1998) *Choices for Life: An Evaluation of Rathbone CI's Work with Disaffected and Excluded School Pupils*. Manchester Metropolitan University: Didsbury Educational Research Centre.

INCLUDE (2000) *Approaches to Effective Practice for YOTs: Engaging Young Offenders in Education, Training and Employment*. London: Youth Justice Board.

Ipsos MORI (2010) *A Review of Techniques for Effective Engagement and Participation*. London: Youth Justice Board.

Jainchill, N., Hawke, J. and Messina, M. (2005) 'Post-treatment outcomes among adjudicated adolescent males and females in modified therapeutic community treatment', *Substance Use and Misuse*, 40: 975–96.

Jermyn, H. (2004) *The Art of Inclusion*, Research Report 35. London: Arts Council England.

Jessor, R. and Jessor, S. (1977) *Problem Behaviour and Psycho-Social Development: A Longitudinal Study of Youth*. New York: Academic Press.

John, P. (1996) 'Damaged goods? An interpretation of excluded pupils' perceptions of schooling', in E. Blyth and J. Milner (eds), *Exclusion from School: Inter-Professional Issues for Policy and Practice*. London: Routledge.

Jones, D. (2002) 'Questioning New Labour's youth justice strategy: a review article', *Youth Justice*, 1 (3): 14–26.

Kaminer, Y., Burleson, J. A. and Goldberger, R. (2002) 'Cognitive-behavioural coping skills and psychoeducation therapies for adolescent substance abuse', *Journal of Nervous and Mental Disease*, 190 (11): 737–45.

Keeling, P., Kibblewhite, K. and Smith, Z. (2004) 'Evidence-based practice in young people's substance misuse services', in D. White (ed.), *Social Work and Evidence-based Practice*. London: Jessica Kingsley.

Kelly, L. (2008) 'Sport-based crime prevention', in B. Goldson (ed.), *The Dictionary of Youth Justice*. Cullompton: Willan.

Kemshall, H. (2008) 'Risks, rights and justice: understanding and responding to youth risk', *Youth Justice*, 8 (1): 21–37.

Kendall, S., Kinder, K., Halsey, K., Fletcher-Morgan, C., White, R. and Brown, C. (2002) *An Evaluation of Alternative Education Initiatives*. London: DfES.

Kinder, K., Halsey, K., Kendall, S., Atkinson, M., Moor, H., Wilkin, A., White, R. and Rigby, B. (2000) *Working Out Well: Effective Provision for Excluded Pupils*. Slough: NFER.

Kroll, L., Woodham, A. and Rothwell, J. (1999) 'The reliability of the Salford Needs Assessment Schedule for Adolescents', *Psychological Medicine*, 29: 891–902.

Krueger, R., Caspi, A., Moffitt, T. and White, J. (1996) 'Delay of gratification, psychopathology, and personality: is low self-control specific to externalising problems?', *Journal of Personality*, 64: 107–29.

Kumpfer, K. (1993) *Strengthening America's Families: Promising Parenting and Family Strengthening Strategies for Delinquency Prevention*. Washington, DC: Office of Juvenile Justice and Delinquency Prevention, US Department of Justice.

Kumpfer, K. and Alvarado, R. (1998) 'Effective family strengthening interventions', *Juvenile Justice Bulletin*, November. Office of Juvenile Justice Delinquency Prevention, Office of Justice Programmes, US Department of Justice.

Lader, D., Singleton, N. and Meltzer, H. (1997) *Psychiatric Morbidity among Young Offenders in England and Wales*. London: Office for National Statistics.

Landenberger, N. and Lipsey, M. (2005) 'The positive effects of cognitive-behavioral programs for offenders: a meta-analysis of factors associated with effective treatment', *Journal of Experimental Criminology*, 1 (4): 451–76.

Latimer, J., Dowden, C. and Muise, D. (2001) *The Effectiveness of Restorative Justice Practices: A Meta-Analysis*. Ottawa: Department of Justice Canada.

Lefevre, M. (2010) *Communicating with Children and Young People*. Bristol: The Policy Press.

Liabø, K. and Richardson, R. (2007) *Conduct Disorder and Offending Behaviour in Young People: Findings from Research*. London: Jessica Kingsley

Liddle, H. A., Rowe, C. L., Dakof, G. A., Ungaro, R. A. and Henderson, C. E. (2004) 'Early intervention for adolescent substance abuse: pre-treatment to post-treatment outcomes of a randomized clinical trial comparing multidimensional family therapy and peer group treatment', *Journal of Psychoactive Drugs*, 36 (1): 49–63.

Lindfield, S. (2001) *Human Rights Act and Parenting Orders: Key Points for Parenting Practitioners*. Brighton: Trust for the Study of Adolescence.

Lindfield, S. and Cusick, J. (2001) 'Working with parents in the youth justice context', in J. Coleman and D. Roker (eds), *Supporting Parents of Teenagers: A Handbook for Professionals*. London: Jessica Kingsley.

Lipsey, M. (1995) 'What do we learn from 400 research studies on the effectiveness of treatment with juvenile delinquents?', in J. McGuire (ed.), *What Works: Reducing Offending*. Chichester: Wiley.

Lipsey, M. and Landenberger, N. (2006) 'Cognitive-behavioral interventions', in B. C. Welsh and D. P. Farrington (eds), *Preventing Crime: What Works for Children, Offenders, Victims, and Places*. Dordrecht, The Netherlands: Springer.

Lipsey, M. and Wilson, D. (1998) 'Effective intervention for serious juvenile offenders: a synthesis of research', in R. Loeber and D. Farrington (eds), *Serious and Violent Juvenile Offenders: Risk Factors and Successful Interventions*. Thousand Oaks, CA: Sage.

Lipsey, M., Wilson, D. and Cothern, L. (2000) *Effective Intervention for Serious Juvenile Offenders*. Washington, DC: Office of Juvenile Justice and Delinquency Prevention.

Littell, J., Popa, M. and Forsythe, B. (2005) 'Multi-systemic therapy for social, emotional, and behavioral problems in youth aged 10–17', *Cochrane Database Systematic Review*, 4, CD004797.

Lloyd, C. (1998) 'Risk factors for problem drug use: identifying vulnerable groups', *Drugs: Education, Prevention and Policy*, 5 (3): 217–32.

Lloyd, E. (1999) *Parenting Matters: What Works in Parenting Education*. Ilford: Barnardo's.

Lloyd, T. (2001) *What Works With Fathers?* London: Working With Men.

Lobley, D., Smith, D. and Stern, C. (2001) *Freagarrach: An Evaluation of a Project for Persistent Juvenile Offenders*, Crime and Criminal Research Findings No. 53. Edinburgh: Stationery Office.

Loeber, R. and Le Blanc, M. (1990) 'Toward a developmental criminology', in M. Tonry and N. Morris (eds), *Crime and Justice*, Vol. 12. Chicago: University of Chicago Press.

Loeber, R. and Stouthamer-Loeber, M. (1986) 'Family factors as correlates and predictors of antisocial conduct problems and delinquency', in N. Morris and M. Tonry (eds), *Crime and Justice*, Vol. 7. Chicago: University of Chicago Press.

Loeber, R., Kammen, W. B. and Manghon, B. (1993) 'Development pathways in disruptive child behaviour', *Development and Psychopathology*, 5: 103–33.

Luthar, S. S. (ed.) (2003) *Resilience and Vulnerability: Adaptation in the Context of Childhood Adversities*. Cambridge: Cambridge University Press.

McAra, L. (2004) *Truancy, School Exclusion and Substance Misuse*. Edinburgh: University of Edinburgh Centre for Law and Society

McAra, L. and McVie, S. (2007) 'Youth justice? The impact of system contact on patterns of desistance from offending', *European Journal of Criminology*, 4 (3): 315–45.

McCart, M., Priester, P., Davies, W. and Azen, R. (2006) 'Differential effectiveness of behavioral parent-training and cognitive-behavioral therapy for antisocial youth: a meta-analysis', *Journal of Abnormal Child Psychology*, 34 (4): 527–43.

McCold, P. and Wachtel, T. (2002) 'Restorative justice theory validation', in E. Weitekamp and H. J. Kerner (eds), *Restorative Justice: Theoretical Foundations*. Cullompton: Willan.

McGarrell, E., Olivares, K., Crawford, K. and Kroovand, N. (2000) *Returning Justice to the Community: The Indianapolis Juvenile Restorative Justice Experiment*. Indianapolis: Hudson Institute.

McGuire, J. (1995) *What Works: Reducing Re-offending: Guidelines from Research and Practice*. Chichester: J. Wiley & Sons.

McGuire, J. (2000) *Cognitive Behavioural Approaches: An Introduction to Theory and Research*. London: HM Inspectorate of Probation.

McGuire, J. and Priestley, P. (1995) 'Reviewing "what works": past, present and future', in J. McGuire (ed.), *What Works: Reducing Re-offending: Guidelines from Research and Practice*. Chichester: J. Wiley & Sons.

McGuire, J., Kinderman, K. and Hughes, C. (2002) *Offending Behaviour Programmes*. London: Youth Justice Board.

McIntosh, S. (2003) *The Early Post-school Experiences of the Unqualified/Low Qualified: Using the Labour Force Survey to Map the 14–16 Year Old Low-Achievers*. London: Centre for Economic Performance.

McIvor, G. (1990) *Sanctions for Serious or Persistent Offenders: A Review of the Literature*. Stirling: Social Work Research Centre, University of Stirling.

MacKenzie, D. (2006) *What Works in Corrections. Reducing the Criminal Activities of Offenders and Delinquents*. Cambridge: Cambridge University Press.

McMahon, G., Hall, A., Hayward, G., Hudson, C., Roberts, C., Fernandez, R. and Burnett, R. (2004) *Basic Skills Programmes in the Probation Service: Evaluation of the Basic Skills Pathfinder*. London: Home Office.

McNeill, F. (2009) *Towards Effective Practice in Offender Supervision*. Glasgow: Scottish Centre for Crime and Justice Research.

McNeill, F. and Batchelor, S. (2002) 'Chaos, containment and change: responding to persistent offending by young people', *Youth Justice*, 2: 1.

Maguin, E. and Loeber, R. (1996) 'Academic performance and delinquency', in M. Tonry (ed.), *Crime and Justice: A Review of Research*, Vol. 20. Chicago: University of Chicago Press.

Marshall, M., Hogg, L. I., Gath, D. H. and Lockwood, A. (1995) 'The Cardinal Needs Schedule – a modified version of the MRC Needs for Care Assessment Schedule', *Psychological Medicine*, 25: 605–17.

Marshall, T. (1999) *Restorative Justice: An Overview.* London: HMSO.

Marshall, T. and Merry, S. (1990) *Crime and Accountability. Victim-Offender Mediation in Practice.* London: HMSO.

Martinson, R. (1974) 'What works? Questions and answers about prison reform', *The Public Interest*, 35.

Mason, P. and Prior, D. (2008) *Engaging Young People Who Offend: Source Document.* London: Youth Justice Board.

Masters, G. (2005) 'Restorative justice and youth justice', in T. Bateman and J. Pitts (eds), *The RHP Companion to Youth Justice.* Lyme Regis: Russell House.

Matrix Research and Consultancy and ICPR (2007) *Evaluation of Drug Interventions Programme Pilots for Children and Young People: Arrest, Referral, Drug Testing and Drug Treatment and Testing Requirements*, Home Office Online Report 07/07. London: Home Office RDS.

Maxwell, G. and Morris, A. (1993) *Family, Victims and Culture: Youth Justice in New Zealand.* New Zealand: Department of Social Welfare.

May, C. (1999) *Explaining Reconviction Following a Community Sentence: The Role of Social Factors*, Home Office Research Study 192. London: Home Office.

Mental Health Foundation (1999) *Bright Futures – Promoting Children and Young People's Mental Health.* London: Mental Health Foundation.

Merrington, S. (1998) *A Guide to Setting Up and Evaluating Programmes for Young Offenders.* Winchester: Waterside Press.

Merton, B. (with Payne, M. and Smith, D.) *et al.* (2004) *An Evaluation of the Impact of Youth Work in England*, DfES Research Report RR606. London: DfES.

Mihalic, S., Irwin, K., Elliott, D., Fagan, A. and Hansen, D. (2001) *Blueprints for Violence Prevention.* Washington, DC: Office of Juvenile Justice and Delinquency Prevention.

Miller, W. R. and Rollnick, S. (2002) *Motivational Interviewing: Preparing People for Change.* London: Guilford Press.

Ministry of Justice (2009) *Re-offending of Juveniles: Results from the 2007 Cohort, England and Wales.* London: Stationery Office.

Mischkowitz, R. (1994) 'Desistance from a delinquent way of life?', in E. Weitekamp and H. J. Kerner (eds), *Cross-National Longitudinal Research on Human Development and Criminal Behaviour.* London: Kluwer.

Moffitt, T. (1993) 'Adolescence-limited and life-course persistent antisocial behaviour: a developmental taxonomy', *Psychological Review*, 100: 674–701.

Moon, J. (1999) *Reflection in Learning and Professional Development: Theory and Practice.* London: Kogan Page.

Moore, D. and Arthur, J. (1989) 'Juvenile delinquency', in T. Ollendick and M. Hersen (eds), *Handbook of Child Psychopathology.* New York: Plenum.

Moore, K. J., Sprengelmeyer, P. G. and Chamberlain, P. (2001) 'Community-based treatment for adjudicated delinquents: the Oregon Social Learning Center's "Monitor" Multi-dimensional Treatment Foster Care program', *Residential Treatment for Children and Youth*, 18: 87–97.

Moore, R., Gray, R., Roberts, E., Merrington, C., Waters, S., Fernandez, I., Hayward, R. G. and Rogers, R. (2004) *ISSP: The Initial Report.* London: Youth Justice Board.

Moran, P., Ghate, D. and van der Merwe, A. (2004) *What Works in Parenting Support? A Review of the International Evidence*, Research Report 574. London: DfES.

Morgan, R. (2006) 'Enabling compliance: more than enforcement', *Youth Justice Board News*, No. 32.

Morgan, R. (2010) 'Children and young people in custody', in W. Taylor, R. Earle and R. Hester (eds), *Youth Justice Handbook: Theory, Policy and Practice*. Cullompton: Willan.

MORI (2004) *MORI Youth Survey 2004*. London: Youth Justice Board.

Morris, A. (2002) 'Critiquing the critics: a brief response to the critics of restorative justice', *British Journal of Criminology*, (42): 596–615.

Morrow, V. (1999) 'Conceptualising social capital in relation to the well-being of children and young people: a critical review', *Sociological Review*, 47 (4): 745–65.

Mortimore, P., Davies, J., Varlaam, A. and West, A. (1983) *Behaviour Problems in Schools: An Evaluation of Support Centres*. London: Croom Helm.

Mouridsen, S. E. and Hauschild, K.-E. (2009) 'A long-term study of offending in individuals diagnosed with a developmental language disorder as children', *International Journal of Speech-Language Pathology*, 11 (3): 171–9.

Muncie, J. (2001) 'A new deal for youth? Early intervention and correctionalism', in G. Hughes, E. Mcloughlin and J. Muncie (eds), *Crime Prevention and Community Safety: New Directions*. London: Sage.

Muncie, J. (2002) 'Policy transfers and "what works": some reflections on the comparative youth justice', *Youth Justice*, 3: 1.

Muncie, J. (2004) *Youth and Crime*. London: Sage.

Munn, P., Lloyd, G. and Cullen, M. (2000) *Alternatives to Exclusion from School*. London: Paul Chapman.

Myner, J., Santman, J., Cappelletty, G. and Perlmutter, B. (1998) 'Variables related to recidivism among juvenile offenders', *International Journal of Offender Therapy and Comparative Criminology*, 42 (1): 65–80.

Nacro (2000) *Proportionality in the Youth Justice System*, Nacro Youth Crime Briefing. London: Nacro.

Nacro (2005) *Housing and Accommodation Issues for Young People in the Criminal Justice System*. London: Nacro.

Nacro (2006) *Effective Practice with Children and Young People Who Offend – Part 1*, Youth Crime Briefing September 2006. London: Nacro.

Nacro Cymru (2006) *Custody and Young People's Living Arrangements*. London: Nacro.

Narain, B. (2001) *Parenting Orders and the Human Rights Act 1998*. London: Aire Centre/Brighton: Trust for the Study of Adolescence.

National Assembly for Wales (2000) *Child and Adolescent Mental Health Services for Wales: Everybody's Business*, Consultation Strategy Document. Cardiff: National Assembly for Wales.

National Association of Probation Officers (2002) *Accredited Programmes Policy*. London: NAPO.

National Institute for Health and Clinical Excellence (2007) *Community Based Interventions to Reduce Substance Misuse among Vulnerable and Disadvantaged Children and Young People*. London: NICE.

National Probation Service (2003) *Closure of Sherborne House – Letter of 14 January 2003 to London Youth Offending Team Managers*. London: National Probation Service.

National Treatment Agency (2005) *Young People's Substance Misuse Treatment Services – Essential Elements*. London: NTA.

National Treatment Agency (2008) *Changes in Offending Following Prescribing Treatment for Drug Use*. London: NTA.

National Treatment Agency (2009a) *Smoking, Drinking and Drug Use among Young People in England in 2008*. London: NHS Information Centre.

National Treatment Agency (2009b) *Substance Misuse among Young People: The Data for 2008–09*. London: NTA.

Newburn, T., Crawford, A., Earle, R., Goldie, S., Hale, C., Hallam, A., Masters, G., Netten, A., Saunders, R., Sharpe, K. and Uglow, S. (2001) *The Introduction of Referral Orders into the Youth Justice System: 2nd Interim Report*. London: Home Office.

Newburn, T., Crawford, A., Earle, R., Goldie, S., Hale, C., Hallam, A., Masters, G., Netten, A., Saunders, R., Sharpe, K. and Uglow, S. (2002) *The Introduction of Referral Orders into the Youth Justice System: Final Report*, Home Office Research Study 242. London: Home Office.

Newburn, T., Shiner, M., Groben, S. and Young T. (2005) *Dealing with Disaffection: Young People, Mentoring and Social Inclusion*. Cullompton: Willan.

Newman, T. (2004) *What Works in Building Resilience?* Ilford: Barnardo's.

Nichols, G. (2007) *Sport and Crime Reduction: The Role of Sports in Tackling Youth Crime*. London: Routledge.

Niven, S. and Stewart, D. (2005) *Resettlement Outcomes on Release from Prison in 2003*. London: Home Office.

Noel, P. (2006) 'The impact of therapeutic case management on participation in adolescent substance abuse treatment', *American Journal of Drug and Alcohol Abuse*, 32 (3): 311–27.

Nuffield Foundation (2004) *Time Trends in Adolescent Well-being*. London: Nuffield Foundation.

O'Mahony, D. and Doak, J. (2004) 'Restorative justice – is more better? The experience of the police-led restorative cautioning pilots in Northern Ireland', *Howard Journal of Criminal Justice*, 43 (4): 484–505.

Office for Criminal Justice Reform (2005) *Code of Practice for Victims*. London: Office for Criminal Justice Reform.

Ofsted (1995) *Pupil Referral Units: The First Twelve Inspections*. London: Stationery Office.

Ofsted (2003) *Annual Report of Her Majesty's Chief Inspector of Schools: Standards and Quality in Education 2001/2002*. London: Stationery Office.

Ofsted (2004) *Out of School*. London: Stationery Office.

Ofsted (2006) *Evaluation of the Impact of Learning Support Units*. London: Stationery Office.

Ofsted (2007) *Pupil Referral Units: Establishing Successful Practice in Pupil Referral Units and Local Authorities*. London: Ofsted.

Ofsted (2008) *Good Practice in Re-engaging Disaffected and Reluctant Students in Secondary Schools*. London: Ofsted.

Ofsted (2009a) *Chief Inspector's Annual Report*. London: Stationery Office.

Ofsted (2009b) *Chief Inspector's Annual Report: Findings on Prisons*. London: Stationery Office.

Ofsted (2009c) *Implementation of 14–19 Reforms, Including the 14–19 Diplomas*. London: Stationery Office.

Olweus, D. (1991) 'Bully/victim problems among schoolchildren: basic facts and effects of a school-based intervention program', in D. J. Pepler and K. H. Rubin (eds), *The Development and Treatment of Childhood Aggression*. Hillsdale, NJ: Erlbaum, pp. 411–48.

Olweus, D. (1993) *Bullying at School: What We Know and What We Can Do*. Oxford: Blackwell.

Pagnin, D., De Queiroz, V. and Saggese, E. G. (2005) 'Predictors of attrition from day treatment of adolescents with substance-related disorders', *Addictive Behaviors*, 30 (5): 1065–9.

Parentline Plus (2006) *The Information, Advice and Support Needs of Black and Minority Ethnic Families.* London: Parentline Plus.

Parker, H., Aldridge, J. and Measham, F. (1998) *Illegal Leisure: The Normalisation of Adolescent Drug Use.* London: Routledge.

Parrish, J. M., Charlop, M. H. and Fenton, L. R. (1986) 'Use of a stated waiting list contingency and a reward opportunity to increase appointment keeping in an outpatient pediatric psychology clinic', *Journal of Pediatric Psychology*, 11: 81–9.

Parsons, C. and Howlett, K. (2000) *Investigating the Reintegration of Permanently Excluded Young People in England.* Ely: INCLUDE.

Pawson, R. (1997) 'Evaluation methodology: back to basics', in G. Mair (ed.), *Evaluating the Effectiveness of Community Penalties.* Aldershot: Avebury.

Pawson, R. (2000) 'The evaluator's tale', in D. Wilson and A. Reuss (eds), *Prison(er) Education: Stories of Change and Transformation.* Winchester: Waterside Press.

Pawson, R. and Tilley, N. (1997) *Realistic Evaluation.* London: Sage.

Pearson, G. (1983) *Hooligan: A History of Respectable Fears.* Basingstoke: Macmillan.

Peile, E. (2004) 'Reflections from medical practice: balancing evidence-based practice with practice-based evidence', in G. Thomas and R. Pring (eds), *Evidence-Based Practice in Education.* Maidenhead: Open University Press.

Peplow, M. (2002) 'Full of goodness', *New Scientist*, 176 (2369): 38–41.

Perry, A., Gilbody, S., Akers, J. and Light, K. (2008) *Mental Health Source Document.* London: Youth Justice Board.

Phoenix, J. (2009) 'Beyond risk assessment: the return of repressive welfarism?', in M. Barry and F. McNeill (eds), *Youth Offending and Youth Justice*, Research Highlights 52. London: Jessica Kingsley.

Pickburn, C., Lindfield, S. and Coleman, J. (2005) 'Working with parents', in T. Bateman and J. Pitts (eds), *The RHP Companion to Youth Justice.* Lyme Regis: Russell House.

Pitcher, J., Bateman, T., Johnston, V. and Cadman, S. (2004) *Provision of Health, Education and Substance Misuse Services.* London: Youth Justice Board.

Pitts, J. (2001a) 'Korrectional karaoke: New Labour and the zombification of youth justice', *Youth Justice*, 1 (2): 3–16.

Pitts, J. (2001b) *The New Politics of Youth Crime: Discipline or Solidarity?* Basingstoke: Palgrave.

Pitts, J. (2001c) 'The new correctionalism: young people, youth justice and new labour', in R. Matthews and J. Pitts (eds), *Crime, Disorder and Community Safety.* London: Routledge.

Polanyi, M. (1969) 'The logic of tacit inference', in M. Grene (ed.), *Knowing and Being: Essays by Michael Polanyi.* London: Routledge & Kegan Paul.

Porporino, D. and Robinson, F. (1992) *Can Educating Adult Offenders Counteract Recidivism?* Ottowa: Research and Statistics Branch of the Correctional Service of Canada.

Pring, R. (2004) 'Conclusion: evidence-based policy and practice', in G. Thomas and R. Pring (eds), *Evidence-based Practice in Education.* Maidenhead: Open University Press.

Prochaska, J. O. and DiClemente, C. C. (1982) 'Transtheoretical therapy: toward a more integrative model of change', *Pscychotherapy: Theory, Research and Practice*, 19: 276–88.

Pullman, M. D., Kerbs, J., Koroloff, N., Veach-White, E., Gaylor, R. and Sieler, D. (2006) 'Juvenile offenders with mental health needs: Reducing recidivism using Wraparound', *Crime and Delinquency*, 52: 375–97

Quinton, D., Pickles, A., Maughan, B. and Rutter, M. (1993) 'Partners, peers and pathways: assortative pairing and continuities in conduct disorder', *Development and Psychopathology*, 5: 763–83.

R *(on the application of U)* v. *Metropolitan Police Commissioner and R (on the application of R)* v. *Durham Constabulary* (2002), reported in *Justice of the Peace*, 166, December.

Rand, A. (1987) 'Transitional life events and desistance from delinquency and crime', in M. E. Wolfgang, T. P. Thornberry and R. Figlio (eds), *From Boy to Man, From Delinquency to Crime*. Chicago: University of Chicago Press.

Raynor, P. (2002) 'What works: have we moved on?', in D. Ward, J. Scott and M. Lacey (eds), *Probation: Working for Justice*. Oxford: Oxford University Press.

Raynor, P. (2004a) 'Opportunity, motivation and change: some findings from research on resettlement', in R. Burnett and C. Roberts (eds), *What Works in Probation and Youth Justice: Developing Evidence-based Practice*. Cullompton: Willan.

Raynor, P. (2004b) 'Seven ways to misunderstand evidence-based probation', in D. Smith (ed.), *Social Work and Evidence-based Practice*. London: Jessica Kingsley.

Rees, C. and Conalty, J. (2004) *Taping the Seams in the Resettlement Process: Successfully Reintegrating Young Ex-offenders into Employment, Education and Training Opportunities*. London: Rainer.

Respect Task Force (2006) *Respect Action Plan*. London: Home Office.

Rex, S. (1999) 'Desistance from offending: experiences of probation', *Howard Journal*, 38 (4): 366–83.

Rex, S., Gelsthorpe, L., Roberts, C. and Jordan, P. (2004) *What's Promising in Community Service: Implementation of Seven Pathfinder Projects*, Home Office Findings 231. London: Home Office.

Reynolds, S. (2000) 'The anatomy of evidence-based practice: principles and methods', in L. Trinder with R. Reynolds (eds), *Evidence-Based Practice: A Critical Appraisal*. Oxford: Blackwell Science.

Richardson, H. and Roker, D. (2002) *An Evaluation of the YMCA England 'Dads and Lads' Initiative*. Report submitted to YMCA, England.

Riggs, P., Baker, S., Mikulich, S.,Young, S. and Crowley, T. (1995) 'Depression in substance-dependent delinquents', *Journal of American Academy of Child and Adolescent Psychiatry*, 34: 764–71.

Robbins, M. S., Liddle, H. A., Dakof, G. A., Turner, C. W., Alexander, J. F. and Kogan, S. M. (2006) 'Adolescent and parent therapeutic alliances as predictors of dropout in multidimensional family therapy', *Journal of Family Psychology*, 20 (1): 108–16.

Roberts, C. (2004) 'Offending behaviour programmes: emerging evidence and implications for practice', in R. Burnett and C. Roberts (eds), *What Works in Probation and Youth Justice: Developing Evidence-based Practice*. Cullompton: Willan.

Roche, D. (2001) 'The evolving definition of restorative justice', *Contemporary Justice Review*, 4 (3–4): 341–54.

Roker, D. and Coleman, J. (1998) 'Parenting teenagers programmes: a UK perspective', *Children and Society*, 12: 359–72.

Ross, A. (2009) *Disengagement from Education among 14–16 Year Olds*. London: DCSF.

Runyan, D., Hunter, W., Socolar, R., Amaya-Jackson, L., English, D., Landsverk, J., Dubowitz, H., Browne, D., Bangdiwala, S. and Mathew, R. (1998) 'Children who prosper in unfavourable environments: the relationship to social capital', *Pediatrics*, 101 (1, Pt.1): 12–18.

Rutter, M. (1997) *Heterogeneity of Antisocial Behaviour: Causes, Continuities, and Consequences*. Lincoln, NE: University of Nebraska Press.

Rutter, M., Giller, H. and Hagell, A. (1998) *Antisocial Behavior by Young People*. Cambridge: Cambridge University Press.

Sackett, D., Richardson, W., Rosenberg, W. and Haynes, R. (1997) *Evidence-based Medicine: How to Practice and Teach EBM*. New York: Churchill Livingstone.

Safer Custody Group (2003) *Draft Guidance on Managing Prisoners Who Self-harm*. London: HM Prison Service.

Sampson, R. and Laub, J. (1993) *Crime in the Making: Pathways and Turning Points through Life*. Cambridge, MA: Harvard University Press.

Sarno, C., Hearnden, I., Hedderman, C. and Hough, M. (2000) *Working Their Way Out of Offending: An Evaluation of Two Probation Employment Schemes*, Home Office Research Study 218. London: Home Office.

Saylor, W. and Gaes, G. (1997) 'PREP: training inmates through industrial work participation and vocational and apprenticeship instruction', *Corrections Management Quarterly*, 1 (2): 32–43.

Schön, D. (1983) *The Reflective Practitioner: How Professionals Think in Action*. New York: Basic Books.

Seddon, T. (2006) 'Drugs, crime and social exclusion: social context and social theory in British drugs-crime research', *British Journal of Criminology*, 46 (4): 680–703.

Sexton, T. L. and Alexander, J. F. (2000) *Functional Family Therapy*. Washington, DC: Office of Juvenile Justice and Delinquency Prevention, Department of Justice.

Shapland, J., Atkinson, A., Atkinson, H., Chapman, B., Colledge, E., Dignan, J., Howes, M., Johnstone, J., Robinson, G. and Sorsby, A. (2006) *Restorative Justice in Practice: The Second Report from the Evaluation of Three Schemes*. Sheffield: Centre for Criminological Research, University of Sheffield.

Shapland, J., Atkinson, A., Atkinson, H., Chapman, B., Colledge, E., Dignan, J., Howes, M., Johnstone, J., Robinson, G. and Sorsby, A. (2007) *Restorative Justice: The Views of Victims and Offenders – The Third Report from the Evaluation of Three Schemes*. London: Ministry of Justice.

Shapland, J., Atkinson, A., Atkinson, H., Dignan, J., Edwards, L., Hibbert, J., Howes, M., Johnstone, J., Robinson, G. and Soresby, A. (2008) *Does Restorative Justice Affect Reconviction? The Fourth Report from the Evaluation of Three Schemes*. London: Ministry of Justice.

Shapland, J., Atkinson, A., Colledge, E., Dignan, J., Howes, M., Johnstone, J., Pennant, R., Robinson, G. and Sorsby, A. (2004) *Implementing Restorative Justice Schemes (Crime Reduction Programme): A Report on the First Year*, Home Office Online Report 32/04. London: Home Office.

Shelef, K., Diamond, G. M., Diamond, G. S. and Liddle, H. A. (2005) 'Adolescent and parent alliance and treatment outcome in multidimensional family therapy', *Journal of Consulting and Clinical Psychology*, 73 (4): 689–98.

Sherman, L. and Strang, H. (2007) *Restorative Justice: The Evidence*. London: Smith Institute.

Sherman, L., Strang, H. and Newbury-Birch, D. (2008) *Restorative Justice Source Document*. London: Youth Justice Board.

Sherman, L., Strang, H. and Woods, D. (2000) *Recidivism Patterns in the Canberra Reintegrative Shaming Experiments (RISE)*. Canberra, Australia: Centre for Restorative Justice, Australian National University.

Simourd, L. and Andrews, D. (1994) 'Correlates of delinquency: a look at the gender differences', *Forum on Corrections Research*, 6: 26–31.

Smith, C. (1996) *Developing Parenting Programmes*. London: National Children's Bureau.

Smith, D. (ed.) (2005) *Social Work and Evidence-Based Practice*. London: Jessica Kingsley.

Smith, R. (2003) *Youth Justice: Ideas, Policy, Practice*. Cullompton: Willan.

Smith, R. (2006) 'Actuarialism and early intervention in contemporary youth justice', in B. Goldson and J. Muncie (eds), *Youth Crime and Justice*. London: Sage.

Snow, P. C. and Powell, M. B. (2004) 'Developmental language disorders and adolescent risk: a public-heath advocacy role for speech pathologists?', *Advances in Speech Language Pathology*, 6 (4): 221–9.

Social Exclusion Unit (2001) *Preventing Social Exclusion*. London: Social Exclusion Unit.

Social Exclusion Unit (2002) *Reducing Re-offending by Ex-Prisoners*. London: Cabinet Office.

Spooner, C., Mattick, R. P. and Noffs, W. (2001) 'Outcomes of a comprehensive treatment program for adolescents with a substance-use disorder', *Journal of Substance Abuse Treatment*, 20 (3): 205–13.

Stathis, S. L., Letters, P., Doolan, I. and Whittingham, D. (2006) 'Developing an integrated substance use and mental health service in the specialised setting of a youth detention centre', *Drug and Alcohol Review*, 25 (2): 149–55.

Staudt, M. (2003) 'Mental health services utilization by maltreated children: research findings and recommendations', *Child Maltreatment: Journal of the American Professional Society on the Abuse of Children*, 8: 195–203.

Steedman, H. and Stoney, S. (2004) *Disengagement 14–16: Context and Evidence*, Centre for Economic Performance Discussion Paper No. 654. London: Centre for Economic Performance.

Stein, L. A. R., Monti, P. M., Colby, S. M., Barnett, N. P., Golembeske, C., Lebeau-Craven, R. and Miranda, R. (2006) 'Enhancing substance abuse treatment engagement in incarcerated adolescents', *Psychological Services*, 3 (1): 25–34.

Stephenson, M. (1996) 'Cities in Schools: a new approach for excluded children and young people', in E. Blyth and J. Milner (eds), *Exclusion from School*. London: Routledge.

Stephenson, M. (2000) 'Inclusive learning', in B. Lucas and T. Greany (eds), *Schools in the Learning Age*. London: Campaign for Learning.

Stephenson, M. (2007) *Young People and Offending: Education, Youth Justice and Social Inclusion*. Cullompton: Willan.

Steurer, S., Smith, L. and Tracy, R. (2001) *Three State Recidivism Study*. Lanham, MD: Correctional Education Association.

Strang, H. (2001) 'Justice for victims of young offenders: the centrality of emotional harm and restoration', in A. Morris and G. Maxwell (eds), *Restorative Justice for Juveniles – Conferencing, Mediation and Circles*. Oxford: Hart.

Strang, H. (2002) *Repair or Revenge: Victims and Restorative Justice*. Oxford: Clarendon Press.

Sutton, C., Utting, D. and Farrington, D. (2004) *Support from the Start*, Research Report 524. London: DfES.

Tait, R. J., Hulse, G. K. and Robertson, S. I. (2004) 'Effectiveness of a brief intervention and continuity of care in enhancing attendance for treatment by adolescent substance users', *Drug and Alcohol Dependence*, 74 (3): 289–96.

Tait, R. J., Hulse, G. K., Robertson, S. I. and Sprivulis, P. C. (2005) 'Emergency department-based intervention with adolescent substance users: 12-month outcomes', *Drug and Alcohol Dependence*, 79 (3): 359–63.

Tarling, R. (1993) *Analysing Offending*. London: HMSO.

Tarling, R., Davison, J. and Clarke, A. (2004) *Mentoring Projects: The National Evaluation of the Youth Justice Board's Mentoring Projects*. London: Youth Justice Board.

Teplin, L. A., Abram, K. M., McClelland, G. M., Dulcan, M. K. and Mericle, A. A. (2002) 'Psychiatric disorders in youth in juvenile detention', *Archives of General Psychiatry*, 59 (12): 1133–43.

Tevyaw, T. and Monti, P. M. (2004) 'Motivational enhancement and other brief interventions for adolescent substance abuse: foundations, applications and evaluations', *Addiction*, 99 (Supp. 2): 63–75.

Thomas, G. (2004) 'Introduction: evidence and practice', in G. Thomas and R. Pring (eds), *Evidence-Based Practice in Education*. Maidenhead: Open University Press.

Thomas, L., Sexton, T. L. and Alexander, J. F. (2000) *Functional Family Therapy*. Washington DC: Office of Juvenile Justice and Delinquency Prevention.

Thomas, S. (2008) *Accommodation Source Document*. London: Youth Justice Board.

Thornberry, T. P. (1987) 'Towards an interactional theory of delinquency', *Criminology*, 25 (4): 863–92.

Thornberry, T. P. (1996) 'Empirical support for interactional theory: a review of the literature', in J. Hawkins (ed.), *Delinquency and Crime: Current Theories*. Cambridge: Cambridge University Press.

Tilley, N. (2006) 'Knowing and doing: guidance and good practice in crime prevention', *Crime Prevention Studies*, 20: 217–52.

Tolbert, M. (2002) *State Correctional Education Programs: State Policy Update*. Washington, DC: National Institute for Literacy.

Topping, K. (1983) *Educational Systems for Disruptive Adolescents*. Beckenham: Croom Helm.

Torgerson, C., Brooks, G., Porthouse, J., Burton, M., Robinson, A., Wright, K. and Watt, I. (2004) *Adult Literacy and Numeracy Interventions and Outcomes: A Review of Controlled Trials*. London: National Research and Development Centre.

Trinder, L. (2000) 'Introduction: the context of evidence-based practice', in L. Trinder with S. Reynolds (eds), *Evidence-based Practice: A Critical Appraisal*. Oxford: Blackwell Science.

Trinder, L. and Reynolds, S. (eds) (2000) *Evidence-based Practice: A Critical Appraisal*. Oxford: Blackwell Science.

Trotter, C. (1996) 'The impact of different supervision practices on community corrections', *Australian and New Zealand Journal of Criminology*, 28: 2.

Truax, R. and Carkhuff, C. (1967) *Towards Effective Counselling and Psychotherapy*. Chicago: Aldine.

Trupin, E. W. (2005) 'Juvenile justice reform and best practices in juvenile systems', *NAMI 2005 Annual Convention*, Austin, Texas, Slide 19.

Trupin, E. W., Stewart, D. G., Beach, B. and Boesky, L. (2002) 'Effectiveness of a dialectical behaviour therapy program for incarcerated female juvenile offenders', *Child and Adolescent Mental Health*, 7 (3): 121–8.

Tye, D. (2009) *Children and Young People in Custody. An Analysis of the Experiences of 15–18 Year-Olds in Prison*. London: HMIP and Youth Justice Board.

Umbreit, M. (1994) *Victim Meets Offender*. New York: Willow Tree Press.

Umbreit, M., Coates, R. and Vos, B. (2001) 'Victim impact of meeting with young offenders: two decades of victim–offender mediation practice and research', in A. Morris and G. Maxwell (eds), *Restorative Justice for Juveniles – Conferencing, Mediation and Circles*. Oxford: Hart.

Underdown, A. (1998) *Strategies for Effective Offender Supervision*. London: Home Office, HM Inspectorate of Probation.

UNICEF (2007) 'Child poverty in perspective: an overview of child well-being in rich countries', *Innocenti Report Card 7*. Florence: UNICEF Innocenti Research Centre.

Unitas (2009) *Summer Arts Colleges: 2008: Outcomes Report*. London: Unitas.

Utting, D. (ed.) (1999) *A Guide to Promising Approaches*. London: Rosebery House/ Communities that Care.

Utting, D. and Vennard, J. (2000) *What Works with Young Offenders in the Community?* Ilford: Barnardo's.

Utting, D., Monteiro, H. and Ghate, D. (2007) *Interventions for Children at Risk of Developing Antisocial Personality Disorder: Report to the Department of Health and Prime Minister's Strategy Unit.* London: Policy Research Bureau.

Viney, L. L. and Henry, R. M. (2002) 'Evaluating personal construct and psychodynamic group work with adolescent offenders and non-offenders', in R. A. Neimeyer and G. J. Neimeyer (eds), *Advances in Personal Construct Psychology: New Directions and Perspectives.* Westport, CT: Praeger/Greenwood, pp. 259–94.

Visser, J. (2002) 'Eternal Verities: the strongest link', *Emotional and Behavioural Difficulties,* 7 (2): 68–84.

Wade, E. (2006) *The Mental Health Needs of Young People Who Offend.* Newcastle: Derwent Initiative.

Waldron, H. B. and Kaminer, Y. (2004) 'On the learning curve: the emerging evidence supporting cognitive-behavioural therapies for adolescent substance abuse', *Addiction* 99 (Supp. 2): 93–105.

Walker, S. (2003) *Working Together for Healthy Young Minds – A Practitioner's Workbook.* Lyme Regis: Russell House.

Wallace, S. A., Crown, J. M., Berger, M. and Cox, A. D. (1997) 'Child and adolescent mental health', in A. Stevens and J. Raftery (eds), *Health Care Needs Assessment,* 2nd series. Oxford: Radcliffe Medical Press.

Ward, T. and Maruna, S. (2007) *Rehabilitation: Beyond the Risk Paradigm.* London: Routledge.

Washington State Institute for Public Policy (2004) *Washington State's Family Integrated Transitions Program for Juvenile Offenders: Outcome Evaluation and Cost-benefit Analysis.* Washington: WSIPP.

Weare, K. (2000) *Promoting Mental, Emotional and Social Health – A Whole-school Approach.* London and New York: Routledge.

Weissberg, R. and Caplan, M. (1998) *Promoting Social Competence and Preventing Antisocial Behavior in Young Urban Adolescents.* Philadelphia: Temple University, Center for Research in Human Development and Education, Laboratory for Student Success.

Whitney, S. D., Kelly, J. F., Myers, M. G. and Brown, S. A. (2002) 'Parental substance use, family support and outcome following treatment for adolescent psychoactive substance use disorders', *Journal of Child and Adolescent Substance Abuse,* 11 (4): 67–81.

Whyte, B. (2009) *Youth Justice in Practice: Making a Difference.* Bristol: Policy Press.

Wikstrom, P. and Treiber, K. (2008) *Offending Behaviour Programmes Source Document.* London: Youth Justice Board.

Wilcox, A. and Hoyle, C. (2002) *Final Report for the Youth Justice Board on the National Evaluation of Restorative Justice Projects.* Oxford: Centre for Criminological Research, University of Oxford.

Wilcox, A., Young, R. and Hoyle, C. (2004) *Two-Year Re-sanctioning Study: A Comparison of Restorative and Traditional Cautions,* Home Office Online Report 32/04. London: Home Office.

Wilkin, A., Hall, M. and Kinder, K. (2003) *Learning Support Unit Strand Study.* Slough: NFER.

Williams, D. J. and Strean, W. B. (2002) 'The transtheoretical model and quality of life promotion: towards successful offender rehabilitation', *Probation Journal,* 49: 3.

Williams, J. D. (2003) *Student Engagement at School: A Sense of Belonging and Participation: Results from PISA 2000.* Paris: OECD.

Williams, J., Clemens, S., Oleinikova, K. and Tarvin, K. (2003) *The Skills for Life Survey: a National Needs and Impact Survey of Literacy, Numeracy and ICT Skills,* DfES Research Brief 490. London: DfES.

Wilson, H. (1980) 'Parental supervision: a neglected aspect of delinquency', *British Journal of Criminology*, 20: 203–35.

Wilson, T. and Kelling, G. (1982) 'Broken windows: the police and neighbourhood safety', *Atlantic Monthly*, March: 29–38.

Witton, J. (2001) *Cannabis and the Gateway Hypothesis*, a review paper prepared for DrugScope's submission to the Home Affairs Select Committee.

Wood, R. J., Drolet, J. C., Fetro, J. V., Synovitz, L. B. and Wood, A. R. (2002) 'Residential adolescent substance abuse treatment: recommendations for collaboration between school health and substance abuse treatment personnel', *Journal of School Health*, 72 (9): 363–7.

World Health Organisation (1994) *International Statistical Classification of Disease and Related Health Problems*. World Health Organisation.

Youth Justice Board (2002) *Building on Success: Youth Justice Board Review 2001/2002*. London: Youth Justice Board.

Youth Justice Board (2003) *Progress Report on the Implementation of the Youth Justice Board's National Specification for Learning and Skills in the Juvenile Prison Estate 2002–03*. London: Youth Justice Board.

Youth Justice Board (2004a) *National Evaluation of the Restorative Justice in Schools Programme*. London: Youth Justice Board.

Youth Justice Board (2004b) *Keeping Young People Engaged Project: Interim Evaluation of Good Practice in Developing Re-engagement Capability for Education, Training and Employment – Year 1*. London: Youth Justice Board.

Youth Justice Board (2004c) *Progress Report on the Implementation of the Youth Justice Board's National Specification for Learning and Skills in the Juvenile Prison Estate 2003–04*. London: Youth Justice Board.

Youth Justice Board (2004d) *Research and Evaluation to Determine the Most Effective Means of Ensuring that Young People in the Youth Justice System are Fully Engaged in Education, Training or Employment*. London: Youth Justice Board.

Youth Justice Board (2005a) 'Diversity in Learning: Establishing the Cognitive Styles and Learning Strategies of Young People in the Youth Justice System'. London: Youth Justice Board (unpublished).

Youth Justice Board (2005b) *Youth Justice Annual Statistics 2003/04*. London: Youth Justice Board.

Youth Justice Board (2005c) *Progress Review on the Implementation of the Youth Justice Board's National Specification for Learning and Skills 2004–2005*. London: Youth Justice Board.

Youth Justice Board (2005d) *Youth Resettlement: A Framework for Action*. London: Youth Justice Board.

Youth Justice Board (2006) *Barriers to Engagement in Education, Training and Employment for Young People in the Youth Justice System*. London: Youth Justice Board.

Youth Justice Board (2007) *Annual Report 2006/7*. London: Youth Justice Board.

Youth Justice Board (2008a) *Assessment, Planning Interventions and Supervision Source Document*. London: Youth Justice Board.

Youth Justice Board (2008b) *Youth Justice Annual Workload Data 2006/07*. London: Youth Justice Board.

Youth Justice Board (2009a) *Youth Justice Annual Workload Data 2007/08*. London: Youth Justice Board.

Youth Justice Board (2009b) *National Specification for Substance Misuse*. London: Youth Justice Board.

Youth Justice Board (2009c) *Youth Justice: The Scaled Approach*. London: Youth Justice Board.

Youth Justice Board (2010) *Youth Justice Annual Workload Data 2008/09*. London: Youth Justice Board.

Youth Justice Board and National Treatment Agency (2006) *YOT Substance Misuse Worker Guidance: Integrating Youth Justice Provision and Substance Misuse Treatment*. London: Youth Justice Board.

Youth Justice Board/Association of Chief Police Officers (2003) *Guide to Good Practice*. London: Youth Justice Board and Association of Chief Police Officers.

Youth Justice Trust (2004) *On the Case: A Survey of Over 1,000 Children and Young People under Supervision by Youth Offending Teams in Greater Manchester and West Yorkshire*. Manchester: Youth Justice Trust.

Index

Added to a page number 'f' denotes a figure and 't' denotes a table

ABC model 205
absenteeism 104, 130, 234
academic attainment
   community-based interventions 119
   desistance 49
   engagement 74–5
   interventions to increase 100–5
   offending 100
   parental involvement 163
   in secure estate 222
   segregated education 111
   teacher attitudes and behaviour 83
   see also low attainment
academic failure 5, 13, 99
accessing services 226–7
accommodation 33, 225
accountability 8, 53, 82, 217, 218
accredited programmes 9, 34, 35, 36
achievement (programme) 91
   see also academic attainment
action stage, of change 65, 87
actuarial assessment 26, 51, 54
actuarial justice 4, 55
addictive-type substance use 148
adolescence 5
adolescence-limited anti-social behaviour 50
advice, substance-related 155
African-Caribbean boys 46
aftercare 225, 227–8
agency 54, 87, 165
aggregation, in RCTs 18, 20
aggression 46, 47, 136, 137, 139
alcohol use/misuse 5, 116, 129, 136, 147, 148,
   156, 158, 225
American Psychiatry Association 127
anger 136, 182, 208, 226
Annual Inspection Report for YOTs (2005–6)
   131, 157, 186
anti-bullying programmes 104
anti-social behaviour 5, 47, 48, 50, 83, 105,
   136, 163, 207, 235

Anti-social Behaviour Intensive Family
   Support Projects 171–2
anti-social behaviour strategy 164
anxiety 47, 128, 129, 137, 138, 224
arrest referral 147, 158
art exhibitions, trips to 92
art of teaching 84
arts 33, 85–6
   see also Summer Arts Colleges
assessment
   challenges for practice 69–70
   effective practice 59–69
   and engagement 75–8
   evidence base 43–56
   of mental health, lack of 131
   of parents 172
   see also needs assessment; risk assessment
assessment tools 44, 143
Asset 4, 9, 23, 43, 49–51, 54, 69
   criminogenic need 27
   criticisms of 51–6, 53, 55
   identification of mental health needs 133,
      141
   judgements about substance misuse 151–2
   reliability and validity 50–1, 208
   risk classification 26
   role in planning 58
   use of 75–6
'at risk' families 166
'at risk' young people 4, 53, 70, 237
attendance
   at programmes 62, 80, 91, 171, 210, 211
   see also school attendance
Attention Deficit Hyperactivity Disorder
   (ADHD) 127
attitudes 48, 83, 85, 110, 208–9
attrition rate (programme) 23, 36, 62, 106, 112,
   210
Audit Commission 54, 57, 58, 70, 117, 132
audit society 7–8
autistic spectrum disorders 136

autonomy 7, 222, 236

Basic Skills Pathfinders programmes 23, 75, 106
befriending role 80
behaviour
  context and 119
  drug use 149
  predictability of 20
  preoccupation with 2
  see also anti-social behaviour; criminal behaviour; delinquency
behaviour modification 205
behavioural change 20, 108, 119, 167, 175, 207, 217
behavioural engagement 74–5
behaviourism 205
Beijing Rules 28
Bercow Report (2008) 101
biogenetic theories 127
biological factors 47
bipolar disorder 136
black young people 219
Blueprints programme 167
body language 81
'boot camp' approaches 213
borderline learning difficulties 129, 224
boundaries 84
bridge course 112–14
brief interventions 158
British Crime Survey 147
bullies/bullying 47–8, 104, 105, 192
burglary 114

Cambridge study 47
Canadian Adult Basic Education programme 107
cannabis 145, 147, 148, 149, 156, 225
Cardinal Needs Schedule 133
Careers Wales 209, 234, 237, 238
case management 36, 60f, 141, 228, 229, 238, 240
cautions 190, 191, 192, 195
'chalk and talk' teaching 117
change
  cycle of 64–6
  identifying and enabling 77
  models 86–8
  potential for 54
  see also behavioural change; social change
Child and Adolescent Mental Health Services (CAMHS) 131, 132, 134, 135t, 137, 143
Child Development Project 103
child poverty 5
child protection register 225
childhood 5
Children and Young Persons Act (1933) 27–8
children's centres 164

choice 8
citizenship responsibilities 53
Class A drugs 145, 158
closure, for victims 194
cocaine 147
Code of Practice for Victims 185, 201
cognitive ability 47, 87, 138
cognitive engagement 74, 75
cognitive theory 205
cognitive therapy 205
cognitive-behavioural approaches 33, 63, 120, 140, 141, 158, 199, 204, 205–6, 210, 215, 237
Common Assessment Framework (CAF) 70
communication
  and engagement 81, 85
  geographical distance and 240
  inter-agency 54
  skills 104
community panel meetings 189, 199–200
community reparation 192, 197, 199
community risk factors 14, 45
community sentences 27
community-based interventions 32–3
  assessment, planning and supervision 66–7
  education and training 119–20
  engagement 92
  mental health 138–40
  offending behaviour 213–14
  parenting 177–8
  resettlement 236–7
  restorative justice 198–9
  substance misuse 155–7
community-level CAMHS 131
completion (programme) 206, 210
compliance (programme) 211
compulsion 80
conduct disorders 5, 127, 128, 129, 130
confidentiality 35, 131, 155
Connexions 70, 121, 209, 234, 237, 238, 241
Conservatives 2
contact with children, maintaining 236
contact time, in supervision 57
contamination 207
contemplation 64–5, 87
continuity in care 227, 229, 230, 234
control 2, 35, 164
coping skills/strategies 4, 33, 93, 138, 155
cost-benefit analysis 65
cost-effectiveness (programme) 171–2
counter-conditioning 87
crack 147, 148, 149
craft knowledge 37
craft of teaching 84
Crime and Disorder Act (1998) 4, 10, 15, 164, 165
Crime Parenting Orders 164
crime reduction, substance misuse treatment 150

Crime Reduction Initiative in Secondary
    Schools (CRISS) 24, 104
criminal behaviour
    early onset 45
    of parents or family members 162–3
    predisposition to 87
criminal careers 50
criminal history 208
Criminal Justice Act (1991) 225
criminal justice system
    detection of mental health needs 143
    mental health problems 130
criminalisation 165
criminogenic need 26–8
    assessment, planning and supervision 61–2
    education and training 115–16
    engagement 82, 90
    mental health interventions 134–7
    offending behaviour programmes 208–9
    parenting programmes 172–3
    resettlement 233–4
    restorative justice 196
    substance misuse interventions 152
cultural resistance, victim involvement in RJ
    200–1
culture 34, 63, 128, 171, 176
custodial sentences 27
custody 220–1
    differential use of 8
    education and training in 19, 29, 106–7
    as inimical to learning and change 119
    justifications for 221–2
    labelling effect 240
    mental health interventions 139
    mental health problems 130
    risk of reoffending 231–3
    as a safe haven 239
    weakening of protective factors 222–3, 239
    see also secure estate

decision-making 4, 53, 104, 119, 120, 193, 227
decisional balance 65
deficit model 88
dehumanisation, youth crime issue 7
delayed gratification 47
delinquency
    biogenetic theories 127
    prediction/predictors 6, 99
    risk factors 13, 45
    see also peer delinquency
delinquent identities 207
delusions 136
demonstration projects 215
Department for Children, Schools and
    Families (DCSF) 102, 121
depression 47, 128, 129, 136, 137, 151, 164,
    224, 227
deprofessionalism 56

desistance 33, 35, 48–9, 77, 82, 88, 94, 190
detachment from education 26, 209, 233
    interventions to prevent 100–5
    offending 115, 116
    scale of 97–100
Detention and Training Orders (DTOs) 15,
    112, 198, 224, 227, 229
deterrence 21, 222
developmental pathways 49–50
developmentalisation 52
Diagnostic Interview Schedule for Children
    128–9
*Diagnostic and Statistical Manual of Mental
    Disorders see* DSM-IV
dialectical behavioural therapy (DBT) 138–9,
    140
diet 47
diplomas, 14–19 year olds 118
disclosure, of personal information 28, 155
discrepancy 35
discretion (practitioner) 36, 216, 217, 218
disorganisation 46–7
diversion schemes 138
diversionary conferences 190
diversity 77, 79, 94, 120, 171, 175, 198
dosage 17, 29–30
    assessment and planning 62
    education and training 116–17
    engagement 90–1
    mental health interventions 137
    offending behaviour programmes 210–11
    parenting programmes 173–4
    RCT assumptions 20
    resettlement programmes 234–5
    restorative justice 197
    substance misuse interventions 152–4
double jeopardy 110
drift 34, 93
Drug Abuse Resistance Education (DARE)
    21, 114
drug action teams 234
drug dependency 147
Drug Treating and Testing Requirements
    158–9
drug use/misuse 5, 47, 116, 129, 136, 145, 147,
    148–9
DSM-IV 127
Dunedin study 46
duration of intervention *see* dosage
dynamic risk factors 27, 56, 90, 208

E2E Young Offender Pilot 112
economic deprivation 46
ecstasy 225
Education Action Zones 108
education agencies, response to mental
    health problems 127t
Education Maintenance Allowance (EMA) 114

Education Parenting Orders 164
education and training 97–123
  challenges for practice 122
  in custody 19, 29, 106–7
  effective practice 115–22
  engagement 74
  evidence base 97–115
  lack of, prior to custody 224
  lack of support to sustain 66
  mental health 130
  prevention/reduction of substance misuse
    156
  RCT evaluation 19
  segregated 33, 92, 107–12, 119
  YJB championing of 54
  see also academic attainment; academic
    failure; detachment from education
education, training and employment (ETE)
    interventions 30, 234
educational support 83
effective practice
  assessment, planning and supervision
    59–69
  definition and application of 10
  education and training 115–22
  engagement 88–95
  guidelines for 25–34
  mental health interventions 133–42
  offending behaviour programmes 207–16
  parenting programmes 172–81
  resettlement 231–9
  restorative justice 195–200
  substance misuse interventions 151–9
Effective Practice Quality Assurance
    Framework 7
efficacy, CAMHS interventions 132
emotional and behavioural difficulties 84, 97,
    111–12, 125
emotional engagement 74, 75
emotional problems/disorders 5, 47, 128, 129
empathy 35, 87, 186, 209, 212, 216
employment 48, 54, 66, 209, 231
  challenges for practice 122
  evidence base 98, 99, 106
  see also unemployment
engagement 72–96
  assessment and 75–8
  definitions 73–5
  effective practice 88–95
  in evaluative processes 34
  evidence base 72–88
  in offending behaviour programmes 210,
    217
  parental aspirations 102
  in parenting programmes 167, 174–5, 176
  relevance of intervention 63
  see also re-engagement
environment, and drug use 149

equity 8
ethical problems, RCTs 20–1
ethnicity 46, 63, 176, 181, 182, 198, 218, 219
European Convention on Human Rights 28,
    165
evaluation culture 24
evaluation of interventions 12, 23, 29, 30, 216,
    239
  see also randomized controlled trials
Every Child Matters 5, 70, 164
Every Parent Matters 164
evidence 11–12
evidence base
  assessment, planning and supervision
    43–56
  education, training and employment
    97–115
  engagement 72–88
  mental health interventions 124–33
  offending behaviour programmes 203–7
  parenting programmes 162–72
  resettlement 224–31
  restorative justice 184–95
  scaled approach 58
  secure estate 220–3
  substance misuse programmes 145–51
evidence-based practice 1, 216
  determining effectiveness 10
  emergence of 3–6
  guidance 36–7
  managerialism 3, 7–8
  practitioners see practitioners
  reflective practice 37–40
  risk and protective factors 12–15
  youth justice context 2
  see also What Works
Excellence in Cities 108
exclusion see school exclusion; social
    exclusion
expectations 30, 35, 48, 84, 91, 103, 118–19
experimental education programmes 117
externalising problems 137, 138
extrinsic motivation 217

face-to-face restorative justice 187–8, 192, 198
facilitators, restorative justice 187, 188
factorisation 51
fair trial, right to a 28, 165
fairness 80–1, 186
families
  chaotic and disrupted backgrounds 225
  maintenance of contact with 236
  working with 90
family discord 26, 90
family group conferencing 188–9, 190, 198
Family Integrated Transitions (FIT) 140
Family Intervention Programmes (FIPs) 164,
    169

family life, right to 165
family relationships 35, 178, 179, 209
family risk factors 14, 44–5, 162–3
family stress 45, 164, 172, 173
family structures 179
family support programmes 164
family systems theory 206
Fast Track 103–4
fathers 176, 181, 182
female offending 46
Final Warnings 27, 28, 186, 191, 195, 200, 204, 208
firm but fair' approach 63, 80, 81
flexibility 215, 218
Freagarrach project 217
fresh start 85
frustration 164, 165, 182, 233
Functional Family Therapy (FFT) 167, 171
further education colleges 105

gateway hypothesis 149
GCSE performance 105, 108
gender 46, 49, 63, 218
generalisation 167
genetics 47
genuineness 216
Good Lives Model (GLM) 88
government targets 29
group work 33, 138, 154–5, 175, 212, 213
group-based parenting programmes 168
guidance 36–7

HAS four-tier model 152, 153t
hazardous drinking 147
health inequalities 5
helping relations 87
heroin 147, 148, 149
high dosage 29, 90, 117
High/Scope Perry project 103
Home Office 12, 24, 100, 176, 212, 225
home visiting 168, 174, 236
home-school links 103
homelessness 26, 178, 225
honesty 82
hope 77
hostility 136
housing need 225
    see also accommodation; homelessness; poor housing
human ecology theory 206
human rights 2, 28, 53, 165
Human Rights Act (1988) 28, 165
hyperactivity 47, 129, 133, 137, 224
hyperkinetic disorders 128, 130

ICD-10 126, 127
implementation (intervention) 22–4, 34, 68, 229, 238

impulsivity 13, 47, 139
incapacitation 221
incarceration 5, 7, 222, 239
incentives, educational participation 103, 114
INCLUDE 99–100
income 5, 44, 45, 103
Incredible Years 167–8
independence 128, 236
Indianapolis experiment 190
indirect mediation 189, 192
individual risk factors 14, 45
individualisation 77
ineffective educational approaches 114–15
informal social control 52
information
    about offending behaviour programmes 211
    exchange 24, 213–14, 230–1, 234
    on learning strategies 235–6
    substance-related 155
    see also management information; personal information
Institute of Psychiatry 5
institutional life 222
intensity of intervention see dosage
Intensive Aftercare Programme (IAP) 228, 230
intensive interventions 207–8
Intensive Supervision and Surveillance (ISS) 4, 15, 29, 99, 112
inter-agency communication 54
inter-agency risk management 50
inter-professional relationships 143
interactional theory 52
internalising problems 137, 138
International Statistical Classification of Disease and Related Health Problems see ICD-10
intervention modality 33–4
    assessment, planning and supervision 67–8
    education and training 120–1
    engagement 93
    mental health 140–1
    offending behaviour programmes 214
    parenting programmes 178–9
    resettlement 237–8
    restorative justice 199
    substance misuse 157–9
interventions
    complexity and unpredictability of 17–18
    effective 232t
    effective practice see effective practice
    evaluations 12, 23, 29, 30, 216, 239
        see also randomized controlled trials
    evidence base see evidence base
    implementation 22–4, 34, 68, 229, 238
    level of see risk classification
    matching to risk factors 15, 16–17t
    planning see planning

primary aim 10
regulation of 4
scaled approach 56–8, 142
see also individual interventions/programmes
intrinsic motivation 217
Ipsos MORI survey 79–85
irritability 136
isolation (social) 5, 164

justice approach 2, 53
Juvenile Rehabilitation Administration 140

key workers 169

labels/labelling 5, 26, 85, 125, 130, 142, 146,
    154, 173, 207, 240
Labour Force Survey data 118
lapse/relapse 65, 66
large-scale RCTs 19–20
law and order 2
learning, paradigms in 38t
learning difficulties 13, 129, 138, 224
learning disabilities 136, 138, 168
learning environments 118
learning opportunities 197
learning outcomes 30
learning strategies 31, 32, 235–6
learning styles 30–1, 32, 117
Learning Support Units (LSUs) 32, 108–9
left-brain dominance 31
life course 49–50
life skills 236
life-course persistent anti-social behaviour 50
Lifeskills '95 programme 230
lifestyle 209
literacy interventions 101, 117, 119, 212
literacy skills 31, 91, 94, 99–100, 112, 113, 116,
    120, 176, 209, 224
local education authorities (LEAs) 121, 234
'looked after' young people 45, 240, 241
low attainment 13, 14, 31, 75, 100, 115, 117,
    130, 163
low dosage 29
low income 44, 45, 103
low mood 136

mainstream education/provision 32, 108, 109,
    110, 111
maintenance stage, of change 65, 66
male offending 46
management information 7
management information systems 24
managerialism 3, 7–8, 53, 54, 67
marginalisation 51
Maryland Scientific Methods Scale 166
masculinity 85
mediators 187
mental, use of term 124

mental disorders 125
    defined 126
    scope and scale of problem 128–30
mental health 124
    definitions 124–8
    language 125
    positivist approach 17
    services 131, 142
        see also Child and Adolescent Mental
        Health Services
Mental Health Foundation 142
mental health interventions
    challenges for practice 142–4
    effective practice 133–42
    evidence base 124–33
mental health problems 125
    agency responses 126–7
    definition 126
    prevalence 128, 133
    young people with DTOs 224
mental illness 126
mental well-being 125
Mentoring PLUS 87
meta-analyses 9, 18, 20, 24, 25, 72
meta-cognition 32
Misspent Youth 57
modelling 154
modifiability 14–15
monitoring 68, 85, 218, 235
mothers 165
motivation 20, 74, 77, 88, 98, 117, 167, 216, 217
motivational enhancement therapy (MET)
    140
motivational interviewing 35, 78–9, 87, 158
Multi-Agency Public Protection
    Arrangements (MAPPA) 50
multi-agency support 169
multi-agency working 142–3, 223, 240
multi-agency YOTs 214
multi-disciplinary approach, mental health
    142
multi-disciplinary training 143
multi-modal approaches 33, 103, 141, 178,
    199, 214
multi-systemic therapy (MST) 140, 150, 155–6,
    167, 171, 204, 206–7
multidimensional approaches 178
Multidimensional Treatment Foster Care 167,
    171
mutual expectations 35
mutual respect 82

National Academy of Parenting Practitioners
    164, 167
National Child Development study 83
national policy, resettlement 226
National Specification for Substance Misuse
    150

National Treatment Agency for Substance
   Misuse 149
need(s)
   displaced by risk 4
   ignoring of individual 2
needs assessment 4, 229
neglect 47, 124, 162
negotiation 35, 75, 82
neighbourhood disadvantage 5
net-widening 5, 26, 89
New Labour 2, 5, 15, 37, 164
non-attendance (school) 13, 21, 22, 46, 97, 98,
   104, 116, 130, 234–5
non-compliance 29, 34, 55, 93
non-possessive warmth 216
normalisation, substance use 148, 151, 159
not in education, employment or training
   (NEETs) 97, 99, 118
numeracy interventions 101, 119
numeracy skills 91, 94, 100, 112, 113, 116, 120,
   176, 224

obsessive behaviour 136
OCJR household survey 147
offending behaviour programmes 4, 203–19
   academic attainment 120
   challenges for practice 216–19
   effective practice 207–16
   evidence base 203–7
   reduction in reoffending 72
Office for National Statistics (ONS) survey
   (2005) 128, 129
Ofsted 46, 84, 85, 108–9, 118, 119, 121
On Track Projects 164
one-to-one work 33, 175, 213
Onset 49
opposition defiant disorder 137
oral skills 102
organisational difficulties, group work 155
out-of-school educational provision 110
Outward Bound programmes 32, 33
Oxford University Report 194

paralanguage 81
parental contact, with children 236
parental involvement 102, 103, 156, 163, 178,
   236
parental responsibility 164
parental stress 172, 178
parental supervision 46
Parenting Contracts 164, 166
Parenting Early Intervention Pathfinder
   (PEIP) 167
Parenting Orders 164–6, 181, 182
parenting programmes 162–82
   challenges for practice 181–2
   core elements 177f
   effective practice 172–81

evidence base 162–72
parenting support 164, 166, 168–9, 170, 173,
   178
Parentline Plus 176
part-time employment 98
participation
   distinction between engagement and 79–80
   educational 100, 107, 114
   in programmes 75, 91, 210, 211
   of victims in RJ 192, 200–1
partnership agencies 68
pathology 47
peer delinquency 32, 47, 61, 83, 109, 116, 239
peer feedback 154
peer risk factors 14, 45
people variables 216
performance indicators 8
persistent offending 45, 46, 100, 115, 204, 208,
   217
personal information, disclosure of 28, 155
personalised learning 83
pharmacological interventions 157–8
Philanthropic Society 222–3
physical abuse 46, 124
physiological explanations, harder drug use
   148
planning
   Asset's role 58
   effective practice 59–69, 208, 209, 229
   evidence base 43–56
planning stage, of change 65
police cautions 190
Police-led Restorative Cautioning Pilots 195
'politics of behaviour' 2
poly-drug use 148
poor housing 44, 45, 164
positive life attitude 87
positivist approach 15–17
post-16 training providers 112
Post-Release Employment Project 107
post-traumatic stress disorder (PTSD) 129,
   136, 224
poverty 5, 124, 164
Powers of Criminal Courts (Sentencing) Act
   (2000) 224
practitioner resistance 34
practitioners
   discretion 36, 216, 217, 218
   limited use of research 8–9
   power of 82
   role, evidence-based practice 35–6, 68
   survey of 79–85
   zombification of 7, 52
   see also supervising officers; teachers
pre-contemplation 64, 66, 87
pre-natal services 168
pre-sentence reports 233
prediction of delinquency 6

predictive utility, of Asset 52–3
pregnancy, early 5
preparation stage, of change 87
presentation style (programme) 175
prevalence, risk and protective factors 14–15
prevention 10, 12, 44, 203, 228
primary prevention 203
primary schools 100–5
privacy, right to 28, 165
pro-social modelling 35, 78–9, 213
pro-social values 74
probation 9, 17, 80
probation officers 35, 78, 104
problem-solving 33, 93, 104, 139, 141, 205,
    212, 213, 237
professional autonomy 7
professional judgement 53, 218
professional specialism 121
professional training 36, 103, 201
professionals see practitioners
Progam Development Evaluation 103
programme fetishism 33
programme integrity 34
  assessment, planning and supervision 68–9
  education and training 121–2
  engagement 93–5
  mental health interventions 141–2
  offending behaviour programmes 215–16
  parenting programmes 180–1
  resettlement 238–9
  restorative justice 199–200
  substance misuse 159
Programme for International Student
    Assessment (PISA) 83
programmes see interventions
progression 75, 87, 234
project management 23
property crime 150, 190, 191, 195, 198
proportionality 27, 58, 90
protective factors 12–15, 45, 67
  custody and weakening of 222–3, 239
  desistance 48–9
  education 115
  family support 178
  parenting behaviours 163, 164, 172
  salience, prevalence and modifiability
    14–15
psychiatry 127t
psycho-educational therapy 158
psychodynamic group work 138
psychology 88, 205
psychometric instruments 31
psychosis 136
psychosocial bias 52
psychotic-like symptoms 129, 133, 224
public life, right to 28
public protection 5, 50
punishment 27, 85, 146, 221, 222

punitiveness 53, 139, 208
Pupil Referral Units (PRUs) 32, 85, 92, 108,
    109–11, 121
purposeful activity, in custody 29

qualitative research 17
quasi-experimental approach, of RCTs 20–1
questioning, skilful 85

randomized controlled trials (RCTs) 17,
    18–22, 24, 25, 75
re-engagement 66, 84–5, 111
reader programmes 101
recidivism
  custody and 223
  evidence-based practice 40
  interventions
    educational 106–7
    effective 232t
    indirect mediation 192
    offending behaviour programmes 205,
      207, 215
  meta-analysis findings 18
  resettlement 230
  risk factors 46, 47
reciprocity 81
reconviction 50
reconviction data 24, 106, 206
reconviction rates 169, 191, 221, 222
records of action, resettlement 234
recruitment, parenting programmes 180
Reducing Burglary Initiative (RBI) 114
Referral Orders 193, 195, 196, 197
referrals, parenting programmes 172, 182
reflective practice 37–40
rehabilitation 12, 44, 88, 222
rehearsal 154
reintegration
  mainstream education 108, 109, 110, 111
  social 206, 223
relapse 65, 66
relapse prevention 140
relationships
  centrality in parenting 35
  desistance 94
  development of effective 80–1
  inter-professional 143
  with service providers 237
  Summer Arts Colleges 95
  see also family relationships; therapeutic
    alliance; working relationships
release on temporary licence (RoTL) 119, 236
remand 130
remove rooms 108
reoffending 50
  post-custody 221
  reduction in
    education 113

offending behaviour programmes 72
   restorative justice 186, 187, 189–93
risk of
   creative ways of dealing with 196
   custody and 231–3
   level of intervention 59
   practitioner perceptions 53
   priority in youth justice 44
   substance misuse and 159
reparation 189, 192, 197, 199
Reparation Orders 186
repressive welfarism 53–6
Reprimands 200
research
   limited use of 8–9
   see also evidence base
research projects 215
researcher involvement, intervention design
   and implementation 34, 93
resettlement
   challenges for 239–42
   definitions 225–6
   dimensions and models 226–31
   effective practice 231–9
   evidence base 224–31
   'wraparound' services and care 139
residential special schools 111–12
residential treatment 156, 157
resilience 35, 48, 77, 120, 222
Respect agenda 5
responsibilisation 193
responsibility 4, 30, 66, 88, 103, 128, 195, 227
responsivity 30–2
   assessment, planning and supervision
     62–6, 76
   education and training 117–19
   engagement 91–2
   mental health interventions 137–8
   offending behaviour programmes 211–13
   parenting programmes 174–7
   resettlement 235–6
   restorative justice 197–8
   substance misuse interventions 154–5
restorative cautions 190, 191, 192, 195
restorative conferencing 188–9, 194, 196, 198
restorative justice 184–202
   benefits to victims 193–4, 197
   challenges for practice 200–1
   defined 184–6
   effective practice 195–200
   evidence base 184–95
   how it works 186–7
   models 187–9
   reducing reoffending 189–93
   in secure estate 194–5
   types and degrees of 190t
Restorative Justice in Schools Programme
   (YJB) 192

restorative practices 185
reversal 34, 93
right-brain dominance 31
rights *see* human rights
risk assessment 4, 44–8, 53, 55, 195, 229
risk categories 44
risk classification 25–6
   assessment, planning and supervision
     59–61
   education and training 115
   engagement 89–90
   mental health interventions 133–4
   offending behaviour programmes 207–8
   parenting programmes 172
   resettlement 231–3
   restorative justice 195–6
   substance misuse interventions 151–2
risk discourse 5
risk factor research (RFR) 5–6, 56
risk factors 12–15, 44–8, 50, 67, 103, 209
   criticism of 5–6
   dynamic 27, 56, 90, 208
   matching interventions to 15, 16–17t
   mental health problems 134–6
   parenting behaviours 164, 172
   peer delinquency 239
   reoffending 231–3
   salience, prevalence and modifiability
     14–15
   substance misuse 146, 147, 154
risk management 4, 50, 60–1
'risk and resilience' model 88
Risk of Serious Harm (ROSH) 50
risk society 3–6
R(M) v. Inner London Crown Court 165
role clarification 35
role play 155
rolling groups 212

Safer Schools Partnership (SSP) 104–5
Salford Needs Assessment Schedule for
   Adolescents (SNASA) 133
salience, risk and protective factors 14–15
scaled approach 56–8, 142
Scared Straight 21
school attendance 234
   see also school non-attendance
school effectiveness 103
school exclusion 21, 22, 46, 61, 97, 108, 156
school factors, and engagement 83
school leadership 103
school non-attendance 13, 21, 22, 46, 97, 98,
   104, 116, 130, 234–5
school risk factors 14, 45
school-based prevention programmes 103
school-focused development projects 24
schools
   probation officers in 104

restorative approaches in 192
see also primary schools; special schools
Screening Questionnaire Interview for
    Adolescents (SQIfA) 133–4
seamless approach 225, 229, 241
Seattle Social Development Project 103
second chance 85
secondary prevention 203
Secure Children's Homes (SCHs) 220, 222
secure estate 28
    cost of beds 220
    distance from home communities 240
    evidence base 220–3
    lack of mental health assessment 131
    mental health interventions 138–9
    parenting support 178
    restorative justice in 194–5, 198
    see also custody
secure training centres (STCs) 100, 213, 220,
    222
segregated education 33, 92, 107–12, 119
self-control 104
self-destructiveness 139
self-determination 77
self-efficacy 35, 49, 151
self-esteem 10, 82, 87
self-fulfilling expectations 30, 119
self-harm 124, 129, 130, 133, 224
self-medication 124, 136
self-reflection 158
self-reliance 138
sentence planning 152–4, 213, 225
sentencing 27, 57, 119, 226
serious harm to others 44, 50, 61
seriousness of offending 27, 100, 147, 152, 191,
    204
service providers, relationships with 237
service users' choices 8
sexual abuse 46, 124, 225
sexuality 63
siblings, delinquent 46
single order 57
site performances, Summer Arts Colleges 94
situational changes, and relapse 66
skills acquisition 4, 32, 33, 91, 93
skills development/training 87–8, 139, 141,
    154
smoking 129, 158, 225
social capital 77, 83
social change 3
Social Competence Promotion Programme
    for Young Adolescents in America 104
social disadvantage 45–6, 55
social exclusion 5, 66, 178
social inclusion 66, 67, 206, 209
social interactions 33, 93
social justice 8
social naivety 136

social networks 77, 156, 160, 206, 207, 238
social policy 4
social reinforcement 87
social services 127t
social skills development 87–8, 154
social work 9, 17, 18, 80
socio-economic conditions 5
source documents *see* Youth Justice Board,
    source documents
special educational needs (SEN) 30, 46, 84, 97,
    125, 130, 224
special needs 168
special schools 108, 111–12
specialist interventions, mental health 132–3
speech, language and communication needs
    101–2
sport 33, 85, 176
standardised assessment 54, 55
standards 8, 48, 67, 141
statementing 97
static risk factors 208
stepping-stone theory 148
stigma/stigmatisation 154, 156, 165, 173, 174,
    178
stimulus control 87
street life cycle 239
Strengthening America's Families
    programme 167
Strengthening Families, Strengthening
    Communities 167–8
strengths-based approach 88
stress 47, 130, 133, 138
    see also family stress; parental stress;
    post-traumatic stress disorder
stress management 104
Strong African American Families
    Programme 174
substance misuse 26, 58, 145–60
    mental health 129, 136–7
    offending/reoffending 208, 233
    prevalence 159
    recidivism 46, 47
    YJB research 130, 150
    young people with DTOs 225
    see also alcohol use/misuse; drug
    use/misuse
substance misuse interventions
    challenges for practice 159–60
    effective practice 151–9
    evidence base 145–51
success criteria, PRUs 109
sufficient duration/sufficient intensity 116
suicide 47, 124, 130
Summer Arts Colleges (case study) 88–95
supervising officers (YOTs) 233–4, 235, 237,
    238
supervision 30, 35, 46, 57, 62, 63, 66, 92
support, post-sentence 241

Sure Start Projects 164
surveillance 235
systematic assessment *see* assessment
systems management 7

tacit knowledge 36, 37
tagging (electronic) 235
targets 8, 29–30, 67, 209
task avoidance 235
teachers 83, 84
technicised practice 51–2
technocratic managerialism 7
Teen Triple P 168
temporary accommodation 225
tertiary prevention 203, 204
Texas Special Needs Diversion Program 138
Text*Now* 101
theft 104
therapeutic alliance 155
thinking skills 32
throughcare 225
tobacco 147, 148, 149, 156
Tomlinson Review 117
training
    YJB parenting programmes 180
    see also education and training;
        multidisciplinary training; professional
        training
transitions
    factors contributing to successful 140
    and substance misuse 156–7
    see also youth transition model
Triple P 167–8
trips, to art exhibitions 92
trust 82
Trust for the Study of Adolescents (TSA) 181
Turner, Reverend J. 222–3

underage drinking 116
unemployment 46, 98, 99
uniqueness fallacy 20
United Nations Convention on the Rights of
    the Child 27, 28, 53–4
United Nations Standard Minimum Rules for
    the Administration of Juvenile Justice 28
universal truths 15, 20

validation 139
value for money 8
value-free 3, 15
vandalism 104
victim illegitimacy/legitimacy 198
Victim Support 199
victim-offender mediation 187–8
victimisation 136
victims
    restorative justice 197–8
        benefits 193–4, 197

entitlement 199
involvement/participation in 192, 200–1
needs priority 195–6
Victims Code of Practice 185, 201
videoconferencing 178, 198, 236
violence, witnessing 136
violence prevention programme 167
violent crime(s) 150, 190, 191
visual hallucinations 136
vocational qualifications 118
vocational training 117
volatility 151
vulnerability 5, 44, 50, 61, 148

Weare 29
welfare 35, 218
welfare principle 27–8
welfarism 2, 5, 53–6
well-being 5, 128
What Works 1, 3, 22, 94, 102
    appeal of 40
    criticisms of 15, 37
    debate about evidence 11
    and implementation 22–4
    philosophical issues 15–18
    programme evaluation 12
    randomized controlled trials 18–22
    risk factor research 5, 6
    in youth justice 9–10
witnessing violence 136
working relationships 76–7
World Health Organisation (WHO) 124–5
'wraparound' services and care 139

'Year Zero' style 2
York Oral Language Programme 102
Young Offender Institutions 220, 222
young people
    engagement of *see* engagement
    negative feelings towards residential
        treatment 156
    numbers involved in youth justice 99
    perceptions, and effective resettlement 241
    perspectives, marginalisation of 51
    reluctance to engage with mental health
        services 142
    self-fulfilling expectations 30, 119
    survey of 79–85
Youth Crime Action Plan 101
youth crime issue, dehumanisation of 7
youth inclusion programmes 21–2, 120
youth justice
    decision-making and restorative justice 193
    interventions *see* interventions
    numbers involved in 99
    over-representation of black young people
        219
    reforms 4

response to mental health problems 127t
Youth Justice Board (YJB) 2, 15, 24, 43, 230
  education, training and employment
    interventions 234
  Effective Practice Quality Assurance
    Framework 7
  effective practice strategy 9
  intervention modalities 33–4
  parenting programmes 170, 171, 173, 175,
    176, 177, 180
  relationship with YOTs 9
  research
    approach to 12
    Asset 50–1
    cognitive behavioural projects 206, 210
    evaluative 23
    reoffending, post-custody 221
    substance misuse 130, 150, 225
  restorative justice
    definition of aims, outcomes and
      principles 185–6
    evaluation of programmes 186
    projects 192, 194
  scaled approach 56–8, 142
  source documents
    accommodation 178
    parenting 166–7, 173
    restorative justice 191
  targets 29–30, 67

youth inclusion programme 21–2
Youth Lifestyles Survey 147
Youth Matters 164
youth offender contracts 27
Youth Offender Panels (YOPs) 196, 199
Youth Offending Teams (YOTs) 6, 27, 28, 149
  Annual Inspection Report (2005–6) 131,
    157, 186
  culture 34
  mental health resources 131
  offending behaviour programmes 214
  parenting programmes 179
  parenting services 166
  parenting support 170
  punitive interventions 53
  relationship with YJB 9
  relationships with practitioners 80
  restorative justice 185, 192, 201
  scaled approach 58
  supervising officers 233–4, 235, 237, 238
Youth Rehabilitation Order (YRO) 57, 58
Youth Resettlement: A Framework for Action
  (YJB) 227
youth transition model 227
youth work 82, 88

zero tolerance 21, 156
zombification of professionals 7, 52